Contemporary Hollywood Cinema

A comprehensive overview of Hollywood today, *Contemporary Hollywood Cinema* brings together leading international scholars to explore the structure, technology, aesthetics and ideology of recent Hollywood cinema. The contributors draw on a wide array of films – ranging from *Batman*, *Bram Stoker's Dracula* and *Blue Steel* to *The Player*, *Pulp Fiction* and *Fargo* – in order to discuss various facets of the contemporary American film scene.

The notion of 'New' or 'post-classical' Hollywood cinema is one that has gained currency in film criticism even as it has eluded detailed study. Contributors consider the idea of the 'New' Hollywood and ask how it differs from the 'Old'. They discuss the growth of independent and package production, the significance of companies like New Line and Miramax, the impact of television and the globalization of Hollywood's markets. They also address such topics as widescreen composition, the pop-music score, Dolby and digital sound and the aesthetic characteristics of the Hollywood blockbuster. Other chapters emphasize issues of race, gender and class, through discussions of the changing fortunes of established genres like the 'woman's picture', as well as emerging trends such as the new black cinema, female action heroines, the 'yuppie horror' film and the family-adventure movie.

Contributors: Michael Allen, Tino Balio, Warren Buckland, Steven Cohan, Pam Cook, Elizabeth Cowie, K. J. Donnelly, Thomas Elsaesser, Douglas Gomery, Barry Keith Grant, Peter Krämer, Tommy L. Lott, Richard Maltby, Steve Neale, Hilary Radner, James Schamus, Gianluca Sergi, Murray Smith, Justin Wyatt.

Steve Neale is Research Professor in Film Studies at Sheffield Hallam University.
Murray Smith is Senior Lecturer in Film Studies at the University of Kent.

Contemporary Hollywood Cinema

Edited by Steve Neale and Murray Smith

London and New York

First published 1998
by Routledge
11 New Fetter Lane, London EC4P 4EE

Simultaneously published in the USA and Canada
by Routledge
29 West 35th Street, New York, NY 10001

Typeset in Perpetua and Bell Gothic by RefineCatch Limited, Bungay, Suffolk
Printed and bound in Great Britain by
Biddles Ltd, Guildford and King's Lynn

British Library Cataloguing in Publication Data
A catalogue record for this book is available from the British Library

Library of Congress Cataloging-in-Publication Data
Neale, Stephen.
Contemporary Hollywood cinema / Steve Neale and Murray Smith.
p.   cm.
Includes bibliographical references and index.
1. Motion pictures—California—Los Angeles.   2. Motion picture
industry—California—Los Angeles.   I. Smith, Murray (Murray
Stuart).   II. Title.
PN1993.5.U65N43   1998
791.43′09794′94—dc21   98–5952
CIP

ISBN 0–415–17010–9 (pbk)
0–415–17009–5 (hbk)

Contents

List of illustrations and permissions

We are indebted to the people and archives below for permission to reproduce photographs. Every effort has been made to trace copyright holders, and any omissions brought to our attention will be remedied in future editions.

Notes on contributors

Michael Allen worked for Rank Video in the early 1980s and, since returning to academia, has developed multimedia study programmes for film studies, and has taught in a variety of institutions. His doctoral thesis was on narrative structure and spatial articulation in the later feature films of D.W. Griffith. He is currently Research Officer at the British Film Institute.

Tino Balio is Chair of the Department of Communication Arts at the University of Wisconsin-Madison, where he also served as Director of the Wisconsin Center for Film and Theater Research from 1966 to 1982. He is the editor of *The American Film Industry* and *Hollywood in the Age of Television*, and author of *Grand Design: Hollywood as a Modern Business Enterprise, 1930–1939* and *United Artists: The Company that Changed the Film Industry*.

Warren Buckland is Lecturer in Film Studies at John Moores University, Liverpool. He is editor of *The Film Spectator: From Sign to Mind* and author of the forthcoming *The Unfinished Project of Film Theory*.

Steven Cohan is Professor of English at Syracuse University. He is co-author of *Telling Stories*, co-editor of *Screening the Male* and *The Road Movie Book*, and author of *Masked Men: Masculinity and the Movies in the Fifties*.

Pam Cook is Professor of European Film and Media at the University of Southampton. She has published widely on gender and film and is editor of *The Cinema Book* and co-editor of *Women and Film: A Sight and Sound Reader*. Her study of costume and identity in British cinema, *Fashioning the Nation*, was published in 1996. Her most recent book is *Gainsborough Pictures* and she is currently writing a BFI Film Classic on the Powell and Pressburger film *I Know Where I'm Going!*

Elizabeth Cowie is Senior Lecturer in Film Studies at the University of Kent and has published on feminism and psychoanalysis, *film noir*, and documentary. Her book *Representing the Woman: Psychoanalysis and Cinema* appeared in 1997.

K. J. Donnelly was a professional musician and is now Lecturer in Film Studies at Staffordshire University. He has published on film music and postmodernism, and has recently completed his doctoral thesis, a study of the impact of popular music on film soundtracks.

Thomas Elsaesser is Professor at the University of Amsterdam, and Chair of the Department of Film and Television. His books, as author and editor, include *New German Cinema: A History, Early Cinema: Space, Frame, Narrative, Writing for the Medium: Television in Transition, Double Trouble, A Second Life: German Cinemas First Decades* and *Fassbinder's Germany*.

Douglas Gomery is Professor in the Department of Radio-TV-Film at the University of Maryland. He is the author of *The Hollywood Studio System, Shared Pleasures: A History of Movie Presentation in the United States*, and of other books examining the economics and history of American media. His column 'The economics of television' is a regular feature of *American Journalism Review*.

Barry Keith Grant is Professor of Film and Director of the Film Studies Program at Brock University in St Catharines, Ontario, Canada. He is the author or editor of eight books, including *Film Genre Reader, The Dread of Difference: Gender and the Horror Film, Voyages of Discovery: The Cinema of Frederick Wiseman*, and *Documenting the Documentary: Close Readings of Documentary Film and Video*.

Peter Krämer is Lecturer in American Film in the American Studies Department at Keele University. His work on aspects of American film history has been published in *The Velvet Light Trap, Screen, Theatre History Studies* and a number of edited collections, including the *Oxford Guide to Film Studies*. He is currently working on a study of the early stage and film career of Buster Keaton, and, together with Alan Lovell, on an edited collection on film acting to be published by Routledge.

Tommy L. Lott is Professor of Philosophy at the University of Missouri, St Louis. He is the author of *Like Rum in the Punch: Alain Locke and the Theory of African-American Culture* and editor of *Subjugation and Bondage: Critical Essays on Slavery and Social Philosophy*.

Richard Maltby is Professor of Screen Studies at Flinders University, Adelaide. He is the author of *Harmless Entertainment* and *Hollywood Cinema: An Introduction*. He is completing a study of self-regulation and the political institutions of American cinema.

Steve Neale is Research Professor in Film Studies at Sheffield Hallam University. He is the author of *Genre* and *Cinema and Technology*, and co-author of *Popular*

Film and Television Comedy. He is currently completing *Genre and Hollywood* for Routledge.

Hilary Radner is Associate Professor in the Department of Communication and Theatre at the University of Notre Dame. She is the author of *Shopping Around: Feminine Culture and the Pursuit of Pleasure*, and co-editor of *Film Theory Goes to the Movies* and *Constructing the New Consumer Society*.

James Schamus is a screenwriter and producer who founded Good Machine with Ted Hope in 1991, and Assistant Professor of Film at Columbia University. He was the executive producer of *Poison* and *Swoon*, co-producer of *Sense and Sensibility*, and co-writer and associate producer of *Eat Drink Man Woman*. In 1997 he received the Prize for Best Screenplay at Cannes for his work on *The Ice Storm*.

Gianluca Sergi is Lecturer in Film Studies at Staffordshire University. He is currently researching a Ph.D. on film sound at Sheffield Hallam University.

Murray Smith is Senior Lecturer in Film Studies at the University of Kent. He is the author of *Engaging Characters: Fiction, Emotion, and the Cinema*, and co-editor of *Film Theory and Philosophy*.

Justin Wyatt is Associate Professor of Media Arts at the University of Arizona. He is the author of *High Concept: Movies and Marketing in Hollywood* and a monograph on Todd Haynes' *Poison*. His work has appeared in journals such as *Film Quarterly*, *Cinema Journal*, *The Velvet Light Trap*, *Sight and Sound*, *Wide Angle* and *Cineaste*.

Acknowledgements

The origins of this book lie in a conference held at the University of Kent in 1995. We would like to thank the University of Kent and South-east Arts for their support, and all the participants at the conference for their valuable contributions. Thanks also to Rebecca Barden at Routledge for her interest in and encouragement of the project, and to Alistair Daniel, Sarah Hall and Vivien Antwi for their work on the manuscript. Kate Slattery and Miri Song have, as ever, been of immense help and put up with all the usual bullshit.

Introduction

Steve Neale and Murray Smith

Fifty years ago government legislation – in the form of the Paramount Decrees –
obliged the small group of companies who controlled the film industry in the
United States to divorce their interests in exhibition from their interests in production and distribution. The Paramount Decrees helped bring about the demise
of the hitherto dominant studio system, and according to many film historians,
helped trigger the series of changes in structure, in practice and in style which
marked the end of a distinct phase in Hollywood's history and the beginning of
something new. However, in the meantime, while critical, theoretical and historical research into studio-era Hollywood continued and spread from the 1960s to
the 1990s, research into the Hollywood that had replaced it remained, at best,
intermittent. As a consequence, and with the important exception of those
ground-breaking studies listed in the bibliography and referred to throughout this
book, the precise nature, indeed the precise temporal parameters, of what we
have decided to call simply 'contemporary Hollywood cinema' remain relatively
unexplored and hence open to debate and further research. This book is designed,
as its title suggests, to reflect on and extend the debate and exploration there has
been so far, and to present new research in the field.

A complicating factor here has been the variability of the terminology used to
discuss the changes in Hollywood, and the assumptions, criteria and periodization
implicit in the terminology. Is the 'Old' Hollywood best described as 'classical'?
Is the 'New' Hollywood most usefully described as 'post-classical', 'postmodern'
(or neither)? Are the most revealing criteria industrial, institutional or aesthetic?
What exactly has changed since the 1940s? These questions are directly addressed
in the chapter by Murray Smith which opens the first of the four different sections –
on historiography, on economics, industry and institutions, on aesthetics and
technology, and on audience and address – into which the book as a whole is
divided. The division is a loose one: topics, themes and terms of debate recur
between, as well as within, the different sections. As the following summaries
indicate, any answers to the questions posed above depend as much on recognizing

the interrelated and multidimensional nature of the factors involved as they do on assessing their relative importance.

Smith compares a range of arguments concerning the putative transition from a classical to a post-classical American cinema. Reviewing the arguments and assumptions of David Bordwell, Janet Staiger and Kristin Thompson's *The Classical Hollywood Cinema*, Smith uses this work as a touchstone for the consideration of alternative perspectives on Hollywood cinema. Smith first examines the proposal that the American film industry after 1948 can be characterized as a 'post-Fordist' industry – one characterized by 'flexible specialization' rather than standardization, the production of smaller runs of more specialized goods for more narrowly defined markets, and thus a greater emphasis on innovation than is said to be typical of Fordist industries. Turning from the post-Fordist thesis, Smith considers a range of arguments in favour of the notion of a 'new' or 'post-classical' Hollywood on the basis of the interconnections between film style and the mode of film production within the film industry, as well as more radical arguments which dispute the 'classicism' of studio era Hollywood, and thus the logic of positing a post-classical period. While Smith defends the framework of *The Classical Hollywood Cinema* against many of the critiques that have been mounted against it, he emphasizes that the varied answers to the question of periodization are to a large extent a function of the different questions posed about, and assumptions brought to, the study of Hollywood by different historians.

Richard Maltby's chapter, an overview of institutional and economic developments in the post-war era, is unusually explicit in just this respect. Beginning with a comparison of, on the one hand, jeremiads for the passing of the 'common language' of a classical American cinema, and on the other hand, Bordwell, Staiger and Thompson's argument that the classicism of Hollywood has to a large extent endured the various changes in the post-war era, Maltby argues that the breadth of our conception of 'Hollywood' makes a crucial difference to the answer we will arrive at on the question of post-classicism. For all its formidable scale and detail, Maltby argues that *The Classical Hollywood Cinema* is nevertheless a partial study of Hollywood, in so far as it is concerned with the relationship between film style and the organization of management and production in the industry, and is ultimately driven by an interest in the aesthetics of Hollywood (as Bordwell himself states in the first chapter of the work). Following the argument of his *Hollywood Cinema*, Maltby proposes a still wider perspective, which gives as much prominence to distribution and exhibition as it does to production, and places economic relations rather than 'product styling' at the fulcrum of debate. Examining the post-war industry from this broad perspective, Maltby focuses on the wake of the Paramount Decrees. The industry was compelled to find a new 'stabilized economics of distribution', and did so by moving into telefilm production, Maltby argues, which became the industry's bread and butter from the late 1950s onwards. It is this underlying stability, bolstered by the expanded markets afforded by home video and other new technologies, which allows for the apparent high risk of the ultra high-budget 'event' movie. These movies exploit the synergies fostered by conglomeration to such an extent that even the partial return to vertical integration in the 1980s takes place in a significantly changed commercial environment, in which the individual film is no longer an adequate token of the larger system of production, distribution and exhibition. Maltby thus suggests that, from this broad and emphatically economic perspective, and in spite of many continuities, the post-war years have indeed seen the gradual emergence of a fundamentally new kind of film industry.

Douglas Gomery opens the second section of the book, 'Economics, industry and institutions', with his chapter on innovations in corporate business practice in the post-war American film industry. Gomery discusses the new strategies pioneered by Lew Wasserman (at MCA-Universal) and Steven J. Ross (at Warner Communications and Time Warner). Both initiated practices which were widely emulated by other corporations, acting as the catalysts for transformations in the industry as a whole. According to Gomery, Wasserman was the architect of many of the novel practices around which the industry re-organized in the 1950s, including the independent marketing of stars like James Stewart and Jack Benny on a deal-by-deal basis. Wasserman's significance as a business innovator continued, however, with Universal's promotion of made-for-TV movies, and perhaps above all, two of the key strategies defining today's blockbuster films: saturation release combined with a vigorous campaign of prime time television advertising. Wasserman's innovations, Gomery argues, helped to put cinema back 'atop the pop culture hierarchy' after many years of perceived decline. The innovations of Ross might be said to have consolidated this new position of power and stability, through the creation of a new form of 'conglomerate' vertical integration, which positioned the film industry at the gateway of an emerging field of new technologies and markets (including publishing, music recording, cable and home video). Gomery argues that the significance of these two waves of corporate innovation are such that we can legitimately talk of *two* 'New' Hollywoods.

Tino Balio provides a broader overview of the contemporary, conglomerated industry in which Ross's activities figure so prominently. Balio begins by noting a factor which appears in many of the essays in this volume: the exponential growth of both domestic and foreign markets in the 1980s which have led to the increasing 'globalization' of Hollywood. These expanded markets opened the way for a variety of new business strategies: the 'horizontal' movement of Hollywood into new foreign markets through the upgrading of international operations; the forging of partnerships with overseas companies; and a simultaneous 'vertical' expansion, in which the major studios struck deals with independent production companies in order both to bolster and vary the nature of their output. Echoing both Maltby and Gomery, Balio's argument brings out the importance of *synergy* in the conglomerated film industry: the enhanced profit potential brought about by the cross-marketing of a commodity or related commodities in multiple media. Balio traces the successive waves of corporate merging in the 1990s, driven not only by the potential benefits of synergy and 'tight diversification' (the concentration of a conglomerate's assets and activities around closely related commodities, rather than the 'loose' diversity of interests characteristic of earlier conglomerates formed in the 1960s, like Gulf + Western), but also, crucially, the impetus to maintain and extend control of distribution as new markets have opened up.

Justin Wyatt takes a closer look at a particular aspect of the contemporary situation reviewed by Balio: the rise of the 'major independent' producer-distributor. Both Balio and Wyatt note that the growth of home video in the early 1980s increased the demand for films, a situation exploited for a time by the 'mini-majors' (companies like Orion and Cannon, which possessed their own distribution arms) and independents (such as Atlantic and Vestron, who were reliant on deals with the majors for distribution). Wyatt notes that video proved to be an unreliable market for these smaller companies, many of whom consequently withdrew from film production. However, two independents – New Line and Miramax – not only survived this period, but flourished in the 1990s. (Indeed, following the success of *The English Patient* in the 1997 Academy Awards, Miramax became virtually a household name.) One factor which marks these companies off is that both started as independent distributors, only later moving into financing and production. Wyatt surveys the contrasting tactics of the two companies: while New Line relied on the development of 'franchise' films – most notably *Teenage Mutant Ninja Turtles* (1990), the popularity and marketability of which sustained two sequels and numerous tie-ins – Miramax consistently sought to exploit the controversial dimensions of the art house films it distributed, in order to maximize 'crossover' potential. The success of both companies led to mergers in the 1990s with major corporations: New Line with Turner, Miramax with Disney. Wyatt concludes by suggesting that, given the clout of these companies and their incorporation within major producer-distributors, even the phrase 'major independent' may overstate their independence. The process by which the major companies have 'swallowed' the most successful independents of the 1990s and come to dominate the new markets opened up by home video, also discussed by Balio, parallels the way in which the initial burst of independent production in the 1950s, serving the new market of television, came to be dominated by the majors soon thereafter.

The three chapters by Gomery, Balio and Wyatt trace an arc through the major studios and into the 'mini-majors' and 'major independents', an arc completed by James Schamus's essay on the world of 'indie' film production. Schamus, a screenwriter and producer who, along with Ted Hope, heads the New York based company Good Machine, describes the difficulties faced by any small, independent company attempting to survive in the contemporary film industry. Assuming the perspective of an investor with a stake in a modestly budgeted independent film, Schamus paints an eye-opening picture of the costs involved not so much in producing a film, but in getting the film marketed and distributed. Schamus underlines a point made by both Gomery and Balio: the mass of profits on films are now derived from nominally 'ancillary' markets. While this is true of all films, in the case of the independent art house film, the key 'back end' is the foreign market (rather than domestic video, etc.). In view of the many costs, complexities and pitfalls involved in the production and distribution of an independent film, Schamus stresses the importance of pre-exhibition sales of distribution rights, rather than the actual success of films at the box office, for a return on the investment that he tracks. The chapters by Wyatt and Schamus together reveal the Janus-faced nature of the 'success' of independent film production in the 1990s. On the one hand, the crossover successes of Miramax and New Line were impressive enough to draw the acquisitive attention of the majors; on the other hand, the success of these companies led to bidding wars which raised the cost of distribution rights sharply. This, in turn, has led to spiralling distribution fees and thus the need for films to make still more money in order to break even or, just maybe, make a profit.

The third part of the book, 'Aesthetics and technology', begins with Michael Allen's survey of technological developments in Hollywood since the end of the Second World War, a survey that covers Dolby, digital sound, computerization and experiments in virtual reality, as well as 3-D, widescreen and colour. Throughout, Allen places an emphasis on ever-more spectacular forms of 'realism' as a driving force in the development of film technology, though he notes both narrative and economic preconditions for the successful adoption of a new technology: the technology will have to be adaptable to narrative purposes for it to generate a sufficient return on the high cost of research and development. The next three chapters each examine a particular area of technology in more detail: Steve Neale focuses on widescreen aesthetics, while K. J. Donnelly and Gianluca Sergi consider music and sound respectively.

Neale looks at a number of the compositional features characteristic of widescreen films since the industry's adoption of CinemaScope in 1953, and in particular since the advent of television – and of other non-widescreen 'windows' – as regular sites of exhibition for the industry's films. Noting the effects of panning and scanning, and the existence since the early 1960s of a 'safe action area' when composing shots and scenes in widescreen formats, he draws attention to a number of distinctive compositional devices in post-1960s widescreen films which suggest an awareness of both. Observing that these devices are more varied than has hitherto been supposed, he goes on to argue that the adoption of widescreen formats in the 1950s itself disrupted 'classical' conventions, and that the period since then has been marked by a complex aesthetic and technological interplay between film and television whose features and terms have barely begun to be explored in detail.

Focusing on *Batman* (1989) and *Batman Returns* (1992), K. J. Donnelly discusses the aesthetic, commercial and industrial roles played by the orchestral and the popular song-based music in and around these and other recent Hollywood films. Comparing and contrasting these roles with those played by music earlier on in Hollywood's history, he demonstrates the extent to which contemporary musical soundtracks and scores reward detailed aesthetic analysis, and he argues in favour of the term 'neoclassical' both as a means of describing the style of many contemporary orchestral scores, and as a way of differentiating these scores, and the practices that surround them, from those of the classical era.

Donnelly refers in passing to John Williams's score for *Star Wars* (1977). *Star Wars* also figures in Gianluca Sergi's chapter, as one of the films which pioneered Dolby stereo sound, and hence as a film which helped inaugurate a fundamental transformation in the production, use and reproduction of sound in Hollywood cinema. Arguing in general for more theoretical attention to be paid to the soundtrack, Sergi notes the extent to which sound is now a major attraction for audiences, a major selling point for cinemas and for multimedia conglomerates, and a major point of aesthetic innovation and experiment. He pinpoints some of the complexities and effects characteristic of the 'post-classical' soundtrack, contrasting them with what he sees as the technical, conceptual and architectural limitations of classical sound, and suggests that their roots lie in the popular musical culture of the 1960s. Sergi and Donnelly also share the view that sound and music are now more obtrusive than they were in classical Hollywood cinema.

Where Donnelly, Neale and Sergi focus on the image and the soundtrack, Warren Buckland and Elizabeth Cowie focus instead on issues of narrative. In contrast to the dismissive stress laid on spectacle and special effects in many accounts of the contemporary Hollywood blockbuster, and in the context of an argument in favour of poetics and an examination of the aesthetic norms of popular films, Buckland highlights the importance of narration and narrative in *Raiders of the Lost Ark* (1981). Stressing the film's episodic narrative structure on the one hand, and the systematic role played by an 'off-screen presence' in the generation of suspense, surprise and spectatorial engagement on the other, he argues that such narrative engagement is a fundamental feature of *Raiders*' aesthetic.

Buckland notes that the roots of *Raiders*' episodic structure lie in the 'B' adventure films and serials of the 1930s and 1940s to which the film pays homage (a point expanded on by Thomas Elsaesser in his chapter, in which he discusses the significance of horror and other 'B'-genres for contemporary prestige or 'event' movies). Buckland also notes that this structure – and these films – tend to be neglected in *The Classical Hollywood Cinema*. To that extent, his argument overlaps with Elizabeth Cowie's. Couched within a critique suggesting that profit rather than adherence to any particular narrative model governed Hollywood's aesthetic practices during the studio era, Cowie argues that Bordwell, Staiger and Thompson overemphasize causal motivation, logical coherence and other 'well-made' narrative features in their account of the Hollywood film. Noting the extent to which they rely on screenwriting manuals as warrant for their argument, and pointing to a number of exceptions to the model these manuals advocate, she argues that Bordwell, Staiger and Thompson tend either to downplay the persisting heritage of those forms of popular entertainment, like vaudeville and melodrama, which eschewed or simply lacked well-made conventions, or else to treat them solely as sources and forms of generic motivation. She suggests instead that Hollywood films be looked at in terms of an assembly or 'package' of aesthetic ingredients.

Finally, Thomas Elsaesser touches on many of the issues central to debates about contemporary cinema – issues of narrative and spectacle, of aesthetics and technology, and of classicism and post-classicism – in an analysis of Francis Ford Coppola's *Bram Stoker's Dracula* (1992). Elsaesser's chapter is also one of the few essays to appeal to the concept of postmodernism. Moreover, in discussing the 'complex hopscotch' between European and American filmmaking, in which he traces the twists and turns of transatlantic exchange over the course of the last thirty years, Elsaesser revisits an issue he had discussed in his earlier work on American filmmaking of the 1970s. Elsaesser sees Coppola's film as a wide-ranging meditation on all these topics and themes. This meditation, he argues, is embedded as much in its technological and aesthetic devices, in its treatment of its source material, and in its allusions to films, paintings and other instances of representation, as it is in any of its overt thematic concerns. Attributing the film's hostile critical reception to features such as these, he argues that it represents an attempt to situate itself, its director and its cinematic heritage within a complex series of cultural developments, traditions and debates.

Focusing on issues of audience, address and ideology, the fourth and final section of the book is also more diverse than the earlier sections, ranging as it does across such topics as ethnicity, gender, sexuality and class, as well as textuality, genre and spectatorship. Tommy Lott opens the section with a survey of recent writing on black independent and Hollywood cinema. Noting the prevalence of a rigid division between the two in these accounts, he questions its validity on empirical and ideological grounds, arguing instead for consistent, but flexible and context-specific analyses of all forms of black American cinema. Noting the extent to which the Hollywood of the studio era not only excluded black filmmakers and black concerns, but often perpetuated or actively promoted racist representations and racist views, Lott focuses in particular on developments since the late 1960s. To the extent that he notes elements of overlap, as well as divergence, between Hollywood and various spheres of black independence since then, his argument echoes the industrially oriented accounts of Balio and Wyatt; to the extent that he refuses simply to condemn Hollywood's output on a priori political grounds, it is echoed by the ideologically oriented analyses of Pam Cook and of Hilary Radner.

Cook and Radner are concerned with feminist issues, and in particular with issues of spectatorship, address and representation. Cook takes the classical women's picture as her starting point. She argues for a revision in attitudes and approaches towards these and other classical films. Noting the shift towards greater visibility in the representation of sex and violence during the post-classical era, she goes on to compare and contrast the treatment of sexual violence in a series of cycles and films from the 1940s through to the mid-1990s. She concludes by noting the greater presence of women as production personnel in the New Hollywood, its increasing fluidity with respect to gender and genre, and the extent to which 'models defined by exclusion and marginalization' are inappropriate to feminist investigations and discussions of New and Old Hollywood alike.

Radner focuses on two recent examples of what she sees as 'a new generation of femmes fatales, of psychofemmes – of women who refuse the violence of men': Sarah Connor (Linda Hamilton) in *Terminator 2* (1991) and Marge Gunderson (Frances McDormand) in *Fargo* (1996). Arguing that they 'defy the Hollywood machinery that all too often reduces femininity to her image', she also notes that they maintain the conventional opposition between masculinity and femininity in which maternity remains a founding characteristic of women and irrational violence a defining characteristic of men. The films thus pose questions as to the persistence of traditional conceptions of gender 'in spite of the increasing plasticity and indeterminacy of the body that defines that terrain'.

Whether or not she figures as one of the new generation of psychofemmes, Steven Cohan places Catherine Trammell (Sharon Stone) in *Basic Instinct* (1992) within the Hollywood tradition of *noir femmes fatales*, and the film as a whole within the regime of more visible and explicit representations of violence and sex noted by Cook. Paradoxically, for all its post-Hays Code notoriety, and despite the attempts by protest groups, reviewers and even the director himself to fix the film's meanings, the sexual politics of *Basic Instinct*, and the nature and significance of Trammell herself, Cohan argues, remain indeterminate. In that respect, and for all their apparent post-classical explicitness, *Basic Instinct* and Catherine Trammell are perhaps not as dissimilar to some of the traditional *films noirs* and *noir femmes fatales* as may appear to be the case at first sight.

The panic engendered by Trammell is in some ways comparable to the panic experienced by the protagonists of the 'yuppie horror' films discussed by Barry Keith Grant. (Indeed, Grant notes that the depiction of 'masculinity in crisis' in these films connects them with a pervasive theme in contemporary Hollywood, also manifested by contemporary 'hardbody' action films.) As Grant points out, yuppie horror protagonists find themselves confronted by their worst middle-class nightmares in a series of 1980s and early 1990s films which often mix conventions derived from the horror film with elements of humour and screwball comedy. Both Robin Wood and, in this volume, Thomas Elsaesser, have argued that the horror film takes on a much more central role in the overall generic regime of Hollywood in the 1970s and 1980s, and Grant's analysis bears out the way in which horror continues to be fused with other genres and adapted to address new audiences and ideologies. Pointing thus to what many have characterized as the generically hybrid nature of many post-classical Hollywood films, Grant explores the extent to which the films themselves vary in their attitudes and in their mix of generic ingredients.

One of the issues raised by the yuppie horror cycle is the issue of address. To whom are – or were – these films directed? Were they made for yuppie consumption, a paradoxical combination, perhaps, of niche marketing and masochistic narcissism? Were they addressed to those who loathe yuppies and yuppiedom, at those willing and able to rejoice in their discomfort? Or, as is consonant with Hollywood's traditions, were they made so as to be available for appreciation and consumption by both groups at once? Combining textual and sociological analysis, the chapter by Peter Krämer that concludes this volume takes audience and address as its central concern. He argues that most of the most popular films produced by Hollywood in recent years can be categorized as 'family-adventure films', films which are far less 'escapist' than may initially appear to be the case. The family-adventure films specifically address the concerns and the members of the modern 'dysfunctional' family, children in particular, but adults as well. In working through scenarios of familial loss and fragmentation, these films, he suggests, engage psychic and social issues alike. The commercial success of these films thus has firm social and cultural, as well as industrial, foundations. Along with the chapters by Buckland, Donnelly and Sergi, Krämer's chapter also challenges the predominant academic view of mainstream contemporary cinema as (to use Maltby's phrase) 'a sequence of emptily expensive, aesthetically impoverished spectacles'.

As will be apparent, the chapters in this volume discuss a number of different aspects of contemporary Hollywood cinema. It will also be apparent that no single answer emerges to any of the questions posed earlier in this introduction: there is no single concept, term or form of explanation that adequately encapsulates all of contemporary Hollywood's important characteristics. The chapters themselves vary not only in the terms that they use and topics they explore, but also in their levels of generality. They thus help to illustrate the pertinence of specific approaches and locally focused research as well as more abstract and generalized discussion. Some of the chapters look backwards as well as forwards; in exploring the contemporary, they also raise questions about the past.

Part I

Hollywood historiography

Chapter 1

Theses on the philosophy of Hollywood history

Murray Smith

At one time, the main tools necessary for picture-making were a megaphone, a strong cranking arm, and a plot.
Only the last has resisted change.

(Weegee and Mel Harris, *Naked Hollywood*)

There have been, I know, a lot of new Hollywoods . . .
(Jon Lewis, *Whom God Wishes to Destroy: Francis Coppola and the New Hollywood*)

Since the 1960s, there has been a proliferation of terms designating more-or-less fundamental shifts in the nature – and thus the appropriate periodization – of Hollywood cinema: the New Hollywood, the New New Hollywood, post-classicism, and more indirectly, post-Fordism and postmodernism. And before these terms came into currency, critics had already noted what they saw as significant shifts in the nature of American filmmaking through terms which have since fallen out of use – Manny Farber's 'New Movie', for example, or the 'maximized' cinema posited by Lawrence Alloway to encompass the period 1946–64. Many of the contributors to this volume assume, argue or imply that the classical Hollywood cinema of the studio era has been partly transformed or wholly superseded.

The watchwords in virtually all analyses of 'classical Hollywood cinema' are *stability* and *regulation*, features which can either be prized for the way in which they enabled a great popular art, or decried for the constraints they imposed upon filmmakers. But just what is said to have been regulated in such a way that a high degree of stability was ensured varies considerably. First, and most obviously, classicism may refer to certain narrative and aesthetic features (the stability of a system of genres, or of continuity principles, for example); or, it may refer to the studio system as a mode of production. Moving out from the films themselves in another direction, 'classicism' may be said to describe a certain kind of spectatorship, one characterized by a high degree of 'homogenization' or psychic regulation.[1]

Although the notion of a 'classical' American cinema had been in circulation for decades, the concept became a focus of theoretical attention in journals such as *Monogram* and *Screen* in the 1970s, and was given far greater substance by David Bordwell, Janet Staiger and Kristin Thompson in their landmark 1985 work *The Classical Hollywood Cinema (CHC)*.[2] Influenced by both André Bazin[3] and – less obviously but perhaps just as significantly – Jan Mukařovský, Bordwell, Staiger and Thompson use the phrase 'classical Hollywood cinema' to refer to a mode of film practice (an aesthetic of 'decorum, proportion, formal harmony' (*CHC*, p. 4)) supporting and supported by a mode of film production (the studio system).[4] 'The label "classicism" serves well', the authors argue, 'because it swiftly conveys distinct aesthetic qualities (elegance, unity, rule-governed craftsmanship) and historical functions (Hollywood's role as the world's mainstream film style)' (*CHC*, p. 4). 'Classical', then, connotes not only particular aesthetic qualities, but the historical role of Hollywood filmmaking as a template for filmmaking worldwide: classical films are classical in the sense that they are *definitive*.

Following Mukařovský, Bordwell, Staiger and Thompson separate several dimensions of form: they write of material, technical, aesthetic and socio-ethical-political ('practical') norms. Each of these can be said to have been highly regulated in the studio era (many material and technical norms, for example, were regulated and stabilized by co-operation among the majors, while many practical norms were regulated by the Production Code). The emphasis of *The Classical Hollywood Cinema* is very clearly and explicitly placed on technical and aesthetic norms, though to that statement we need to add two qualifications. First, material and 'practical' norms are considered, though only to the extent that these impinge upon technical and aesthetic norms (the norm of the union of a heterosexual couple is examined as an instance of Hollywood's interest in narrative closure, for example). Second, there is an important principle of interdependence in operation: not only between the mode of production and mode of film practice, but also, implicitly at least, among the various norms. One might argue, for example, that the technical norms of narrative closure and shot/reverse-shot editing are interdependent with the aesthetic norms of 'unity' and 'harmony'. This extends into a kind of holistic principle (also evident in Bazin): the idea that the regulated stability of each of the formal norms, along with the ordered nature of the mode of production, generates a greater overall level of stability than the sum of each of these levels. There is, to recall Bazin's metaphor, an overall 'equilibrium profile' which arises from the stability achieved in each of the institutional and formal dimensions.

Where Bordwell, Staiger and Thompson argue that the classical style has 'persisted' since 1960 (the date at which the detail of their study ends) in spite of the shift to package production, and the later process of conglomeration,[5] other authors have argued that the classical aesthetic gradually dissipated with the breakdown of the studio system (and, for some authors, the wider emergence of postmodernity). Indeed, for almost as long as Hollywood has been conceptualized as a 'classical' cinema, there have been claims regarding the end of the classical period. Probably the first such claim was implicitly made by Bazin, who suggested that the classicism of 1930s Hollywood began to give way to a 'baroque' cinema in the 1940s, a cinema of greater self-consciousness and stylization, in the form of, for example, 'superwesterns' like *Duel in the Sun* (1946), *High Noon* (1952), and *Shane* (1953). In 1952 Manny Farber lambasted the 'new mannerist flicker', which seemed more concerned with thematic seriousness and stylistic ostentatiousness than with the traditional Hollywood virtue of entertaining storytelling.[6] In 1971 we find one of the earliest uses of the phrase 'post-classical', which explicitly takes its cue from Bazin. Contemplating Bazin's characterization of American cinema in the late 1930s as a cinema of 'classical perfection', Lawrence Alloway noted 'it follows that the later developments must be post-classical. Extending the morphology of styles implicit in Bazin's formula, the movies I grew up with [in the 1940s and 1950s] were baroque, Hellenistic, overblown, late.'[7] In an argument that in some ways prefigures an aspect of the study by Bordwell, Staiger and Thompson, Alloway rejects this thesis, claiming instead that Hollywood films of the 1940s and 1950s intensified or 'maximized' the themes and formal possibilities established in the 1930s, rather than overthrowing them.

There are essentially two ways of understanding the thesis that the classical mode of practice persisted beyond the breakdown of studio system. The first, and more circumspect, argument involves the claim that one or more aspects of the system described above persists: classical narrative structure, for example, but not the practical norms with which it was associated in the 1930s and 1940s. This is a view which stresses the multi-faceted nature of Hollywood and accepts that change may well be uneven, occurring at different rates and at different moments across these facets.[8] The second, and much stronger, claim is that it is not merely isolated elements of the system that persist, but that the equilibrium obtaining among and across the various levels – that supervening feature which adds greatly to the sense of stability in the system as a whole – has also persisted. This stronger claim is much more difficult to defend, though it is not clear that anyone, including Bordwell, Staiger and Thompson, wishes to make it: they admit, for example, 'that the force of the classical norm was reduced somewhat' (*CHC*, p. 10) after 1960, even if many formally classical films continued to be made; and more recently, Thompson has argued that certain technical and aesthetic norms associated with classical filmmaking have persisted, not that the broader overall stability has endured.[9]

The question of the existence of a distinctive post-classical cinema – like the question of the existence of a classical cinema – is, then, one with both empirical and conceptual dimensions. Nothing approaching the scale and rigour of *The*

Classical Hollywood Cinema has been undertaken on the empirical aspect of this question, and this volume cannot claim to make more than a very modest contribution towards it. What I want to focus on here, however, are the conceptual aspects of the issue – aspects which, it should be underlined, are never eradicated by empirical work, no matter how thorough. If there is no agreement at this point on whether there is a post-classical cinema, or on which features of such a cinema are the features which mark it off from a preceding classical cinema, we can at least sketch out what sorts of criteria would be important in answering these questions. Hollywood, as a total institution, is a multi-faceted creature: which of its facets are of most significance in understanding its evolution? Are the most important criteria those of changes in technology, narrative form, or the use of style? Should changes in the mode of production of films, or changes in their marketing, distribution and exhibition have greater priority? Is the positing of an 'epochal' transition only warranted by a global assessment in which all of these factors play a role and undergo change? In what remains of this essay, I want to explore these questions – questions about the assumptions and criteria present in arguments concerning classicism and post-classicism. I will do this through an examination of two arguments – or rather, one argument, and a second family of arguments – in favour of the idea that the classicism of the studio era has given way to something new. The first argument roots itself very much in the nature of industrial organization, while the second family of arguments stresses the interdependence of the aesthetics of Hollywood films with their mode of production.

Vertical disintegration and post-Fordism

The equilibrium profile of classicism – its high level of stability – will only be disrupted, Bazin argued, by a 'geological movement', as a result of which 'a new pattern' will be 'dug across the plain'.[10] Bazin's metaphor provides a way into the argument that the most significant development in the post-war Hollywood system is the shift away from the Fordist principles around which it had been organized during the studio era. For the proponents of the 'post-Fordist thesis', the Paramount decrees of 1948 constitute a seismic 'movement' which fundamentally alters the 'pattern' of Hollywood.

Although the concept of post-Fordism is relatively obscure within film studies, it has a direct bearing on debates regarding the shift to package production. The notion of post-Fordism was coined by sociologists studying shifts in the nature of capitalist production, particularly after the Second World War when in many industries the strategies of Fordist mass-production (economies of scale through standardization and a detailed division of labour) were revised as a result of changes in market conditions. In a series of articles, Michael Storper and Susan

Christopherson have used the development of the US film industry after 1948 as a case study of post-Fordism. As they apply the concept to post-war Hollywood, post-Fordism involves a shift from a largely undifferentiated mass market served by a limited array of standardized, mass-produced commodities, to that of a more heterogeneous range of specific markets to which more specialized products can be profitably sold. The 'initial shock' of the Paramount decrees, which forced the major studios to sell off their exhibition arms, dramatically raised 'the level of uncertainty [and] instability' in the market for film, Storper argues.[11] Loss of control over exhibition encouraged the trends (already underway) towards fewer but more expensive films, and 'independent' package production. The details of this process of vertical disintegration are relatively well-known within film studies. Storper's analysis does, however, draw our attention to a number of less well-understood features of the post-war industry. The rise of package production leads to a growth in the number of independent film companies – both independent production companies (small production companies without a corporate relationship with a distribution company[12]), as well as specialist firms serving various aspects of preproduction, production and postproduction (talent agencies, special effects houses, catering firms, etc.). These specialist firms then adapt the products and services they offer to the needs of a variety of clients, a process Storper refers to as *product variety* (as distinct from product differentiation), in order to ensure their own long-term viability. The organization of production is now 'flexibly specialized' in the sense that, relative to a typically Fordist mode of production, the specialized units are far more capable of adapting to shifts in market need (or of the needs of a variety of 'niche' markets). This can be seen as parallel with the effect of horizontal integration at the corporate level: as film companies became incorporated within larger conglomerates, with interests in other entertainment fields, so the risk attached to film production – relatively greater because of the ever-increasing investment in individual films – was dissipated by the other products and assets of the conglomerate. A vital part of Storper's analysis, however, is that corporate control of the organization of production, and of the process of vertical disintregration, is absent once the process reaches a certain point:

> A process of replacement of internal economies is set into motion, and beyond a certain point the large firms can no longer reverse it, because no single firm can assert enough control for a long enough period of time. Disintegration, in this manner, may begin with subcontracting, but it may end with the appearance of a network of independent supplier firms and a flexibly specialised system.[13]

Questions from a variety of angles can be posed with respect to this analysis. First, because films are not absolutely identical – two formulaic genre films still have many more significant differences than do two cars of the same model, produced on an assembly line – the 'Fordist' nature of the mode of production in the studio era was always somewhat compromised. (In recognition of this, Bordwell, Staiger and Thompson write of 'serial manufacture' rather than 'mass production' (*CHC*, p. 92).) Indeed, many descriptions of post-Fordist strategies apply at least as well to the studio era as to the period after 1948; consider, for example, the statement that 'flexible automation uses general-purpose machines to produce a variety of products'.[14] In spite of the emphasis on the homogeneity of the Hollywood audience in the 1930s and 1940s, along with the idea that cinemagoers went to the cinema as much as part of a ritual of attendance as to see particular films, the variety of genres and the range of stars testified to and catered for a range of different audience tastes; and as we have already noted, the individual film is distinctive to a degree that most mass-produced commodities are not.

Matthew Bernstein's arguments concerning the continuities and similarities between 'unit production' and 'semi-independent' package production in the studio era add further weight to the queries. Bernstein demonstrates that 'independent' production companies with distribution agreements with the majors (such as Selznick, Goldwyn and Wanger) functioned, in almost all cases, in exactly the same way as studio production units. This, in turn, implies that the shift to package production in the 1950s was not as fundamental as many commentaries – including Storper's – suggest, since 'semi-independent' package production had long been a practice, albeit a minority one, used by the studios.[15] The challenge to Storper's thesis raised by this line of thinking, then, concerns the appropriateness of the US film industry as a case study for the shift to post-Fordism, given its 'non-Fordist' peculiarities in the era when it was supposedly run along Fordist lines.[16]

According to Storper, the 'hallmarks of Fordist industries' are 'vertical integration, mass production, and stable oligopolistic market structures'.[17] In spite of the shifts in the organization of production that he details, however, the oligopolistic nature of the American film industry has not been undermined. This fact has been leapt upon by various critics, who have berated Storper for failing to discuss the crucial role of distribution in the maintenance of the oligopolistic control of the industry as a whole by a small group of major corporations.[18] The reason for the sharpness of the disagreement here lies ultimately in the different focus of Storper's argument, and those of his critics who stress the importance of finance and distribution. Storper is interested, precisely, in the organization of production within industries which have moved away from (quasi-)Fordist, vertically integrated, assembly line models of manufacture. Although the shift from the Fordist mode of production is evidently related to the nature of the product and habits of consumption as well, these remain, for Storper, matters of secondary interest.

More seriously, though, Storper's work fails to account for the trend towards vertical *re*-integration evident in the 1980s and 1990s (see the chapters by Maltby, Gomery and Balio in this volume).

Storper makes few detailed claims about the impact that vertical disintegration had upon film form and style. He does, however, note that the industry responded to disintegration by intensifying product differentiation (through the introduction of widescreen etc.), ushering in a period of 'constant innovation'. This development is in keeping with the 'new pluralism of products' and 'new importance for innovation' said to be characteristic of post-Fordism more generally,[19] and is surely at odds with a central implication of classicism: '"Classical" works conform.'[20] However, the enduring control of the industry by the major film companies, exercised now through the financing and distribution of films, continues to act as a major constraint on such innovation and diversity. As has been documented by both Bernstein and Tino Balio, greater freedom of expression – in thematic, formal and stylistic terms – is by no means guaranteed by the package system. 'Hollywood's unit and semi-independent production . . . offered only the *potential* for procedural autonomy and distinctive filmmaking, if the right historical circumstances . . . enhanced that potential. . . . This is why the semi-independents' departure from the studio system "is more apparent than real".'[21] Others have argued that this continued dominance not only constrains US 'independent' filmmaking, but also reinforces American cultural hegemony abroad. The possibility of distinctive national and regional film cultures is eroded by the globalization of the Hollywood aesthetic.[22]

On the one hand, then, the 'freedoms' of the post-divestment era were, to a greater extent than is often recognized, already present in the studio era; and on the other hand, the 'constraints' and controls of the studio system were maintained, albeit through different legal and corporate mechanisms, in the age of package production. Storper's claim about the relative increase in the significance and power of independent firms essentially applies to *supplier* firms within the domain of film production. There can be little doubt that, in terms of 'final market concentration', the major film companies have in general maintained their market share throughout the period in question. Indeed, one might well argue that the US film industry is an example not of post-Fordism, but of *industrial dualism*, in which independent production companies act at once as 'shock absorbers' and research arms ('pilot fish') for the majors, 'by attracting risk capital and creative talent which the majors can then exploit through their control of distribution'.[23]

Post-classicism, neoclassicism and
the New Hollywood

The post-Fordist argument is, then, essentially an argument about the nature of industrial organization, with only inchoate implications about the form of films themselves. By contrast, the second cluster of arguments I will examine places greater emphasis on aesthetic questions: either through an exclusive attention to them, or more commonly, through arguments concerning the interdependence of the form of Hollywood films and their mode of production – a key assumption, as we have seen, in the work of Bordwell, Staiger and Thompson. I will refer generally to these arguments as arguments for a 'post-classical' period, though, as we will see, a variety of terms have been used to name the new period.

Post-classicism is a term of relatively recent coinage. The notion of the 'New Hollywood' has been around quite a lot longer – or at least, it has been subjected to far greater intensity of discussion and revision of meaning since being coined. Peter Krämer has traced back the earliest uses of the phrase to 1959,[24] but the academic adoption of the concept occurred in the 1970s, when it came to be applied to the period of relative experimentation in the late 1960s and 1970s in Hollywood, made possible by the economic insecurity of Hollywood, still casting around for forms of durable and predictable appeal after the massive post-war decline in audiences, and the more immediate problems of overproduction in the mid- to late 1960s. One of the key accounts of this period was Thomas Elsaesser's 1975 essay 'The pathos of failure', which reflected on the 'New Hollywood' of directors like Altman, Hellman and Spielberg, against the background of earlier writings on the classical Hollywood cinema by Elsaesser and his colleagues in the journal *Monogram*.[25] The causal dynamics and key features of this phase of American filmmaking are now well-known: incorporating elements drawn from European art cinema, these films depicted uncertain, counter-cultural and marginal protagonists, whose goals were often relatively ill-defined and ultimately unattained, in contrast to the heroic and typically successful figures around which classical films revolved.

This 'New Hollywood' – or what David James calls the 'American art film' – represented a trend in dialectical tension with the blockbuster films of the era, most notably the disaster film cycle. While a few films like *Bonnie and Clyde* (1967) and *Easy Rider* (1969) were very successful, many of these films were based on relatively complex narrative premises, lacked major stars, and some, like *MacCabe and Mrs Miller* (1971), exhibited a deliberately rough-hewn, 'primitive' quality. The blockbusters and the 'art' films are also dialectically related in terms of narrative. Elsaesser argued that the 'unmotivated hero' eroded the very narrative fabric of these films: writing of the opening of *The Mean Machine* (1974), Elsaesser wonders whether he 'has seen the last 15 minutes of the previous film, or the pre-credit scene to a flashback movie that never follows'.[26] In developing projects such as *Star Wars* (1977) and *Raiders of the Lost Ark* (1981), Lucas and Spielberg are said to have been seeking a return to narrative tautness and transitivity. Ironically, however, as we will see, some critics see these films as manifesting another form of narrative malaise.

The work of Elsaesser and his associates at *Monogram* seems to have been highly influential on the historiography of Bordwell, Staiger and Thompson, who among other things fleshed out the hypothesis of an extended classical period beginning in the mid-1910s, continuing beyond the Paramount decrees and into the 1960s. With respect to the question of just how significant the innovations of the New Hollywood were, however, there is an important difference. While Elsaesser maintains that these films retained an underlying architecture drawn from the genre film, as well as the emotional punch characteristic of Hollywood films throughout their history, his argument implies that the period marks a funda-mental break with the classical Hollywood cinema. The new prominence of 'mar-ginal' audiences for Hollywood, along with the critical and cynical attitudes ascribed to these groups, undermined the 'can do' ideology which Elsaesser argued was implicit in classical narrative form itself. These 'transitional' films seemed to be harbingers of a wholly new kind of American filmmaking. Like Elsaesser, Bordwell and his colleagues argue for the continuing role of genre conventions, around which the elements from art cinema are moulded. But Bord-well distinguishes his argument from that of the *Monogram* writers in proposing that this amounts to an example of stylistic assimilation, rather than overall formal transformation: the underlying system of conventions – at the level of functions, rather than devices – remains the same (*CHC*, pp. 373–5).[27] In a sense, Bordwell's argument can be seen as the reiteration, within his own theoretical framework, of Bazin's famous remark concerning the 'fertility' of the 'classical art' of American cinema 'when it comes into contact with new elements'.[28]

The notion of the New Hollywood, however, underwent a strange mutation, ending up designating either something diametrically opposed to the American art film, or something inclusive of but much larger than it. On this view – articulated most concisely by Thomas Schatz – the thematic, narrative and stylistic innova-tions of the late 1960s and 1970s were but one phase of a gradual and ongoing reorientation and restabilization of the film industry, finally achieved after 1975. This new stability was secured not by the flirtation of American cinema with the art cinemas of Europe, but by what has sometimes been termed – again extending the analogy with art history – *neoclassicism*: a return to genre filmmaking, but now marked by greater self-consciousness, as well as supercharged by new special effects, saturation booking, engorged production budgets and, occasionally, even larger advertising budgets. Although some 'arty' projects continued to be sup-ported by the studios into the late 1970s – *Days of Heaven* (1978), *Apocalypse Now*

(1979), *All that Jazz* (1979), *Heaven's Gate* (1980) – the direction of the industry
had been set by the monumental success of those 'hyperbolic simulations of
Hollywood B-movies', *Jaws* (1975) and *Star Wars*.[29] Many of the features of these
neoclassical 'event' movies are borne out of the horizontal integration now
existing between film producers and other entertainment companies, in which
films are 'designed with the multimedia marketplace and franchise status in
mind'.[30] While Schatz has argued that these films are unlike classical Hollywood
films in their emphasis on 'visceral, kinetic and fast-paced' plotting at the expense
of character, one might argue instead that such films draw on a different strain of
the legacy of studio era Hollywood – the serial B-film, most obviously in *Star Wars*,
the *Indiana Jones* series, and in the British remake of *Flash Gordon* (1980).

In an argument which parallels Schatz's in several respects, Justin Wyatt has
argued that the economic and institutional changes in Hollywood since 1960 'have
irrevocably altered the forms of product from Hollywood'.[31] Given the principle
of interdependence between form and industrial context, there is one institutional
change in particular which we might expect to have had an impact on the form of
Hollywood films. Following on the process of conglomeration, and the emergence
of cable, satellite, and home video markets, the bulk of the profits on most films
are now derived from these 'ancillary' markets rather than from theatrical box
office.[32] Why should this development be of such moment – of any greater
significance than all the other changes since 1948? When the bulk of profits is
derived from sources other than the theatrical market, it is reasonable to assume
that the pressures from these 'secondary' markets will command more attention
in the making of the product.[33] One example of this concerns the changes in
widescreen compositional practices due to the significance of the television market, discussed by Steve Neale in this volume; according to Wyatt, a more dramatic
set of formal changes has been driven by the synergies with music marketing
(music videos and soundtrack albums) and advertising, resulting in what he terms
a 'modular' aesthetic, which tends to stall and 'fragment' narrative form.

Wyatt locates the modular aesthetic in the immensely popular and influential
'high-concept' film, a term and a form that came to prominence in the 1970s. A
high-concept film is one which places a great emphasis on style and 'stylishness',
revolving around a simple, easily summarized narrative based on physically typed
characters, which in turn affords striking icons, images and snappy plot descriptions as marketing 'hooks'. The high-concept film is heavily reliant upon stars, and
gives great prominence to its soundtrack (usually a mixture of original scoring and
pop songs), which is marketed separately as one or more soundtrack albums
associated with the film (as discussed by K. J. Donnelly in Chapter 9 of this
volume in relation to the first two *Batman* films). In addition, music videos often
rework aspects of the film in order to promote both the film and the music. These
are the factors that give rise, he argues, to the modularity of the high-concept

film, in which sections of the film are apt to exceed the requirements of the narrative and take on a quasi-autonomous function, in contrast to the economical 'knitting' of segments in the classical film.

High-concept films are the most overtly 'market driven' films made by Hollywood, according to Wyatt. As the major film companies became absorbed within larger conglomerates, so the potential for synergies between the previously separate entertainment industries could be realized. As several essays in this volume make clear, the 'big screen' film is now just the beginning of a profit stream involving television, home video, CDs, computer games, clothing and so forth. Wyatt places a special emphasis on marketing: it is not merely that the mode of production has changed, but that the stress on the marketing and 'pitching' of individual films, and the convergence between fiction films and advertising, has directly affected the form of these films. The influence of advertising is evident, for example, in the development of product placement, soundtrack marketing and television advertising of new releases, as well as the gleaming, over-polished visual style of directors weaned on advertising, and the substitutability among film performers, stars and fashion models.

Other authors take a less measured stance on the impact of marketing and advertising on narrative. Richard Schickel claims that 'Hollywood seems to have lost or abandoned the art of narrative'; most contemporary films, he suggests, offer little more than 'a succession of undifferentiated sensations, lucky or unlucky accidents, that have little or nothing to do with whatever went before or is about to come next'.[34] From such an account, one would be forgiven for thinking that a Dada film like *Entr'acte* (1924) had become the model of Hollywood filmmaking. Reports of the death of narrative in Hollywood filmmaking, however, are surely much exaggerated (and usually either impressionistic speculations or generalizations based on a single or very few examples). Narrative has not disappeared, but the new technologies and new markets have encouraged certain kinds of narrative, traceable to serials, B-adventures and episodic melodramas. Given the potential profits to be made from computer games, for example, it should not surprise us that action-adventure films – like *The Lost World* (1997) – are perceived as potential high-earners, since their chase scenarios dovetail easily with the formats of such games. But even here, narrative is still omnipresent. There may be less attention to detailed character motivation, greater emphasis on spectacle – the kinds of features that Thomas Schatz stresses – and even straightforward narrative sloppiness, but narrative has certainly not disappeared under a cloud of special effects. In action films, the plot advances *through* spectacle; the spectacular elements are, generally speaking, as 'narrativized' as are the less ostentatious spaces of other genres. As the chapters by Peter Krämer and Warren Buckland in this volume demonstrate, careful narrative patterning – a prerequisite for the kind of emotional response associated with classical narratives – is still very much in evidence in the biggest blockbusters of our time; and as K. J. Donnelly demonstrates, the conglomerate, multimedia nature of the industry does not necessarily shatter a film into a string of wholly unconnected sounds and images. The dinosaurs in Spielberg's recent films are not just impressive spectacles, but creatures of terror and wonderment – characters, antagonists, in a tale. It is this emotional dimension which, among other things, makes the movies memorable, and thus fosters the 'memorialization' of the experience through further purchases – be it games, videos, clothing or theme parks. It is not so much, then, that narrative has been displaced by the new technologies and markets of the last fifteen to twenty years, as that the demands and opportunities provided by them have led to an emphasis on certain genres and episodic forms of narrative. The modular segments of which Wyatt writes are not merely held in check by the narratives of such films, but given meaning by them. Just as the 'big screen' movie experience plays a far greater role in driving the profitability of the multimedia marketplace than theatrical ticket sales would suggest,[35] so the movie provides a primary narrative baseline which both endows isolated movie icons with meaning and emotional resonance, and provides a backdrop against which to toy with these associations in other media contexts.[36]

The continuity of Hollywood

Many critics throughout the post-war period have, then, argued that Hollywood filmmaking had crossed, or was on the brink of crossing, a threshold into a new epoch. Equally, however, there have been many critics who have cautioned against overhasty judgements regarding such fundamental shifts, suggesting that superficial changes are likely to obscure our view of underlying continuities. From this point of view, historians of the 'New' or post-classical Hollywood, while correctly recognizing new phases or trends in product differentiation, are not warranted in positing a break with classicism. Indeed, the very regularity with which declarations of new epochs have been made, the sheer number of 'New Hollywoods' that one finds posited over the course of film history, recommends this more sober view: if things are always 'new', nothing is ever really new. There *is* a constant process of adjustment and adaptation to new circumstances, but this is an adaptation made on the basis of certain underlying and constant goals: the maximizing of profits through the production of classical narrative films. Rather than looking for a fundamental break between classicism and a putative post-classicism, we would do better to look for smaller-scale changes and shifts, at both the institutional and aesthetic levels, within a more broadly continuous system of American commercial filmmaking.[37] It is not that change has not occurred, but that the scale of change has consistently been overestimated.

There is a related historiographical position which has not been articulated in such a unified fashion and as a consequence has received far less attention. This thesis is similar to the argument that the Hollywood system has maintained essentially the same character from the teens to the present day – with the vital additional proviso that we should *not* think of this enduring system as in any sense 'classical'. The 'weighting' of the analysis towards aesthetic questions, inevitably introduced by the use of art-historical language, is rejected. Like its near twin, this argument acknowledges the endurance of the profit motive, but demurs from the premise that this has been or is always best fulfilled by the appeal of classical narrative form. Many individual Hollywood films, and perhaps entire genres, of the studio era, so the argument goes, are not characterized by the formal harmony or 'decorum' which forms the main justification for the appellation 'classical'. The norms of narrative classicism, while certainly expressed as goals within screenwriting manuals and more informal Hollywood lore, are compromised and interrupted by other forms of interest: the drive towards comedy (and other emotions), the display of stars, the impetus towards sheer spectacle.[38] Richard Maltby and Ian Craven, for example, discuss Hollywood in terms of a 'commercial aesthetic' that is 'too opportunistic to prize coherence, organic unity, or even the absence of contradiction among its primary virtues', an analysis that 'sits uneasily with the stylistically determined view of a movie's organization implicit in the idea of classicism'.[39] In the terminology of *The Classical Hollywood Cinema*, classically harmonious narrative is not the 'dominant' of any era of Hollywood filmmaking, even if it is present as one key compositional principle.[40] This, of course, removes altogether the motivation for positing a 'post-classical' era, since the aesthetic features of so-called 'post-classical' cinema are revealed to have been an aspect of so-called 'classical' cinema all along.

A charge sometimes levelled at Bordwell, Staiger and Thompson is that, for all the wealth of historical detail contained in their work, the description of the classical Hollywood mode becomes an ahistorical one. The classical system they posit becomes so abstract, generalized and encompassing that anything can be assimilated and nothing can make a difference.[41] Dirk Eitzen, for example, has argued that underlying the study by Bordwell, Staiger and Thompson are a set of functionalist principles, principles which are most apt for the study of long-term historical processes. But to the extent that a functionalist account is designed to explain how a given system perpetuates itself and remains stable over long periods, historical development may appear to be sidelined.

While Eitzen notes that such functionalism is much more robust and subtle than its detractors claim, and that it is perhaps the only theory which accounts for long-term historical development while avoiding teleological assumptions, he nevertheless points out that functionalism has its limitations. These limitations become apparent precisely in the study of briefer historical episodes, when the intentions and interventions of both individual and institutional agents – the things that account for the events which force the system either to reorient itself, or collapse – take on more weight than the longer-term patterns and constraints.[42] Arguing along similar lines, Henry Jenkins suggests that there is a 'necessary process of experimentation and accommodation which surrounds the adoption of alien aesthetic norms into the dominant classical system',[43] a process which Bordwell, Staiger and Thompson tend to downplay in favour of the ultimate assimilation of 'alien' elements within the existing system. In its eagerness to avoid overstatement regarding the 'subversiveness' of this film or that genre, the functionalist bent of *The Classical Hollywood Cinema* perhaps flattens the local and immediate experience of change and discontinuity.

As the Annales historians have taught us, however, history consists of many layers which change at very different rates, and stasis is as much a fact of history as is change. Bordwell, Staiger and Thompson do not 'banish' history; rather, their account implies that there are various levels of historical change and development. There is a history of devices, but this is distinct from the history of the functions of devices, and from the history of the relations between the systems within which they function (*CHC*, pp. 6–7, 9–10). The mode as a whole – the 'total style' – which encompasses all of these levels, *can* be subverted: it is just that the standards for such subversion are high indeed – the continuity of classicism is argued for in part by contrasting the American art film with more radically different kinds of cinema, such as the 'counter-cinema' of Jean Marie Straub and Danièle Huillet. To argue that Elsaesser's New Hollywood fails to mark an epochal divide is, thus, hardly to argue that a shift had not occurred at a less fundamental level.

This problem – a lack of clarity about what aspect of Hollywood is being discussed – is one that has frequently afflicted debate around classical and 'post-classical' Hollywood. Critics have often argued at cross-purposes with one another, rushing to judgement without checking the scope of the problem or being clear about the purview of their arguments. No matter what other factors are relevant – including the careful empirical study of a representative body of films – assessing the plausibility of arguments concerning classicism and post-classicism will require that we begin by considering the breadth and nature of the claims being made.

Notes

1 Miriam Hansen, 'Early cinema, late cinema: permutations of the public sphere', *Screen*, vol. 34, no. 3 (Autumn 1993), pp. 197–210. Hansen even suggests that one sign of the end of this regulated, classical spectatorship is the rise in complaints about talking in movie theatres (p. 198).

2 David Bordwell, Janet Staiger and Kristin Thompson, *The Classical Hollywood Cinema: Film Style and Mode of Production to 1960* (New York: Columbia University Press,

1985). All subsequent page references in the main text are to this edition, abbreviated as *CHC*, followed by page number(s).

3 For André Bazin, the stability and 'maturity' of Hollywood filmmaking in the 1930s, in terms of subject matter (a range of genres with established conventions), style (conventions of editing, cinematography, sound, etc.) and technological development, as well as its worldwide success as 'a common form of cinematic language', warranted its description as a 'classical art'. André Bazin, 'The evolution of the language of cinema', in *What is Cinema?* vol. 1, trans. Hugh Gray (Berkeley: University of California Press, 1967), pp. 28–30.

4 Although this interdependence is not absolute: 'the Hollywood mode of production . . . while congruent in some respects, cannot be simply superimposed upon stylistic history' (*CHC*, p. 9). The emphasis on style (albeit in relation to mode of production) is implicit in the very word 'classical' – we would be unlikely to label an industrial practice 'classical' if it were not associated with a commodity apt to be described in aesthetic and art historical terms. The art historical origins of the term 'classical' are plainly visible in the key definitions of it in the first few pages of *The Classical Hollywood Cinema*, and are stressed by Bordwell when he insists that 'the history of an art' may periodize history differently from histories prioritizing political or social matters (p. 9).

5 The same sort of continuity is argued for from an economic and institutional perspective by Douglas Gomery, 'The American film industry of the 1970s: stasis in the "New Hollywood"', *Wide Angle*, vol. 5, no. 4 (1983), pp. 52–9.

6 André Bazin, 'The evolution of the western', in *What is Cinema?* vol. 2, trans. Hugh Gray (Berkeley: University of California Press, 1971), pp. 149–57; Manny Farber, 'The Gimp', in *Negative Space* (New York: Praeger, 1971), p. 71.

7 Lawrence Alloway, *Violent America: The Movies, 1946–64* (New York: MOMA, 1971), p. 11.

8 For general historiographical discussions of these issues, see David Hackett Fisher, *Historian's Fallacies: Toward a Logic of Historical Thought* (New York: Harper and Row, 1970), p. 146; and Robert C. Allen and Douglas Gomery, *Film History: Theory and Practice* (New York: Knopf, 1985), pp. 48–9.

9 Kristin Thompson, 'Narrative structure in early classical cinema', in John Fullerton (ed.), *Celebrating 1895* (University of Luton/John Libbey, forthcoming). Thompson specifically argues for the persistence of a kind of temporal 'golden mean', which dictates that a large-scale portion of narrative should last between twenty and thirty minutes.

10 Bazin, 'The evolution of the language of cinema', p. 31.

11 Michael Storper, 'The transition to flexible specialisation in the US film industry: external economies, the division of labour and the crossing of industrial divides', in Ash Amin (ed.), *Post-Fordism: A Reader* (Oxford: Blackwell, 1994), p. 217.

12 This is the definition provided by Janet Staiger in 'Individualism versus collectivism', *Screen*, vol. 24, nos. 4–5 (July–October 1983), pp. 68–9; and reiterated in *The Classical Hollywood Cinema*, p. 317.

13 Storper, 'Flexible specialization in the US film industry,' p. 218. The notion of 'flexible specialization' is derived from the work of Michael Piore and Charles Sabel; see especially *The Second Industrial Divide: Possibilities for Prosperity* (New York: Basic Books, 1984). A very useful discussion of 'flexibility' in relation to film and other media can be found in Michael Curtin, 'On edge: culture industries in the neo-network era', in

Richard Ohmann (ed.), *Making and Selling Culture* (Hanover: Wesleyan University Press/University Press of New England, 1996), pp. 181–202.

14 Robin Murray, 'Fordism and post-Fordism', in Stuart Hall, David Held and Tony McGrew (eds), *Modernity and its Futures* (Cambridge: Polity Press, 1992), p. 218.

15 Matthew Bernstein, 'Hollywood's semi-independent production', *Cinema Journal*, vol. 32, no. 3 (Spring 1993), pp. 50, 54.

16 Indeed, the post-Fordist thesis has been challenged on home territory by those who point out that the production of cars incorporated the need for 'flexible specialization' from the late 1920s onwards; 'it is thus to be seriously doubted whether mass production has ever consistently corresponded to the Fordist paradigm'. Mark Elam, 'Puzzling out the post-Fordist debate: technology, markets and institutions', in Amin (ed.), *Post-Fordism*, p. 55.

17 Storper, 'Flexible specialisation in the US film industry', p. 195.

18 Asu Aksoy and Kevin Robins, 'Hollywood for the 21st century: global competition for critical mass in image markets', *Cambridge Journal of Economics*, vol. 16 no. 1, pp. 7, 13, 16. In fairness to Storper, it should be noted that this anomaly in the argument was acknowledged by him, though he does downplay its significance: Storper, 'Flexible specialisation in the US film industry', p. 222, note 9.

19 Murray, 'Post-Fordism', p. 218.

20 Richard Maltby and Ian Craven, *Hollywood Cinema: An Introduction* (Oxford: Blackwell, 1995), p. 7.

21 Bernstein, 'Semi-independent production', p. 51; see also p. 52, note 4. Bernstein is quoting Richard Dyer MacCann, 'Independence with a vengeance', *Film Quarterly*, vol. 15, no. 4 (1962), p. 4. Also of relevance are Tino Balio, *United Artists: The Company That Changed the Film Industry* (Madison: University of Wisconsin Press, 1989); and Tino Balio, 'When is an independent producer independent? The case of United Artists after 1948', *The Velvet Light Trap*, no. 22 (1986), along with other essays in this issue by Bernstein, Kevin Hagopian and Ed Lowry.

22 Aksoy and Robins, 'Hollywood for the 21st century', p. 20. See also Tino Balio, '"A major presence in all of the world markets": the globalization of Hollywood in the 1990s', this volume, pp. 58–73. Other authors, however, have discussed some of the 'localizing' responses to the global power of the Hollywood aesthetic. See, for example, Curtin, 'On edge', p. 187; and Dana Polan, 'Globalism's localisms', in Rob Wilson and Wimal Dissanayake (eds), *Global/Local: Cultural Production and the Transnational Imaginary* (Durham: Duke University Press, 1996), pp. 255–83.

23 Nicholas Garnham, quoted by Aksoy and Robins, 'Hollywood for the 21st century', p. 11; see also Curtin, 'On edge', p. 197; and chapters 4–6 by Balio, Wyatt and Schamus of this volume.

24 Peter Krämer, 'Post-classical Hollywood', in John Hill and Pamela Church Gibson (eds), *The Oxford Guide to Film Studies* (Oxford: Oxford University Press, 1998), p. 296.

25 Thomas Elsaesser, 'The pathos of failure: American films in the 70s – notes on the unmotivated hero', *Monogram*, no. 6 (1975), pp. 13–19.

26 Elsaesser, 'The pathos of failure', p. 16.

27 In his early overview of arguments concerning the 'New Hollywood', Steve Neale signalled a similar scepticism. '"New Hollywood Cinema"', *Screen*, vol. 17, no. 2 (1976), p. 120.

28 André Bazin, 'On the *politique des auteurs*', in Jim Hillier (ed.), *Cahiers du Cinema: The*

1950s – Neo-Realism, Hollywood, New Wave (London: Routledge and Kegan Paul, 1985), p. 258.

29 J. Hoberman, *Vulgar Modernism: Writing on Movies and Other Media* (Philadelphia: Temple University Press, 1991), p. 284.

30 Thomas Schatz, 'The New Hollywood', in Jim Collins, Hilary Radner and Ava Preacher Collins (eds), *Film Theory Goes to the Movies* (New York: Routledge, 1993), p. 35. See also the essay by Tino Balio in this volume. For an analysis which draws upon the notion of 'neoclassicism', see the essay by K. J. Donnelly on the first two *Batman* films, Chapter 9 of this volume.

31 Justin Wyatt, *High Concept: Movies and Marketing in Hollywood* (Austin: University of Texas Press, 1994), p. 16.

32 See Douglas Gomery, Chapter 3 of this volume, p. 52.

33 James Schamus, Chapter 6 of this volume, p. 94.

34 Quoted in Schatz, 'New Hollywood', p. 33; see also chapters 2 and 6 by Richard Maltby and James Schamus in this volume. For another account which argues that Hollywood films have suffered a breakdown of narrative due to the influence of advertising, see Mark Crispin Miller, 'Advertising: end of story', in Mark Crispin Miller (ed.), *Seeing Through Movies* (New York: Pantheon Books, 1990), pp. 186–246.

35 Peter Krämer, 'The lure of the big picture: film, television and Hollywood', in John Hill and Martin McLoone, *Big Picture, Small Screen: The Relations between Film and Television* (Luton: University of Luton/John Libbey, 1996), pp. 9–46.

36 Schatz, 'New Hollywood', pp. 33–4.

37 This is the line of argument taken by Douglas Gomery in 'Toward a new media economics', in David Bordwell and Noël Carroll (eds), *Post-Theory: Reconstructing Film Studies* (Madison: University of Wisconsin Press, 1996), pp. 407–18.

38 See Rick Altman, *The American Film Musical* (Bloomington: Indiana University Press, 1987); Henry Jenkins, *What Made Pistachio Nuts? Early Sound Comedy and the Vaudeville Experience* (New York: Columbia University Press, 1992); Dirk Eitzen, 'Comedy and classicism', in Richard Allen and Murray Smith (eds), *Film Theory and Philosophy* (Oxford: Clarendon Press, 1997), pp. 394–411; and Elizabeth Cowie, Chapter 12 of this volume.

39 Maltby and Craven, *Hollywood Cinema*, pp. 35 and 37.

40 Maltby's position in Chapter 2 of this volume is somewhat different to that in his earlier book with Craven. In this volume, he argues that though the potentially disunifying presence of the 'commercial intertext' has been present throughout Hollywood history, the pressures threatening to fragment narrative unity and stylistic coherence have increased.

Christopher Williams has similarly argued against the aptness of the adjective 'classical', though with no particular stress on the commercial factors which, for Maltby, lead to the loss of formal 'decorum': 'After the classic, the classical and ideology: the differences of realism', *Screen*, vol. 35 no.3 (1994), pp. 284–5. Like Andrew Britton ('The philosophy of the pigeonhole: Wisconsin formalism and "the classical style"', *CineAction!*, no. 15 (Winter 1988/9), pp. 47–63), Williams is more concerned to stress the diversity of aesthetic strands within Hollywood cinema. It should be noted here, however, that Bordwell, Staiger and Thompson neither deny the existence of non-narrative impulses within Hollywood films, nor that many of the streams running into Hollywood filmmaking were anything but classical (*CHC*, p. 4). But they do argue that classical narrative requirements acted as the 'constructive principle' in Hollywood filmmaking. Robin Wood justifies the term 'classicism' in a somewhat similar way, albeit in a critical language informed by psychoanalysis rather than Formalism, in *Hollywood from Vietnam to Reagan* (New York: Columbia University Press, 1986), pp. 48–9.

41 See Elizabeth Cowie, Chapter 12 of this volume; and Maltby and Craven, *Hollywood Cinema*, p. 218.

42 Dirk Eitzen, 'Evolution, functionalism, and the study of American cinema', *The Velvet Light Trap*, no. 28 (Fall 1991), pp. 82–3.

43 Henry Jenkins, 'Historical poetics', in Joanne Hollows and Mark Jancovich (eds), *Approaches to Popular Film* (Manchester: Manchester University Press, 1995), p. 114; see also Murray Smith, 'Technological determination, aesthetic resistance', *Wide Angle*, vol. 12, no. 3 (July 1990), pp. 92–3.

Chapter 2

'Nobody knows everything'

Post-classical historiographies and consolidated entertainment

Richard Maltby

Griffin (Tim Robbins):	[The story] lacked certain elements that we need to market a film successfully.
June (Greta Scacchi):	What elements?
Griffin:	Suspense, laughter, violence, hope, heart, nudity, sex, happy endings. Mainly happy endings.

The Player (1992)

As a classical metanarrative, the history of classical Hollywood cinema lacks only one element: a happy ending. Its resolution is problematic, untidy and uncertain. Among its chroniclers, there is no consensus as to when (if ever) classical Hollywood ended. But whenever its final scenes are set, they are seen to act out a prolonged decline. The metaphors of evolution that brought Hollywood from primitivism to maturity are replaced by notions of decadence and decay. The last three decades of Hollywood's history are most often presented as a story of failed promise: the promises made to, or at least believed by, that generation of critics who espoused cinema as 'the most important art of the twentieth century,' and constructed its study as an academic discipline.[1] In his historical survey of American cinema, John Belton entitles the section on contemporary Hollywood 'The failure of the new', and invokes Fredric Jameson in support of his account of contemporary Hollywood as 'stylistically youthful and inventive but politically conservative', constrained by 'the inability to say anything that has not already been said. . . . The authentic expression of ideas that took place in the past is today replaced by quotation and allusion to that authentic expression.'[2] By the 1980s, he concludes, the continuity of the Hollywood tradition had begun to fall apart:

> Each new film existed in an aesthetic vacuum, though it continued to compete with the box-office statistics of its predecessors. Audiences who expected little were enthralled by the little they got. And they had even

less with which to compare. If you have never seen *Intolerance*, *Sunrise*, *Citizen Kane*, *The Searchers*, or *Vertigo*, you can't expect more than *Batman Returns*.[3]

Even more despairingly, James Bernardoni has analysed the 'New Hollywood' as the product of four aesthetic fallacies misinterpreting the virtues of classical cinema and resulting in the collapse of significance and the violation of film's obligation to convey a sense of credible reality.[4]

In this story of failed romance, a self-confessed nostalgia colours the account of the *traison des auteur-comptables* who deserted the radical political and aesthetic possibilities of the 'New Hollywood', which Joseph Gelmis conceived in 1970 as being no less than 'a technical and aesthetic revolution in movies which will inevitably restructure human consciousness and understanding'.[5] In the passage from the Old to the New Hollywood, argues Bernardoni, 'something real and important has been lost': the complex 'common language' of classical Hollywood, which reached 'a peak of aesthetic consolidation in the American cinema of the late forties and fifties', as an art form that 'seemed permanently embedded in the American culture'.[6]

The study of Hollywood as an academic discipline has been constructed by two generations of scholars: a first who, 'in their youth during the 1960s, fell in love with Hollywood in its sunset years';[7] and a later group, whose decisive encounter with cinema took place in the heated atmosphere of the early 1970s, when Hollywood's crisis of overproduction was understood as a Renaissance because, as John Milius declared, 'now, power lies with the film-makers'.[8] While many of the earlier generation were never seduced by the Movie Brats, the second group have endured the disillusionment of watching what should have been 'a new mythology for the disaffected 1960s generation' lose whatever countercultural content it once had and become 'increasingly, albeit unintentionally, complicit with the rehabilitation of patriarchal authority'.[9] For the last two decades, academic criticism has predominantly viewed mainstream cinema as a sequence of emptily expensive, aesthetically impoverished spectacles, literally and metaphorically restricted within the 'safe action area' required by the small screens of multiplexes, video and pay-TV. In a contemporary version of the eternal conflict between art and commerce for the soul of cinema, the economic opportunities provided by globalization and the new technologies of distribution are seen as aesthetic contractions requiring the application of a formula to 'make it simple and keep it moving'.[10] Betrayed by Spielberg, those academic critics who have not retired into the eternal verities of Alfred Hitchcock or the universal human truths of Howard Hawks seek alternative comforts in a postmodern Arden, where interpretation and identity may be as free and as labile as you like.

Bernardoni's 'common language' is a less complexly analysed equivalent of the 'mode of film practice' explored by David Bordwell, Janet Staiger and Kristin Thompson in *The Classical Hollywood Cinema*. Their conclusions are, however, noticeably different from his. In the final part of their book, they argue that since 1960 the classical style has demonstrated its capacity to maintain itself through variation and assimilation. The New Hollywood can be explained as a process of stylistic assimilation:

> As the 'old' Hollywood had incorporated and refunctionalized devices from German Expressionism and Soviet montage . . . the 'New' Hollywood has selectively borrowed from the international art cinema.[11] . . . [It has bent] art-film devices to causally or generically motivated functions . . . [But t]he classical premises of time and space remain powerfully in force, with only minor instrumental changes [and] even the most ambitious directors cannot escape genres.[12]

In their account, the mode of production also absorbed technological innovations and restabilized itself, assigning the new techniques to already canonized functions.[13] Further, they argue that the modifications in the American film industry since 1960 have had only minor effects on the mode of production.[14] Conglomerate ownership, they suggest, leads to decentralized management control, leaving control over the mode of production with individual package units, and the package-unit system operating in essentially the same way.

There is something wrong with both these pictures. As Janet Wasko argues, the feature film business no longer exists in its own right.[15] Contemporary Hollywood is a fully integrated part of a much larger and more diversified entertainment software industry, the second largest net export industry in the US economy, dominating its global market to an extent comparable only with the position of Hollywood at the height of the late silent era. In economic terms, at least, this is anything but a story of decline, regardless of whether the product being so successfully marketed is fundamentally inferior to, or fundamentally the same as, the classically functional/elegant Hollywood product of 1917–60. The Hollywood of high concept, ultra-high budget production – after *Star Wars*, video, pay-cable, deregulation and globalization – bears the same names as classical Hollywood, but it understands its economics, its audiences and its products in dramatically different ways. Post-classical Hollywood describes the end result of the changes initiated by the Paramount decrees, the establishment of a new relationship with the television industry, and the switch of its attention to a younger audience. In this New Hollywood the major companies, acting primarily as financiers and distributors, have gradually come to terms with a fragmentation of the audience, a concern with ideas of demographics and target audiences derived from market research, globalized markets and new delivery systems. The names, moreover, are only half the same: Time Warner–Turner; Disney–ABC; News Corporation/Fox; Viacom/Paramount; Sony–Columbia.

Since 1950 the audience attending American movie theatres has grown younger: by 1979 every other ticket was bought by someone aged between 12 and 20, and another 30 per cent of ticket sales were to people in their twenties.[16] The changes to Hollywood are not all demographic, but they are most starkly revealed by statistics. In 1977 *Star Wars* took over $500 million at the box office, but the income from sales of ancillary goods far exceeded that figure, as well as extending the life of the product and guaranteeing the success of its sequels. In the early 1980s, worldwide sales of *Star Wars* goods were estimated to be worth $1.5 billion a year, while *Batman* (1989) made $1 billion from merchandizing, four times its box-office earnings. The growth of ancillary markets in video and television since 1980 has meant that by 1995, less than 20 per cent of total film revenues came from the domestic box office.[17] Paradoxically, this has not greatly diminished the strategic importance of that sector, since the ancillary markets are themselves dominated by feature films, and the American domestic theatrical market remains crucial in determining the value of a product in subsequent outlets. It does, however, require that movie production be seen as the creation of entertainment software that can be viewed through several different windows and transported to several different platforms maintained by the other divisions of tightly diversified media corporations. Both the economic and aesthetic boundaries of contemporary Hollywood are difficult to define, but like the aesthetics of synergy, the corporate economics of transnational media conglomerates differ considerably from the economics of a single industry which, with whatever additions, the film industry remained until 1948.

For perhaps three decades in this century, Hollywood, the American film industry's synonym for itself, appeared to have a unified identity. That identity was determined by the existence of a relatively stable, vertically integrated oligo-poly dominating all three sectors of the industry, but it has almost always been perceived as inhering in the form of its principal product, the feature film.[18] The history of Hollywood has most frequently been constructed as if it were the history of a narrative form, an evolution of stylistic norms, thematic or ideological paradigms and technological changes. Accounts describing this almost organic process stress the internal coherence of the diachronic object 'Hollywood' and equally, through their emphasis on its specific formal features, differentiate it from other related cultural products and processes.

The Classical Hollywood Cinema provides the exemplary instance of this practice. Economics, style and technology are drawn together in a narrative tracing the evolution of a discrete and unified object: classical Hollywood's 'mode of film production'. Although *The Classical Hollywood Cinema* acknowledges that the forces of oligopoly demonstrate economic determination in the final instance, its authors' primary interests lie elsewhere: 'in the last analysis,' they argue, 'stylistic factors can explain the most specific and interesting aspects of Hollywood film-making.'[19] In their preface, they define the object of their study as a mode of film practice, which 'consists of a set of widely held stylistic norms':

> These formal and stylistic norms will be created, shaped, and supported within a mode of film production – a characteristic ensemble of economic aims, a specific division of labor, and particular ways of conceiving and executing the work of filmmaking . . . to see Hollywood filmmaking from 1917–60 as a unified mode of film practice is to argue for a coherent system whereby aesthetic norms and the mode of film production reinforced one another.[20]

Economic determination is not explicitly denied by such a formulation, but the primary interest remains with questions of style and modes of practice: one cannot, they maintain, 'reduce alternative styles to their productive contexts'.[21] In this analysis, the stylistic concept of 'mode of film practice' encompasses the 'mode of film production', which requires examination in order 'to situate the styles historically'.[22]

> While economic practices are an important condition of existence for Hollywood's production practices, equally significant was the film industry's commitment to particular ideological/signifying practices. . . . While in the last instance economic practices may have been determinant . . . ideological/signifying practices continually influenced the necessity to divide labor and to divide it in its particular configuration.[23]

The Classical Hollywood Cinema concentrates explicitly on the production of films and in practice, the term 'mode of production' refers specifically to the management systems and the division of labour within the production industry, not to any broader totality embracing distribution or exhibition.[24] Other writers have criticised this formulation for implying the relative autonomy of the object 'Hollywood' from the broader social history of twentieth-century American capitalism.[25] In *Hollywood in the Information Age*, Janet Wasko suggests this approach assumes that 'a study of the industry and its technological development is only important to the extent that it contributes to the close examination of film texts'.[26] There is not, of course, a stark and absolute opposition between the history of a narrative form and the history of a cultural industry. As Janet Staiger observes, 'No film historian has ever questioned that the American film industry was an instance of the economic system of capitalism.'[27] There has, however, been a fairly clear division between a practice of textual analysis that has either avoided historical contextualization or engaged in it only minimally, and an economic film history that has largely avoided confronting the movies as formal objects. *The Classical Hollywood Cinema* integrates stylistic and economic factors to an extent not previously attempted, and it would be churlish to suggest that its narrative is not grand enough. But to address the question of when Hollywood became 'New', one must ask not simply where the novelty of New Hollywood might be situated, but also what criteria are being used to judge change in the Hollywood system. The different approaches manifest themselves in the varying accounts of continuity and change as well as in the distinct accounts of determination.

Classical Hollywood produced a full range of products used in the presentation of an evening's movie entertainment; the majors were frequently accused of 'full-line forcing', obliging independent exhibitors to buy not simply blocks of feature films, but also the same company's shorts and newsreels. With the partial exception of animation, however, these aspects of American film industry practice have been relegated to the margins of its history. The major Hollywood corporations are now equally involved in the production and distribution of a chain of inter-related cultural products: books, television shows, records, toys, games, videos, T-shirts, magazines, as well as tie-ins and merchandizing arrangements with the entire panoply of consumer goods. These, too, can be dismissed as marginalia in a history of style, but the interdependency of cultural production and distribution – what is often called 'synergy' – has made it increasingly difficult not only to distinguish the film industry from other media or entertainment industries, but also to understand the movies themselves as cultural and 'textual' objects.

The ever more 'sophisticated' critical tools of our analysis advise us that the movies at the centre of this matrix should themselves be complex objects, but too often we find that we can render them sufficiently complex to justify the investment of our critical energies only through the ingenuities of our analysis.[28] The energies of these objects are often directed more to the pursuit of synergy than to that of narrative coherence. At one point in *Jurassic Park* (1993), the camera tracks past the Jurassic Park gift shop, showing us a line of T-shirts, lunch boxes and other souvenirs identical to the ones available for purchase in the lobby of the theatre, in toy shops, on cereal packets. This is not accidental: as a cinematic object and experience, and therefore as a 'text', *Jurassic Park* is constructed under the obligation to provide a range of merchandising and marketing opportunities or 'hooks'. As Steve McBeth, vice president of consumer products for Disney, said of the little rubber replica of the Flounder from *The Little Mermaid* (1989) in a McDonald's Happy Meal, 'it extends the entertainment experience for the child – it's a way of letting the fun of the movie continue'.[29] 'Extending the entertainment experience' is what we might call commercial intertextuality.[30] Almost every ultra-high budget movie produced in contemporary Hollywood is, among other things, an advertising space for the placement of consumer products, defended not only as a budgetary instrument but as a form of capitalist realism: thus the Teenage Mutant Ninja Turtles eat Domino's Pizza to make both themselves and, in a different sense, the pizza more *credible*.[31] Domino's Pizza paid for participating in this commercial realism because product placement delivers a demographically desirable audience to advertisers at very low cost. Where the classical industry generally declined to permit advertising in its products or its exhibition sites, because 'propaganda [including commercial propaganda] disguised as entertainment would be neither honest salesmanship nor honest showmanship', the products of the New Hollywood take their fees up front.[32] Since 1975, movies have become increasingly commodified, both in themselves as objects forming part of a chain of goods, and as 'multipliers' for the sale of other products. They also rely more heavily on advance audience analysis to identify market opportunities not only for their own advertising, but also for that of their collaborators in licensing and merchandizing. In these aspects of their aesthetic organization, they have moved ever closer to the heavily commodified aesthetic of broadcasting, 'by which the viewer is led not into a work for consideration of its thematic and ideological elements, but away from the text itself into those commercial frames that surround it'.[33]

A history of Hollywood constructed as the history of a narrative form may not be able to account satisfactorily either for these changes or for their effects: the phenomena of multiple formats, repeat viewings and modularity question the centrality of narrative and the concept of a 'univocal reading' solicited by the classical film.[34] An alternative historical framework, privileging economic relations rather than product styling, would provide a different account. Such an alternative account should not eliminate questions of form; but it will place them differently, constructing them in terms of what I have elsewhere called a 'commercial aesthetic'.[35] As Graham Murdock has observed, the economic determines in the first instance rather than the last: 'it is a necessary starting point for analysis but not a destination.'[36]

From very early in its history, the central structuring tension within the motion picture industry has been not in the competition between the major companies, but between the small number of large producer–distributor companies and the large number of small, independent or 'unaffiliated' exhibitors – a normal business distinction, in other words, between manufacturers and retailers. The period of broadly stable vertical integration of production, distribution and first-run exhibition that economically underpinned classical Hollywood's mode of production can be seen as one phase in this history, a phase terminated by the Paramount decrees in 1948. The major companies comprising what Will Hays called the 'organised industry' consciously and consistently sought to defer public attention away from anxieties about oligopoly control and trade practices onto issues of film content; displacing concern, quite literally, from economic base to ideological superstructure. Most of the critical and historical accounts of Hollywood which have emphasized production and product to the exclusion of industrial process have unwittingly tended to perpetuate the industry's politically motivated act of deferral. But the history of the American cinema is not the history of its products any more than the history of railroads is the history of locomotives. The development of locomotives forms part of the history of railroads, but so, for example, do government land policies and patterns of agricultural settlement. Perhaps learning an historiographical lesson from the canted emphases of film history, historians of American television have recognized the importance of a contextual institutional history from the outset of their endeavours.[37]

In *The Oxford History of World Cinema*, Geoffrey Nowell-Smith writes of 'the growth of *competing* forms of mass media, and especially television' since 1960, and speaks of radio, television and video as 'challenge[s] to cinema's monopoly'.[38] But the movies have never in their history had a monopoly in the business of turning pleasure or leisure into a purchasable product, and it would be more accurate to describe television and video as alternatives to cinema rather than as competitors or rivals. The conjuncture of television's emergence with the implementation of divorcement did, however, permit a publicly repressed hostility between production and exhibition to reappear as a much more explicit discourse of hostility between the film and television industries, sustained in part by the cinema's commercial need to justify its cost premium by differentiating the two media. That discourse, together with the relative neglect of television history, elevated Hollywood's sustained hostility to television into a shibboleth comparable to Warner Bros.' innovation of sound, supported by little more than anecdotal evidence and the citation of a few scenes from 1950s movies. Recent histories have revised these perceptions, demonstrating a much closer and more mutually dependent relationship between the two industries and their products. This work allows us to recognize that an overview of Hollywood's post-war industrial history must emphasize convergence, consolidation and synergy among the audio-visual entertainment industries.[39]

In such an account, the Paramount decision features as a pivotal event. From the 1920s the major companies' oligopoly power had resided in their domination of both distribution and first-run exhibition, and therefore of the relationship between them. Divorcement separated these interests, obliging the majors to find ways of controlling the industry through the conduit of distribution and allowing them to regard the plight of exhibitors with far less concern than before, so long as their own profits remained reasonably healthy. The Paramount decision was also pivotal to the initial relationship between the film and television industries. The government's anti-trust suit against the majors stimulated anxieties that they might also attempt to control television, unless they were resisted by regulation.

Accordingly, from the mid-1940s onward the Federal Communication Commission (FCC) restricted the majors' involvement in broadcasting, and in particular hindered the development of pay-TV, which the film industry had recognized as a potential additional mode of exhibition.[40]

The FCC's resistance ensured that, during the 1950s and 1960s, it was the production sector of the film industry that became most integrally involved in television, while the experiments with subscription and theatre television gradually withered away. The steady decline in movie audiences pitted exhibitors against television as an outlet, but for the studios themselves television production replaced in both volume and quality the formulaic output of programmers, B-features, shorts and newsreels – the other lines of classical Hollywood's output – that had serviced the economies of scale in plant and personnel and justified the studio system.[41] In several cases, including Columbia's Screen Gems, the subsidiary company responsible for the production of shorts was converted into the television subsidiary. By the mid-1950s, the centre of television production had moved from New York to Los Angeles, where the major studios joined independent telefilm companies and talent agencies as key providers of prime-time programming in what Christopher Anderson has called 'the consolidation of American television'.[42] Filmed material came to replace live programming as the dominant television form because it was durable, and therefore capable of earning profits on subsequent-run syndication. Telefilm production financing rapidly came to depend on residuals from syndication; if this was an economic lesson in part learned from the film industry, television reciprocally taught the movies the residual value of their libraries.[43] At the same time that they were concentrating film production on a smaller number of increasingly costly features, the major Hollywood studios were producing 40 per cent of network programmes by 1960, while 80 per cent of that year's prime-time schedule was generated in Hollywood.[44] In 1959, *Broadcasting* magazine observed that instead of television being 'the dreaded destroyer' the movie production industry had feared, it had 'turned out to be the good provider'.[45]

The independent exhibitors who had encouraged the Justice Department's anti-trust suit also wanted to prevent the majors from using broadcasting as an alternative form of exhibition. Their interest coincided with that of the network broadcasters, who sought to protect the existing broadcasting system and extend its organization into television. This alliance, and the production industry's response in relation to the screening of movies on television, indicates the extent to which the film industry's structural tensions between production–distribution and exhibition were transferred to the new form. Until 1953, neither the scale of network coverage nor the number of television sets in use were sufficient to support high-priced programming, and the production industry's initial attitude to releasing their product to the new medium was summarized by Barney Balaban in 1953: 'television can have Paramount product when it can pay for it.'[46] When television had achieved sufficient market penetration to justify high-cost programming, the networks initially resisted using movies because they were reluctant, as David Sarnoff put it, to 'weaken TV as a medium', by becoming 'just a new system of distribution' for Hollywood.[47] While the networks downplayed their use of theatrical movies, the majors sold their pre-1948 films to individual stations, either directly or indirectly. When, in 1961, major films were released to the networks relatively soon after their first theatrical run, their success cemented the victory of filmed programming over live TV, and promoted demand for new hardware in the form of colour television sets.[48]

The major film companies had been deprived of the opportunity to control television distribution by government regulation, and remained restricted within their limited role as suppliers of product to the networks. However, the period 1953–65 marks Hollywood's growing influence over the networks in developing the hybrid forms of commercial programming. But while the two industries negotiated mutually beneficial and interdependent relationships through the development of filmed television, the networks' oligopoly power ensured that they controlled the terms of these relationships, and the major film companies' attempts to create alternative means of distribution through pay-cable continued to meet government resistance into the late 1970s. The majors were, indeed, far from being the most adept players in establishing television operations, in part because they continued to see television production as a way of preserving the studio system. The independent producers and talent agencies that diversified into programme packaging and distribution innovated and prospered, most visibly with MCA's purchase of Universal in 1962.

Most statistics indicating 'Hollywood's' decline in the 1950s and 1960s refer to attendance and box-office receipts. Divorcement had, however, severed the direct connection between exhibition and the other branches of the industry, and the prohibition on block-booking had undermined the economies of scale which sustained the distribution companies' financial dealings with the small independent exhibitors whose audiences were most vulnerable to the alternative lures of television. In fact, as Michelle Hilmes suggests, Hollywood – the production industry – 'appears to have been able to have its cake and eat it too' during the 1950s and 1960s, using television as an additional exhibition site for its otherwise obsolete and commercially valueless product, dominating the television series market, and developing an alternative economic strategy for feature film production and distribution to the classical production schedule of a weekly release from each of the major studios.[49] As the major companies demanded increasingly high prices for sales to television in the mid-1960s, the networks began to develop alternative formats: the made-for-TV movie in the late 1960s, and later the miniseries. Movies premiering on television could be produced for less than the charge for screening a blockbuster, and drew comparable or better ratings. By 1970 made-for-TV movies had become a mainstay of network programming.[50]

The blockbuster strategy developed as a form of product differentiation, in combination with widescreen and colour, through the concentration of production resources on fewer movies in the 1950s. It was firmly established in the following decade, when feature film output dropped to as little as 130 movies a year. Before 1960, only twenty movies had grossed over $10 million in the domestic market; by 1970, more than eighty had. For the successful, the profits were enormous, far greater than those made under the studio system. In 1965, *The Sound of Music*, which was made for $8 million, earned $72 million in the US and Canada alone. (In 1971 *Love Story*, the year's top-grossing film, earned more money in domestic rentals than the next three highest-earners combined.) The successes of such movies as *The Godfather* (1971), *The Poseidon Adventure* (1972) and *The Exorcist* (1973) confirmed the blockbuster principle by which the industry's profits were concentrated into a handful of enormously successful movies in each production season. Three-quarters of the movies released failed to recoup their costs at the box office, but for the major companies, increasingly operating as distributors and financiers in a system of 'vertical disintegration', television provided a compensatory degree of stability absent from the theatrical market, while the risks of both film and television production were principally borne by independent producers.[51]

The majors also learned to offset the risks of production by cutting operating costs, adopting defensive marketing tactics and pre-selling films to distributors. In the mid-1970s they began to capitalize on the value of ancillary markets by negotiating television sales in advance of production, so that their revenues could be taken into account in calculating budgets, a lesson in part learned from the deficit financing of prime-time television production. By the mid-1970s the post-Paramount attitude of regarding each production as a one-off event had reached a point where none of the majors any longer possessed a recognizable identity either in its personnel or its product. The flexibilities of post-Fordist production, however, remain firmly integrated into the stabilized economics of distribution, which has been a more substantial legacy of the crisis of the late 1960s than any greater freedom for the individual filmmaker.[52]

The period from 1966 to 1969 saw an upheaval in company ownership more substantial even than that of the early 1930s. As the television networks granted feature films a central position in their programming, the book value of the majors' film libraries rose to between two and three times the market price of their stock, making them ripe for take-over. Initially, the conglomerates taking over the major companies were widely diversified corporations: Kinney National, which took over Warner–Seven Arts in 1969, was a New York based conglomerate engaged primarily in car rental, car parks, construction and funeral homes. As Douglas Gomery details in Chapter 3 in this volume, under Steven Ross it also moved into publishing, merchandizing tie-ins and creative talent management, concentrating its entertainment industry interests in Warner Communication Inc. in 1972, and establishing the pattern in which film production and distribution companies have become components in multimedia conglomerates geared to the marketing of a product across a number of interlocking media. The merger with other media concerns, particularly the record industry, was in a sense only an extrapolation of the majors' post-Paramount commitment to a power-base in distribution – or what we might more generally think of as software publishing – rather than in production.

In the late 1960s the film production industry entered a cycle of overproduction that led to the financial crisis of 1969–71. Although this crisis is usually represented as the result of the industry's 'directionless floundering' in search of a successful formula to attract an audience with which it had lost touch, it had in fact more to do with the industry simply spending too much money on production to make profits.[53] New entrants into production and distribution – CBS, ABC and National General – increased the supply of films and bidded aggressively for talent and properties, escalating budgets to a level insupportable by theatrical demand. At the same time, in 1968 the networks suddenly stopped buying films, leaving the theatrical market oversupplied with product. In the restructuring that followed only Disney and MCA escaped without deficits; Fox and Columbia were potential candidates for receivership. The three new companies closed.[54] Under pressure from their bankers, the majors retrenched, closing branch offices, combining studio facilities, arranging joint foreign distribution and briefly cutting their production budgets. Over the next five years the industry returned to equilibrium, with the only section not doing well being theatrical exhibition. By 1975, the level of production had fallen back to around 120 movies a year.

The period of instability coincides with the 'Hollywood Renaissance', repeating a phenomenon observable from the movies of the early 1930s: that periods of economic instability in Hollywood appear also to be periods of relative instability in the movies' codes of representation. Understood as opportunities for experimentation and formal innovation, such periods prove particularly receptive to critical attention. As in the early 1930s, a significant stimulus to the revision of representational codes was the decision in November 1968 to replace the Production Code with a ratings system. Provoked by two Supreme Court decisions upholding the rights of local governments to prevent children being exposed to books or movies considered suitable only for adults, the MPA introduced ratings in an attempt to circumvent a flood of state and municipal legislation establishing local schemes for film classification.

The period following the introduction of classification in November 1968 was, inevitably, one of uncertainty, as the boundaries of classification, and the economic implications of different ratings, were established. One consequence was that independent distributors were briefly able to gain wider access to the domestic exhibition market, taking a 30 per cent share of it in 1970. The most contentious issue presented by classification was the commercial viability of the 'X' category. Movies classified 'X' were not given a Seal, and were therefore not covered by the MPAA's commitment to provide legal support to all films under the Seal. By the end of 1969, 47 per cent of exhibitors declared that they would not play an 'X', and several newspapers refused to advertise them.[55] Within the MPAA, this was taken to mean that the boundary between 'R' and 'X' had been inappropriately set, and in early 1970 it was realigned by increasing the indicated age restriction from 16 to 17, allowing for a broadening of what could be included in the 'R' category. The concomitant effect, however, was to confirm the opinion that 'X' was defined as 'a dumping ground for movies which warrant no official notice from the industry or consideration from general audiences', an opinion effectively confirmed by CARA Director Eugene Dougherty's comment that 'when we broadened the R category, we hoped no serious film-makers would want to go beyond the limits of the R'.[56] In 1972, Stephen Farber observed that the 'stigmas attached to the X rating' required filmmakers to cut their films to achieve an 'R' if they were to 'achieve nationwide release and reach an intelligent diversified audience'. Whatever the MPAA's Declaration of Principle had claimed about the rating system's objective of encouraging 'artistic expression by expanding creative freedom', in practice 'the pressures to avoid an X may in fact constrain [it] as much as the old Production Code'.[57]

The constraints were, however, different in nature. Designed as a means of labelling movies according to the degree of explicitness in their representation of sex, violence or language, the ratings system became a marketing device, inciting such representations up to the limits of the permissible. The introduction of ratings accelerated the trend that Linda Williams dates from the release of *Psycho* (1960), 'when the experience of going to a mainstream film began to be constituted as a sexualized thrill: a sort of sado-masochistic roller-coaster ride whose pleasure lay in the refusal completely to re-establish equilibrium'.[58] Mainstream Hollywood's move into the production of high-budget exploitation movies in the early 1970s would not have been possible without ratings.

The underlying importance of the introduction of the ratings system, however, lay in its formal acknowledgement that the industry was no longer attempting to appeal to an undifferentiated audience. It is clear in retrospect – and was presumably equally clear to production and distribution executives at the time – that Hollywood had been catering to a plurality of audiences since at least the early 1950s. Suburbanization had redrawn demographic maps, leaving the exhibition industry with many inappropriately located theatres. Prevented from any substantial expansion of their theatre stock by the Paramount decrees, the major chains

had been obliged to leave the provision of suburban exhibition sites to independent developers.[59] Although the drive-in theatres they built were initially marketed
at suburban family audiences, they were most heavily used by teenagers, and
exploitation companies developed to provide product specifically for this market,
aiming their output, according to AIP's 'Peter Pan syndrome', at the 19-year-old
male.[60]

The mainstream industry remained reluctant to abandon a concept of the
undifferentiated audience, but it is critically naive to presume that distribution and
production executives were unaware of, or unresponsive to, their audiences'
demographic composition. There was a reliable – albeit gradually diminishing –
audience for the biblical blockbusters of the 1950s and the musicals and Doris Day
comedies of the 1960s, playing in the gradually decaying picture palaces in urban
centres. As late as 1975, these 1,000 first-run theatres provided 60 per cent of
domestic box-office revenues.[61] Underlying the production crisis of the late
1960s, however, was a need to reconstruct and relocate the site of movie-going in
line with the radical transformation in American retailing brought about by the
building of suburban shopping centres in the 1960s and shopping malls in the
1970s. The new chains of mall theatres – General Cinema, American Multi-
Cinema – serviced a younger audience, and the experimentation of the early
1970s can in one sense be seen as a sequence of attempts to find both production
and distribution formulae to appeal to this newly configured primary audience.[62]

The strategies that eventually proved successful were adapted from those pioneered by exploitation companies like AIP in the previous decade: saturation booking – releasing a movie simultaneously to a large number of theatres – was
combined with national television advertising, most decisively for *Jaws*, which
opened simultaneously on 464 screens in the summer of 1975.[63] Following the
success of *The Godfather* and *The Exorcist*, the majors had also committed themselves to producing and distributing the kind of overtly sensationalist material they
had previously left to independents like Roger Corman. The majors' product –
The Omen, *Carrie* (both 1976) – however, had the budgets and production values of
blockbusters.[64] The shift in content to exploitation genres was, like the use of
saturation booking and the relocation of the site of moviegoing, part of what
Thomas Doherty has called the 'juvenilization' of American cinema, and ultimately a consequence of the juvenilization of its primary audience.

During the 1980s several new companies – United Artists Communications,
Plitt Theatres, Cineplex Odeon – developed national theatre chains to join those
established in the 1970s. Invariably, the new theatres were multiplexes, increasing
the number of screens in the United States to a point where, by 1990, there were
more available screens than there had been since the height of audience attendance
in the late 1940s. Together with national television advertising, the availability of a
large number of relatively small theatres drove the change in distribution patterns:

the saturation booking strategy replaced classical Hollywood's subsequent-run system. By 1990, it was not uncommon for a movie to be saturation-booked in 2,000 theatres, necessitating the provision of ten times as many prints as might have been made of an A-feature released in 1940.[65] Multiplexes allowed for frequent reconfigurations of the number of seats available for each movie in order to maximize the use of space: a prestige movie might open on four or five screens at one site, while outside the peak attendance times of summer and Christmas spare screens were occasionally used for revivals and foreign films.[66] This increased distribution costs by expanding both print costs and publicity budgets, and expenditure on publicity frequently exceeded the cost of production by the late 1970s: *Alien* (1978) cost $10.8 million to produce and $15.7 million to advertise.

From the physical revival of the American theatrical market in the 1970s, the industry has seen a succession of new markets develop: American home video and pay-TV from the early 1980s, the European theatrical market from 1985, new geographical markets in Asia and Eastern Europe since 1990. The availability of new delivery systems in the 1980s resulted in a further cycle of mergers as both film and television companies sought to gain control of the new technologies. On the surface, the movie industry appeared to react to video with the same hostility as they had apparently reacted to television in the early 1950s: in 1976, Universal and Disney brought a lawsuit against Sony claiming that its Betamax machine encouraged infringement of copyright and arguing that its manufacture should be prohibited. But by the time the Supreme Court ruled in Sony's favour that home recording constituted 'fair use', the production industry had reached an accommodation with the makers of the hardware, recognizing the profits to be made by developing video as a subsequent release market – one that exceeded the size of theatrical exhibition by 1986. During the 1980s the number of VCRs rose from under 2 million to 62 million, or two-thirds of all households, and the sales of pre-recorded videos increased from 3 million units in 1980 to 220 million in 1990. In the same period, the number of subscribers to pay-cable grew from 9 million to 42 million.[67]

From 1975 the global entertainment market has expanded, and there is no sign of that expansion stopping in the near future. In 1980 Europe had one-third as many screens per capita as there were in the US, and most of these were old. As part of a concerted policy by the American majors and their European partners to rebuild and renovate cinemas, 500 new multiplex screens were built in Britain during the 1980s, and there was a similar expansion elsewhere in Europe and in Japan, which is now the largest single national market for American movies outside the US. Between 1984 and 1989, the total world market for filmed entertainment doubled in size. The overseas non-theatrical market grew in the late 1980s as a result of the deregulation of state broadcasting and the growth of cable, and most of all by the spread of video as a second-run exhibition window. By 1989 video was the largest source of Hollywood's overseas revenue. The deregulation of much European television resulted in an enormous increase in the number of commercial television stations and satellite services. By 1989, Western European television reached a larger market (320 million people, 125 million households) than US television (250 million people, 90 million households). A movie may now make as much as 90 per cent of its revenue outside the US. In 1996, the value of the majors' film libraries was estimated at a figure fifteen to twenty times the value placed on them in 1980; over the same period, television libraries have increased in value at twice that rate.[68] The development of further new delivery technologies and synergies through the home entertainment functions of computers and the Internet will continue to provide expanding opportunities for the repackaging and recirculation of entertainment software.

Convergence and globalization have resulted in the American film industry no longer necessarily being owned by Americans, although its product has, if anything, become more exclusively American in perspective.[69] The ownership changes of the late 1960s left the industry in fairly stable structural shape through the 1970s, when the companies affiliated with conglomerates – Paramount, Warner Bros., Universal, United Artists, maintained a bigger market share than those – Columbia, MGM, TCF – that were not. During the 1980s, four companies – Warner Communications Inc. (WCI), Gulf + Western (Paramount), Disney and MCA (Universal) – dominated production and distribution. All four companies were diversified operations with interests in related businesses in publishing and music, but they shed most of their operations that were less connected to software distribution. They also all had fairly stable management teams throughout the decade. A second tier of companies, with fluctuating shares of the market, were similarly connected to ancillary markets: MGM/UA, Columbia (owned for most of the decade by Coca-Cola), and Twentieth Century Fox. A new wave of mergers was triggered in 1985 by Rupert Murdoch's acquisition of TCF and Metromedia Television, the largest group of independent stations in the country, as the first move in creating a fourth US television network, in itself a platform for a global television, publishing and entertainment corporation. The expansion of News Corp., and of Bertelsmann in Germany, set off further mergers. In 1989 Sony bought Columbia in order to be able to market a software library alongside its own new equipment, in one version of 'synergy'. Responding with an alternative version of synergy based on the remarketing of talent through a range of media, Warner Communications merged with Time Inc., which owned Home Box Office, the largest pay-cable television service in the United States, to create Time Warner Inc., the world's largest media conglomerate. In its first Annual Report the new corporation declared that 'no serious competitor could hope for any long-term success unless, building on a secure home base, it achieved a major presence in all of the world's important markets'.[70] The integration of television and film interests has continued. In 1993 Paramount Communications, the only studio other than Disney not to change hands during the 1980s was acquired by cable company Viacom, Inc.; in 1995 Disney acquired the ABC network and Time Warner, in response, took over Turner Broadcasting as the base for a potential fifth American network. News Corporation has continued to expand, particularly into the Asian market. American telecommunications legislation in 1996 will in all likelihood increase the speed of convergence of the software, computer and telecommunications industries. In all these fields, the likely outcome is an industry dominated by a few giant concerns, each 'controlling a vast empire of media and entertainment properties that amounts to a global distribution system for advertising and promotion dollars'.[71]

Globalization and the new markets have made the majors increasingly stable, whoever actually owns them. Through the development of new markets and synergies, their combined revenues have been growing at a remarkably steady rate of 9 per cent per annum since 1980, from $4 billion in 1980 to $15 billion in 1995.[72] Economically, their most effective strategy has been the ultra-high-budget film. The majors' average negative cost rose from $9.4 million in 1980 to $26.8 million in 1990 and $39 million in 1995, and average costs for prints and domestic advertising rose from $4.3 million in 1980 to $11.6 million in 1990 and $20 million in 1995, with an additional $10 million spent on foreign advertising.[73] Ultra-high budgets, generated by spiralling star salaries and the costs of spectacular special effects, act as effective barriers to entry into the profits from synergy, securing the majors' control of the most profitable sectors. The existence of stable secondary markets has made the risk-taking involved acceptable, by providing a financial cushion for movies that fail at the theatrical box office: while the commercial failure of *Heaven's Gate*, at a cost of $35 million, brought about the sale of United Artists in 1980, *Waterworld*, produced in 1995 for an alleged cost of $200 million, would eventually recoup its costs in secondary markets.[74] While in the late 1960s only one movie in ten made a profit, by 1985, the existence of secondary markets in cable television and video ensured that half the films with negative costs over $14 million went into profit.

However, these profits were available – or at least, predictably available – only to a certain kind of product, known for most of the 1980s and 1990s as 'high concept'. The term and the meta-concept originated with the made-for-television movie in the 1970s, which needed stories that could be promoted and summarized by a thirty-second television spot. A high-concept movie has a straightforward, easily pitched and easily comprehended story. While producers of high-concept movies emphasize their idea's uniqueness, their critical detractors stress the extent to which they rely on the replication and combination of previously successful narratives: *Robocop* is *Terminator* meets *Dirty Harry*. Production executives might reasonably justify high concept as a way of packaging previously tested and reliable ingredients, particularly for the global market. Screenwriter Howard Rodman has observed that 'When you are writing a screenplay, one of the things you are doing, in a sense, is writing a prospectus for a stock offering', and in the mid-1980s executives at United Artists talked, accurately enough, of high concept as being a fiscally responsible way of making films.[75]

Justin Wyatt describes high concept as the central development within post-classical Hollywood, a style of 'post-generic' filmmaking based on the simplification of character and narrative, and a strong match between image and music track throughout the film. Portions of the movie are often presented as extended montages which are, in effect, music video sequences available for reconfiguration in other windows. The physical design or look of the films frequently reflects the graphic design and layout of contemporary advertising, which can be easily replicated in the high-tech trailers, television commercials or publicity stills. In formalist terms, much of the content of high concept functions as 'excess': the 'look'; the music track's interruption of the narrative; the self-conscious allusion to other films and television programming; the detached performances of stars appearing as something closer to a TV show 'guest' than a character (the *Batman* series' villains, for example); the hyperbolic physiques of many of the protagonists, deployed in equally hyperbolic spectacles of action; the 'ironic' distancing effects created by the investment in a star persona – a 'walking, talking brand-name' like Schwarzenegger – rather than in characterization. As Wyatt argues, 'the particular configuration of "excess" on the one hand, and drained characters and genre on the other' distinguishes high concept from previous Hollywood forms:

> The modularity of the films' units, added to the one-dimensional quality of the characters, distances the viewer from the traditional task of reading the film's narrative. In place of this identification with narrative, the viewer becomes sewn into the 'surface' of the film, contemplating the style of the narrative and the production. The excess created through such channels as the production design, stars, music, and promotional apparatus enhances this appreciation of the films' surface qualities.[76]

But it may be more appropriate to suggest that rather than there being a plethora of excess attached to a stock narrative, high concept represents a form of product styling designed to function – in McLuhan's terms – 'coolly' in both 'hot' and 'cool' media environments. The idea of 'cool' consumption – incorporating an element of detached viewing – pervades the culture of the primary audience group targeted by these products: much of Bill, Ted, Wayne and Garth's 'excellence' resides in the detached imperial certainty with which they know that the world of contemporary American teenage experience will remain impervious to encounters with aliens, corporate capitalism or history. Designed to accommodate multiple acts of consumption across different formats, high concept has little commercial investment in narrative except as a vehicle for the movie's other pleasures, and equally little commitment to a classical hierarchization of a narrative system over those of space and time. Tie-in products – novelizations, soundtrack albums, TV spin-offs – have no obligation to preserve the narrative line of the 'original' against the obvious economic benefits of multiplication, which maintains the product range in the marketplace and encourages repeat viewings.[77] As Robert Vianello remarks of the TV narrative, 'it must be at once a suitable "environment" for commercials and a mechanism for delivery of an audience of certain demographic composition . . . [it] has a far greater socioeconomic purpose than the rather provincial scope of the motion picture industry', delivering a unified narrative as an end in itself.[78]

Neither all high-concept nor all blockbuster movies are ultra-high-budget movies. The system retains large and sometimes fatal elements of unpredictability, as befell Carolco with the failure of *Cutthroat Island* in 1996. William Goldman's axiom that 'nobody knows anything' holds true.[79] But fiscal responsibility encourages the producers and distributors of ultra-high-budget movies to follow the reliable formulae of high concept. There are, obviously, other levels of production operating in contemporary Hollywood, but the ultra-high budget movie remains the engine that drives the distribution system, and the object around which the majors concentrate their control over what Douglas Gomery calls 'the means of presentation'.[80] The economic principles of its organization derive from the marriage of the film and television industries. One indication of how far the movie industry's structures have moved from those of classical Hollywood is the almost unnoticed return of vertical integration in the mid-1980s. The strengthening of the theatrical market coupled with the *laissez-faire* attitude of the Reagan administration towards anti-trust issues convinced the majors to test the terms of the Paramount decrees. In 1986 Columbia purchased some theatres in New York; within a year, MCA, Paramount and WCI had bought or acquired stakes in important theatre chains throughout the country, acquiring more than 3,500 of the 22,000 screens in the US – about the same percentage as they held in 1938. The distributors' return to ownership in the exhibition sector was, however, less an attempt to re-create the vertical integration of classical Hollywood than the addition of another element in the strategy of what Wall Street analyst Harold Vogel has called 'entertainment industry consolidation'.[81] If, as Douglas Gomery argues in Chapter 3 of this volume, the strategies of tight diversification pioneered by WCI and Time Warner constitute a reconstruction of vertical integration, they do so in a markedly changed commercial environment in which no single product provides the focus for analysis in its passage through the vertically integrated system. 'Synergy' is an alternative conceptualization: while vertical integration describes the economic relationship between business sectors, 'synergy' instead imagines a 'creative' and horizontal relationship between practices and products, between hardware and software, between media, and between interpretations. It is now the governing economic logic of New Hollywood's tightly diversified media conglomerates, and the likely future developments in the new technologies of distribution will only add further layers to this process.

To contemporary observers of contemporary Hollywood, the ultra-high-budget movie appears an inescapable object, however reluctant we may be to pay it critical attention. But critics may take solace by revisiting classical histori-ography to contemplate the movies omitted or elided from most accounts of Hollywood's past. Kim Newman typically declares that 'the truly important and outstanding movies of the period' of the 1950s were the now canonical objects such as *Kiss Me Deadly* (1955) or *The Searchers* (1956), created out of 'the involve-ment of major talents with formerly low-esteem genre material . . . [which] now stand as far more resonant and rewarding than, say, best picture Oscar winners *Around the World . . . in 80 Days* (1956) or *Ben-Hur* (1959).[82] What is certainly and consistently true of the history of classical Hollywood as presently written is that the industry's prestige product has been excluded from the critical canon as criticism seeks to construct a Hollywood cinema worthy – thematically, aesthetic-ally, ideologically – of study. Equally, much of the industry's most popular prod-uct – the star vehicles of Marie Dressler, Shirley Temple, Deanna Durbin and Betty Grable, to take four instances at random – has been omitted from the historical record. John Belton observes that in the 1980s, 'the films that proved to be the most successful financially were those that reassured rather than disturbed the public', as if this had not always been the case.[83] The contemporary concentration of budgetary resources into fewer and more prominent objects may make it more difficult to discard these movies, but it may be that they are presently seen as more aberrant in the *longue durée* than they should be, not because of their own proper-ties but because of what is excluded from accounts of earlier periods. The alterna-tive, of course, is to re-examine the assumptions underlying the status of classical Hollywood's canonic works in the light of more thorough institutional histories.

Notes

1 James Bernardoni, *The New Hollywood: What the Movies Did with the New Freedoms of the Seventies* (Jefferson, North Carolina: McFarland Press, 1991), p. 1.
2 John Belton, *American Cinema/American Culture* (New York: McGraw-Hill, 1994), pp. 296, 311.
3 Belton, *American Cinema/American Culture*, pp. 317–18.
4 Bernardoni, *The New Hollywood*, pp. 11–12.
5 Joseph Gelmis, *The Film Director as Superstar* (Harmondsworth: Penguin, 1970), p. ix.
6 Bernardoni, *The New Hollywood*, pp. 3, 217, 222.

7 Laura Mulvey, 'Americanitis: European intellectuals and Hollywood melodrama', in *Fetishism and Curiosity* (London: British Film Institute, 1996), p. 19. Writing in 1971, Nicholas Garnham described his book on Samuel Fuller as 'a labour of love, a love born in the dark womb of Sunday afternoon moviehouses in rain-drenched provincial towns and the seedier areas of London . . . the culmination of an odyssey whose islands are ancient cinemas named Rex, Imperial, Tolmer, whose sirens are named Fuller, Boetticher, Siegel, Ray, Mann and Aldrich.' Nicholas Garham, *Samuel Fuller* (London: Secker and Warburg, 1971), p. 7.

8 Quoted in Jim Hillier, *The New Hollywood* (London: Studio Vista, 1993), p. 7.

9 Elizabeth G. Traube, *Dreaming Identities: Class, Gender and Generation in 1980s Hollywood Movies* (Boulder, Colorado: Westview Press, 1992), p. 3. See also the essays by Peter Biskind and Mark Crispin Miller in *Seeing Through Movies*, ed. Mark Crispin Miller (New York: Pantheon Books, 1990), which argue that the 1980s were an 'epoch of revision', in which the aesthetic experimentation and cultural criticism evident in Hollywood movies of the 1970s were systematically repudiated or revised out.

10 Quoted in Janet Wasko, *Hollywood in the Information Age: Beyond the Silver Screen* (London: Polity, 1994), p. 236. This opinion is not, of course, restricted to academia. For instance, in his analysis of the contemporary industry, Martin Dale bemoans 'the lack of a new talent wave' comparable to that of the early 1970s: 'It seems that the present generation has neither a voice, nor anything to say.' Martin Dale, *The Movie Game: The Film Business in Britain, Europe, and America* (London: Cassell, 1997), p. 21.

11 David Bordwell, Janet Staiger and Kristin Thompson, *The Classical Hollywood Cinema: Film Style and Mode of Production to 1960* (London: Routledge and Kegan Paul, 1985), p. 373.

12 Bordwell, Staiger and Thompson, *The Classical Hollywood Cinema*, p. 375.

13 Ibid., p. 339.

14 Ibid., p. 368.

15 Wasko, *Hollywood in the Information Age*, p. 250.

16 The audience has 'greyed' somewhat since this extreme. On average in Europe and North America, one-third of the audience in the mid-1990s were teenagers, another third were in their twenties, and the rest over thirty. Dale, *The Movie Game*, p. 5.

17 As Martin Dale points out, the core of the theatre-going audience – the 'avids' who attend once a week – comprise 3.5 per cent of the American population, but buy 60 per cent of the tickets for new releases. 'The film audience is therefore a very particular substratum of society'. Dale, *The Movie Game*, p. 5.

18 Michelle Hilmes suggests that 'the direct sale economics of the theatrical film imply a . . . unified formal structure that reflects the undivided nature of the product sold'. Michelle Hilmes, *Hollywood and Broadcasting: From Radio to Cable* (Urbana: University of Illinois Press, 1990), p. 117.

19 Bordwell, Staiger and Thompson, *The Classical Hollywood Cinema*, p. 367.

20 Ibid., p. xiv.

21 Ibid., p. 384.

22 Ibid., p. 382.

23 Ibid., pp. 88–9.

24 Ibid., p. 93.

25 Andrew Britton, 'The philosophy of the pigeonhole: Wisconsin formalism and 'the classical style', *CineAction!*, no. 15 (Winter 1988/9), p. 48.

26 Wasko, *Hollywood in the Information Age*, p. 17.

27 Bordwell, Staiger and Thompson, *The Classical Hollywood Cinema*, p. 88.

28 See, for example, Cathy Griggers, '*Thelma and Louise* and the cultural generation of the new butch-femme', in Jim Collins, Hilary Radner and Ava Preacher-Collins (eds), *Film Theory Goes to the Movies* (London: Routledge 1993), pp. 129–41; Chris Holmlund, 'Cruisin' for a bruisin': Hollywood's deadly (lesbian) dolls', *Cinema Journal*, vol. 34, no. 1 (Fall 1994), pp. 31–51.

29 Quoted in James Twitchell, *Peepshow America*, p. 141.

30 *Batman*, suggests Eileen Meehan, 'is best understood as a multimedia multimarket sales campaign'. Eileen Meehan, ' "Holy commodity fetish, Batman!": the political economy of a commercial intertext', in Roberta E. Pearson and William Uricchio (eds), *The Many Lives of the Batman* (London: British Film Institute, 1991), p. 52.

31 According to Patrick Denin, a marketing co-ordinator, product placements 'are more credible than endorsements because they portray someone using a product in real life'. Domino's product placement in the movie did not inhibit Pizza Hut from a tie-in arrangement that included a commercial and coupon offer with the videocassette release of *Teenage Mutant Ninja Turtles*. Wasko, *Hollywood in the Information Age*, pp. 190, 197.

32 Will Hays, 1938, quoted in Margaret Thorp, *America at the Movies* (London: Faber, 1946), p. 161.

33 Hilmes, *Hollywood and Broadcasting*, p. 141.

34 Bordwell, Staiger and Thompson, *The Classical Hollywood Cinema*, p. 374.

35 Richard Maltby, *Hollywood Cinema: An Introduction* (Oxford: Blackwell, 1995), pp. 27–46, 485.

36 Graham Murdock, 'Critical inquiry and audience activity', in Brenda Dervin, Lawrence Grossberg, Barbara J. O'Keefe and Ellen Wartella (eds), *Rethinking Communication, Volume 2: Paradigm Exemplars* (Newbury Park, Ca.: Sage, 1989), pp. 229–30.

37 It is, however, also fair to note Christopher Anderson's comment that in many histories of television, 'the programs are fairly insignificant, envisioned less as symbolic forms than as the residue of economic relations or the reflection of social issues'. Christopher Anderson, *Hollywood TV: The Studio System in the Fifties* (Austin: University of Texas Press, 1994), p. 11.

38 Geoffrey Nowell-Smith, 'Introduction: the modern cinema', in Geoffrey Nowell-Smith (ed.) *The Oxford History of World Cinema* (Oxford: Oxford University Press, 1996), p. 464. My emphasis.

39 Anderson, *Hollywood TV*, p. 5. See also William Boddy, *Fifties Television: The Industry and Its Critics* (Champaign: University of Illinois Press, 1990).

40 Douglas Gomery, 'Failed opportunities: the integration of the US motion picture and television industries', *Quarterly Review of Film Studies*, vol. 9, no. 3 (Summer 1984), p. 227.

41 By 1955, at least ten times as much film was being generated in Hollywood for television as for theatrical exhibition. Robert Vianello, 'The rise of the telefilm and the networks' hegemony over the motion picture industry', *Quarterly Review of Film Studies*, vol. 9, no. 3 (Summer 1984), p. 213.

42 Anderson, *Hollywood TV*, p. 12; Lynn Spigel and Michael Curtin, 'Introduction', in Lynn Spigel and Michael Curtin (eds), *The Revolution Wasn't Televised: Sixties Television and Social Conflict* (London: Routledge, 1997), p. 3.

43 Curiously, the majors themselves were far slower in learning the value of residuals in financing programming than were the more successful independents such as Desilu

and Revue. In part this was due to their initial commitment to using television programming to cross-promote their feature output. Anderson, *Hollywood TV*, pp. 60, 212–13.

44 Mark Alvey, 'The independents: rethinking the television studio system', in *The Revolution Wasn't Televised*, p. 139.

45 'Hollywood in a television boom', *Broadcasting* (26 October 1959), pp. 88–90; quoted in Alvey, 'The independents', p. 141.

46 Quoted in Hilmes, *Hollywood and Broadcasting*, p. 122.

47 Hilmes, *Hollywood and Broadcasting*, p. 163. Quotations from David Sarnoff, *Business Week* (3 March 1956), p. 115.

48 Douglas Gomery, *Shared Pleasures: A History of Movie Presentation in the United States* (London: British Film Institute, 1992), p. 250.

49 Hilmes, *Hollywood and Broadcasting*, p. 165.

50 Gomery, *Shared Pleasures*, p. 252.

51 Mark Alvey argues that 'the production systems and financial arrangements of the telefilm industry beyond the mid-1950s replicated the new realities of the motion picture business. The telefilm was inextricably bound to the Hollywood system, but it reflected the package-oriented structure of the contemporary film industry more than the studio system of old.' Seventy per cent of prime-time fiction shows were produced by independents in 1963. Alvey, 'The independents', p. 143. Contrary to most accounts of unpredictability, Martin Dale argues that the 'demand curve' for films in the US theatrical market has remained fairly stable since the 1960s, with about ten films grossing over $100 million (in 1995 prices), another ten grossing over $50 million, and a further forty grossing over $20 million. Dale, *The Movie Game*, p. 22.

52 A 'post-Fordist' account of Hollywood production is provided by Michael Storper, 'The transition to flexible specialisation in the US film industry: external economics, the division of labor and the crossing of industrial divides', *Cambridge Journal of Economics*, vol. 13 no. 2 (1989), pp. 273–305. See also Wasko, *Hollywood in the Information Age*, p. 16.

53 Kim Newman, 'Exploitation and the mainstream', in *The Oxford History of World Cinema*, p. 514.

54 Bankers calculated that around the end of the 1960s, producers were spending approximately twice as much on production than the market could return to them. Tino Balio, 'Introduction to Part II', in Tino Balio (ed.), *Hollywood in the Age of Television*, (Boston: Unwin-Hyman, 1990), p. 260.

55 Stephen Farber, *The Movie Rating Game* (Washington, DC: Public Affairs Press, 1972), p. 47.

56 Charles Champlin, quoted in Farber, *The Movie Rating Game*, p. 48.

57 Farber, *The Movie Rating Game*, pp. 50–1.

58 Linda Williams, 'Sex and sensation', in *The Oxford History of World Cinema*, p. 493.

59 The major chains were not permitted to acquire theatres without court permission, which was regularly refused when they proposed closing a downtown movie theatre and replacing it with one in the suburbs. Gomery, *Shared Pleasures*, p. 89.

60 Thomas Doherty, *Teenagers and Teenpics: The Juvenilization of American Movies in the 1950s* (Boston: Unwin-Hyman, 1988), p. 157.

61 Axel Madsen, *The New Hollywood* (New York: Crowell, 1975), p. 94.

62 Gomery, *Shared Pleasures*, pp. 93–9.

63 In 1959 distributor Joe Levine released *Hercules* simultaneously on 600 screens, grossing $20 million. Dale, *The Movie Game*, p. 32.

64 Belton, *American Cinema/American Culture*, p. 304.

65 In 1995, 153 movies were released to more than 800 screens; these films earned over 95 per cent of all theatrical revenues. Dale, *The Movie Game*, p. 32.

66 The calendar of the viewing year has shifted substantially since the early 1970s, when movies were still being released regularly throughout the year. The summer season now accounts for half the annual domestic box office. The other peak times are the Christmas and Easter vacations, which also draw on the most reliable sector of the audience, teens out of school. See Gomery, *Shared Pleasures*, p. 105; and Peter Krämer, Chapter 19 of this volume.

67 Thomas Schatz, 'The New Hollywood', in *Film Theory Goes to the Movies*, p. 25.

68 The total accounted value of the majors' 16,000-plus titles is probably $6–8 billion, and their annual worldwide earnings probably in excess of $1 billion. Dale, *The Movie Game*, pp. 24–5.

69 The retreat from 'runaway' production at the end of the 1960s marked the return to a representation of the foreign as exotic hardly different from that of Hollywood in the 1930s – in the *Indiana Jones* trilogy, for example. In industry league tables of popularity, American stars predominate to a far greater extent than was true in classical Hollywood.

70 Quoted in Wasko, *Hollywood in the Information Age*, p. 49.

71 *Wall Street Journal* (7 March 1989), p. B1. Quoted in Michelle Hilmes, 'Pay television: breaking the broadcast bottleneck', in *Hollywood in the Age of Television*, p. 315.

72 Dale, *The Movie Game*, p. 19.

73 Dale, *The Movie Game*, p. 31.

74 The science fiction adventure *Willow*, produced by George Lucas in 1988, cost $55 million and grossed only $28 million in American theatres. But it earned an additional $18 million in video sales, and $15 million in television sales. Combined with its foreign earnings of $42 million in cinemas and $22 million in video and television sales, its earnings from ancillary markets ensured its profitability. Nicholas Kent, *Naked Hollywood: Money, Power and the Movies* (London: BBC Books, 1991), p. 60.

75 Rodman quoted in Kent, *Naked Hollywood*, p. 121.

76 Justin Wyatt, *High Concept: Movies and Marketing in Hollywood* (Austin: University of Texas Press, 1994), p. 60.

77 Repeat viewings have been central to high concept since *Star Wars*. *Star Wars* opened in May 1977. By August, four in ten viewers had already seen it twice or more.

78 Vianello, 'The rise of the telefilm', p. 217.

79 William Goldman, *Adventures in the Screen Trade* (New York: Warner Books, 1983), p. 39.

80 Gomery, *Shared Pleasures*, p. 257.

81 Harold J. Vogel, *Entertainment Industry Economics* (Cambridge: Cambridge University Press, 1990), p. 15.

82 Kim Newman, 'Exploitation and the mainstream', p. 511.

83 Belton, *American Cinema/American Culture*. p. 312.

Part II

Economics, industry and institutions

Chapter 3

Hollywood corporate business practice and periodizing contemporary film history

Douglas Gomery

Proper periodizing of Hollywood history after the coming of sound remains an unsettled matter. We must grapple with this key issue: what is the best way to divide the history of the American film? The most straightforward and obvious causal factor – the coming of television – is fraught with historiographical contradiction. Indeed if the literature on television history tells us anything, it is that the process of how the coming of television changed Hollywood is complex and will require many more studies.[1]

There is a wide variety of argument as to when the post-studio system era began. Some historians argue a 'new' Hollywood commenced as early as May 1948 when the Paramount US Supreme Court decision forced the major studios to sell off their theatre chains. In contrast, David Bordwell, Janet Staiger and Kristin Thompson's landmark study, *The Classical Hollywood Cinema: Film Style and Mode of Production to 1960*, proposes a boundary after television had taken its place in nearly every household in the United States.[2] In between – for any number of dates during the 1950s – numerous other events, from 1953's coming of widescreen images to the 1950s ending of blacklisting, have been taken as *the* signal that a new period of Hollywood history had commenced.

In this chapter I shall argue that the study of a more systematic and productive periodization of Hollywood history begins with an examination of changes in Hollywood's business practices: how the continuously powerful corporations that have long dominated American cinema altered how they have been organized and run. During the final half of the twentieth century, Hollywood has significantly transformed itself as new owners and managers have adapted new and different business tools. By understanding how these corporate strategies have changed, historians of Hollywood can better understand how the 'film industry' as business, social and cultural practice has continued to dominate mass entertainment image making.[3]

To begin to understand how motion picture industry business practice has changed and transformed Hollywood in the post-studio era, I propose we start by examining the changes wrought by two bold, pioneering business innovators. Both brought to the forefront the tactics and organizing principles that others have widely imitated since and indeed today function as part of normal industry behaviour. This is not to make these two business executives into 'great men', but to recognize their innovations in business practices as methods by which to begin to sort out when and why Hollywood as an industry has fundamentally changed over time.

During the 1950s and 1960s, Lew Wasserman led the development of Hollywood style independent film and television production, and initiated the first 'New' Hollywood. A generation later Steven J. Ross transformed Warner Communications into the ultimate vertically integrated media conglomerate, Time Warner, and initiated a second 'New' Hollywood. By analysing the pioneering innovations in business strategy of Lew Wasserman and Steven J. Ross, historians can properly periodize recent Hollywood history, and understand there exist two 'new' periods in Hollywood history during the second half of the twentieth century.

The transition to independent production

The innovation of business practices that would transform Hollywood after the studio era came from Lew Wasserman. Beginning as an agent, Wasserman moved into independent television and film production, took over a whole studio, Universal, and by the 1970s showed the industry how to use a flexible system of production and distribution. In the process Hollywood reinvented itself. Five achievements rank Wasserman as the leading executive of his age:

1 Wasserman initiated independent radio and television series production based in Hollywood. He sold his clients as properties to networks, and turned MCA into the leading independent producer of primetime radio and television.

2 Wasserman entered the film industry directly by buying a film library – Paramount's – and thereby began a new era in which studios prospered by milking long-term value from their libraries of older films and TV shows.

3 Wasserman then bought a studio – Universal – so MCA could make the broadcast television shows directly while still distributing independently made and financed feature films.

4 Wasserman pioneered movies made for television even as Universal produced and syndicated half-hour- and hour-long broadcast television shows. With TV movies Universal became the largest network supplier of network broadcast television programming, reaching a crest in 1977 by providing *Roots*, the most popular TV show of its era.

5   With his broadcast TV base solid and highly profitable, Wasserman returned to the feature film and pioneered the blockbuster motion picture, setting trends that with the exploitation of *Jaws* (1975) through *ET: The Extraterrestrial* (1982) redefined what it meant to make a successful Hollywood feature film.

All these innovations are now common industry practice. Yet Wasserman brought them to Hollywood not as a studio executive protégé, but as the president of a leading talent agency looking for deals for his clients. Born on 15 March 1913 in Cleveland, Ohio, he did not apprentice in Hollywood but came to power through an indirect route. In 1930, after graduating from Cleveland's Glenville high school, Wasserman skipped college, and began earning serious money for his family as a publicity director for the Mayfair Casino, a Cleveland nightclub, just as the Great Depression commenced. Booking dance bands, Wasserman met Jules Stein, the president and founder of the Music Corporation of America (MCA), a Chicago based talent agency. Stein hired Wasserman in 1936, and placed his protégé in charge of MCA publicity. Through the late 1930s Wasserman generated hundreds of press releases each week on behalf of clients from Tommy Dorsey to Artie Shaw.[4]

Stein moved Wasserman to Southern California in 1938 to book bands into Hollywood films. Wasserman expanded agency business by taking on disgruntled motion picture actresses Bette Davis and Joan Crawford, but MCA's breakthrough came in 1945 when it acquired the prestigious Hayward agency with 200 clients, most notably James Stewart. By the early 1950s Wasserman had become legendary through his clever, calculating deals on behalf of Jack Benny and James Stewart in which he 'incorporated' them and 'sold' the enterprises to radio networks and then Hollywood studios so the client had to pay less than half the taxes required for salaried individuals.

This innovative business practice led to widespread independent production, which in time would revolutionize Hollywood. Wasserman first used it to take radio's *Amos 'n' Andy* (written and acted by Freeman Gosden and Charles Correll) and sell them as a corporation, in 1948, to CBS for $2 million plus a share of future profits. Their hit show had been on the air for two decades, yet for the first time Gosden and Correll became millionaires. Jack Benny was impressed, and followed suit. Benny's case would set an industry precedent as he took his hit radio show from NBC to CBS, and became a multi-millionaire in the process. Soon stars lined up to have Wasserman perform his magic for them. Benny aptly summed up client feeling when he wrote: 'The president of MCA was Lew Wasserman, a dynamic gentleman who combines a shrewd business sense with a real creative show business flair and who takes a strong personal interest in his clients.'[5]

Wasserman surpassed his mentor Jules Stein and initiated a new era in the film

industry when he applied the same principle to motion picture finance and production. He began with client James Stewart. Wasserman 'sold' Stewart to
Universal-International for *Harvey* (1950) and *Winchester '73* (1950). It is not so
important whether Stewart was or was not the first actor to accept a percentage
deal, but for these two particular films his success made headlines for the share
Stewart received (one estimate states he ended up with half the income from
Winchester '73). Agents for other actors, actresses and directors noticed this and
thereafter demanded a stake in the films they made. The initial deal was risky
because at the time Universal-International was a small, languishing company. But
both films did well and Wasserman and Stewart went on to work his percentage
deals at other studios (MGM and Paramount in particular) as they bid one studio
against another for Stewart's services. The Hollywood movie business would
never be the same again.[6]

By the middle of the 1950s, through his shrewd deal making Lew Wasserman
stood at both the heart of Hollywood television production and moviemaking. He
had proven so successful that MCA was packaging hundreds of 'products' every
year, and so Wasserman soon reasoned it would be more economical to purchase
an ailing Universal studio than continually pay rent. When in 1962 MCA bought
Universal the United States Department of Justice (under Attorney General
Robert F. Kennedy) asked MCA to sell off its agency business or risk an anti-trust
suit for possible monopolization through a conflict of interest. The government
threatened to argue that MCA should not represent clients and also own the
studio for which the clients worked. Lew Wasserman chose production and
divested MCA of its agency business.[7]

Wasserman loathed the circumstances which allowed him to get into such trouble
with the government over the MCA take-over of Universal studios. Thereafter he
parlayed his considerable corporate clout into substantial political influence. As a
member of the Democratic political party, Wasserman supported the ambitions of
Lyndon Baines Johnson, and by doing so became a Washington insider during the
1960s. Later he helped finance the presidential ambitions of both Jimmy Carter
and Bill Clinton. Visible presidential appointments were tendered; Wasserman
turned them all down. He only accepted a trusteeship of the John F. Kennedy
presidential library, and a position on the Board of the John F. Kennedy Center for
the Performing Arts.

It was in Hollywood that through the 1960s and 1970s Lew Wasserman fashioned a mighty media-making machine based on movie and television production.
Indeed as soon as MCA acquired Universal, he ploughed millions of dollars into a
series of modern office towers adjacent to the studio lot from which Wasserman
and his underlings supervised the construction of a score of new sound stages, and
two new colour-processing laboratories. Wasserman brought top film and television talent to the new Universal, including Alfred Hitchcock who loved to stop

productions and exchange Wall Street tips with his boss. Universal's *To Kill a Mockingbird* (1962) won the best actor Oscar for Gregory Peck, and so much television production commenced that Universal by the mid-1960s was the busiest lot in Hollywood.

Wasserman's final innovations in business practice would come during the early 1970s when he reasoned something new had to be done to add more profitability to feature filmmaking. He coupled mass-saturated advertising on prime-time television with simultaneous bookings in new shopping mall cineplexes across the United States with the release of *Jaws* in 1975. The film created a sensation and with it Universal initiated the era of the blockbuster feature film, and forever altered the Hollywood film landscape. Advertising on broadcast television became the key to turning a feature film into a blockbuster, enabling the studio distributor to milk millions and millions of dollars from 'ancillary rights'.[8]

Jaws was not the first film sold by and through broadcast television, but its million-dollar success proved that this strategy was the one that would re-define Hollywood. The Wasserman-led Universal money-making machine reached its climax and closure with *ET* in 1982, bringing the company that was languishing two decades earlier revenues that needed to be measured in billions of dollars. Again Hollywood – as an industry of cinema, not the source of most prime-time television – stood atop the pop culture hierarchy, able with a single film to initiate a truly widespread popular culture phenomenon leading to infusions of dollars. With its innovation of broadcast television production, and blockbuster filmmaking and distribution, by the 1970s MCA/Universal – Lew Wasserman's creation – stood at the apex of a renewed Hollywood moving image business.[9]

The era of the vertically integrated media conglomerate

During the 1970s, however, other executives quickly copied Wasserman's innovations. Indeed the late 1970s and early 1980s proved a period of transition, whereby first the studio executives had to grapple with the new television forms of cable TV and home video. Lew Wasserman led one camp which fought these new technologies.[10] In contrast Warner's Steven J. Ross would lead a new set of entrepreneurs to innovate the business strategies by which the Hollywood companies could and would take full and complete advantage of all possible television 'windows of release' in every market in the world. Ross built on what Wasserman had created and then took Hollywood to a new era of vertically integrated conglomerate power that led to more economic might and profits than had ever been realized in the studio era of the 1930s or the Wasserman era of the 1950s and 1960s.

Beginning with the take-over of an ailing movie studio, Warner Bros., Ross carefully crafted the model vertically integrated media conglomerate, Time

Warner, one that by the early 1990s ranked as the biggest and most powerful media empire in the world. Ross demonstrated how Hollywood could serve as the base to dominate a plethora of media industries – from television and film, from home video to cable TV, from publishing to theme parks. In the process he led Hollywood to re-invent itself once again, and establish a new historical era.[11]

Ross showed that while feature films would still begin their marketing life in theatres, a true blockbuster is really determined as millions are added from home video, pay-TV and cable TV. In Lew Wasserman's era movie theatres supplied more than three-quarters of the revenue for an average Hollywood feature film. By the time Ross had innovated new marketing and distribution arms where skilled business school trained executives worked their magic, movie theatres provided but about one-quarter of the ultimate total. Lew Wasserman saw the video era begin with little money expected or collected from sales and rentals of videocassettes. As the twentieth century ends the figure is moving past $20 billion. The former 'ancillary' monies had become the leading contribution to the revenue stream of a Hollywood blockbuster.[12]

Steven J. Ross (born Steven J. Rechnitz on 5 April 1927) grew up in the Flatbush section of Brooklyn, New York. Unlike Lew Wasserman, he did attend college for two years, but in the heady days after the Second World War went to work for an uncle in New York's garment district. Like Wasserman Ross did not train in Hollywood, but learned business strategy in the funeral and parking lot industries, joining the family business when he married. Indeed Ross had passed his fortieth birthday before all these operations were consolidated into Kinney, Inc.

The Hollywood of the fully vertically integrated mass-media corporation began in July of 1969 when Ross's Kinney Corp. took over Warner–Seven Arts at a cost of $400 million and renamed it Warner Communications, Inc. Thereafter, through the 1970s, Ross expanded the divisions of the company to embrace all new forms of release. In the process he created the late twentieth-century proto-type media conglomerate as Warner pioneered cable TV's Home Box Office, and took Hollywood companies into the business of directly operating cable TV systems. For Ross these new TV technologies were not to be fought but embraced, for they were simply more outlets for Warner Bros.' Hollywood studio productions. Ross looked to total vertical integration, the ownership of means of production, distribution and presentation to the public.

Through the next two decades Ross expanded the studio operations and acquired new divisions in order to integrate vertically his ever-growing media conglomerate. To Wall Street Warner seemed to be a 'cable TV company' because of its innovation of HBO and Cinemax, and Warner cable multiple system cable operations. Ross bragged he did not care about the magazine side of Time, Inc. when he took over that company; he simply wanted Time, Inc.'s vast cable TV business.

The Time merger was simply another step in logically expanding the 'ancillary markets' for Warner's television programmes and films, furthering vertical integration, making ever more money, and in the process remaking Hollywood.[13]

The 1990 creation of Time Warner caused a great deal of complaining from the Time, Inc. side. Former *Time* magazine editor Richard M. Clurman aptly titled his resentment: *To the End of Time: The Seduction and Conquest of a Media Empire* (New York: Simon & Schuster, 1992). Connie Bruck's *Master of the Game: How Steve Ross Rode the Light Fantastic from Undertaker to Creator of the Largest Media Conglomerate in the World* (New York: Simon & Schuster, 1994) came closer to capturing Ross the deal maker. Yet neither appreciates Ross's formidable accomplishments as a corporate chiefton, a rare CEO who could adapt and innovate.

Throughout his two decades of Hollywood innovation of new business practices, Ross continually sought to take greater and greater advantage of the power which vertical integration offered: reducing costs of sales and transactions, and thereby increasing profits. His vertically integrated corporation would sell films and TV shows to 'itself', and thus not have to absorb the expenses associated with bidding for product from others. Thus even if the new Warners sold no more than in the past, with lower costs the company would make ever more profit.[14]

Ross also recognized that conglomeratization enabled Warners to maintain its growing economic power and keep out the competition. Cross-subsidization, in particular, enabled his ever-growing power in more and more media markets to take profits from a thriving area and invest and innovate in another. Single-line competitors did not have this luxury and so only other media conglomerates, which were willing to match Ross step for step, could survive.

Reciprocity also enabled Ross to choose to whom he would sell and then only deal with those companies that co-operated with other Warner units. For example, the Paramount studio had to tender its top movies to Time Warner's HBO because if Paramount did not, Time Warner's cable franchises would not book Paramount's Sci-Fi cable channel.

In the end, the vertical integration of media conglomerates generated considerable profits from a wide spectrum of mass-media enterprises, including theme parks, recorded music, publishing, and film and television production, distribution and exhibition. The significant change in the last sixth of the twentieth century has been the relentless building up of considerable vertical power by spending millions to acquire interests in movie theatres, cable television operations, over-the-air television stations, and even TV networks. Controlling the markets has become vital for the long-term survival and prosperity of any Hollywood operation. Ross recognized the importance of market control and led Hollywood in this direction, and into a new era.[15]

Ross's final experiment, planned during the months before his death, would be Time Warner's Orlando, Florida trial in 4,000 homes – offering a full service,

500-channel cable television, complete with video games and movies on demand, multiple interactive shopping channels, and information including news and reference guides as desired. This would be the ultimate vertically controlled outlet for Time Warner's ever-growing array of moving image products. That this experiment did not work and was ended by the corporation in 1997 signalled the end of the Ross era at Time Warner and the beginning of the epoch of his hand-picked successor, Gerald Levin.[16]

Through all his attempts at seeking new forms of business practice Ross knew talented creators were vital to making the products he alone could fully exploit downstream. Ross wooed the Clint Eastwoods and Steven Spielbergs. In turn they were loyal to him. Steven Spielberg, for example, dedicated *Schindler's List* (1993) to Ross. Spielberg told interviewers that he thought Schindler reminded him of Ross, and Spielberg had Liam Neeson study home movies of Ross. Like most of those who Ross tempted into the Warner empire, Spielberg was truly mesmerized. Here was a business CEO the equal of any character Spielberg had ever created in the movies: '[Ross] had silver-screen charisma, much like an older Cary Grant or a Walter Pidgeon. He had style. . . . He had flash.'[17]

Conclusions and the future

Steven J. Ross showed Hollywood that the best basis for corporate ownership and operation was the media conglomerate. The other Hollywood movie companies saw what happened and over the next twenty years tried to initiate their own form of conglomeratization. Ross inspired a generation of Hollywood executives. For example, although we associate Hollywood companies with film and television, the leading book publisher in the world is Simon & Schuster, owned by Viacom's Paramount division. Disney's Capital Cities/ABC division not only represents one of the world's leading broadcast TV networks, but also functions as a major publisher of magazines.

Ross's 'best' pupils have been Michael Eisner of Disney and Rupert Murdoch of Twentieth Century Fox. Both revitalized moribund companies into media conglomerates that alone can match the assets accumulated by Time Warner. Murdoch, owner of the Twentieth Century Fox studio, stands as the leading symbol of media power for those who question its role in modern society and culture. We are still living with what Steven J. Ross wrought as Eisner and Murdoch continue to react to Ross's innovations in business practice.

For historians of Hollywood I argue that we must recognize that there have been *two* New Hollywoods. Through the 1950s and 1960s Lew Wasserman re-crafted the independent mode of filmmaking and brought broadcast television production and exploitation into the Hollywood 'film' industry. Thereafter as the twentieth century proceeded to its close Steven J. Ross replaced Wasserman as

Hollywood's leading innovator of new business practice. Are we possibly on the verge of a new era? I think not. Critics who find fault with Hollywood's excess power look to the coming of some new technology to alter Hollywood's long-held economic hegemony. Yet for technical change to make a difference it must be tied to the innovation of fundamental business practice, and there are no signs of change on this front as the twentieth century comes to an end and the mighty media conglomerates of Hollywood hold more economic sway than they ever have in their history.

Notes

1 For my thinking about issues of historiography I have relied on two key works: Anthony Selden (ed.), *Contemporary History: Practice and Method* (Oxford: Basil Blackwell, 1988), which surveys the problems of researching and writing the history of recent decades, and David Hackett Fischer, *Historian's Fallacies: Toward a Logic of Historical Thought* (New York: Harper and Row, 1970) which examines periodization and most other fundamental historiographic concerns.

2 David Bordwell, Janet Staiger and Kristin Thompson, *The Classical Hollywood Cinema: Film Style and Mode of Production to 1960* (New York: Columbia University Press, 1985).

3 I deal with the historiographic issues surrounding these claims in my essay 'Culture and industry: recent formulations in economic history', *Iris* (Paris), vol. II, no. 2 (Spring 1985), pp.17–29. The leading exponent of the analysis of business practice is Alfred D. Chandler, as summed up in his monumental work *The Visible Hand: The Managerial Revolution in American Business* (Cambridge, Mass.: Harvard University Press, 1977). See also Thomas K. McCraw (ed.), *The Essential Alfred Chandler: Essays Toward a Historical Theory of Big Business* (Boston: Harvard Business School Press, 1988). For a careful application for another industry, see George David Smith, *The Anatomy of a Business Strategy: Bell, Western Electric, and the Origins of the American Telephone Industry* (Baltimore: Johns Hopkins University Press, 1985).

4 For Lew Wasserman there are no archives of personal papers, diaries, or accessible corporate files. Instead the historian must rely on the public record: corporate annual reports, government Security and Exchange records, and extensive commentary in the financial press, as best exemplified by the day-to-day coverage in the *Wall Street Journal*. On Jules Stein, start with the profile in Michael Pye's *Moguls: Inside the Business of Show Business* (New York: Holt, Rinehart and Winston, 1980).

5 Jack Benny and Joan Benny, *Sunday Nights at Seven* (New York: Warner Books, 1990), p. 238. Benny's daughter Joan took her father's unpublished and incomplete autobiography and added her own stories of growing up in Hollywood to create *Sunday Nights at Seven*. Benny wrote that he took and appreciated Wasserman's advice on everything, from any and all contracts to hiring talent to negotiations for bookings for live appearances. In 1961 when MCA took over Universal studios, Benny sold his TV production company to Universal for nearly $3 million in MCA stock, becoming in effect Lew Wasserman's partner. See also Melvin Patrick Ely's *The Adventures of Amos 'n' Andy: A Social History of an American Phenomenon* (New York: Free Press, 1991).

6 Biographers of Lew Wasserman's clients usually properly credit him. For James

Stewart's appreciation dip into the dozens of citations in Donald Dewey's *James Stewart: A Biography* (Atlanta: Turner Publishing, 1996). Alfred Hitchcock was another long-time Wasserman client as can be seen in Donald Spoto's *The Dark Side of Genius: The Life of Alfred Hitchcock* (Boston: Little Brown 1983), and Stephen Rebello's *Alfred Hitchcock and the Making of Psycho* (New York: Dembner Books, 1990). In both books we learn Hitchcock vacationed with Wasserman, exchanged advice about finances, and in the end became a major stockholder of MCA.

7 The take-over of the Universal studio by MCA in the early 1960s caused a wave of interest. Bill Davidson's two-part article, 'MCA', *Show*, February 1962, pp. 50–3 and *Show*, March 1962, pp. 68–71 offers many details. Thereafter there have been few serious writings about the very private Lew Wasserman who neither sought nor desired publicity. The business press did its best, but only when Wasserman deemed it in his best interest to be profiled. See, for example, the unsigned 'How MCA gets its teeth into profits', *Business Week*, 18 August 1975, pp. 98–9, and Peter J. Schuyten's 'How MCA rediscovered movieland's golden lobe', *Fortune*, November 1976, pp. 122–4, 212–24. Both tell much, but leave out even more. Better analysed has been Wasserman's role in the American political process as laid out in Ronald Brownstein's *The Power and the Glitter* (New York: Pantheon, 1990).

8 The addition of television production significantly transformed Hollywood. But this transformation was no simple, straightforward matter. Consider two celebrated 'firsts', neither of which led to long-run successes for their enterprises. In 1954 Howard Hughes sold RKO's library of movies to TV and broke a co-operative log-jam. Yet this cash infusion offered only a one-time fix for RKO, and soon thereafter Hughes's company was out of the production business. A year later Warner Bros. innovated studio production of TV series with *77 Sunset Strip*, *Maverick* and *Cheyenne*. But this pioneering effort did not revitalize Warners, and within a decade the company was sold to outsiders (Seven Arts from Canada, and then later to Kinney from New York). Neither of these firsts helps much in beginning seriously to study Hollywood's long-term transformation.

9 Lew Wasserman's role in the remaking of Universal pictures has been recently treated in Bernard F. Dick, *City of Dreams: The Making and Unmaking of Universal Pictures* (Lexington: The University Press of Kentucky, 1997), Chapter 10. Since Dick's real interests are in film auteurs, not business practices, he relies on the interpretations of others. Thus we read of detail about alleged mob ties, but never learn what difference this made in corporate history or the transformation of the Hollywood industry. No overarching explanation of Lew Wasserman's or Universal's contributions are ever made. Indeed, according to Dick, Wasserman lorded over a down era in the otherwise rich history of the Universal company.

10 Lew Wasserman opposed home video; see James Lardner, *Fast Forward: Hollywood, the Japanese, and the VCR Wars* (New York: Norton, 1987), pp. 24–9, 110–14.

11 The considerable accomplishments of Steven J. Ross are recent and thus like all of contemporary history elusive at best. Despite extensive press coverage surrounding the Time and Warner merger, and his supposed excessive salary, there exists a single scholarly, footnoted, logical account devoted to the rise of Time Warner: Robert Gustafson, '"What's happening to our pix biz?" From Warner Bros to Warner Communications, Inc.', in Tino Balio (ed.), *The American Film Industry*, revised edition (Madison: University of Wisconsin Press, 1985), pp. 574–602.

12 For more on the blockbuster and its impact in the modern Hollywood, see Douglas

Gomery, 'The contemporary American movie business', in Alison Alexander, James Owers and Rod Carveth (eds), *Media Economics: Theory and Practice* (Hillsdale, New Jersey: Lawrence Erlbaum Associates, 1993), pp. 273–8.

13 For Steven J. Ross there exist no archives of personal papers, diaries or corporate files. As in the case of Wasserman, the historian must rely on the public record (see note 4).

14 Here Ross re-created a phenomenon that worked with movie theatres during the studio era where the Hollywood studio distributed films to itself. See Douglas Gomery, *The Hollywood Studio System* (New York: St Martin's Press, 1986), pp. 6–21.

15 The importance of vertical integration provides the concluding chapter to my book *Shared Pleasures* (Madison: University of Wisconsin Press, 1992), pp. 294–9.

16 Dan Trigoboff, 'Full service network out of service', *Broadcasting and Cable*, 5 May 1997, p. 68.

17 Connie Bruck, *Master of the Game: How Steve Ross Rode the Light Fantastic from Undertaker to Creator of the Largest Media Conglomerate in the World* (New York: Simon & Schuster, 1994), p. 178. See also p. 362.

Chapter 4

'A major presence in all of the world's important markets'

The globalization of Hollywood in the 1990s

Tino Balio

Introduction

During the 1980s, the worldwide demand for films increased at an unprecedented rate, the result of such factors as economic growth in Western Europe, the Pacific Rim, and Latin America, the end of the Cold War, the commercialization of state broadcasting systems, and the development of new distribution technologies. To capitalize on these conditions, Hollywood entered the age of 'globalization'. As described by Time Warner, globalization dictated that the top players in the business develop long-term strategies to build on a strong base of operations at home while achieving 'a major presence in all of the world's important markets'.[1] In practice, this meant that companies upgraded international operations to a privileged position by expanding 'horizontally' to tap emerging markets world-wide, by expanding 'vertically' to form alliances with independent producers to enlarge their rosters, and by 'partnering' with foreign investors to secure new sources of financing. Achieving these goals led to a merger movement in Hollywood that has yet to run its course.

The domestic market

Home video, a fledgling technology early in the 1980s, became the fastest growing revenue stream in the business. In 1980, only around two of every 100 American homes owned a VCR; ten years later, about two-thirds did.[2] Although the theatrical box office reached a new high of $5 billion in 1989, retail video sales and rentals had surpassed that figure by a factor of two.[3] Capitalizing on the appeal of their hit pictures and film libraries, the majors were able to extract the lions' share of the revenues from the home video market; today, home video can account for up to one-third of the total revenue of a major studio.[4]

Home video naturally stimulated demand for product. Domestic feature film production jumped from around 350 pictures a year in 1983 to nearly 600 in

1988. Surprisingly, the majors played a small role in the matter; in fact, the number of in-house productions of the majors held steady during this period, between seventy and eighty films a year.[5] The influx came from the so-called 'mini-majors' – Orion Pictures, Cannon Films and Dino De Laurentiis Entertainment – and from independents like Atlantic Release, Carolco, New World, Hemdale, Troma, Island Alive, Vestron and New Line who were eager to fill the void. These companies entered the business knowing that even a modest picture could recoup most of its costs from the pre-sale of distribution rights to pay-cable and home video.

Rather than producing more pictures, the majors exploited a new feature film format, the 'ultra-high-budget' film.[6] Popularized by Carolco Pictures, the independent production company that invested $100 million in Arnold Schwarzenegger's *Terminator 2: Judgment Day* (1991) to create a vehicle that grossed $204 million domestic and $310 million foreign, ultra-high-budget pictures started a spending spree which boosted average production budgets to new highs.[7] Contrary to common sense, pictures costing upwards of $75 million became conservative investments. Containing such elements as high concepts, big-name stars, and visual and special effects, such pictures reduced the risk of financing because (1) they constituted media events; (2) they lent themselves to promotional tie-ins; (3) they became massive engines for profits in ancillary divisions like theme parks and video; (4) they stood to make a profit in foreign markets; and (5) they were easy to distribute.

Ease of distribution was linked to saturation booking. Defined as the practice of releasing new films simultaneously in every market of the country accompanied by a massive national advertising campaign, saturation booking was designed to recoup production costs quickly. Standard practice at least since Universal's release of *Jaws* in 1975, saturation booking boosted print and advertising costs to over $12 million per film on the average during the 1980s; during the 1990s, studios were spending $35 million and more to promote new films.[8] The strategy generated 'ultra-high' grosses; for example, in 1989, six pictures grossed over $100 million in the US, among them *Batman* (Warner, $250 million), *Indiana Jones and The Last Crusade* (Paramount, $195 million), *Lethal Weapon 2* (Warner, $147 million) and *Honey, I Shrunk the Kids* (Disney, $130 million).[9] As *Variety* remarked, the majors 'want to knock off a bank, not a candy store'.[10]

The foreign market

The growth of the overseas market during the 1980s resulted from the upgrading of motion picture cinemas, the emancipation of state-controlled broadcasting, the spread of cable and satellite services, and the pent-up demand for entertainment of all types. At one time, theatrical rentals constituted nearly all of the foreign revenues of American film companies, but by 1989 they accounted for little more than a quarter. The major sources of revenue overseas for Hollywood product had become home video, theatrical exhibition and television, in that order.[11]

The largest influx came from Western European television following the liberation of the broadcast spectrum and the growth of privately owned commercial television stations and cable and satellite services. But the largest single source of overseas revenue for Hollywood was from home video. In Western Europe, the number of VCRs sold rose from around 500,000 in 1978 to 40 million, or nearly one-third of all households, ten years later. By 1990, video sales in Western Europe reached nearly $4.5 billion, with the lion's share generated by Hollywood movies.[12] More recently, the international home video market was fuelled by a surge in revenues from the Asia-Pacific region, which grew by more than 20 per cent in 1994 alone.[13]

Like the United States, Europe's video business was fuelled by hits. Europe's theatrical market improved steadily over the decade and by 1990 yielded around $830 million in film rentals for American distributors – about half of the film rentals they collected at home.[14] The overseas market as a whole had also improved and by 1990 nearly reached parity with the US domestic market.[15] By 1994, the overseas market surpassed the domestic in film rentals for the first time.[16]

Two factors boosted the foreign box office: better cinemas and more effective marketing. Outside the US, nearly every market was under-screened. Western Europe, for example, had about one-third the number of screens per capita as the United States, despite having about the same population.[17] And most of its theatres were old and worn. To resuscitate moviegoing, the American majors and their European partners launched a campaign during the 1980s to rebuild and renovate exhibition in Great Britain, Germany, Italy, Spain and other countries.

Taking advantage of the advertising opportunities created by commercial television, Hollywood pitched its wares as never before. Whole markets, such as West Germany, were opened up to television advertising. And new channels, such as MTV Europe which reached 15–20 million homes, offered opportunities for niche marketing.[18] Spending lavishly on advertising, the majors were able to bolster their ultra-high-budget pictures in theatrical and in ancillary markets and overwhelm smaller, indigenous films that could not compete in such a high-stakes environment.

Hollywood's response to globalization

The first wave of mergers

Hollywood maintained its dominant position in the worldwide entertainment market by engaging in another round of business combinations beginning in the 1980s. The new urge to merge departed significantly from the merger movement of the 1960s, which ushered the American film industry into the age of conglomerates. During the 1960s, motion picture companies were either taken over by huge multifaceted corporations, absorbed into burgeoning entertainment conglomerates, or became conglomerates through diversification. The impetus behind this merger movement was to stabilize operations by creating numerous 'profit centers' as a hedge against a business downturn in any one area.[19] The quintessential sixties conglomerate was Gulf + Western. The parent company of Paramount Pictures as of 1966, Gulf + Western owned or had interests in a range of unrelated industries such as sugar, zinc, fertilizer, wire and cable, musical instruments, real estate and scores of others.

The merger movement of the 1980s was characterized in part by vertical integration, the desire to control the production of programming, the distribution of programming, and even the exhibition of programming. Although the trend seemed a throwback to the glorious days of the studio system, the rationale for merging was 'a faith in synergy, a belief that one plus one could equal three'. Described another way, synergy was supposed to function like a good marriage, in which 'each partner would bring qualities that when combined would magically create something better than either could achieve alone'.[20]

A prime example of the vertical integration trend was the move by film companies into exhibition. The revival of the US theatrical market, coupled with the *laissez-faire* attitude of Ronald Reagan's administration towards anti-trust issues, prompted the majors to test the terms of the Paramount decrees and 'take another fling with vertical integration'.[21] The logic seemed to be this: since only a few movies do most of the business at the box office, why not go into exhibition and profit from the hits? Columbia Pictures started the trend in 1986 by purchasing a small group of theatres in New York City. Within a year, MCA, Paramount and Warner Bros. bought or acquired stakes in important chains around the country.[22]

More significantly, the new merger movement was characterized by horizontal integration – a desire to strengthen distribution. Film industry analyst Harold Vogel described the benefits of controlling distribution as follows:

> Ownership of entertainment distribution capability is like ownership of a toll road or bridge. No matter how good or bad the software product (i.e., movie, record, book, magazine, tv show, or whatever) is, it must

pass over or cross through a distribution pipeline in order to reach the consumer. And like at any toll road or bridge that cannot be circumvented, the distributor is a local monopolist who can extract a relatively high fee for use of his facility.[23]

Rupert Murdoch started this trend by acquiring Twentieth Century Fox in 1985. Murdoch was the head of News Corp., an Australian publishing conglomerate that owned newspapers and magazines in Sydney, London, New York and Chicago valued at over $1 billion. Acquiring a controlling interest in Twentieth Century Fox for $600 million, Murdoch embarked on a strategy 'to own every major form of programming – news, sports, films and children's shows – and beam them via satellite or TV stations to homes in the United States, Europe, Asia and South America'.[24]

To strengthen Fox's presence in US television, Murdoch set out to create a full-blown fourth TV network, Fox Broadcasting, to challenge the three entrenched American TV networks, ABC, CBS and NBC. And he did so with the knowledge that the US's Federal Communications Commission (FCC) wanted to foster more competition in television broadcasting. Murdoch made his first move by acquiring Metromedia Television, the largest group of independent television stations in the country, for $2 billion.[25] Murdoch then waged a costly three-year battle to assemble a network of over 100 independent stations capable of reaching nearly all TV homes. Developing counter-programming aimed at young adults to supply those stations, Fox Broadcasting lost hundreds of millions the first three years, but in 1989 it staged a turnaround with two hit series – *America's Most Wanted* and *Married . . . with Children*.[26] More recently, Fox enhanced its reputation as a programmer by backing such series as *The Simpsons* and *The X Files* and by bidding $1.6 billion to steal away the rights to broadcast National Football League games that CBS had held for four decades.[27]

Companies such as Gulf + Western (Paramount) and Warner Communications focused on distribution by 'downsizing' their businesses. For example, Warner Communications under the direction of Steven J. Ross had evolved into a diversified entertainment conglomerate involved in a wide range of 'leisure time' businesses such as film and television, recorded music, book publishing, cable communications, toys and electronic games, and other operations. In 1982, Warner decided to restructure its operations around distribution and sold such non-essential companies as Atari, Warner Cosmetics, Franklin Mint, Panavision, the New York Cosmos soccer team, and Warner's cable programming interests in MTV and Nickelodeon.

The 'downsized' Warner Communications emerged as a horizontally integrated company engaged in three areas of entertainment: (1) production and distribution of film and television programming; (2) recorded music; and (3) publishing. In addition to owning one of Hollywood's most consistently successful studios, a formidable film and television library, and the largest record company in the world, Warner had acquired the distribution systems associated with each of its product lines, including Warner Cable Communications, the nation's second biggest cable operator with 1.5 million subscribers. Warner added considerable muscle to its distribution capability when it merged with Time Inc. in 1989 to form Time Warner, the world's pre-eminent media conglomerate valued at $14 billion.[28]

Time Warner touted its merger 'as essential to the competitive survival of American enterprise in the emerging global entertainment communications marketplace'.[29] It had in mind not only the take-over of Twentieth Century Fox by Australia's News Corp., but also the anticipated acquisition of Hollywood studios by Japanese electronics giants. The first such take-over occurred in 1989, when Sony acquired Columbia Pictures Entertainment (CPE) for $3.4 billion. Sony had previously entered the US entertainment software business in 1987 when it purchased CBS Records for $2 billion. Columbia Pictures Entertainment had 'bumped along on a downhill path' and experienced frequent management turnovers under its previous owner, Coca-Cola Co. But Sony considered the CPE acquisition, which included two major studios – Columbia Pictures and TriStar Pictures – home video distribution, a theatre chain, and an extensive film library, as a means of creating synergies in its operations.[30] As *Variety* put it, 'The hardware company's strategists had concluded that all their fancy electronic machines would have souls of tin without a steady diet of software'.[31] To strengthen CPE as a producer of software, Sony spent lavishly to acquire and refurbish new studios and to hire Peter Guber and Jon Peters to set a course for the company.[32]

The second take-over of a Hollywood studio by a Japanese firm occurred in 1990, when Japan's Matsushita Electric Industrial Company, the largest consumer electronics manufacturer in the world, purchased MCA for $6.9 billion. Like its rival Sony, Matsushita 'thought the entertainment "software" business could provide higher profit margins than the intensely competitive, and now largely saturated, consumer electronics appliance business'.[33] And like Sony, Matsushita thought that synergies could exist between the hardware and the software business.

The parent of Universal pictures, MCA had embarked on an acquisitions binge in 1985 in an effort to offset its lagging film and television operations. In two years, the company spent $650 million to acquire toy companies, music companies, a major independent television station and a half interest in Cineplex Odeon Theaters. The diversification strategy was designed to strengthen MCA's existing positions and to extend the company into contiguous businesses. MCA's investments showing the greatest promise were the Universal Studios Tours located near the company headquarters outside of Los Angeles and near Disney World in Orlando, Florida.

International partnerships

Hollywood's second response to globalization was to seek an international base of motion picture financing. To reduce its debt load, Time Warner restructured its film and cable businesses and created Time Warner Entertainment as a joint venture with two of Japan's leading companies, electronics manufacturer Toshiba and trading giant C. Itoh. The deal netted Time Warner $1 billion and was unprecedented.[34] Following the lead of some independent producers, Twentieth Century Fox pre-sold the foreign rights to two high-profile 'event' films, Danny DeVito's *Hoffa* (1992) and Spike Lee's *Malcolm X* (1992), to reduce its exposure in these films.[35] Another common practice was to seek out co-production deals to take advantage of film subsidies in overseas markets. Studios chose this option mostly with 'unusual material' – which is to say a picture that was not a sequel, that did not have a major international star, or that did not have an 'unflaggingly high-concept' – such as Universal's *Fried Green Tomatoes at the Whistle Stop Cafe* (1991) and Paramount's *1492* (1992). [36]

To finance television programming, the majors invested in foreign media industries. When the European Union decided against removing trade barriers and tariffs on movies and television programmes in 1992 as anticipated, Time Warner, Turner, Disney, Viacom and NBC re-evaluated their relationship to this market. No longer did these companies think of Western Europe only as a programming outlet: instead they considered it as another investment source and formed partnerships with European television producers, broadcast stations, cable and satellite networks and telecommunications services. Time Warner, for example, invested in satellite broadcasting in Scandinavia, FM radio in the UK, and pay-TV in Germany and Hungary. And Disney formed joint ventures to produce children's programming in France, Germany, Italy and Spain.[37]

Domestic partnerships

Finally, Hollywood responded to globalization by competing for talent, projects and product for their distribution pipelines. The competition typically took the form of partnerships with the new breed of independent producers. Represented by the likes of Carolco, Castle Rock, Morgan Creek and Imagine Entertainment, these newcomers differed from the failed mini-majors of the 1980s – such as Orion, De Laurentiis and Cannon – in several important ways: (1) the newcomers ran 'lean machines' with only skeletal staffs rather than emulating the structure of the large studios; (2) most concentrated exclusively on filmed entertainment rather than branching out into TV; (3) most produced only a few high-quality productions each year rather than large rosters aimed at different segments of the market; (4) most distributed domestically through the majors rather than organizing their own distribution arms; and (5) most raised their production financing by keeping their eyes on the burgeoning foreign market rather than on home video deals.[38]

After the breakdown of the studio system during the 1950s, the majors regularly formed alliances with independent producers to fill out their rosters and to create relationships with budding talent. A deal might involve multiple pictures, complete financing, worldwide distribution, and a fifty-fifty profit split. Deals like these are still common, but TriStar's partnership with Carolco, Columbia Pictures' with Castle Rock and Time Warner's with Morgan Creek departed from traditional film industry practice in certain key respects: they typically involved partial financing, domestic distribution and lower distribution fees. Partnerships took this form because the majors not only needed more pictures to increase market share but also a means of sharing the risks and potential benefits of distributing ultra-high-budget pictures.[39]

Take the case of TriStar's alliance with Carolco Pictures. After aligning with TriStar, Carolco delivered three big-budget blockbusters in a row, *Total Recall* (1990), *Terminator 2: Judgment Day* (1991) and *Basic Instinct* (1992). To finance its pictures, Carolco originally made a public offering of stocks but later sold stakes in the company to Japan's Pioneer Electronics, France's Canal Plus, Britain's Carlton Communications, and Italy's Rizzoli Corriere della Sera.[40] Carolco's strategy was to cover as much of the production costs for a picture as possible by pre-selling the ancillary rights piece by piece, country by country. In this manner, Carolco was able to cover nearly all the $100 million budget, including Arnold Schwarzenegger's $12 million fee, for *Terminator 2*. TriStar Pictures paid Carolco $4 million for domestic distribution rights and had first call on the rentals until the advance was recouped, after which it levied a smaller-than-usual distribution fee. Thus the partnership lowered the risks of production financing for Carolco and enabled TriStar to share in the profits of an ultra-high-budget picture without going out on a limb.[41]

Walt Disney and Turner Broadcasting took a different tack to acquire product by moving into the specialized art film and American independent markets. In 1993, Disney linked up with Merchant–Ivory and Miramax Films, two of the most successful art film companies in the business. According to Peter Bart of *Variety*, Disney's strategy was 'to foster an eclectic slate of projects':

> While rival entertainment companies pursue the Time Warner model to become diversified, albeit debt-ridden, hardware-software conglomerates, Disney is determined to become the largest producer of intellectual property in the world. As such, the studio is committed to an astonishing sixty-films-a-year release schedule starting in 1994.[42]

Disney's deal with Merchant–Ivory, the producer of *A Room With a View* (1985), *Howard's End* (1992) and other British prestige films, was a conventional product development deal that provided partial financing in exchange for domestic distribution rights. Disney's deal with Miramax consisted of an $80 million buy-out in which Disney acquired Miramax's library of 200 art films and agreed to finance the development, production and marketing of Miramax's movies.

Founded as a distribution company by Harvey and Bob Weinstein in 1982, Miramax had 'become a logo that brings audiences in on its own'. Adopting a straight acquisition policy from the start, Miramax rose to the front ranks of the independent film market by releasing hits year in and year out that received prestigious film festival awards, including Oscars, and set box-office records. Miramax's roster included Steven Soderbergh's *Sex, Lies and Videotape* (1989), Neil Jordan's *The Crying Game* (1992), Alfonso Arau's *Like Water for Chocolate* (1993) and Jane Campion's *The Piano* (1993). The first two pictures became big crossover hits; *Like Water for Chocolate* grossed $21 million to become 'the all-time foreign language box-office champ' in the United States and *The Piano* received an incredible eight Academy Award nominations and three Oscars, including best original screenplay.

After becoming a fully autonomous division of Disney's distribution arm, Miramax continued to dominate the independent film market. In 1993, Miramax initiated a programme of production financing and expanded into the genre market through a subsidiary called Dimension Pictures. In 1994, Miramax had two big mainstream hits, Quentin Tarantino's *Pulp Fiction* and *The Crow*, which together grossed well over $100 million domestic. In 1996, Miramax maintained its cachet in the prestigious art house scene by releasing *Il Postino*, which surpassed the $21 million mark set earlier by *Like Water for Chocolate*. And by 1996, Miramax's overall track record enabled Disney to recoup its $80 million investment in the company.[43]

In an attempt to become a major motion picture producer, Turner Broadcasting moved into the independent film market by acquiring New Line Cinema and Castle Rock Entertainment in 1993 at a combined cost of $700 million.[44] Castle Rock made its reputation during the early 1990s producing top-shelf pictures such as *City Slickers* (1991), *A Few Good Men* (1992) and *In the Line of Fire* (1993). In contrast, New Line under the leadership of Robert Shay and Michael Lynne made its fortune during the 1980s producing and distributing genre pictures aimed at adolescents – for example, the *Nightmare on Elm Street* horror series and *Teenage Mutant Ninja Turtles* (1990). In 1990, New Line branched out from its traditional slate of inexpensive niche films and created a division called Fine Line Features to produce and distribute art films and offbeat fare. Within two years, Fine Line rose to the top independent ranks by backing such American ventures as Gus Van Sant's *My Own Private Idaho* (1991), James Foley's *Glengarry Glen Ross* (1992) and

Robert Altman's *The Player* (1992) and by releasing such English-language imports as Derek Jarman's *Edward II* (1991) and Mike Leigh's *Naked* (1993).[45]

Acquiring New Line Cinema and Castle Rock Entertainment, Turner Broadcasting manoeuvred itself into the front ranks of Hollywood and positioned itself for global expansion.

The second wave of mergers

The merger movement entered a second phase in 1993 and involved cable and network television. Pay-TV had become a mature business by 1990.[46] Home Box Office growth levelled off at around 17 million subscribers and other large pay services, including Showtime, the Movie Channel and Cinemax, showed slight declines.[47] Home video took a toll, as did the deregulation of cable in 1984. Deregulation allowed cable operators to raise the prices of basic cable services, with the result that subscribers tended to watch basic channels such as the USA Network and Turner Network Television at the expense of the pay channels. And by 1993, basic cable services themselves had hit a plateau, the result of a static pool of viewers and market fragmentation created by added channel capacity of up to 300 channels on some services.[48]

Conditions in the cable industry prompted Viacom Inc., a leading TV syndicator and cable network company, to acquire Paramount Communications for $8.2 billion in 1993. Spearheading the second largest merger ever in the media industry after Time Warner's, Viacom's 70-year-old chairman Sumner Redstone united Viacom's MTV and Nickelodeon cable channels, Showtime pay-TV service, television syndication companies, and a string of television stations with Paramount's formidable holdings in entertainment and publishing.[49] The following year, Viacom acquired Blockbuster Entertainment, the world's largest video retailer with over 3,500 video stores and various side businesses – purchase price, $7.6 billion. Like Time Warner, Viacom had become a completely integrated entertainment conglomerate.

Changes in the regulatory climate put the TV networks into play. During the 1980s, the old-line television networks – ABC, CBS and NBC – were hard hit first by independent stations, then by cable television, and then by the proliferation of cable channels. Because the number of television viewers in the country has remained static, network TV ratings declined and so did earnings.[50] Adding to the woes of the networks were restrictive FCC regulations. In place for two decades, the FCC's financial interest and syndication rules precluded ABC, CBS and NBC from producing a significant portion of the prime-time programming they broadcast, which had the effect of depriving them of the significant profits hit shows earned in syndication.

However, when the FCC voted to suspend the so-called 'finsyn' rules after

1996, the networks took on their old allure. Since the networks would likely reduce the number of programmes they ordered from outside producers and rely more on in-house projects after the expiration of the FCC rules, big suppliers like Time Warner and Disney might be hard hit. To avoid this, conventional wisdom had it that Hollywood studios would attempt to acquire the networks to 'assure themselves of a guaranteed outlet for their product'.[51]

None of the big three networks had changed hands since 1986, when the General Electric Company bought RCA, the parent company of NBC. On 31 July 1995, however, Disney announced that it would acquire Capital Cities/ABC in a deal valued at $19 billion. The merger brought together the most profitable television network and its ESPN cable service with Disney's Hollywood film and television studios, its theme parks and its vast merchandising operations.[52]

The day following the Disney deal, Westinghouse Electric, an early broadcasting pioneer, announced that it had agreed to pay $5.4 billion for CBS, the last major television network to change ownership. If the Disney deal had programme distribution as its target, the Westinghouse deal was for station market share. Michael H. Jordan, the chairman and chief executive of Westinghouse, said the deal would create a 'premiere top-notch outstanding company with 15 television stations and 39 radio stations that combined would give it direct access to more than a third of the nation's households'.[53]

The aftermath

The first mergers played themselves out with mixed results. After launching a fourth television network in the US, Rupert Murdoch's News Corp. went into direct broadcast satellite distribution. He turned his sights first on Great Britain, where he introduced Sky Television, a four-channel satellite service in 1988 at a cost of about $540 million. After spending additional millions acquiring motion picture rights to compete with his competitor, the British Satellite Corporation, Murdoch ultimately merged the two satellite services to create BSkyB that became 'the distribution gatekeeper for programmers in Britain'.[54]

Wanting to replicate his success in Britain, Murdoch bought control of Star TV, an Asian satellite business based in Hong Kong, and then either purchased or formed joint ventures to acquire or construct satellite services in Europe, Latin America and Australia. Today, Murdoch's News Corp. ranks among the world's largest communications companies with annual revenues of over $9 billion. As *The Economist* magazine put it,

> Nobody bestrides the global media business like Rupert Murdoch. His empire may not be the biggest. . . . Yet there is no doubting . . . who is the media industry's leader. What is breathtaking about News Corp is its

global reach, its sweeping ambition and the extent to which it is the creature of one man.[55]

Sony Pictures Entertainment performed reasonably well until 1993, but the following year took a $3.2 billion loss on its motion picture business, reduced the book value of its studios by $2.7 billion, and announced that 'it could never hope to recover its investment' in Hollywood.[56] Nobuyuki Idei, the Tokyo-based president of Sony Corp., took direct control of the company's Hollywood operations and installed new talent to effect a turnaround. Sony's two Hollywood studios soon returned to profitability, but not to top-tier status. The reason: Sony had neither forged connections with cable television nor had it acquired theme parks or consumer product chain stores to extend the franchises developed by its studios.[57]

The Matsushita–MCA marriage foundered as well, but for different reasons. By producing a string of hits that included two Steven Spielberg blockbusters, *Jurassic Park* (1993) and *Schindler's List* (1993), MCA become a financial bright spot in the Matsushita empire as it confronted the recession in Japan and the rising value of the yen (which would make exports more expensive). For its part, MCA hoped the merger would provide it with the financial leverage to acquire CBS and Virgin Records and the economic wherewithal to build a Universal Studios theme park in Japan. Matsushita rejected the proposals, with the result that, 'in the brave new world of vertical integration, MCA found itself alongside Sony at a competitive disadvantage compared to such rivals as News Corp. and Disney'. The rejection also created a rift with MCA's top management, chairman Lew Wasserman and president Sidney Sheinberg, who claimed that MCA's Japanese owners 'did not understand either the corporate nuances of MCA or the dynamic change of the United States media business'.[58] Admitting defeat, Matsushita agreed to sell a majority interest of MCA to Seagram, the giant Canadian liquor company, for $7 billion in April 1995.[59]

Burdened with $11 billion of debt after the merger, Time Warner lost money two years in a row and was plagued by clashing corporate styles among its top management following the death of Chairman Steven J. Ross in December 1992. Under the leadership of Gerald Levin, Ross's successor, Time Warner spent heavily to expand its cable television operations. Viewing 'cable as a crucial distribution technology for the so-called information highway', Levin wanted Time Warner's cable operations to become 'full-service networks', carrying not only television programming, but also telephone service, video-on-demand and home shopping services.[60]

Regaining its title as the largest media company in the world in September 1995, Time Warner bought out Turner Broadcasting System for $7.4 billion. The acquisition enlarged Time Warner's programming and distribution capacity. Among the synergies envisioned by the merger was the creation of a mammoth

combined film production and distribution conglomerate that might easily dominate the business. But Turner's film companies did not live up to expectations and
were awash in red ink by 1996.[61] After the merger, Time Warner took drastic
action and folded Turner Pictures into Warner Brothers and put New Line
Cinema up for sale. Although the measures stemmed the bleeding, Time Warner
has continued to struggle under a burden of debt.

Following the merger with Paramount and Blockbuster, Viacom enjoyed the
extraordinary earnings of *Forrest Gump* but in 1995, Paramount's profits dropped
sharply and the studio had to write off $140 million on poorly performing pic-
tures. To lighten its burden, Viacom took drastic action. Downsizing its operations, Viacom sold its Madison Square Garden sports and entertainment empire
and its cable television systems, leaving it essentially a content company, aside
from its Blockbuster Entertainment video and music stores. Redstone apparently
decided that 'entertainment "content" – that is, programming – drives the entertainment business – not distribution'.[62]

Conclusion

Globalization hastened the concentration of the media by emphasizing economies
of scale. Every year, a few offbeat pictures and smaller art films produced either by
independents or by subsidiaries of the majors win wide critical acclaim and enjoy
significant box-office success – witness *Fargo*, *The English Patient* and other Oscar
nominees for best picture in 1997. Hollywood, nevertheless, remains committed
to megapics and saturation booking, which have the combined effect of dominating most of the important screens around the world to the detriment of national
film industries.[63]

During the 1990s, companies merged, partnered and collaborated as never
before to tap all the major markets of the world. Although some of the assumptions that propelled the mergers proved false – linking electronics manufacturers
(hardware) and film studios (software) did not create the synergy to stimulate
VCR sales – the big got bigger. Small firms both in the US and abroad have been
driven out of business or have been merged with burgeoning giants, repeating a
pattern all too familiar in film industry history.

Digital compression and other new technologies will permit cable systems to
transmit hundreds of channels simultaneously and allow subscribers to dial up
programming on demand. But where will the new programming come from to fill
all these new channels? Will cable networks simply cannibalize one another in an
attempt to maintain audience share? Will pay-per-view and direct broadcast satel-
lites with 300 channels of programming simply fragment TV audiences? In short,
will the synergies of merging a Disney with a Capital Cities/ABC be worth the
price?

And how much untapped potential still exists abroad? As a media industry report recently said:

> The popular notion is that there is a vast wealth of untapped potential in foreign countries for the media and entertainment industry. However, relatively few countries have disposable income per capita as high as it is in the US; cultural barriers and potential local government restrictions could be a very major problem; and competition is intense for foreign markets and making foreign inroads requires sizeable amounts of capital.[64]

Answers to questions such as these will determine the outcome of Hollywood's globalization.

Notes

1 Time Warner Inc., *1989 Annual Report* (New York: Time Warner Inc., 1990), p. 1.
2 Tom Bierbaum, 'Booming '80s behind it, vid faces uncertainty', *Variety*, 10 January 1990, pp. 31, 32.
3 Marc Berman, 'Studios miss boat on vid demographics', *Variety*, 24 September 1990, p. 15.
4 Bierbaum, 'Booming '80s', pp. 31, 32.
5 Lawrence Cohn, 'Only half of indie pics shot will see the screens in '90', *Variety*, 30 May 1990, p. 7.
6 Jeffrey B. Logsdon, *Perspectives on the Filmed Entertainment Industry* (Los Angeles: Seidler Amdec Securities Inc., 1990), p. 11.
7 Ted Johnson and Anita M. Busch, 'Mega-moolah movies multiplying', *Variety*, 29 April–5 May 1996, pp. 1, 53. Only four films besides *Terminator 2* cost $100 million or more in the period 1990–6: *Last Action Hero* (1993), *True Lies* (1994), *Batman Forever* (1995) and *Waterworld* (1995). Carrying a price tag of more than $175 million, *Waterworld* became the most expensive film ever made.
8 Gary Levin, 'Studios gamble on big bucks ad buys', *Variety*, 18–24 March 1996, pp. 11, 12.
9 'The 1980s: a reference guide to motion pictures, television, VCR, and cable', *The Velvet Light Trap*, no. 27 (Spring 1991), pp. 77–88.
10 Leonard Klady, 'Why mega-flicks click', *Variety*, 25 November–1 December 1996, pp. 1, 87.
11 From 1985 to 1989, videocassette revenues increased from $1.5 billion to $3.25 billion; theatrical film rentals rose from $800 million to $1.25 billion; and TV sales grew from $300 million to $800 million. Logsdon, 'Perspectives on the filmed entertainment industry', p. 49.
12 Geoff Watson, 'Sell-through salvation', *Variety*, 16 November 1992, p. 57.
13 Don Groves, 'Veni, video, vici', *Variety*, 3–9 April 1995, pp. 1, 46.
14 Terry Iliot, 'Yank pix flex pecs in new Euro arena', *Variety*, 19 August 1991, p. 1.
15 Geraldine Fabrikant, 'Hollywood takes more cues from overseas', *New York Times*, 25 June 1990, p. C1.

16 Leonard Klady, 'Earth to H'wood: you win', *Variety*, 13–19 February 1995, pp. 1, 63.
17 Iliot, 'Yank pix flex pecs', p. 1.
18 Don Groves, 'U.S. pix tighten global grip', *Variety,* 22 August 1990, pp. 1, 96.
19 Tino Balio (ed.), *The American Film Industry* (Madison: University of Wisconsin Press, 1985), p. 443.
20 Calvin Sims, '"Synergy": the unspoken word', *New York Times*, 5 October 1993, pp. C1, C18.
21 Richard Gold, 'No exit? studios itch to ditch exhib biz', *Variety*, 8 October 1990, pp. 8, 84.
22 Paul Noglows, 'Studios stuck in screen jam', *Variety*, 9 March 1992, pp. 1, 69. The move into exhibition was precipitous. Industry analysts have claimed that the majors grossly overspent to re-enter exhibition and that the timing was wrong – the reasoning being that the domestic exhibition market was heavily over-screened (unlike foreign markets) while admissions have stayed constant.
23 Harold Vogel, 'Entertainment industry', *Merrill Lynch*, 14 March 1989 (single page newsletter).
24 Geraldine Fabrikant, 'Murdoch bets heavily on a global vision', *New York Times*, 29 July 1996, pp. C1, C6–7.
25 In order to comply with FCC regulations governing the ownership of TV stations, Murdoch became a US citizen.
26 'Chernin yearning to get Fox some Hollywood respect', *Variety*, 19 August 1991, p. 21.
27 Bill Carter, 'Fox will sign up 12 new stations; takes 8 from CBS', *New York Times*, 24 May 1994, p. A1.
28 Time Warner, *1989 Annual Report.*
29 Richard Gold', Sony–CPE union reaffirms changing order of intl. showbiz', *Variety*, 27 September–3 October 1989, p. 5.
30 Charles Kipps, 'Sony and Columbia', *Variety*, 27 September–3 October 1989, p. 5.
31 Gold, 'Sony–CPE union', p. 5.
32 Signing the Peter Guber–Jon Peters production team alone cost Sony $700 million and was one of the most expensive management acquisitions ever.
33 Andrew Pollack, 'At MCA's parent, no move to let go', *New York Times*, 14 October 1994, p. C1.
34 Jonathan R. Laing, 'Bad scenes behind it, Time Warner is wired for growth', *Barron's*, 22 June 1992, p. 8.
35 'Newest H'wood invaders are building, not buying', *Variety*, 21 October 1991, p. 93.
36 Richard Natale, 'Risky pix get a global fix', *Variety*, 28 September 1992, p. 97.
37 Richard W. Stevenson, 'Lights! Camera! Europe!', *New York Times*, 6 February 1994, p. C1.
38 Peter Hlavacek, 'New indies on a (bank) roll', *Variety*, 24 January 1990, pp. 1, 7.
39 Hlavacek, 'New indies on a (bank) roll', pp. 1, 7; Richard Natale, '"Lean" indies fatten summer boxoffice', *Variety*, 12 August 1991, pp. 1, 61.
40 David Kissinger, 'Judgment day for Carolco', *Variety*, 2 December 1991, pp. 1, 93.
41 Richard W. Stevenson, 'Carolco flexes its muscle overseas', *New York Times*, 26 June 1991, pp. C1, C17.
42 Peter Bart, 'Mouse gears for mass prod'n', *Variety*, 19 July 1993, pp. 1, 5.
43 Greg Evans and John Brodie, 'Miramax, mouse go for seven more', *Variety*, 13–19 May 1996, pp. 13, 16.

44 J. Max Robins and Judy Brennan, 'Turner may tap Sassa to run film venture', *Variety*, 23 August 1993, p. 9.

45 Bernard Weinraub, 'New Line Cinema', *New York Times*, 5 June 1994, p. F4.

46 Stated another way, the rate of growth in pay-TV subscribers declined for the first time from around 10 per cent in 1988 to 5 per cent in 1989. Geraldine Fabrikant, 'Pay cable channels are losing their momentum', *New York Times*, 28 May 1990, p. 25.

47 Fabrikant, 'Pay cable channels are losing their momentum', p. 25.

48 John Dempsey, 'Wanted: viewers for new cable channels', *Variety*, 3–9 January 1994, pp. 1, 67.

49 Geraldine Fabrikant, 'A success for dealer on a prowl', *New York Times*, 13 September 1993, p. A1.

50 Bill Carter, 'Cable networks see dimmer future', *New York Times*, 22 July 1991, pp. C1, C6.

51 Geraldine Fabrikant, 'Media giants said to be negotiating for TV networks', *New York Times*, 1 September 1994, p. A1.

52 Geraldine Fabrikant, 'Walt Disney acquiring ABC in deal worth $19 billion', *New York Times*, 1 August 1995, p. A1.

53 Geraldine Fabrikant, 'CBS accepts bid by Westinghouse; $5.4 billion deal', *New York Times*, 2 August 1995, p. A1.

54 Fabrikant, 'Murdoch bets heavily on a global vision', pp. C1, C6–7.

55 'Murdoch's empire: the gambler's last throw', *The Economist*, 9 March 1996, pp. 68–70.

56 James Sterngold, 'Sony, struggling, takes a huge loss on movie studios', *New York Times*, 18 September 1994, p. A1.

57 Martin Peers and Anita M. Busch, 'Sony sizes up size issue', *Variety*, 16–22 August 1996, p. 86.

58 Geraldine Fabrikant, 'At a crossroads, MCA plans a meeting with its owners', *New York Times*, 13 October 1994, p. G13.

59 Geraldine Fabrikant, 'Seagram will buy 80% of big studio from Matsushita', *New York Times*, 7 April 1995, p. A1.

60 Geraldine Fabrikant, 'Battling for the hearts and minds at Time Warner', *New York Times*, 26 February 1995, p. F9.

61 TBS announced that it would have to take a $60 million write-off for Castle Rock's first-quarter performance in 1996 and that New Line had a $19 million negative cash flow at the end of that period. Dan Cox, 'New Line sees red', *Variety*, 11–17 November 1996, pp. 1, 73.

62 Mark Landler with Geraldine Fabrikant, 'Sumner and his discontents', *New York Times*, 19 January 1996, p. C1.

63 The theatrical market has not become homogenized, however, because producers still must strive for novelty to capture the attention of audiences. As one media analyst dryly put it, 'poorly-produced programming compromises both content and distribution profit margins – witness how poorly produced programming has affected the asset value of Viacom or has taken Ted Turner out of play'. In 'Media mergers don't add up', *Nat West Markets*, 2 January 1996, pp. 1–5.

64 'Media mergers don't add up', pp. 1–5.

Chapter 5

The formation of the 'major independent'

Miramax, New Line and the New Hollywood

Justin Wyatt

While much of the economic film history of the New Hollywood has focused on the conglomeration of the industry and the globalization of media production, the industrial structure has changed not just for the major studios, but also for those distributors on the margins, the independent film and video distributors. In this chapter, I intend to analyse how the marketplace for independent film (films not released by the majors) has shifted in the past two decades by considering the development of the two largest independent companies, New Line Cinema and Miramax Films. The case studies of New Line and Miramax illuminate the diverse distribution, marketing and advertising methods developed and co-opted by the independents to weather an increasingly competitive economic climate. Perhaps strongest evidence of the two companies' success in traversing the marketplace can be seen by the recent mergers between these independents and major companies which have provided both New Line and Miramax with substantial financial backing.

In terms of independent production, the video and cable boom initially seemed to create an increased demand for product. As one industry analyst commented in 1987,

> Why are there suddenly so many new companies joining the low-budget bandwagon – companies like Cinecom and Island, Goldwyn and Alive, Skouras, Cineplex, Atlantic, Vestron and Spectrafilm? The answer is home video. For one thing, the independent home video companies need products to fill their pipelines. Since the studios already have their own video companies, new movie forces need to be created.[1]

This boom can be evidenced through the dramatic increase in independent production in the second half of the 1980s, particularly from 1988 on. Considering all films receiving MPAA ratings, independent films increased from 193 in 1986 to 277 in 1987 and to 393 in 1988.[2] The figures for 1989 through 1991 also remained close to the 400 mark.

This period of increased production was marked by a substantial growth in negative costs and by the widespread failure of most independent films: between 1986 and 1989, the years coinciding with the film production boom, negative costs doubled, while film rentals for independent companies dropped 33 per cent.[3] Even those companies which were able to launch one or more breakthrough films overextended their assets and weakened their longevity in the marketplace. Vestron earned about $63 million in domestic gross for *Dirty Dancing* in 1987, but then proceeded to double production. With failures ranging from art house films (Ken Russell's *Gothic* (1986), John Huston's *The Dead* (1987)) to teen pics (*Dream a Little Dream* (1989), *Big Man on Campus* (1989)), the company had financing cut from Security Pacific National Bank, and was forced to shut down production and distribution in 1989.[4] Similarly, Cinecom, after *A Room With a View* (1986), and Skouras, after *My Life As a Dog* (1987), were unable to replicate their initial major success. Other independent companies, such as New Century/Vista, Circle, Cineplex Odeon, Spectrafilm and Weintraub Entertainment Group, could not produce even one breakthrough success.

Video also has proven to be an unreliable market for the independents. Indeed, both rental and 'sell-through' (purchased directly for the home) videos have been characterized as 'A' title businesses. As Strauss Zelnick, former president and chief operating officer of Twentieth Century Fox, comments on this phenomenon,

> Because video is released after theaters, the success in video tracks the success in theaters like every other market. Certain pictures outperform in video, but that would never induce you to make a picture because if it fails at the box office, video will not 'fix' the failure. A movie will perform in accordance with its performance at the box office which means you won't make enough money to justify the decision.[5]

Theatrical successes drive the push at every additional market window so that 'A' titles are most likely to translate to video and cable successes. Consider that among the top ten sell-through titles in 1991, five were distributed by Buena Vista (Disney Classics), with the remaining titles all grossing over $75 million theatrically.[6] While the video market expanded, independent companies were not the beneficiaries of this growth in the long run. Part of this phenomenon is explained by the shift towards sell-through spending in the video market: while rental spending also increased between 1985 and 1992, the amount allocated to sell-through videos multiplied seven times during the period.[7] Only certain titles are launched with a sell-through approach: namely those videos which have already proven their appeal at the theatrical box office. Films that are star based and family oriented (and therefore possess repeatability in home use) also have a greater chance of being sell-through items.[8] These factors tend to privilege in the video market major releases with a track record of box office performance. Consequently, many of the independent companies initially 'helped' by video and cable eventually severely cut production (for example, Cinecom and Cannon) or exited the market altogether (for example, Island, Alive, FilmDallas, Skouras, Vestron, Atlantic Releasing, Avenue, DEG). By 1992, the top-grossing imports were distributed only by New Line, Miramax, Goldwyn, and the dying Orion Classics.[9]

New Line and Miramax have been able to withstand this shakeout by consistently developing movies with the potential to cross over beyond the art house market. The companies differ in the methods employed for long-run survival though. Whereas New Line has continually favoured gradual expansion and diversification only following breakthrough successes, Miramax's presence is based much more on marketing and targeting audiences beyond a narrow art house niche. In the process, both companies have been able to develop respectable market shares and some commercially impressive cross-over films.

New Line Cinema and franchising

Formed in 1967 by Robert Shaye, New Line Cinema began as a non-theatrical distributor focusing on the market for 'special events' on college campuses. Through such films as *Reefer Madness* (1936) and *Sympathy For the Devil* (1970) and a lecture series representing among others William Burroughs, Norman Mailer and R.D. Laing, New Line maintained a constant presence until 1973 when Shaye decided to open a theatrical distribution arm.[10] Shaye targeted his product narrowly, distributing, as described by *Variety*, 'arty and freak' films. 'Arty' translates to films by Lina Wertmuller (*The Seduction of Mimi* (1974)), Claude Chabrol (*Wedding in Blood* (1973)) and Pier Paolo Pasolini (*Porcile* (1969)), while 'freak' would include *Reefer Madness*, *The Texas Chainsaw Massacre* (1974) and *Pink Flamingos* (1972). Shaye opened some of these films, such as *Pink Flamingos*, in a midnight screening pattern, followed by a larger theatrical release. By 1974, the New Line Cinema distribution slate mixed foreign, sexploitation, gay cinema, rock documentaries and 'midnight specials' reserved exclusively for midnight exhibition. The intent behind these choices was to tap those markets which would be ignored by the majors, and to maximize the difference of New Line's product from more traditional commercial film.

In 1978, New Line began a limited policy of film production inspired by two major factors. As the market for art films became more established, a greater number of distributors entered the marketplace and competition became more intense within this market. As a result, 'the bidding auction' for film distribution encouraged the price to rise. New Line had already begun to advance money (albeit the small amount of $150,000) in pre-production deals to acquire the completed pictures for distribution.[11] Shaye's decision to enter production was facilitated by access to a fresh source of production funds: Chemical Bank and a group of private investors supplied a $5 million loan based on New Line's consistent track record.[12] Vowing to limit budgets to under $2 million, Shaye maintained that his decision to enter production was also motivated by the growing availability of money from television, syndication, foreign territories and other subsidiary markets.[13]

Over the next decade, New Line continued to augment their distribution slate with pickups, often forming long-term alliances with production companies. For example, New Line signed an exclusive three-year deal with the British company Working Title Productions giving New Line all North American rights, excluding home video.[14] Even more significant from a financial standpoint, New Line entered into a distribution partnership with Carolco Pictures, under which New Line agreed to release lower-budget Carolco features separate from their features for TriStar Pictures.[15] During the decade, New Line also managed to translate the low-budget exploitation film *A Nightmare on Elm Street* (1985) into a wildly profitable six-part series by developing the iconic value of Freddy Krueger. Breaking from the expected decay from film to film in a series, *Nightmare III* (1987) grossed $15 million more than *Nightmare II* (1985) and *Nightmare IV* (1988) grossed $7 million more than *Nightmare III*. Revenue from the franchise was funnelled back into the company rather than into hasty and sizeable production and distribution expansion; as Shaye commented, 'We are a highly efficient operation with significantly low overhead. One *Elm Street* annually suffices to pay for it. We do not need to make pictures merely to support our distribution apparatus, so we can be selective in our judgments'.[16]

The *Nightmare* franchise was augmented by New Line's most successful film – the most successful independent film ever made – *Teenage Mutant Ninja Turtles*, grossing $135 million in 1990. The film moved New Line from a loss position in 1989 to a $5.3 million profit for the first half of 1990.[17] Picking up the completed film, New Line's share of ticket sales amounted to only 15 per cent, yet this figure, added to the *Nightmare* franchise, transformed the company.[18] Based on a comic book about crusading radioactive reptiles, the film possessed a wide level of awareness given the comic book and a host of assorted merchandised items: in 1989, a year prior to the film's release, over 100 companies licensed *Turtles* merchandise totalling approximately $350 million. Immediately on release, New Line executives began referring to the Turtles as a franchise – *Turtles II* was released a year after the first film and *Turtles III* two years later. The lag on the third film did not lower the box office revenue. As New Line marketing and distribution president Mitchell Goldman described at the release date of *Turtles III*, 'There's no question that we knew the turtles weren't what they once were.

However, there's a second generation of children who are 3 or 4 years old and who love the turtles. We knew the videocassettes, TV show, and toys were still selling well.'[19]

New Line's franchises recall Paramount's adherence to 'tent pole' movies: in the mid-1980s, Paramount built their release schedule around commercial tent poles, like the *Indiana Jones*, *Star Trek* and *Beverly Hills Cop* movies, which could support less viable projects.[20] For New Line, the franchise permitted two developments: the creation of a home video division and a separate distribution arm, Fine Line Features, devoted to more specialized, hard-to-market films. While many New Line films had been distributed through RCA/Columbia Pictures Home Video, the benefits of retaining video rights were clear: control of another window of release and the advantage of further coordination of the theatrical-video release programme.

As early as 1983, New Line announced that they would split their product into mainstream and speciality items.[21] Ira Deutchman, former marketing and distribution president of independent distributor Cinecom, was chosen to be the president of Fine Line Features, the specialized division of New Line launched in 1990. Distancing himself from the failed 'classics divisions' of the major studios, Deutchman highlighted the market appeal of the potential Fine Line films: 'We're looking for films that perhaps take a little more immediate special attention to launch them into the marketplace, a little more time to find their audiences, but they have more market, more crossover potential than classics-oriented films.'[22] The move has allowed New Line to produce more commercial fare and to hire stars as insurance for their films. Most conspicuously, in 1994, New Line's product included two Jim Carrey vehicles, the comedy/special effects movie *The Mask* and another film for which they paid $7 million for his talents, *Dumb and Dumber*. Ridiculed in the press at the time (Carrey had appeared in only one successful film, *Ace Ventura: Pet Detective* (1994), when the deal for *Dumb and Dumber* was signed), both films became blockbusters, with *The Mask* making $119 million and *Dumb and Dumber* $127 million domestically.[23] Fine Line Features enjoyed early success with the art house hit by Robert Altman, *The Player* ($21.7 million) in 1992, but their track record since has been less auspicious: top grossers for each year include Altman's *Short Cuts* ($6.1 million in 1993), the documentary *Hoop Dreams* ($7.8 million in 1994), *The Incredibly True Adventure of Two Girls in Love* (a dismal $2.2 million in 1995), and finally a breakthrough hit with *Shine* at the end of 1996 ($36 million). Shaye vowed to concentrate on acquiring distribution rights for Fine Line Features, rather than being an active producer.[24] This decision was motivated by the lower revenue potential associated with specialized art house films. By separating product between the two arms, Shaye has been able to create a market identity for each company and to allocate advertising/distribution expenditures consistent with each film's potential pay-off.

Miramax Films and marketing media controversies

Miramax Films, run by Harvey and Bob Weinstein, also started by mining the college audience, through booking rock concerts and roadshow concert movies.[25] Their experience in film distribution began with acquiring distribution rights to films which, at the right pickup price, would enable them to reap at least a small profit. Consider Billie August's *Twist and Shout* (1986): with the North American rights acquired for $50,000, Miramax was able to nurture the film to about $1.5 million at the box office.[26] *I've Heard the Mermaids Singing* (1987), *Working Girls* (1987) and *Pelle the Conqueror* (1988) were all successes for Miramax in the mid-1980s.

Miramax became more visible with the acquisition of Steven Soderbergh's *sex, lies and videotape*, which they advanced $1.1 million for the North American theatrical rights alone. Appropriately enough the film was produced through pre-selling the video rights to RCA–Columbia Home Video. Winning the Audience Award at the Sundance Film Festival and the Palme d'Or at Cannes, *sex, lies* was sold by Miramax as a sexy and intense comedy about relationships: ad images displayed Peter Gallagher and Laura San Giacomo embracing, and James Spader and Andie MacDowell about to kiss. Highlighting the critical acclaim also, Miramax realized a gross of over $26 million domestically. The film's success can be attributed to its topicality: many critics considered the film as primarily centred on the relationship between culture and technology in the age of 'safe sex'. With Graham (James Spader) videotaping interviews by women talking about their sex lives and his professed total reliance on masturbation as a sexual outlet, the film represents the intersection of the latest 'new technology' with sex, or rather with a form of sex that is completely safe. As Karen Jaehne astutely noted, 'Soderbergh wants Graham to explode the neo-conservative Eighties with video the way David Hemmings did the swinging Sixties with photography in *Blowup*.'[27] Soderbergh's technique was to start by exploring the limited sexual boundaries available in the 1980s, a move that was calculated to some extent by the director. When queried on the difficulty of the project in terms of funding, Soderbergh explains, 'Well, on the one hand, it may seem like a risk. On the other, remember that we've got four relatively young people drenched in sexuality in a film that can be made for $1.2 million.'[28] Given the critical triumph, prizes and aggressive marketing by Miramax, the gross destroyed the previous benchmark for an art house hit. Independent marketing executive Dennis O'Connor, who has worked at Strand Releasing and Trimark Pictures, believes that the marketplace for independent or specialized film has changed drastically since the time of *sex, lies and videotape*. In terms of box office, whereas the mark of an independent success used to be a gross of about $3 million, the figure currently is closer to $10 million.[29] Perhaps because of his film's role in this phenomenon, Soderbergh now has mixed feelings:

The positive aspect is that it shows that 'art movies' can be a viable commercial product. They don't have to remain ghettoized as an art film. The bad thing is that it's established an unrealistic benchmark for other films. That's unfortunate. All you have to do is look at the Sundance Festival in the following years after *sex, lies* won, and you see films which may have been passed over since 'it's just not another *sex, lies*.' I actually think that my next two movies (*Kafka* and *King of the Hill*) will hold up better over time. I just feel that *sex, lies* is so much the beneficiary of being of that time that it's become so dated, like a Nehru jacket![30]

The experience with *sex, lies* has been replicated on many occasions by the company – more specifically, selling a product which lends itself to media-induced controversy. Repeatedly Miramax has maximized the publicity created by challenging the MPAA ratings system: Miramax films *Scandal* (1989), *The Cook, The Thief, His Wife and Her Lover* (1989), *Tie Me Up! Tie Me Down!* (1990) and *You So Crazy* (1994) all received X (or NC17) from the ratings board, with Miramax publicly announcing the injustice of the ratings system for independent companies compared to the majors.[31] While in some cases, cuts were made to obtain the R rating, most often (*Cook, Tie Me Up!*) Miramax chose to release the film unrated. Despite this fact, Miramax wagered often lengthy campaigns – all heavily reported in the media – against the 'arbitrary and capricious' ratings system which would assign an X to, for example, *Tie Me Up!*[32]

This ratings battle also has occurred with Miramax's advertising, with the company receiving reprimands from the Classification and Rating Administration of the MPAA.[33] After releasing Peter Greenaway's *The Cook, The Thief, His Wife and Her Lover* unrated – yet foregrounding the letter X in the ad copy, 'X as in . . . ' – Miramax sought to advertise Greenaway's *Drowning By Numbers* (1987) through a silhouette of a naked man and woman embracing matched with a critic's quote stating, 'Enormously entertaining. No, no one gets eaten in this one.'[34] The MPAA believed that the combination was too suggestive for widespread advertising. Amid wide coverage in industry trades, Miramax surrendered the R rating for the film, rather than alter the advertising.

Enormous publicity was generated by the campaign for *The Crying Game* which, unlike the original British ad campaign, centred on a shot of supporting actress Miranda Richardson with a smoking gun. For its North American opening in November 1992, the tag line proclaimed 'Play it at your own risk. Sex. Murder. Betrayal. In Neil Jordan's new thriller nothing is what it seems to be.' By January, the ad line was replaced with the following: 'The movie everyone is talking about, but no one is giving away its secrets.' Miramax wanted to stay away from the film's political elements and instead position it as a thriller based around a core secret (the gender of the character Dil, played by Jaye Davidson, revealed halfway through the film). This major secret was responsible for the film's cross-over success; due to the barrage of publicity and press coverage growing from the secret, an amazing $62.5 million was grossed by this film which would seem to be firmly within the boundaries of the art cinema.[35] As *Variety* describes Miramax's marketing campaign, 'Miramax sold the film as an action-thriller with a big "secret". If it had been realistically pegged as a relationship film with gay connotations, it might never have broken beyond the major cities.'[36]

As with *sex, lies and videotape*, *The Crying Game* benefited from engaging its audiences in current and timely issues – in this case, the national debate over homosexual rights, specifically the proposal to end the ban on gays serving in the military.[37] In many ways, the film's thriller plot line is secondary to the romance between Dil and Fergus (Stephen Rea) which addresses the blurry line between attraction and repulsion, not to mention constructed and essential differences across sexual, gender, class and national lines. As with the 'gays in the military' issue, the film confronts the fears of straight men being considered a sexual object by someone of the same gender. Less commented on during the release were the sexual politics inherent in such a position. While Jordan does feature an unlikely 'romantic' pairing of IRA member with a transvestite hairdresser, the film does nevertheless embody many clichés and stereotypes of gayness: the in-the-closet relationship, the continual drug-taking and nightclubbing, and the mental/psychological instability invoked by the character of Dil. Therefore, while the gimmick certainly placed and maintained the film in the domestic market, the cross-over popularity of the film must be considered in terms of its ideological stance. *The Crying Game* simultaneously allowed viewers to engage the subject of gayness while reinforcing 'traditional' and discriminatory views, all within the larger genre of the thriller.

The strategy of refocusing an advertising campaign also surfaced with Miramax's highest grossing film, *Pulp Fiction*. The campaign was designed to cross over as soon as possible from an art house audience to a wider action-thriller clientele. The trailer demonstrates this approach: the preview begins solemnly by announcing that the film has won the Palme d'Or at the Cannes Film Festival and that it has been one of the most critically acclaimed films of the year. Suddenly gunshots appear through the screen, and a fast-paced barrage of shots from the film stressing the action, sexuality and memorable sound bites. Through the trailer, Miramax has been able to sell to the art house audience through the film's credentials, but, more significantly, an image was created of the film as being full of action, comedy and sex. This approach no doubt broadened the film's audience without alienating those drawn by the critical acclaim. This strategy can also be evidenced in *Pulp Fiction*'s one-sheet which defines the term 'pulp fiction' for those unfamiliar – a process clearly aimed at educating the masses who might have been alienated by an 'obscure' title.

Figure 5.1 Samuel L. Jackson, John Travolta and Harvey Keitel in Quentin Tarantino's *Pulp Fiction* (1994). Courtesy of Buena Vista and the Kobal Collection

The impact of New Line and Miramax can be illustrated through the case of director Robert Altman.[38] Despite a strong critical reputation, a series of commercial failures in the late 1970s and the relatively disappointing box-office gross of the pre-sold, marketing-oriented *Popeye* in 1980, created a hostile climate for Altman within the major studios. Altman's only film for a major studio since *Popeye* was made in 1983 for MGM – *O.C. and Stiggs* – which was released in a handful of theatres four years later, and then directly to home video. Since his estrangement from the majors, Altman has been forced to work in other media (cable for *The Laundromat* (1985) and *Tanner '88* (1988), network television for *The Room* (1987), *The Dumb Waiter* (1987) and *The Caine Mutiny Court-Martial* (1988)) and for independent studios (Cinecom for *Come Back to the Five and Dime, Jimmy Dean, Jimmy Dean* (1982), United Artists Classics for *Streamers* (1983), Cannon for *Fool For Love* (1986), New World for *Beyond Therapy* (1987), Hemdale for *Vincent and Theo* (1990), Fine Line for *The Player* (1992) and *Short Cuts* (1993), Miramax for *Ready to Wear* (1994)).

Altman's return to media prominence relates directly to the efforts of New Line/Fine Line and Miramax in promoting and publicizing Altman's films. New Line chose to release *The Player* in 1992 through their art house distribution arm Fine Line Features, rather than directly through New Line Cinema. This choice indicates that the film, while probably among the most 'accessible' of Altman's career in terms of character and narrative, remained a challenge in terms of placement within the marketplace. On release, Universal's Tom Pollock commented that the film's 'unbridled hostility' towards the studio system could have been turned into a 'brilliant marketing ploy had a "major" distributed it'.[39] I would argue that Fine Line's marketing strategy for *The Player* did indeed centre on Altman's alienation and independence from the studio system. Altman's 'iconoclastic' past and his return to form after a decade away from Hollywood centred many of the publicity opportunities developed by Fine Line.[40] While foregrounding Altman as auteur has been a consistent focus for selling his films, this effect with *The Player* was augmented by repositioning Altman as a famous director returned to form. This approach was repeated in 1993 with Fine Line's release of Altman's *Short Cuts*, with the advertising centred almost entirely on the match between Altman and the writings of Raymond Carver. The tag line describes, 'From two American masters comes a movie like no other.'

Miramax's selling of *Ready to Wear* expands this strategy even further. Miramax Films has thrived due to its marketing savvy, particularly the ability to apply 'exploitation' techniques to art house product. Their approach follows from several earlier Miramax campaigns. Miramax's ads for *Ready to Wear* ran without prior approval by the MPAA, creating a media frenzy over the scantily clad model Helena Christensen in the one-sheet. While the MPAA had banned the image from the film's advertising, the issue was extended even further when Columbia Records continued to utilize the shot in promotion for the soundtrack CD.[41] Since the posters included the line 'See the Movie', the MPAA believed that the ads constituted movie promotion, and threatened to revoke the movie's R rating. Miramax hired high-profile attorney Alan Dershowitz to represent their case, with Dershowitz and Helena Christensen appearing at a press conference on 15 December, ten days before the film's première.[42]

An ensemble comedy/satire of the fashion industry, with a narrative structure close to the crisscrossing of Altman's *Nashville* (1975), *A Wedding* (1978) and *H.E.A.L.T.H.* (1979), *Ready to Wear*'s release was propelled not only by the ad controversy, but also by a title change less than a month prior to release.[43] Miramax marketing vice-president Marcy Granata explained that the change from *Prêt-à-Porter* to *Ready to Wear* was motivated by the feeling that Americans would find the original title 'difficult to pronounce and even harder to define'.[44] Altman concurred with the shift: 'Miramax is a company with incredible gut instincts about this kind of thing.'[45] These comments seem curious from the director whose biggest commercial success was *M*A*S*H*, a title which no doubt proved perplexing initially for many moviegoers in 1970. However, Altman realized the publicity opportunity presented by suddenly translating a title which had been covered in the press for over a year. The media controversy generated by the shift allowed the film to garner more press coverage as a means to compete in the competitive year-end release schedule.[46]

Life under conglomeration

If Miramax and New Line represent the most ambitious and seasoned independents, their current claim to the label 'independent' is much more tenuous. In May 1993, Disney acquired Miramax, while the Turner Broadcasting Corporation merged with New Line. Paying close to $60 million for Miramax, Disney acquired the Miramax film library (over 200 features) and the talents of the Weinsteins who signed contracts for a five-year period.[47] Disney agreed entirely to finance the development, production and marketing of Miramax's features. The benefits for the Weinsteins include better ancillary deals in markets such as home video and pay television. The brothers estimate that by aligning with Disney they will be able to extract in excess of $750,000 to $2 million per film. Bob Weinstein cites the example of two Miramax children's films – *Arabian Knight* (1993) and *Gordy* (1995) – which failed theatrically but were saved by aggressive selling at the video window by Disney: 'We were rescued by Disney in home video. Now, that's a clear case of synergy.'[48] Ted Turner acquired New Line Cinema, along with Castle Rock Entertainment, to provide fresh programming for Turner's television networks, TBS and TNT.[49] New Line/Fine Line was acquired for about $600 million, while Castle Rock cost Turner $100 million in cash and about $300 million in assumed debt.[50]

The intent for both Disney and Turner was to leave New Line and Miramax as separate from the allied companies. In this manner, both New Line and Miramax would be able to maintain some autonomy. This position is significant given the lessons learned from the 'classics' divisions of the major studios in the early 1980s. Established to distribute specialized product, the classics divisions, such as Triumph Films (Columbia) and Twentieth Century Fox International Classics, entrusted distribution for their films to the studios' domestic distribution arm.[51] Focusing their energy on the mainstream (and more costly) films, domestic distribution bungled release after release from the classics divisions. New Line and Miramax have retained control of distribution and marketing for their releases. The most impressive difference given their new affiliation was a greater access to funds and more latitude in production decisions.

Indeed, these major independents, Miramax and New Line, have served to polarize the market for independent film. Miramax, in particular, has become even more aggressive in buying distribution rights to completed films, with their efforts increasing the price for product. As Ira Deutchman of Fine Line comments, '[The Disney era] Miramax has definitely affected the marketplace. People are buying films earlier and earlier, and paying more and more.'[52] Marcus Hu of the independent company Strand Releasing repeats this observation: 'It's tough when you find a Miramax buying up stuff like *Clerks*. If *Crush* had come out this year, a bigger company would have snapped it up.'[53] Even executives at Miramax admit that this syndrome is problematic: acquisitions vice-president Tony Safford comments, 'We think other people have overpaid. We are all having to make strategic decisions that may involve overpaying because of lack of product.'[54]

Since the mergers in 1993, against professed intentions, corporate domination has somewhat constrained both Miramax and New Line despite their greater access to capital. With Miramax, the policy of marketing through media controversy has occasionally created friction with Disney. In 1995, this conflict was evidenced with the releases both of *Priest*, a British film directed by Antonia Bird about a conservative gay priest fighting inner and outer battles to gain peace, and *kids*, Larry Clark's exposé of debauched youth in New York. In a move that was described by William A. Donohue, president of the Catholic League, as placing 'salt on the wounds of believers', Miramax scheduled the release of *Priest* for Good Friday. Miramax, expressing surprise at the vehemence with which the film was being protested, shifted the release date amid a great deal of publicity. A representative headline over the incident read, 'Protest Delays Wide Release of Priest; Miramax Bows to Catholic Group and Reschedules Controversial Film's General Distribution Till After Easter'.[55] Advertising maximized the controversy: the title carried the letter 't' in the shape of the cross, while the ad line referenced both the gay priest's secret and the secondary tale of incest which the priest must expose: 'In the world of rituals, in a place of secrets, a man must choose between keeping the faith and exposing the truth.' Given Miramax's affiliation with Disney, the effects persisted though: several stockholders, including the Knights of Columbus and Senator Bob Dole's wife Elizabeth Dole, sold stock in Disney soon after the *Priest* scandal. The Knights of Columbus, selling $3 million of Disney stock, cited the company's ties to Miramax and *Priest*, while a Dole spokesman commented, 'Mrs. Dole was surprised to learn that Disney owned Miramax and Hollywood Records and has decided to sell her stock.'[56]

kids was able to maintain an almost consistent flow of publicity and promotion from its appearance at the Sundance Film Festival in January 1995 through its release in July. Ostensibly a cautionary tale, *kids* follows a day in the life of 17-year-old Telly, a 'virgin surgeon' whose mission in life is to seduce virgins. One of his earlier conquests, Jennie, discovers that she is HIV-positive and, while Telly is pursuing more girls, Jennie tries to find Telly to tell him the news. Playing into the media's most florid depiction of forgotten urban youth, the film's *cinéma verité* style furthered the critics' and reviewers' beliefs that Clark was depicting only a thinly veiled reality: as *New York* magazine titled their cover story on the film, 'What's the Matter with *kids* Today?'[57] *kids* received an NC17 rating (for 'explicit sex, language, drug use, and violence involving children') from the Motion Picture Association of America. Contractually Miramax, as a subsidiary of Disney, cannot release NC17 films. Thus the Weinsteins were forced to form another company, Shining Excalibur Pictures, just to release *kids*. Although some industry analysts viewed this move as an attempt by the Weinsteins to distance themselves from Disney, the brothers denied any such intention.[58]

Whereas Miramax has been able to continue its strategy of marketing through controversy, albeit with occasional institutional difficulties, New Line's fate under the Turner regime has been more precarious. The long-term differences in their life under conglomeration can be appreciated by contrasting two releases from 1996, Miramax's *Trainspotting* and Fine Line's *Crash*. *Trainspotting*, a mixture of hyperbolic music video visuals with a downbeat tale of heroin addiction among a set of friends in Scotland, became the second most popular British feature in UK box-office history and was adopted by Miramax for North American release. The Weinsteins partly dubbed the film to make the Scottish accents more comprehensible and sold it more along the lines of disillusioned youth than on heroin addiction. The trailer shifted the narrative trajectory to the heist of the last third of the film, limiting mention of drugs to an absolute minimum, while the print ad positioned the film in terms of lifestyle choices for the young ('Choose life. Choose a job. . .' through to 'Choose rotting away at the end of it all'). While the film's advertising diminished the role played by heroin in the narrative, a secondary level of publicity detailed the 'heroin chic' culture of emaciated and drugged fashion models and the rise of heroin use among the young. The result was a solid gross of $16.5 million, not a cross-over hit, but certainly a respectable art house box-office figure.

David Cronenberg's *Crash* describes a subculture of people sexually aroused by car accidents, following a young couple's descent into this world after their own crash. Admittedly, the subject matter strictly limited the film to art house exhibition, but New Line's owner Ted Turner reportedly delayed the release of the film after finding it distasteful: the release date was moved from October 1996 to March 1997, putting *Crash*'s American release after many other territories, including Canada and France. Turner's intervention in his subsidiary companies over 'difficult' projects had already impacted Anjelica Huston's television film *Bastard Out of Carolina*, depicting the rape of a 12-year-old by her stepfather. Huston's film was dropped from Turner's TNT cable network after Turner called the film 'extraordinarily graphic' and 'inhumane'.[59] Apart from shying away from controversy, the merger of Time Warner with Turner Broadcasting in 1996 further complicated New Line's position through making New Line directly compete with Warner Bros. for feature films. By mid-1996, industry trade papers reported that New Line was for sale by Time Warner as a result of this conflict of interest.[60] Around the same time, the Weinsteins extended their deal with Disney for another seven years.[61]

While historically New Line and Miramax were able to develop strategies – franchises and aggressive marketing/publicity – to maintain a consistent market presence, their merger with the larger companies has created a curious hybrid, the 'major independent'. The major independents have fragmented the marketplace for independent film further and further – through producing films parallel to the majors and through stressing art house acquisitions which have the potential to cross over to a wider market. While New Line and Miramax have gained financial backing through their affiliations, the remaining unaffiliated companies have experienced greater difficulty in acquiring product at a reasonable price. The net effect is a contraction in the market for independent film, bolstering the status of the majors and major independents, and creating an increasingly competitive market for those smaller companies. This movement towards the major independent as a market force constitutes a key shift in the industrial parameters of independent film, studio moviemaking and the New Hollywood. These two companies, seemingly on the margins of Hollywood, actually illustrate a number of the ways through which the New Hollywood has been refigured in industrial, aesthetic and institutional terms.

Acknowledgement

I wish to thank Ian Conrich and Conny Ford for sharing research materials on New Line Cinema with me.

Notes

1 David Ansen, Peter McAlevey and Katrine Ames, 'Hollywood goes independent', *Newsweek*, 6 April 1987, p. 66.
2 '23 year indie production pulse', *Variety*, 26 June 1991, p. 77.
3 Lawrence Cohn, 'Domestic market for indie pix soft', *Variety*, 22 February 1989, p. 22.
4 Al Stewart, 'Vestron saying nixed loan triggered woes, sues bank', *Variety*, 23 August 1989, p. 59.
5 Richard Ohmann (ed.), *Making and Selling Culture* (Hanover: Wesleyan University Press, 1996), p. 26.
6 Independent New Line Cinema released *Teenage Mutant Ninja Turtles 2: The Secret of the Ooze* (title #6), while title #10 – *Sweatin' to the Oldies* – was an exercise tape.
7 According to Video Store Magazine Market Research, sell-through spending was $641 million in 1985, climbing to $4,450 million in 1992.
8 Paul Verna, 'The great sell-through vs. rental debate', *Billboard*, 4 January 1992, p. V10.
9 'Top grossing imports for '92', *Variety*, 11 January 1993, p. 63.
10 'Arty and "freak" films packaged to theatre trade by New Line; sex, too', *Variety*, 4 July 1973, p. 6.
11 'Negative pickups a new policy for N.Y.'s New Line Cinema', *Variety*, 11 August 1976, p. 26.
12 'Pickup costs, other factors propel New Line to enter production', *Variety*, 28 June 1978, p. 6.
13 Ibid.

14 'New Line, Working Title in 3-year deal', *Variety*, 31 May 1989, p. 21.

15 Claudia Eller and Max Alexander, '*Turtles* vid heads for sell-through as New Line catches screen sequel', *Variety*, 18 July 1990, p. 3.

16 Myron Meisel, 'New Line's nightmare spurs ambitious expansion program', *The Film Journal*, April 1986, p. 37.

17 Judy Brennan, '*Turtles* a hero for New Line in first Half', *Variety*, 1 August 1990, p. 27.

18 Ronald Grover, 'Nightmares, turtles – and profits', *Business Week*, 30 September 1991, p. 52.

19 Martin Grove, 'New Line's future is filled with franchises', *The Hollywood Reporter*, 25 March 1993, p. 5.

20 For an analysis of Paramount's strategies in designing these commercial tent poles, see Justin Wyatt, 'High concept as product differentiation', *High Concept: Movies and Marketing in Hollywood* (Austin: University of Texas Press, 1994), pp. 104–7.

21 'New Line restructured for 24-pic annual goal', *Variety*, 29 June 1983, p. 4.

22 Claudia Eller, 'New Line forms new label for specialty releases', *Variety*, 10 December 1990, p. 5.

23 Data on domestic New Line and Miramax grosses have been supplied by Entertainment Data, Inc.

24 Claudia Eller, 'New Line forms', p. 5.

25 Anne Thompson, 'Will success spoil the Weinstein Brothers?', *Film Comment*, July/ August 1989, p. 73.

26 Ibid., p. 75.

27 Karen Jaehne, Review of *sex, lies and videotape*, *Cineaste*, vol. 17, no. 3 (1990), p. 38.

28 Harlan Jacobson, 'Truth or consequences', *Film Comment*, July/August 1989, p. 23.

29 Dennis O'Connor, telephone interview, 19 May 1995.

30 Steven Soderbergh, telephone interview, 26 October 1994.

31 Miramax sold off distribution rights to *You So Crazy* to the Samuel Goldwyn Company in March 1994. As a subsidiary of Disney, a Motion Picture Association of America member, Miramax was forbidden to release the film without a rating.

32 Richard Huff, 'Shackles on *Tie Me Up?*: Kunstler calls X rating arbitrary', *Variety*, 27 June 1990, p. 10.

33 Will Tusher, 'Distrib forfeits R on *Numbers* due to ad flak', *Variety*, 27 May 1991, p. 3.

34 Ibid.

35 Caryn James, '*The Crying Game* wins at gimmickry', *The New York Times*, 31 January 1993, p. H11.

36 Michael Fleming and Leonard Klady, '"Crying" all the way to the bank', *Variety*, 22 March 1993, p. 68.

37 A month before the release of *The Crying Game* in North America, President-elect Bill Clinton announced that he planned to reverse the bans on homosexuals in the military as his first policy decision. For a chronology of events and issues leading to this point, see Scott Tucker, 'Panic in the Pentagon', *Humanist*, vol. 53 (June 1993), p. 41. The national furore over this proposal is covered in Bruce B. Auster, 'The Commander and Chiefs', *U.S. News and World Reports*, 8 February 1993, pp. 37–40.

38 For a more complete account of the relationship between Altman and the larger

industrial structure of the New Hollywood, see Justin Wyatt, 'Economic constraints/economic opportunities: Robert Altman as auteur', *The Velvet Light Trap*, no. 38 (Fall 1996), pp. 51–67.

39 Peter Bart, 'Altman's revenge', *Variety*, 10 February 1992, p. 5.

40 As Altman commented in an interview just before the release of *The Player*: 'This film hasn't been released yet. This film, less than 3,000 people have seen it – in the world. I've got more mail from those screenings than on all the other films I've made in my lifetime. Twenty, thirty films . . . and everybody's writing about it; every goddam magazine that you could pick up has it as my "comeback". This is my third comeback, whaddya gonna do on my next one?!' ('The movie you saw is the movie we're going to make', *Film Comment*, May/June 1992, p. 28).

41 Claudia Eller, 'Is Altman dressed for success?', *The Los Angeles Times*, 7 December 1994, p. F1.

42 Greg Evans, '*Ready* to dress down MPAA', *Variety*, 15 December 1994, p. 6.

43 Miramax also sold *Ready to Wear*, in a similar fashion as Fine Line's release of *The Player*, as the work of an acclaimed director – a one-sheet for the film suggests that Altman will 'do' to the fashion industry in *Ready to Wear* what he has done to the military in *M*A*S*H*, country music in *Nashville*, and the film industry in *The Player*.

44 Greg Evans, '*Pret* fret nets translation', *Variety*, 1 December 1994, p. 6.

45 Ibid.

46 It should also be noted that Miramax shifted the release date as well – from 21 December to 25 December. This move was not explained by Miramax, although as Greg Evans points out, 'Pix released on the 25th get a crack at Christmas Day moviegoers before reviews, word-of-mouth or B.O. reports get a chance to settle in.' The implication is that Miramax made both changes in an effort to maximize the marketability of a film which they perceived as uncommercial.

47 Claudia Eller and John Evan Frook, 'Mickey munches on Miramax', *Variety*, 3 May 1993, p. 60.

48 Claudia Eller, 'The synergy between unlikely partners Miramax and Disney has surprised many – including Miramax and Disney', *The Los Angeles Times*, 1 December 1995, p. D1.

49 Anita Sharpe, 'Turner film ventures gets mixed results', *The Wall Street Journal*, 11 August 1994, p. B1.

50 Claudia Eller, 'Media's mega-deal makers', *The Los Angeles Times*, 18 July 1996, p. D6.

51 Alicia Springer, ' Sell it again Sam', *American Film*, March 1983, p. 55.

52 John E. Frook, 'Call Harvey Mickey Mouth', *Variety*, 29 November 1993, p. 75.

53 Mary S. Glucksman, 'The state of things', *Filmmaker*, Fall 1994, p. 29.

54 John Brodie, 'Harvey's hefty cash lends fest some flash', *Variety*, 23 May 1994, p. 63.

55 John Dart, 'Protest delays wide release of *Priest*', *The Los Angeles Times*, 25 March 1995, p. Metro 1.

56 'Disney link to assailed movie spurs Dole's wife to sell stock', *The Los Angeles Times*, 3 June 1995, p. A16.

57 Lynn Hirschberg, 'What's the matter with *kids* today?', *New York*, 5 June 1995, pp. 36–41.

58 Elaine Dutka, 'Miramax circumvents *kids* controversy', *The Los Angeles Times*, 29 June 1995, p. Calendar 2.

59 Warren Berger, 'A harsh story finally avoids a harsh fate', *The New York Times*, 15 December 1996, p. H37.

60 Turner's reported pricing of New Line stalled some potential bidders for the company; see Dan Cox and Martin Peers, 'New Line goes back in time', *Variety*, 10 April 1997, p. 1.

61 Claudia Eller, 'Miramax's production duo extending run with Disney', *The Los Angeles Times*, 10 May 1996, p. 5.

Chapter 6

To the rear of the back end
The economics of independent cinema

James Schamus

Let me write the following from a purely small business point of view – from the perspective of an independent film producer working out of New York who makes 'specialized' films intended for upscale art house theatrical release. And let us assume for the purposes of this chapter that my motivations in pursuing a producing career are purely economic, and that I and my partners are rational economic agents attempting to extract maximum value from the efforts of ourselves, our collaborators and our employees. From this perspective, and with those assumptions, let me add one more assumption – that you, my reader, would not mind turning your academic and critical interest in cinema into something of a money-making sideline, and that I am here to help steer you and your investment pounds, dollars or ecus in the right direction, in the direction of one of those fabulously successful independent films we have all read about these past few years. We have heard that a film's mode of production bears some relation to its mode of representation. Perhaps the many modes of financing independent films bear some relation to their meaning. So let us scan the money trail that leads towards and away from these films, with an ear for discerning what we might call independent cinema's own particular 'poetics of late capitalism'.

Mainly, however, we will simply adumbrate the prices of things and the costs of doing business, compiling not-so-epic lists of transactions and purchases. We shall deal with four main areas. First, we shall take a look at what share of the box office you, as an investor, might be able to get your hands on if you have been fortunate enough to finance a runaway hit. Second, we shall look at the international film sales food chain to see where you, as a successful financier, might figure. Third, we will take a look at what a 'no-budget' independent film really costs to get into the marketplace. You have probably heard stories about $7,000 or $25,000 movies that go on to play at your local multiplex, and those stories are more or less true. But there is a more true story that I will tell you shortly. And fourth, we shall take a look at the current market conditions that are accompanying the consolidation of independents into studio-owned and affiliated entities or their new international counterparts such as Polygram and Canal-Plus.

Gross

Let us say you have financed a $1 million independent film that I and my partner at Good Machine, Ted Hope, have produced. And let us say that *Variety* has just reported that our $1 million independent film has hit, over the past weekend, the $10 million mark at the US domestic box office. My assistant's voice comes through on the speakerphone, to inform me that you are on the line, with a bottle of champagne in hand. Before you uncork that bottle, I had better explain to you a few facts about the film business.

That $10 million – known as the film's 'gross' – was collected by the exhibitors at the doors to their theatres. Those exhibitors have made a series of deals with the film bookers who work at the distribution company to whom Ted and I, the producers, have licensed the film. Oddly, no one pays much attention to these exhibition deals when the time comes for the distributor to 'settle' and collect – the amount of money the distributor will be able to extract from the cinema owners has as much to do with the promise of future business and current market clout as anything else. Theatre owners like to hold on to the majority of the box-office gross until they reach their weekly 'nut' – the amount they claim to need to pay their overhead costs. After the nut is reached, the distributor generally lays claim to the vast majority of box-office revenues. To reach this nut is no mean feat, as most cinemas claim a weekly overhead of well over $5,000. One would assume, however, that most successful Hollywood blockbusters would maintain weekly per-cinema averages well over this mark. That is why it comes as some surprise when, studying the weekly grosses published in *Variety*, you notice that, indeed, few if any of the mega-hits maintain those kinds of numbers. What is the story, you might ask. Is there some not-for-profit foundation out there subsidizing the release of Arnold Schwarzenegger films? The answer to that question leads to the acknowledgement of a simple but telling axiom upon which the rest of the film business is founded these days. That axiom is: Movie theatres are not in the business of exhibiting movies. If they were in that business, they would long ago have gone under. They are, instead, in the far more lucrative business of selling paper cups full of flavoured sugar water at astronomical prices to people who spend just enough time sitting in darkened rooms to notice that their blood sugar level requires a boost.

Still, the cinema owners do lay claim to a hefty share of the box office. Without getting into the byzantine structure of exhibition deals, however, one can assume that, if a film has done moderately well, a major studio will be able to collect around 50 per cent of the gross and a moderately strong independent will be able to collect between 35 per cent and 45 per cent. What is collected is known as 'rentals' – the sums actually received by the distributor from the theatrical exploitation of the film.

Now I, the producer of this wildly successful $1 million independent film, have made a deal with a distributor about how those rentals should be split up. Assuming a $10 million gross and a successful collection of 40 per cent of that sum by the distributor, I will be sharing rentals of $4 million. What is the deal I have made with the distribution company? In North America, that deal would probably go something like this. The distribution company would first take a fee off-the-top, a fixed percentage of the rentals, probably 30 per cent. This provides the distribution company with an incentive to do a bang-up job – the higher the gross, the higher the rentals, and thus the higher their fee. After the fee is deducted, the costs of distribution and marketing are reimbursed. These costs, abbreviated as 'p&a' – prints and advertising – cover everything from the design and printing of posters (called 'one-sheets'), the striking and shipment of release prints, the cost of print, radio and TV advertising, the care and feeding of stars and other talent as they travel promoting the film, and the various other costs (promotional giveaways, parties, trailers, residual payments, if any, to guild actors, musicians, etc.). What remains after the distributor's fee and the reimbursement of p&a costs is called 'profits' or sometimes 'net profits', and I, the wildly successful independent producer, depending on the deal I made, might well be entitled to 100 per cent of those profits. That's right – 100 per cent. From the sums owed to me as the producer I will then pay the negotiated profit participations with my director, writer, stars and financiers. Usually, the financier will be able to recoup the cost of the film first, plus interest or at least a fixed bonus. Once this point has been reached – 'payout' – the film will then be in profit to the producer, at which point a standard deal might be that half the profits go to the financier and the other half will be divided according to negotiated deals among the producer and the talent – the so-called 'producer's net profits'.

Let us do some more calculations, then, to see who will get what when our $1 million film hits $10 million at the box office, thus earning $4 million in rentals. From that $4 million the distributor will take its 30 per cent fee ($1.33 million), thus leaving $2.66 million from which the p&a will be deducted, with the remainder counted as profit. Of course, the marketing costs associated with this small independent film will be nowhere near those of even an average Hollywood studio film. Let us say for the sake of example that the p&a is less than one-sixth of the Hollywood average, which this year has reached $20 million. That would mean a p&a charge of just, say, $3 million.

Thus, I can now proudly take your call to report that our wildly successful $1 million independent film, having just topped $10 million at the box office, is in profit to the tune of – *negative* $333,000. There is not even enough money in the distributor's coffers to pay for all the p&a. In other words, at least according to the balance sheet, we owe the distributor money (let us hope I never sign a deal in which that would legally be the case).

All of which leads us to axiom number two of today's independent film business, something which expresses what might be called the economic ontology of the cinema today: There is no such thing as 'the cinema'. For that series of shadows thrown on to the reflecting screen at the front of the sugar-water drinking hall is not a 'film' at all – it is simply an advertisement for what you in fact financed – a television and video programme (as well as, if you have a real breakthrough hit, a video game, a lunch-box, a theme-park ride, and, in the case of *Sense and Sensibility* (1996), an 'elegant keepsake box – jewellery and gloves not included').

From time to time a *Jurassic Park* (1993) can actually turn a profit at the box office, but for the vast majority of films an exhibition run in cinemas is simply an advertising campaign that lends an aura of cinematic legitimacy to the 'back end' ancillary exploitation of the film on various forms of television and other media – video rental and sales, pay and basic cable, broadcast television and satellite transmission, aeroplane and cruise ship projection. This 'back end' long ago became the front end in terms of financing and ultimate revenues. And such being the case, the supposed 'identity' of the filmic text comes increasingly under the dissolving pressures of its various revenue streams. Do *Volcano* (1997), *Mission: Impossible* (1996) or *ID4* (1996) need 'classical Hollywood' narrative construction, when it is precisely the fragmentation of their narratives into soundtrack albums, somatic theme-park jolts, iconic emblems stuck on T-shirts, and continuous loops of home entertainment that are really what is being sold? I don't think so.

Food chain

You might argue, however, that independent, art house films really are films, and to a certain extent you would be right, given that no one has yet to propose a *Poison*-inspired prison theme-park concession or a *Wedding Banquet* (1993) green-card marriage service. But in fact 'independent' films, at least in America, emerged in a commercial context in the early 1980s that was financially driven first by a healthy public TV market in Europe that purchased licences to many non-Hollywood films (ZDF in Germany, then C4 in Britain), followed by the first wave of capital that flowed into the emerging home video business. For a few years, with now-defunct companies like Vestron squandering hundreds of millions of dollars snapping up product to stuff into video boxes, low-budget independents could almost be guaranteed at least a few hundred thousand bucks in advances on video rights. In North America, numerous small independent distributors (Cinecom, Avenue, Island, Aries, etc.) mushroomed into existence in order to service these deals, with the understanding that a theatrical release increased the value of the video titles.

In general, though, American (and, even more certainly, 'foreign') independent films are 'ancillary-resistant'. They have a harder time finding places on the shelves of the large video rental chains; they rarely get free-TV deals; and they hardly ever figure significantly in those large television syndication packages that end up as your local television station's 'midnight' or 'million-dollar' movie. If they are going to profit at all, they had best beat the odds and at least come close to breaking even theatrically – a feat, as we have seen, that is nearly impossible. With these kinds of facts facing the independent film producer and investor, what is it that keeps hope alive, such that over 700 feature films were produced independently in the United States last year? That hope lies abroad, in the aggregate of all the back ends known as 'foreign'.

The fact is that, as an investor, you should simply never hope to reap profits from the potential box-office success of a film. Far more important to you, in terms of return on investment, is the deal-making success of the producer with whom you are working. That success will often be determined by the amount of money the producer can get up front from the various distributors around the world in the form of advances or minimum guarantees against the producer's and your share of the eventual profits. Perhaps a distributor, in the case of a runaway success, and *if* that distributor happens to be honest or afraid enough, will some day send 'overages' – profits due over and above the minimum guarantee paid for the film. But don't count on it. In the world of independently financed film, box-office success and investment success bear little real relation to each other. What you want more than good box office is good sales.

How is an independent film sold? If it is made by a reputable producer with some 'name' elements involved – stars, a director with a proven track record, big special effects, etc. – a film can be pre-sold to distributors at the package stage (script, cast, director, budget, schedule). Often, a packaged film might have to wait actually to go into production before distributors bite – they might distrust that the advertised package will in fact be delivered. Or, the film can be sold at one of the numerous (and ever-growing) international film festivals and markets – independent producers hope that 'festival fever' and positive 'buzz' will propel their modest efforts to greater-than-expected sales numbers. Or, a film can be screened privately for distributors and sold through one-on-one discussions.

'Sold' is, as a rule, a misnomer. If one does one's job correctly, one doesn't 'sell' the film at all – one 'licenses' its exploitation, in a certain territory, for a certain amount of time, in certain media – and in consideration of the grant of this licence one agrees to share the income derived from the various exploitation activities permitted under the contract. Each deal in each territory requires negotiation on all these points. Take a territory such as Germany, for example. Who among the eight or so viable independent theatrical distributors is the right one for this film? Who is honest? Who will release the film most creatively? (Why are the answers to those two questions so often different in many territories?) How long should the licence be for? (At Good Machine, we have negotiated licences as short as two years and as long as twenty-five years.) How do we define the territory? (Germany, or, more often, 'German-speaking territories', including Austria and German-speaking Switzerland?) But if we include German-speaking Switzerland, what happens to our 'French-speaking' deal? Which television station in Switzerland will have the first rights to the film? Will we allow the distributor to dub the film, or simply subtitle it? Will the distributor be granted other rights besides theatrical, such as video and television? Will they get interactive or electronic rights? What should the 'splits' – the division of profits – be, and how often should they be accounted for and paid? And, the most important question for the investor, how much should the distributor advance to us as a minimum guarantee of our profit share?

Now, take this series of questions (and add on about forty more) and multiply them by the number of territories you hope the film to be sold to – Japan, Korea, Spain, France, the UK, etc. Then ask yourself how many producers, after the daunting task of financing and making a film, also want to take on the job of selling it.

Enter the sales agency, the company which specializes in licensing independent films and collecting on the contracts. Often, sales agents themselves will advance to the producer a portion of the film's budget as a way of securing sales rights to the title. The agents will then go into the marketplace, sometimes at the package stage, sometimes with the finished film, and conduct the business arrangements, closing deals in each territory and making collections on the money owed. What do sales agents charge for this service? If they have had no hand in financing the film and are themselves not putting up an advance, their fees can be as low as 5 per cent – sometimes even lower. If, however, they put cash into the project and have some leverage over the producers, their fees can go north of 25 per cent of all sums advanced and all additional sums paid as overages by the distributors who license the film. In addition, the sales agent will pass on the sales and festival costs and the costs of delivering the film – and these charges can often be extremely high.

Assume, for example, that you have just spent the last of your million dollars completing the film when you hear that it has been accepted to world-première at the Cannes Film Festival. You of course immediately accept this extraordinary honour, and your sales agents begin to prepare. Cannes will require not one but two prints of your film, subtitled in French. Pay the lab; pay a service to produce a timed or 'spotted' dialogue list of your film; pay a translator; pay a subtitling service; and pay shipping and customs to get the prints to France. The festival will cover air fare and hotel for three nights for your director. The festival lasts two weeks. Add five or more nights of hotel for the director at $200 to $400 a night (*if* you can find a room). And remember to bring your stars, yourself, and the usual assortment of hangers-on (flights, hotel, not to mention $70 taxi rides from the Nice airport to Cannes). Make provision for food and drink (orange juice at the Majestic bar costs about $12 a glass these days). And don't forget press packets and stills and colour slides for the 4,000 accredited press members who will be there (it will cost more to ship the packets than to create them). Unless you wish to do all the scheduling for your director's and stars' press interviews, you'd best hire a publicist and help pay for their office and assistant. They will of course advise you on where to throw your after-screening party, and the sales agent will let you know where to take the forty or so most important buyers out to dinner. Perhaps if they are organized they will also help make the fabulously expensive video masters of the clips from the film you will need to give out to the electronic media. And because most buyers might miss your official screenings, you will need to pay the market section of the festival to screen the film at least two more times (bring a third print for this purpose), and you will need to advertise in the daily trade press in order to publicize those market screenings. Add the posters, stickers, party invitations, cellular phone rentals and bribes for the *maitre d*'s, and your budget is more or less complete. The total? Easily $150,000, and that is for a 'modest' presence at Cannes. Can Cannes be done for less? Certainly, it's been done for $15,000 to $40,000 but beware – in terms of sales you often get what you pay for. So when you get invited to Cannes, you probably will have only one real consolation: at least you weren't invited to Venice, which is *really* expensive.

What does this mean for you, the investor who financed our $1 million film? It means that in order for you to break even the sales agent will have to make sales far exceeding the film's actual cost, not only to cover their 25 per cent fee but also to cover what might in the long run add up to as much as a quarter of a million dollars in expenses. In other words, for you to get your money back the film would have to collect over $1.5 million – and you would still not be in profit. Even if the film does $2 million in sales – *double* its cost – your profits would still be fairly measly: the sales agent would deduct $500,000 in fees and probably $250,000 in expenses, thus leaving $1.25 million, a million of which would go to pay you back and the remainder of which would be split between you and the producer and other participants, giving you $125,000 in profit. Given how long it takes to make, sell, deliver and collect on an independent film, you might not see that profit until well over two years after you invested in the film, giving you a return on your investment of less than 5 per cent per annum. You can do better with an insured money market account. And that's a *success*.

Delivery

Why, then, would anyone invest in independent film? The answer to that question is probably the same as the answer to the question of why anyone would play black-jack in Las Vegas. As a producer, all I can do is to work relentlessly at keeping every one of these costs as low as possible. Can we make a $1 million film for less by keeping shooting days to a minimum, rewriting the script to avoid costly scenes, deferring talent costs, hiring inexperienced but talented and motivated crew? If so, perhaps we can end up with a *Wedding Banquet*, which cost $750,000 but which looked like it cost more. Can we drive a bargain with a reputable sales agent, or, better yet, can we dive in and try to sell the film ourselves? By being our own sales agents, or by co-agenting with others, we can drive the fees down (and pocket some of them ourselves, in any case), and we can directly control sales costs. On *Wedding Banquet*, for example, we premièred the film at the Berlin festival, a much less expensive place to launch a film than Cannes, and we sold the major territories ourselves, eventually teaming with a reputable agent who worked economically out of Zurich to handle the smaller territories as well as some of the bigger ones where she had excellent connections. (She was also able to advise us on which crooks to stay away from.)

Thus, while *The Wedding Banquet* appeared to the rest of the world like a wildly profitable film because of its tremendous box office, it was wildly profitable to us and to its financier, Central Motion Picture of Taiwan, well before and regardless of its theatrical release. Lest you think I am taking this occasion simply to brag, let me point out that we have also made our share of flops, of which there are two distinct types. The first type of flop might perform terribly at the box office, but for whatever reason sold well either at the package stage or at the festivals, so that in fact we and our investors might have already pocketed our profits, *Wedding Banquet*-style, long before the film's release. This is the profitable flop (at least it is profitable to us, if not to the distributors to whom we sold it). The second type of flop is the real flop, the film we cannot even convince distributors to take a chance on. And if the entire budget of such a film has been financed out of your pocket, you might end up losing all your money.

Given the potential for such risks, it is understandable that the American independent scene is often stirred and inspired by tales of 'no-budget' films – films made so cheaply that there is virtually no significant economic risk involved in their production (we ourselves brought to market the most notable recent example of such a film, *The Brothers McMullen* (1996)). But with all the hoopla surrounding films like *El Mariachi* (1992) ('Made for $7,000!') it is probably worth keeping in mind the barest minimum cost of seeing a no- or micro-budget film through its initial theatrical release. While it is still possible through the usual begging, borrowing and stealing to get a print of a 16mm feature film on to a film

Figure 6.1 Publicity poster for *The Wedding Banquet* (1993). Courtesy of Goldwyn Entertainment Co.

festival screen for something around $40,000, what happens when a distribution company asks to buy the film from you? What exactly are you selling to them, and what will it cost to deliver to the distribution company what it needs in order to release the film? In other words, when Harvey Weinstein from Miramax 'buys' our film at Sundance, as he did *Walking and Talking* (1996) a couple of years ago, what, physically, does he get? He certainly isn't simply purchasing the print that he just saw.

What he will need is both the physical elements from which release prints can be struck, as well as all the supporting legal clearances and publicity materials needed for the cinema release. He will also need video and other elements for the eventual release of the film on TV, cable, video, aeroplanes, etc.

Chances are, you showed up at the festival with a newly minted 'answer' or 'corrected' print, made off of the actual cut negative spliced together from the actual negative film that ran through the camera. Printing off of the cut negative is a tricky and dangerous process – the splices can come undone at any time, resulting in the printing machine eating a good portion of your (irreplaceable) film. Thus the need to go to a single-strand negative, a process which requires the creation of an 'interpositive' print, which is then, in effect, re-photographed frame by frame to create an 'internegative', from which is struck a 'check-print' in order to quality-control the colour timing. If the check-print is good, 'release prints' can then be made from the interneg. The total cost to get from the original negative to the check-print stage: about $45,000.

But, of course, you must first get your 16mm film blown up to 35mm. While there are a couple of hundred screens in the United States that can accommodate 16mm projection, it is pretty much a lost format in the rest of the world. Worse still, 16mm projectors tend to eat movies whole. The cost to blow up a 16mm to get it to a 35mm internegative? About $35,000.

For international distribution, your soundtrack will have to be broken down into constituent elements, such that the dialogue track can be ripped out and replaced by dubbed dialogue in various territories (remember, in Italy they even dub their own movies). This means technically cleaning up your location sound recording, and replacing many of the actual sound effects recorded on location during dialogue scenes, such as door slams, chair sqeaks, etc., with purchased or re-recorded effects. Otherwise, when the dialogue gets ripped out, so too will the ambient sounds. The same goes for music – it must be placed on its own separate track.

When the film is completely remixed onto separate tracks, known as 'music and effects' or 'm&e', you must create duplicate master tapes, in addition to the fully mixed original language optical track that will accompany the internegative. (In most cinemas, the sound is still read off the optical track, that cardiogram-like continuous chart that runs alongside the picture and that sometimes, when the projection messes up, gets onto the screen. It is part of the paradoxical technology

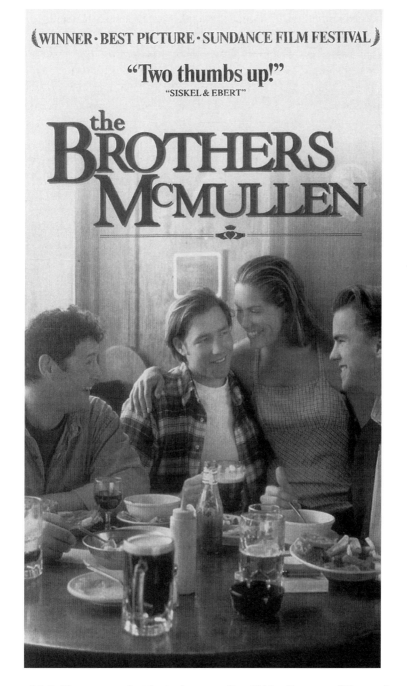

Figure 6.2 Publicity poster for *The Brothers McMullen* (1995). Courtesy of Twentieth Century Fox

that transforms sound into image and then back into sound. Video, of course, began as a sound-recording medium, and the technology surrounding video production and consumption is much more 'aural' than film – but these details will have to be reserved for another study.) In any case, the preparation of an m&e and accompanying sound materials can easily come to an additional $40,000.

As we discussed above, the theatrical release of the film is simply a way-station en route to more important and lucrative media like television and video. The cost of transferring the film to a master video: $25,000. You will also need high-quality black and white publicity stills and colour slides, a final script and spotted dialogue list, and all the legal work that will establish your copyright in the film and the underlying material on which it is based: signed agreements from all actors and extras, and successfully negotiated agreements for the music you use in the film (these last can be astonishingly complicated, as you need rights to both the music and its performance, not to mention possible rights to use the songs on soundtrack albums and on trailers and TV ads). The distributor might also require that you purchase 'e&o' insurance – errors and omissions – in case legal problems emerge regarding these rights. (For example, for Tom Kahn's film *Swoon* (1994) we once bought the rights to a Cole Porter song from – oops – someone who didn't own them but who was happy to have cashed our cheque none the less. We caught the fraud in time to replace the music before its release.) The legal work on all this can run into tens of thousands of dollars itself, and music rights can go anywhere from $1 to, on a recent film we produced, $400,000.

All in all, for an international release of a 'no-budget' independent film, you had best assume a total pre-release cost of between $300,000 and $500,000 – before sales and festival costs. For many film school graduates (and their parents) the most daunting dilemma is not whether one should spend $25,000 getting the film into 'the can'; it is whether, after the distribution rights have been sold to Miramax for, say, $200,000, mum and dad will be able to afford to 'deliver' the film so that it can be released.

Mega-independence

If there is one underlying topic all of the above is concerned with, it is the insertion of 'independent' capital into the flow of products and exchanges that makes up the current international film market. I have by default been using the term 'independent film' to mean 'independently financed film', that is, a film financed by capital that is not provided by or guaranteed by the distribution companies that will eventually exploit the film (be they motion picture studios, cable or TV companies). As you can see, the marketplace is very open to the insertion of such capital into the flow of things. But it is very closed-minded when it comes to extracting such capital back out in the form of profits.

Independent production companies like Good Machine are caught between the demands of Capital on the one hand and the Market on the other. Capital claims ownership of our films as at least one hedge against near-certain losses, and the companies that control the actual traffic in our films (exhibitors, distribution companies, sales agents) grab huge chunks of the revenue flows before sending us our measly 'profits'. To survive, we must make constant border forays in each direction, holding on to long-term ownership interests in our pictures when we can and grabbing as much control of the revenue streams as is feasible, for example, when we sell the international distribution rights to our films ourselves. (These days, controlling the means of production is not the issue – controlling the means of distribution is.) And when we are asked to give up ownership or distribution rights, as when we work on bigger-budgeted studio films, we do what everyone else in Hollywood does – we stick our hands out and try to get as big up-front producing fees as we can, knowing that we will probably see very little more even if the film is a big hit. And more and more, as the studios finance and distribute 'independent' films, independent producers find themselves rather dependent employees.

This is because the 'independent' cinema has quickly become a victim of its own success, a success that has made the independent film game look more and more like a microcosm of the studio business. Six years ago, for example, a North American theatrical box-office gross of $2 million was a more than respectable achievement for a low-budget independent film. Today, it is an increasingly difficult barrier to break, but a barrier that is, at the same time, an economically insignificant joke for all but the most marginal players. Six years ago a distributor might have hit the $2 million mark by cycling twenty or so prints of a film on a continuous, long-term roll-out that would, over the course of as many as sixty weeks, see the film play in as many as 300 markets. Today, even a small film might open on six to twenty prints within its first two weeks, breaking to ten or twenty cities within a month. And this faster, wider release will of necessity require a significant advertising budget in order to reach out to the film's core audience quickly. That core audience will have to start talking fast, spreading the proverbial word of mouth to a larger, cross-over audience within a month's time, so that the distributor can justify an increasingly costly marketing campaign (including TV or cable spots, radio advertising, and national print media) which in turn will convince the larger exhibitors to book the film nationally on upwards of 200 to 400 screens.

Five years ago *Howard's End* (1992) broke the $20 million mark and played on screens in North America for over a year, sometimes playing in a single cinema for nearly that entire time. Today, it would probably need to hit that box-office mark within twenty weeks, supported by a marketing campaign exponentially more expensive, before being thrown off its screens by the next 'indie hit' to come along.

Look at it from the consumer's point of view. Not long ago, sophisticated viewers had each week a choice between a large number of Hollywood films and one, maybe two, new art house releases. Choosing the art film was a matter of simply asserting one's identity as an upscale viewer. Recently, there were many weeks in which four, five, six, sometimes seven 'speciality' films opened simultaneously in the major markets. How to choose? You will probably veer towards the newest, 'hottest' indie title, the one reviewed in your morning paper, the one with the biggest ad.

Given these market conditions, the companies that distribute and finance art house fare have had to remake themselves in the light of successes such as Miramax's *Pulp Fiction* (1994) and *Il Postino* (1994). In order to service and promote potential 'break-out' independent hits, these companies must carry large staffs and significant overheads – and in order to pay the rent at headquarters they will of necessity have to seek to acquire or produce big hits, not just critically acclaimed and nicely profitable films. What, after all, does a half a million dollar profit on a film mean when you have to shell out 15 to 30 million dollars a year in overhead and feature film development costs?

While some outfits, such as Sony Pictures Classics (run by the same savvy management team that ran Orion Pictures Classics until billionaire owner John Kluge let the Orion construct fall apart) continue to focus on lower-cost approaches to releasing independent fare, even they are being forced into ever-wider, ever-faster, ever-more-expensive release strategies. As the risks increase, companies require deeper pockets and more heavy-hitting 'strategic alliances'. With the acquisition of October Films by Universal in the summer of 1997, the last of the significant independent distributors went the way of the studios. Perhaps some of the newer players will rise to revitalize low-cost distribution. But perhaps not. In the meantime, Good Machine will continue to adapt, working for the monster when it lets us make films like *The Ice Storm* (1997) (which was financed by Fox Searchlight), and financing, making and, we hope, selling our own low-budget movies to whoever is left to buy them.

We will attempt judiciously to play the managed growth game by trying to make sure that we exist to make movies rather than make movies to exist. With a staff of twenty, forty phone lines, a computer network, offices that need to be cleaned, two photocopying machines and a kitchen, there is an 'institutional logic' that creeps into our decision-making and 'corporate planning' that is new, necessitated as much by the demands of a voracious overhead as by the needs and desires of the people who pay their own rent by working at the company (we had, for example, our first maternity leave this year).

Where do we get the money to pay our bills? About a third of our overhead is paid for by a 'first-look' arrangement with Fox. This is a deal whereby we give the studio a first crack at whatever we develop; if they pass, we are free to set the project up elsewhere. Another third of our overhead comes from sales fees and profit participations on films we have already made and retained some sales rights to. And the last third comes from producing and administrative fees that we make on the films we produce. This year, we are also selling a small minority stake in the company to raise financing for a more aggressive (and expensive) foreign sales arm, and have also begun a music division.

At the end of the day, Good Machine faces the same 'grow or die' pressures as any small business staking its claim in the post-late capitalist landscape. As such, we spend most of our time on managerial duties that are little different from those faced by sausage factory owners and McDonald's franchisees around the world. And, by the way, we also make movies, although very little in this chapter would give you any indication of what *that* is about.

Part III

Aesthetics and technology

Chapter 7

From *Bwana Devil* to *Batman Forever*
Technology in contemporary Hollywood cinema

Michael Allen

The development of cinema technologies over the past four decades has been the result of a complex interaction between industrial needs (in both production and exhibition), product differentiation, economics and audience expectation. Industrial needs are focused around developing equipment and techniques, both to increase production efficiency and reduce costs, and to create a more attractive viewing environment. These in turn must both be seen in relation to product differentiation, the creation of a significantly new type or style of film which will draw crowds to the box office. That unique product might be very expensive to produce, in which case an important question is raised: will the expense involved in developing new equipment and new techniques towards creating a unique end-product be recouped when that product is released? Audience expectations feed into this equation, by generating a desire to experience the 'new', or demand a more ambitious, more extravagant, or a more intense version of what has already been witnessed. These issues will be explored through a historical survey of the technological developments in widescreen, sound, colour, editing and interactive virtual reality.

Widescreen[1]

Widescreen formats are as old as cinema itself. Throughout the silent period, restless experimentation produced a plethora of widescreen and large image systems as diverse as Fox's 70mm Grandeur, Paramount's Magnafilm, Warner's 65mm VitaScope and Abel Gance's Polyvision, description of which lies outside the scope of this chapter. The failure of these systems, by the early 1930s, was due partly to industry resistance to further conversion costs in the wake of the coming of sound; the serious adoption of widescreen systems in the 1950s was, in turn, due to an industry ready for innovation in the face of the coming of television.

The first of these, Cinerama, was originally developed by Fred Waller in 1939. In prototype form, which he called Vitarama, it was a mechanism designed to project a patchwork of large-image, still pictures onto a curved screen for the Eastman Kodak exhibit at the New York World's Fair. During the Second World War, he adapted Vitarama into the Waller Flexible Gunnery Trainer: five synchronized projectors which threw a continuous moving image of attacking enemy planes onto a spherical screen. After the war, Waller reduced the five projectors to three, and developed a screen, consisting of 1,100 vertical stripes, which could be angled to maximize light reflection. This research was initially funded by Rockefeller and Time before they withdrew their support in 1950. Waller then went into partnership with Lowell Thomas and Mike Todd – who formed Thomas-Todd to make Cinerama features, the first of which was *This is Cinerama*, released in 1952. Entrepreneurial investment had resulted in a new and different product which proved to be an immediate sensation, drawing large crowds to watch its almost exclusively documentary product at a limited number of sites. However, it was not taken up by a major studio until a decade later, when MGM used it for *How the West Was Won* (1962).

The first Cinerama process utilized three cameras in production and three projectors in exhibition. During shooting, three cameras, fitted with 27mm wide-angle lenses, were mounted such that the outer two were angled outwards from the frontal axis. During projection, the three projectors were placed close by one another, and were arranged so that the two outer projectors faced *inwards*, with their beams intersecting; the right-hand projector throwing its image to the left third of the screen, and the left-hand projector to the right third of the screen. This enabled the three projected images, in theory, to line up without any discernible overlap. The first Cinerama screens had a curve depth of over 16 feet, and had a 146° (horizontal) by 55° (vertical) field of vision (the parameters of human vision are 180° and 90°, respectively). It ran at 26 frames per second (although this was changed to 24fps in the Super-Cinerama system of 1960, essentially in order to capture MGM as a client).

The wide angle produced noticeable distortion, making it unsuitable for close-ups, and the image proved hard to light due to its extreme width. The three-strip configuration also severely restricted the use of panning or tracking shots, as registration of the three moving images would be impossible to maintain. Last, even under optimum conditions, visible seams were noticeable where the three images joined. Together, these various characteristics of Cinerama made it more applicable to non-fiction, rather than fictional narrative, filmmaking. Consequently, documentaries, such as *This is Cinerama* (1952), which were usually of a spectacular nature, initially dominated the output.

Such a system was inherently cumbersome, impractical and expensive, and this meant that it was seen as a special event or showcase format, drawing large crowds continuously to a small number of specialist theatres. By the mid-1960s something like ninety-five Cinerama theatres had been built, some using Buckminster

Fuller's geodesic dome design. Although Cinerama operated only in a relatively small number of cinemas, it was profitable: the first five Cinerama travelogues grossed $82 million, even though they could only be seen in twenty-two theatres.

By the late 1950s, the need for industrial efficiency had resulted in the three-camera setup being replaced by a single camera. The three separate film strips, each covering a third of the image width, would then be struck from this single film strip. This enabled fictional narratives to be made more easily: *How the West Was Won* (1962) was filmed partly in 65mm, and then optically separated into three film strips for Cinerama presentation. In June 1963, Cinerama moved to Ultra Panavision, a 65mm negative with an anamorphic compression of 1.25:1, and a single film strip for both sound and vision. This move robbed Cinerama of the very thing which made it unique, and forced it to compete in the marketplace with other single-strip widescreen processes.

Unlike Cinerama, CinemaScope was, from the beginning, developed *within* the film industry. It was initially the product of the Twentieth Century Fox company, whose research department had been experimenting with wide film formats for a number of years, finally being spurred into concrete action by the success of Cinerama. On 2 February 1953, Fox announced that all future productions would be shot in CinemaScope. Previews of the new process coincided with that year's Oscars, which meant that a large number of industry heads were in town. The process was favourably received by those who attended the demonstrations and, by the end of March, Fox had over 1200 orders from exhibitors around the country. The first demonstrations of CinemaScope in Britain took place in June and July 1953. Particularly important to note is the speed of development, which was less than ten months from Fox's first tests to the première of the first CinemaScope feature, *The Robe* (1953).

Essentially, CinemaScope was built upon the Hypergonar lens, which had a compression ratio of roughly 2:1, and was developed by Henri Chrétien in 1929. By using this lens, Fox was able to produce an image with a 2.77:1 aspect ratio, which was almost the same as that achieved by Cinerama. When unsqueezed in projection, the image was 2.66 times as wide as it was high. Chrétien's anamorphic lens was attached to the front of the camera's own standard lens, and both had to be focused separately. This made sharp focus difficult, especially since the early versions of the lens had variable compression factors for different distances between camera and object; a phenomenon which caused visual distortion, especially in tracking shots. In addition, it was decided to include both stereomagnetic sound (see below) and curved projection screens. In April 1953, Fox contracted with Bausch & Lomb to make anamorphic camera and projection attachments. The sums involved were significant: $2.5 million, plus $625,000, in cash, for re-tooling costs. The money was well spent, as the new lens design improved light transmission by 20 per cent, and reduced distance compression variations. A further significant development came when Arriflex developed a hand-held CinemaScope camera in 1954.

In addition to anamorphic lenses and magnetic stereo soundtracks, Fox initially insisted on installing its own 'Miracle Mirror' screens into theatres as an essential element in the exhibition package. Fox's intention was to market CinemaScope as a multi-technological format, involving anamorphic lenses, colour, custom screens, and stereomagnetic sound. However, after considerable resistance from exhibitors who simply couldn't afford the prohibitive conversion costs of projector, sound and screen, Fox relented and dropped parts of the CinemaScope deal.

For big exhibitors, CinemaScope was the answer to a dream, enabling them to present a seductive big-screen spectacular event for which they could charge more at the box office. From its inception, 200 to 250 theatres per week converted to CinemaScope and the rise was exponential: 3,500 theatres by April 1954, 13,500 by mid-1955. Industrial need had been allied to economic need to produce a cheaper, less cumbersome widescreen process which could satisfy growing audience demand. Fox also pursued an aggressive campaign to persuade other studios to adopt the system. MGM was the first to be persuaded. On the other hand, several studios stood out against it. Warners, proving to be the most cautious of the major studios of this period, first tried to develop its own system – Warner-Scope, then WarnerSuperScope – before capitulating after the release of *The Robe* in November 1953. Paramount developed VistaVision, which proved to be a viable and profitable alternative system (see below).

An extension to CinemaScope came in the form of CinemaScope 55, which was developed in 1955, prompted by the appearance of Todd-AO, a 65/70mm system, in the same year (of which more later). CinemaScope 55 had a negative area of 36.22 × 46.44mm, 50 per cent more than Todd-AO. Although it required large cameras for filming, and special projectors for 70mm roadshow presentations, it could use normal projectors for general release because its large film strip was then printed down to 35mm, giving conventional image dimensions but increased image resolution. Early releases included *Carousel* and *The King and I* (both 1956). In the event, CinemaScope 55 was a relative failure largely because, with the reduction of the 70mm original down to 35mm, there was little noticeable difference.

Following initial demonstrations, early in 1951, of the Natural Vision system developed by the Gunzburg brothers, 3-D premièred less than two months after CinemaScope in 1952, with the film *Bwana Devil*. Within weeks, Columbia and Warners had signed to the system. Paramount, MGM and Universal, however, announced plans to develop their own alternative systems. Early 1953 saw the release of the first wave of 3-D features, most notably *House of Wax* by Warners. 3-D employed two cameras during shooting, each with differently coloured polarizing filters on their lenses, and set at slightly different positions to the action. During exhibition, two projectors set at similarly varying positions cast superimposing images onto the screen. Spectators wore polaroid viewers, normally cardboard spectacles, to separate the two images into one eye each, thereby creating a 3-D image in the brain. The heyday of 3-D lasted barely a year; in addition to the destructive effect of proliferating systems clashing in the marketplace, like other systems employing cumbersome elements, it proved too inefficient to facilitate widespread distribution.

The large-image format, Todd-AO, was developed in 1955, under a partnership between the entrepreneur Mike Todd and the engineering firm American Optical. It was a non-anamorphic system, employing a three-blade dissolving shutter with an opening of 170° which furnished an aspect ratio of 2.2:1, and used a 22 × 48.6mm negative (four times the standard). A 65mm negative was used during production, this being slightly printed up to a 70mm print for screening. The extra 5mm was used to carry the six magnetic soundtracks needed for stereo sound. Consequently, both bigger cameras, and bigger, brighter projectors were required, making the system non-standard. Running at thirty frames per second, it was projected onto a deeply curved 52 × 26 foot screen. At the centre of the design was a 128° bug-eye lens (which gave a 140° field of view) plus three other lenses (eventually all mounted on one camera). Since the sound was recorded and projected at 90 feet per minute, and the film strip ran at a faster speed, the sound recording interlocks had to be redesigned to keep the two in sync during the creation of the final release print.

Todd-AO solved certain technical problems inherent in earlier widescreen systems, correcting the distortion caused by projection by introducing corrective optical distortions into the projection prints. It also ushered in new economic methods: a notably cautious production process, which required, among other strategies, selecting sure-fire subjects and pre-selling films. Exhibition involved multi-track stereo, with five tracks feeding speakers behind the screen, the sixth providing surround sound, and the seventh the information which controlled the other six. The combination of the huge, high-definition images, together with the sophisticated stereo soundtrack, made Todd-AO a spectacular, high-end cinema experience. It sought, like Cinerama, to satisfy public demand for new, special-attraction events. Eventually, CinemaScope came to satisfy the mass-market for widescreen product, while Todd-AO catered for the specialist, top-tier theatres. In the event, only fifteen Todd-AO films were produced in sixteen years.

Another anamorphic system, compatible with all widescreen formats, Panavision was developed in 1953–4 by Robert Gottschalk. It involved a pair of prisms which moved in relation to each other to alter the horizontal expansion factor: projectionists could use the lens at one setting for flat films, and at a series of intermediate settings for anamorphic films with squeeze ratios between 1.1 and 2.

Settings were changed by turning a knob on the lens. By 1957, a special camera lens had been developed which dramatically reduced the distortion inherent in CinemaScope, and made the image much brighter, both because of Panavision's smaller negative size and because its lens prevented light loss by creating an oval shaped light-beam, which more closely echoed the rectangle of the film-frame. By the early 1960s, Panavision Inc. could offer anamorphic zoom lenses as well as twelve different fixed focal length lenses. The system was adopted as an industry standard in 1959 by several major studios, and eventually by Fox in 1968.

Both Super Panavision and Ultra Panavision developed out of the earlier MGM Camera 65 system. Ultra Panavision employed a 70mm system with anamorphic optics. Its squeeze ratio was 1.25:1, but, because its picture area was already 2.25:1, the unsqueezed projection aspect ratio was only slightly larger, at 2.76:1. It required exhibitors to invest in 70mm equipment. Super Panavision used a 2.25:1 ratio, similar to Todd-AO, and spherical rather than anamorphic lenses. Both ran at a standard 24fps, making them more compatible with other 70mm systems than Todd-AO. Ultra Panavision was used, in its Camera 65 form, to film *Raintree County*, which was released in October 1957, and, as Ultra Panavision proper, for *Mutiny on the Bounty*, released in November 1962. Super Panavision 70 was used to photograph *Exodus* in 1960, and *West Side Story* in 1961. Within a few years, Super and Ultra Panavision 70 had cornered the market in high-prestige and blockbuster features.

VistaVision, a non-anamorphic system whose roots lay in the 1928 Panoramico Alberini system developed by the Briton George Hill and the Italian Filoteo Alberini, appeared in 1954, and was capable of being projected in any theatre, in ratios between 1.33:1 and 2:1. It was a wide-area, 35mm negative, which was notable for being exposed horizontally rather than vertically, as in conventional cameras. Each image was recorded onto a wide, eight-sprocket-hole, two-frame image on the film strip, using the Paramount Lazy 8 Butterfly Camera. During printing, it was reduced onto conventional 35mm frames to give sharp images, and a good depth of field. This made it compatible with conventional projection systems. It was initially planned to release features in three formats: regular 35mm, horizontal double frame and anamorphic; in the event, only the first of these was taken up. SuperScope projection attachments were used for the screening process. VistaVision stressed height rather than width, and was, therefore, less a widescreen than a big-screen process. It also used Perspecta Stereo Sound, which was an inexpensive, mono-compatible optical audio system that separated its stereo channels with electronic subaudible cues.

IMAX developed into a viable format between two World Expos: Montreal (1967) and Osaka (1970). Originally, though in some ways like Cinerama, IMAX consisted of several separate 70mm images, synchronized together. This was achieved by developing a 70mm frame which, like VistaVision, passed horizontally rather than vertically through the projector. The 49mm × 70mm frame gives three times the exposed surface area of conventional 70mm. The IMAX sound system is separate from the film strip itself, initially on six-channel 35mm magnetic film, and subsequently on a system of CDs (a curious return to the sound-on-disc system of early sound film; see also the DTS sound system below). The exhibition sites have dozens of loudspeakers positioned around the theatre space. This enabled sound to be as accurately positioned as the visual image, with sound cues being deployed to control the viewer's focus towards the action taking place in different areas of the screen. The other huge-image film system, OMNIMAX, which premièred in August 1973, uses an extreme wide-angle, fish-eye lens. The films are then projected onto hemispheric screens angled above and below rather than in front of the audience. This extends the image beyond the field of human vision, effectively immersing the audience in the experience.

The image size of both IMAX and OMNIMAX inevitably influences the type of subjects chosen for their films. Like early Cinerama, documentaries, especially those showing spectacular natural history, are favoured. Certain framings have to be carefully considered, because the audience is viewing the film image from a position lower than in conventional cinemas, and shots, generally, have to be longer, to give the audience time to assimilate the images and sounds. Narrative films are ill-suited to these huge-format systems. Close framings are impossible, which in turn disables the emotional intensities built via shot/reverse-shot strategies in narrative films.

Moreover, both IMAX and OMNIMAX theatres have to be custom-built. While initially seeming a discouraging factor, certainly considering the historical resistance of the exhibition sector to building costs involved in previous innovations such as sound and widescreen, this phenomenon might actually suit modern social practices. For example, IMAX screens are currently being installed in American shopping malls, to provide a one-hour entertainment/diversion/rest from the rigours of an all-day visit to this modern 'compendium' consumer space. The acceptance of IMAX could therefore signal a significant change in contemporary viewing practices. Although expensive to create both the films themselves and the theatres in which to show them, IMAX and OMNIMAX films are seen to justify their high costs because they offer their audience a significantly different viewing experience.

Expo '86 saw the first appearance of 3-D IMAX. Both during filming, when the twin camera set-up shoots the scene from fractionally different positions, and during screening, when two projectors set at slightly different positions superimpose their two images over one another, polarized filters are used to identity the separate images. The audience wears polaroid viewers to produce the 3-D effect. Initially, as with the other systems, 3-D IMAX's subjects were documentary in nature. The year 1995, however, saw the release of the first feature in 3-D IMAX: *Wings of Courage*, a period mountain adventure story, directed by

Jean-Jacques Annaud, and starring Val Kilmer, Tom Hulce and Charlie Sheen. A 350 lb double camera rig was used, with two lenses set an eye-span distance apart. The cumbersome nature of the rig, together with the painstaking preparation process required to ensure focus and synchronization, resulted in an average of only four set-ups a day, and the consequent heavy pre-planning meant that filming lacked any kind of spontaneity or improvisation. Four lens settings were used – 30mm, 40mm, 60mm and 120mm; however, because the 3-D effect was lost at distances over 50 feet, a 2-D IMAX camera image (printed twice) was used for the longer framings, including the aerial photography. Although a significantly different end-product is produced, the technical difficulties inherent in the system are such that it is debatable whether 3-D IMAX features will develop into more than an occasional experiment.

Sound[2]

While stereo sound had been technically possible since the early days of cinema, it became a significant potential element of the cinematic process from the 1930s onwards, with the growth of complex, multi-layered music score recordings. These recordings employed multi-miked, multiple-track recordings, which were then mixed down to a single, complex and multi-layered track. Two- and three-track soundtracks (mixed down to a single track on the final print) were used in *Applause* in 1929; *The Adventures of Robin Hood* in 1938; and *The Wizard of Oz* in 1939. In 1940, VitaSound, premièring with *Santa Fe Trail*, employed a '3-D' sound system which was installed in two flagship theatres, and distributed its sound through three separate speakers – left, right and centre of screen – with dialogue in the centre, and music in stereo from left and right speakers. In 1942, Disney's *Fantasia* employed three-track stereo on a separate 35mm sound-reel. Labelled FantaSound, it was installed in only fourteen theatres, and *Fantasia* was not generally released in stereo until 1956.

Magnetic sound was developed post-war, from equipment captured at the end of the Second World War in Nazi Germany. It began to be used in filmmaking in 1949, with camera/recorder synchronizing equipment available from 1950. Between 1952 and 1954, there was a concerted attempt by sections of the film industry to replace optical sound with magnetic sound. It became a feature of Cinerama, CinemaScope and Todd-AO. In 1952, fully directional stereo sound was introduced to large popular audiences through Cinerama. Sound engineer Hazard Reeves adapted the German magnetic sound recording techniques, improving the clarity, tone and dynamic range of the sound, as well as achieving less degradation through the various generations produced during post-production. As noted above, Cinerama sound employed seven discreet channels of sound onto a single film strip, fully coated with magnetic oxides. During projection, sound was carried to three speakers behind the screen, and three more positioned around the auditorium. A seventh carried the control and synchronization information. CinemaScope prints had four discreet soundtracks transferred from a four-track full-coat master, one track at a time. This proved an expensive process, and the soundtrack wore badly, degrading long before the print. The stereo sound was modelled on a mixture of research during the mid-1930s by Bell Telephone, Disney's experiments on its animated feature *Fantasia* (1940), and the magnetic stereo system developed for Cinerama. The problem with adding four tracks of stereo magnetic sound onto a single strip of 35mm film was one of available space. This was solved by reducing the size of perforations on the 1.33/7:1 Academy format film strip.[3] Two stereo tracks were laid on either side of the image frame, and the filmmasks, which reduced the frame area visible on screen, were eliminated. These various design changes were possible because of the advent, in 1948, of acetate film stock, which was tougher and didn't shrink during repeated usage. Also influential was a shift from Technicolor, which bled in transfer, to Eastman Color to improve image quality in terms of sharpness. When exhibitors complained about the attempts by Fox to force them into upgrading their systems for magnetic stereo sound, optical versions of the film soundtracks were also produced. Initially separate, the two different soundtracks were then combined onto one strip – Magoptical – which was the combination of optical and magnetic sound on a single print. The magnetic soundtrack carried the stereo sound on film, the optical track provided mono backup. This further reduced the image ratio from 2.55:1 to 2.35:1 to accommodate the extra soundtrack.

Different studios developed distinctively different sounds – Fox had a built-in delay between the front and rear channels, to give an expansive depth of sound; Warners a big, brassy, bright sound. Universal also saw the potential of stereo sound apart from supporting the widescreen process. Its *The Glenn Miller Story* (1953) re-recorded Miller's original mono recordings in four-track stereo. Other studios produced similarly alternative, 'pseudo-stereo' effects, by grafting additional tracks onto existing soundtracks.

By the late 1950s, 25 per cent of American cinemas – over 10,000, mostly first-run – had converted to stereo sound, producing 75–80 per cent of the total box-office income for any feature release. Stereo separated the first-run theatres from the remainder. The relaxing of its stereo-only policy by Fox led to the widespread adoption of CinemaScope as the industry standard by 1958, and began the gradual decline of magnetic stereo: mag-optical prints slowly gave way to optical over the next decade. CinemaScope's four-track, 35mm stereo magnetic sound was gradually eclipsed by a variety of 70mm formats, including Todd-AO, and Panavision, which featured six-track optical stereo sound. Prohibitively expensive as a system, it was rejected by the smaller theatres, which used a simpler four-track version. Consequently, stereo became identified as a first-run, road show format. Exceptions to this norm were generally unsuccessful. Paramount developed PerspectaSound, in association with Fairchild Camera; an optical soundtrack in which the sound was shifted back and forth across speakers, achieving the illusion of directional sound, through the inclusion of a control track. It was defeated by fluctuations in projector speed causing loss of control track accuracy. As cinema declined during the 1960s, mono increasingly replaced stereo as a less expensive exhibition sound format.

In 1974, Sensurround, developed in partnership between MCA and RCA, made a brief impact upon the industry, premièring with *Earthquake* (which was also shot in Super Panavision). Huge sub-woofers pumped sub-audible level decibels into the auditorium at dramatic moments in the film, to create vibrations which had a physical effect upon the spectator. The MagOptical soundtrack carried a combination of stereomagnetic, and Sensurround optical, tracks.

Far more significant, in 1975, Dolby introduced its Cinema Surround Sound Processor, spurred on by new talent appearing in the industry, together with the growth in popularity of special effects genres. It was, essentially, a four-channel process that for the first time introduced an element of *directional* sound between its front and surround channels, by adapting the bilateral, variable density optical sound which had been standard since the 1930s into a stereo process. The two optical tracks were mixed into a 'golden' matrix, from which the Dolby Surround Decoder extracted four more or less distinct channels – Left (L), Right (R), Centre (L+R) and Surround (L-R). To these, the Decoder then added Dolby B noise reduction, as well as a standardized delay for the surround track. A special optical stereo eye fitted to the front of conventional projectors played back the decoded sound signal. Although the professional Dolby A process was first used on *A Clockwork Orange* (1971), this more general Dolby system was first employed on *Star Wars* (1977).

THX is a set of standards proposed by a branch of the George Lucas company, Lucasfilm, to be used to assess the quality of sound reproduction in cinemas and, more recently, in home entertainment systems. In 1980, using some of the enormous profits generated by *Star Wars*, George Lucas hired Tomlinson Holman, a Boston-based electronics designer, to design and build the Skywalker Sound Facility, which included a number of film sound dubbing stages. He engineered a proprietary cross-over network for the horn speakers typically used in theatre sound reproduction. The acronym *THX* is derived both from Lucas's first feature film, *THX1138* (1970) and, rather tortuously, from *Tom Holman eXperiment*. THX first appeared in 1983, with *The Return of the Jedi* (1983). Elaborate yearly inspection and certification procedures were developed under TAP (Theatre Alignment Program) to check final prints, theatre projection and sound equipment, and initial showings of features. The theoretical aim of these procedures is to provide theatregoers with exactly the same sound as that which the sound mixers had heard on the dubbing stage. The patented technology had to be leased by theatres from THX. To date, some 700 theatres worldwide have converted to THX.

Essentially a development of the 1990s, digital sound involves converting the analogue sound signal into a series of discreet binary values (a combination of 0s or 1s). The conversion into pure numerical values makes the signal far less prone to distortion or corruption during the various stages it has to undergo from original soundstage to cinema auditorium. Dolby Stereo Digital sound appeared in 1992, digitally encoding/imprinting the sound information onto the actual film sound-track. Cinema Digital Sound involves six discrete channels of sound, digitally encoded and optically printed onto the film soundtrack along with a control channel and SMPTE timecode. During projection, this digital information is decoded through a decoder which separates out the sound information, timecode and control information once again. Sony Dynamic Digital Sound, premièred in June 1993 with *The Last Action Hero*, is the most expensive system to install, at $14,000, and employs eight discrete channels: five behind the screen, two stereo surrounds and a sub-woofer. It is also the only one of the systems to have a digital backup soundtrack should the main soundtrack fail. By the end of 1995, it had been installed in 3,000 theatres in the States. Also in 1993, Digital Theatre Systems premièred with *Jurassic Park*. Co-owned by Universal and Steven Spielberg, it is the cheapest to install ($6,000) and has the largest number of installations (3,300 worldwide). The audio system is separate from the film strip, having been recorded onto digital compact disc, and replayed on a CD-ROM machine that reads an optical timecode track on the film strip in order to keep sound and image in synchronization. The CD format means the sound requires less compression than if it were on the film strip, and results in high-fidelity quality. An analogue version of the soundtrack is also present on the film strip itself, so that, if the CD system fails, the conventional soundtrack can automatically take over. Deals have already been struck with major production companies, including Amblin, MGM/UA, Universal, New Line and Paramount.

Colour[4]

The dominant pre-1950s colour system was Technicolor, which consisted of three separate colour rolls, together with a fourth sound roll. The system was complex and, consequently, expensive. Technicolor technical advisers had to be assigned to each production using the system. The development of Technicolor monopacks – single film-rolls with multiple colour-sensitive layers – was seen as very desirable. Consequently, in 1931, a patent was issued for Technicolor to develop a mono-pack film, which became known as Kodachrome. It took over a decade before, in 1942, Twentieth Century Fox released *Thunderhead*, which was shot on monopack and printed by Technicolor. By the late 1940s, Cinecolor among others were also considering monopack productions.

In 1950, Eastman Kodak introduced Eastman Color colour negative and print films, a simpler, less expensive system which layered its three primary colours onto one film-roll. The year 1951 saw Eastman Color's first full-length colour film, the documentary *Royal Journey*, made by the National Film Board of Canada, and the first fictional feature, *The Sword of Monte Cristo*. By 1953, a fully integrated process had been perfected, consisting of colour negative, separation positives, false sensitized internegative and release print film. Among its other benefits, Eastman Color could, for the first time, be used with tungsten lights. With the appearance of the improved Eastman Color in 1953, Technicolor phased out its three-strip camera as a negative source and moved over to a single monopack camera. By 1955, the name Technicolor stood only for the processing laboratory which printed from Eastman Color negative, each of the three layers being processed separately through filters.

From 1956, all 35mm production in the States was on Eastman Color negative, having been franchised to processing labs under a variety of trade names, including Color by Deluxe, WarnerColor and Trucolor. Thereafter, the history of Eastman Color is one of a process of gradual improvement. In 1956, the Bell and Howell additive colour printer allowed automatic control of light regulation for each individual shot. The year 1959 saw the appearance of the Hazeldine colour analyser, which enabled more accurate colour grading via a scanning colour television camera, producing a read-out of corrections which could be used later in the printing stage. This automated process replaced the earlier 'trial-and-error' technique, which was prone to wastage and inefficiency. The same year saw the development of a high-speed colour negative film, with an exposure index of 50. In 1962, improvements were made in the quality of film grain, as well as the development of a new print film with fourfold speed increase. In 1968, a higher-speed colour negative appeared, with an exposure index of 100.

Steadicam[5]

Although experiments began in 1969–70, it took until 1973 for Garrett Brown, an independent inventor, to develop a prototype counterbalanced camera jig, which he christened 'Brown's Stabilizer'. The Cinema Products Corporation bought up the invention, marketing it as Steadicam. The demo reel which Brown produced attracted the attention of both John Avildsen, who was then preparing *Rocky* (1976), and especially Stanley Kubrick, who was so impressed with the potential of the mechanism that he eventually used it in several scenes of *The Shining* (1980). The time-lag between first appearence and industry acceptance was partly due to the difficulty in training competent operators.

The Steadicam rig works by virtue of several interrelated phenomena: the expanding of its components and consequent shifting of the centre of gravity outside the camera; the attachment of the operator at the centre of gravity with a three-axis gimbal, so that the operator's movements are not transmitted to the camera; the removal of weight from the operator's arms via a sprung and hinged arm attached to the operator by a special vest (which isolates the camera from its lateral and vertical movements); and the viewing of the image via a video monitor rather than by the operator pressing his eye to the viewfinder. Movement is potentially unlimited, allowing mobility from 4 inches to 6 feet in height, 360° of tilt and 270° of pan. Lens control – zooms, focus and iris – is effected via a servo motor controlled by radio. Although initial use was noticeably in horror films, mainstream adoption of Steadicam has resulted in its cross-genre use. Today, Steadicam is a standard part of the filmmaker's armoury, allowing smooth tracking shots to be taken of actors in spaces too restricted for dolly use, and is also perceived to be a potential cost-cutting device because it allows camera set-ups to be tried with little loss of time or money.

Editing[6]

Editing techniques, stabilized during the Classical Hollywood period, remained basically unchanged until 1972, when the first Rank Flying Spot Scanner for NTSC applications appeared, changing post-production methods in North America. It replaced the film printer and allowed a film, for the first time, to be edited on videotape. By the 1980s, laserdisc technology was threatening to replace the more cumbersome tape-based systems. In 1983, the Laser Edit system, marketed by Laser Edit Inc., appeared, employing 'Direct Read After Write' technology which allowed film footage to be recorded onto the laserdisc and immediately viewed. Also in 1983, LucasArt's EditDroid, a nonlinear offline laserdisc system, which resembles a flatbed film editing table rather than a desktop computer, began to have a significant impact upon the industry.

With both systems, the film footage was transferred onto laserdiscs. The system's laser-beam reading mechanism could then, under computer control, seek any point in the footage within seconds, and play it immediately against a second selection, with no perceptible gap between the two. Whole sequences could thereby be 'virtually' edited together – the edited sequence did not 'physically' exist, as was the case with conventional editing, but existed only in the moment of replay. The start- and end-frame points of each edit, however, could be stored so that the sequence could be repeated as often as required. One advantage of both systems was that they allowed several editors and assistants to work side-by-side simultaneously. Therefore, the fundamental drive in developing these new editing technologies has been to make the editing process cheaper, more efficient and more creatively flexible.

Figure 7.1 Digital Edit Program. Courtesy of Michael Allen, and Adobe Systems UK Ltd

The 1990s have brought the introduction of digital compression into editing technologies. In the 'digital domain', film footage is first transferred to video, then digitally grabbed onto a computer and stored as a file. Such footage requires an enormous amount of storage space: approximately 27Mb per second of film. (At this ratio, a full feature film would consume 2.5Tb of computer storage space.) In 1989, the Macintosh-based Avid Media Composer appeared, and in 1993, the Film Option software, which, for the first time, allowed the playback of digitized images at 24fps, instead of the previous 30fps of NTSC television. In 1996, the D-Vision nonlinear editing system appeared, which allows a 'videographer' on-set to digitize footage *as it is shot*, in real-time, and rapidly put together rough cuts. This is especially useful on multi-camera shoots in foreign locations, where re-shoots are not possible if errors are discovered in the editing room back at the studio. With the advent of digital technology, response speed of the equipment is now such that the element determining the time-span of the editing process is now the decision-making capabilities of the editor. The speed and ease of assembly also means that more time can be devoted to experimentation, with less time spent on the mechanics of editing.

Computer-based graphics[7]

Computer-based graphics systems have a complex multiple parentage in the military, business and computer science fields. In 1957, the 'father of computer animation', John Whitney, Sr adapted a Second World War anti-aircraft gun controller to paint light onto movie film by manipulating pinholes and television shadow masks. Around the same time, Lee Harrison produced Lissajous designs (simple multi-lined geometrical shapes which flow around the screen in predetermined directions) using an analogue computer. In the early 1960s, Harrison made a machine called the Animac, which generated puppet-like figures out of high-speed wiggly lines. These could be animated by attaching an electric harness to a live dancer and displaying the results on high-resolution cathode ray tubes. The response from the film industry was muted; interest would only become serious when real, solid objects could be created. In 1967, the Mathematical Applications Group Inc. (MAGI) solved the problem of synthesizing objects. With their Synthavision system, each object was built up from basic shapes (spheres, boxes, ellipsoids, and so forth). These were then modified to produce a smoother final image, movement was added, and the lighting of the objects adjusted on a frame-to-frame basis. The results were then outputted to a colour film recorder on 35mm or VistaVision.

The real breakthrough, however, would be to get a computer waveform to manipulate the entire TV image, rather than just the direction of the single electron beam; namely, to imitate pans, zooms, tilts, and so forth. The system first able to achieve this, Scanimate, appeared in the mid-1970s, and magnetically manipulating the entire raster (a panel-grid of small holes inside a video monitor, through which the electron-beam is directed onto the screen to produce the scanned image) to produce a range of effects. It was used on *Logan's Run* (1976), *Demon Seed* (1977) and *Star Wars* (1977). Its successor, Caesar, had a small *digital* computer controlling its analogue functions, and could be used to produce lengthy sequences of animated characters.

In 1973, Information International Inc. ('triple-I') created Yul Brynner's robot vision for *Westworld*, a mosaic effect produced by progressively reducing the amount of pixel detail in the image. In 1976, the same company was responsible for Peter Fonda's synthetic head and the samurai materialization for *Futureworld*. To digitize Fonda's head, a grid of reference lines was physically drawn on the actor's face, and the co-ordinates of the intersections plotted. These reference points were then used to build the replica, simulated, objects. Interestingly, this technique is still in use, albeit in a more powerful, sophisticated way: the computer-generated toy figures in *Toy Story* (1996) began as real-world 3-D objects, whose contours were scanned at selected points and the co-ordinates fed into a computer which could then use the statistics to generate a wholly cybernetic replica.

In the late 1970s, computer graphics were being developed largely within academic institutions, which were the only organizations with sufficient access to mainframe or mini computers for the purpose of generating images. One of the first results of this research was *Alien* (1979), in which the computer-generated images are used to represent the within-film computer read-outs and displays of statistics and data. The only genuinely computer-generated image was a wireframe representation of the planet surface. The research work which led to these effects had been carried out at the Royal College of Art. Similarly, in America, many of the effects on *Star Wars* were created at the University of Illinois, although Lucas's effects arm, Industrial Light and Magic (formed in 1975 with John Dykstra at its head) also produced effects work on the film. By the time of *The Empire Strikes Back* (1980), Industrial Light and Magic had been 'reborn', relocating to San Francisco after disagreements had caused Dykstra to leave and form his own company, Apogee Inc. The rapid formation of new effects companies is evidence of the movement of effects production into the centre of the film industry.

Flash Gordon (1980) signalled the arrival of compositing, an electronic version of the technique previously achieved using optical methods in a studio's processing laboratory, in which two separate images are combined to form a new original. The system used was analogue, rather than digital, and involved two film scanners for the scenes to be composited, an analogue mixing device similar to a video switcher, a monitor, and a film printer with 4,000 lines of resolution. Modern compositing systems are digital. Electronic compositing is seen to have an economic as well as an aesthetic *raison d'être*; images which would either be impossible or hideously expensive to produce on set can be created, and endlessly manipulated, within a digital computer environment.

Tron (1982), although a box-office failure, is a significant film in the history of computer-generated effects in films. It represents the first large-scale use of computer graphics in a feature; in all, some twenty minutes of the film consist of computer-generated images. However, *Tron*'s effect on the industry was as much negative as positive. Following the film's failure, computer graphics were temporarily exiled from the main body of the film industry, since few producers or directors had sufficient faith to use them in their features and audience interest was not sufficiently strong to persuade the film industry to continue exploring their potential. This exile meant that the development of computer-generated imagery and effects took place outside the film industry, in both academic-based research institutions, and advertising agencies where visual innovation was of central importance.

It took until the late 1980s for effects produced by computer to return to the centre of the film industry. When they did, digital had replaced analogue processes. In the interim, a plethora of independent specialist effects houses emerged; the only ones able to afford the high-end equipment. These companies were employed to create short, highly concentrated and extremely expensive sequences in films and advertisements. Even now that computer-generated effects are central to Hollywood's production methods, the independent effects-house model is very much the one being followed. Modern production methods have created 'service differentiation' – specialist companies handling specific aspects of the production process. This is especially prevalent in high-effects movies, but is also generally true, and is the result of modern production complexities in combination with pressured time-frames. The extremely tight production deadline on *Batman Forever* (1995), for example, forced the effects supervisor to package out the special effects work to fourteen separate external specialist companies, who could then work simultaneously on sections of the film. The problem then became one of maintaining consistency across the differing product produced by these various 'houses'; a problem solved by creating a further level of production management.

One particular type of digital effect – morphing – has almost become an emblem for the entire field in the public imagination. In morphing, two successive objects are taken and merged into a single flowing image that at any given point represents a digital average of the two. On a frame-to-frame basis, corresponding points on the two images are selected, and the computer calculates where those points have to move in order to get from one to another. The process involves five stages: (1) the scanning of the imagery into computer; (2) the creation of mattes for each object; (3) bluescreen;[8] (4) the morphing of the images together; and (5) transfer of the completed computer 'footage' back onto film. Doug Smythe is credited with writing the original morphing software, in 1987. It was first used in *Willow* (1988), in a brief sequence which simulated the transformation of a goat into a woman. In the more ambitious *The Abyss* (1989), consideration was given to computer animation, replacement animation, clay animation and mattes before computer graphics was chosen. Clear resin models, stills from the actual sets and actors' faces were all scanned into the computer, in order to create the pseudopod water-alien which rippled and changed its shape through three-dimensional space. This was the first time the technique was used as animation towards elementary character development rather than simple image transformation. The work, which took eight months, finally consisted of twenty effects shots, lasting seventy-five seconds of screen time. The huge investment in terms of time, money and labour was justified both in terms of advancing the technical capabilities of the film industry, and in creating a significantly different product which would attract the interest of audiences.

The big breakthrough for digital morphing came in 1991, with *Terminator 2: Judgment Day,* where the scale and popular foregrounding of the computerized digital effects forced the film industry to see that such effects, although complex and expensive, were capable of generating substantial box-office returns. The film also extensively employed two other substantial areas of computer technology.

The first applied a later version of the proprietary software used for the pseudopod in *The Abyss* to create, animate and texture the hi-tensile 'enemy' cyborg. The second, digital compositing, was used both to put the computer-generated character into the same space as the human actors, and to 'paint out' the poles and wires used in the stunts. While in retrospect *Terminator 2* demonstrates the complex interaction between various kinds of effects-work in the production of the final footage, such was the experimental, and therefore risky, nature of the computer effects that traditional backups were prepared for every effect, just in case the computer-based techniques failed.

Having started out providing spectacular effects in sci-fi and fantasy films, digital effects are today put to a variety of uses in most larger-budget feature releases: from the compositing of Forrest Gump into the same space as President Kennedy or the removal of Gary Sinese's legs by digitally painting out his limbs frame by frame, in *Forrest Gump* (1994), to the digital creation of the Norwegian army in the snowy landscape in Branagh's *Hamlet* (1996). Eighty per cent of the prequel to the *Star Wars* trilogy, currently filming at Leavesden Studios in England, will be composed of digital effects. Footage is beamed by satellite to Industrial Light and Magic and Skywalker Sound in the States, where it is edited and sent back, again via satellite, to the production site in England.

Virtual Reality[9]

As described above, the idea of simulating reality with wide screens and stereoscopic effects became very attractive to the motion picture industry during the 1950s. In a sense, Virtual Reality (VR) inverts the process, using small screens directly in front of eyes and individual headphones, rather than large screens in spacious auditoria, to achieve the experience of immersion. It works on the principle of totally enclosing the user's sensory capabilities (mainly the head, but also the hands) in high-technology equipment (headsets and datagloves), thus, theoretically, depriving him/her of real-world sensory stimulation. A simulated environment is then created via computer, to replace this newly lost real world. Users of Virtual Reality are simultaneously in two realities: the virtual world, experienced via their eyes, ears and hands, and the real world, generally experienced, or at least sensed, through the rest of the body.

VR began in very elementary form in the 1930s, with the 'Link Trainer' flight simulator. It has been around in the sense we now know it since the 1960s, when government funding agencies such as the National Science Foundation, as well as the Air Force, Navy and NASA, began financing much of the work at the university research centres which built many of the earliest VR systems. The military was initially interested in developing VR as a method of testing missile guidance systems. Later, both military organizations and NASA used VR to create battle or flight simulations which could test out methods and strategies without endangering personnel. In 1965, Ivan Sutherland described (rather than actually built) 'The Ultimate Display', a VR headset whose concept was ahead of the technological sophistication required to construct it. In 1985, the NASA/Ames Aerospace Human Factors Research Division developed a full head-mounted display. By 1991, Jonathan Waldern had developed the first true, commercially available VR system, now being used for interactive sci-fi games (at the Rock Garden, Covent Garden and the Trocadero in London).

Initial development of all of these systems was by small, independent innovators, who were gradually bought up by the giant companies. By the end of 1991 Virtual Reality had become a commercial reality, and a screen-based game using Mattel's Power Glove (based on VPL's DataGlove) was being sold in America. The most popular public arena for VR is currently in theme parks, where it augments and intensifies the thrills of the rides (which are often based on a blockbuster feature film). Sim-cabs suspended on hydraulics, with passengers wearing helmets, and true-to-life sound and wind effects generated, give the impression of being in the 'real' space of the fiction. The 'heightened-experience', spectacular, non-narrative nature of VR links it back to earlier multi-sensory systems such as Cinerama and IMAX. In doing so, it demonstrates that the traditional two-hour fictional feature film is only one of several audio-visual entertainment formats attractive to audiences. Indeed, the opportunity to purchase a variety of different 'alternative viewing' experiences is one of the impetuses which maintains research and experimentation in each of the formats. Only by continually improving on current capabilities will each sector of the audio-visual entertainment industry remain sufficiently interesting to its paying public to warrant its investment.

Conclusion

The drive behind much of the technical development in cinema since 1950 has been towards both a greater or heightened sense of 'realism' and a bigger, more breathtaking realization of spectacle. Both of these impetuses have been realized through the development of larger, clearer, more enveloping images; louder, more multi-layered, more accurately directional sound; and more subtle, 'truer-to-life' colour. The intention of all technical systems developed since the beginning of the 1950s has been towards reducing the spectators' sense of their 'real' world, and replacing it with a fully believable artificial one. In cases where a real-life equivalent is clearly impossible, such as the morphing effects in *Terminator 2*, the pictorial quality of the effect must be sophisticated and 'photo-realistic' enough to persuade the audience that if, for example, a tiled floor transformed into a human figure in real life, it would look exactly like its screen depiction does. A great deal of the technical developments witnessed in the film industry over the past four decades has been dedicated to persuading audiences that the simulated and the artificial are the real and actual, that they *can* believe their own eyes (and ears). The often enormous costs of perfecting any such system is justified if the product created using that system attracts a sufficiently large paying audience. This increased, and substitutive, realistic effect is seen to be what the public both wants and expects from the cinematic experience. It can operate equally in ordinary or fantastic (sci-fi, musical) fictional worlds, with each system competing with others on its ability to create a more believable artificial world. The arena within which that artifical world is designed to operate now covers theme parks, Virtual Reality sites and Science and Technology exhibitions as well as cinemas.

But each new system must also satisfy the industrial requirements of efficiency and economy: will it allow practitioners to do their work more quickly and with less effort, and does it ultimately result in budget savings? Even when the new technology being used is initially very expensive, as was the case with the first digital special effects systems in the late 1980s, the expectation is that it will justify, eventually, the investment by resulting either in cheaper production methods, or very large box-office returns. Whether the system in question is developed within the film industry itself, or outside of it by independents, as in the case of Cinerama, special effects and VR, the new system either disappears if it proves unfeasible to adopt, or is eventually absorbed by the industry and normalized as one of its options. This cycle of new development/assimilation/absorbtion/new development in the service of realism and spectacle has been a part of the film industry's identity since its inception, and will no doubt continue to be so in its future.

Notes

1 See, for example: Charles Barr, 'CinemaScope: before and after', in Mast and Cohen (eds), *Film Theory and Criticism* (Oxford and New York: Oxford University Press, 1974); André Bazin, 'Three essays on widescreen', *Velvet Light Trap*, no. 21 (Summer 1985); John Belton, 'CinemaScope: the economics of technology', *Velvet Light Trap*, no. 21 (Summer 1985); John Belton, 'Glorious Technicolor, breathtaking CinemaScope, and stereophonic sound', in Tino Balio (ed.), *Hollywood in the Age of Television* (Boston: Unwin Hyman, 1990); John Belton, *Widescreen Cinema* (Cambridge, Mass. and London: Harvard University Press, 1992); Brad Chisholm, 'Widescreen technologies', *Velvet Light Trap*, no. 21 (Summer 1985); Richard Hincha, 'Selling CinemaScope: 1953–1956', *Velvet Light Trap*, no. 21 (Summer 1985); Stephen Huntley, 'Sponable's CinemaScope: an intimate chronology of the invention of the CinemaScope optical system', *Film History*, vol. 5, no. 3 (September 1993); David Katz, 'A widescreen chronology', *Velvet Light Trap*, no. 21 (Summer 1985); Fred Waller, 'The archeology of Cinerama', *Film History*, vol 5, no. 3 (September 1993).

2 See, for example: Rick Altman, *Sound Theory/Sound Practice* (New York and London: Routledge, 1992); Michael Arick, 'In stereo: the sound of money', *Sight and Sound*, vol.

57, no. 1 (Winter 1987–8); John Belton, '1950s magnetic sound: the frozen revolution', in Rick Altman (ed.), *Sound Theory / Sound Practice*; John Belton and Elizabeth Weis, *Film Sound: Theory and Practice* (New York: Columbia University Press, 1985); Edward Buscombe, 'Sound and color', *Jump Cut*, no. 17 (April 1978); Evan William Cameron (ed.), *Sound and the Cinema* (New York: Redgrave Publishing Co., 1980); Reinhard Denke, 'Wired for sound', *Moving Pictures* no. 185 (12 May 1994); Bob Fisher, 'Cinema digital sound: the next step', *American Cinematographer*, vol. 71, no. 9 (September 1990); Michael Fremer, 'THX: what it is, and what it ain't', *Perfect Vision*, vol. 6, no. 21 (Spring 1994); Jim Mallick, 'The THX theatre alignment program', *Perfect Vision* vol. 6, no. 21 (Spring 1994); Stephen Neale, *Cinema and Technology* (London: BFI/Macmillan, 1985); Daniel Sweeney, 'THX-rated: the end of a high end audio quality?', *Perfect Vision*, vol. 6, no. 21 (Spring 1994).

3 The 1.33:1 format is an adaptation of the 1.37:1 format, the loss of 0.04 in. being due to the addition of the soundtrack running alongside the image frame.

4 See, for example: John Belton, 'Glorious technicolor, breathtaking CinemaScope, and stereophonic sound'; Gorham Kindem, 'Hollywood's conversion to color: the technological, economic and aesthetic factors', *Journal of the University Film Association*, vol. 31, no. 2 (Spring 1979); Stephen Neale, *Cinema and Technology*.

5 Brooke Comer, 'Steadicam hits its stride', *American Cinematographer*, vol. 74, no. 2 (February 1993); Jean-Pierre Geuens, 'Visuality and power: the work of the steadicam', *Film Quarterly*, vol. 47, no. 2 (Winter 1993).

6 Les Paul Robley, 'Digital offline video editing: expanding creative horizons', *American Cinematographer*, vol. 74, nos. 4–7 (April–July 1993); Janet Wasko, *Hollywood in the Information Age* (Cambridge: Polity Press, 1994); John Watkinson, *An Introduction to Digital Video* (Oxford: Focal Press, 1994).

7 Robin Baker, 'Computer technology and special effects in contemporary cinema', in Philip Hayward and Tana Wollen (eds), *Future Visions: New Technologies of the Screen* (London: British Film Institute, 1993); Frank Beacham, 'Movies for the future: storytelling with computers', *American Cinematographer*, vol. 6, no. 4 (April 1995); Andrew Cameron, 'Dissimulations: the illusion of interactivity', *Millennium Film Journal* no. 28 (Spring 1995); James Cameron, 'Technology and magic', *CineFex*, no. 51 (August 1992); Bob Fisher, 'Dawning of the digital age', *American Cinematographer*, vol. 73, no. 4 (April 1992); Janine Pourroy, 'Through the proscenium arch', *Cinefex*, no. 46 (May 1991); Janet Wasko, *Hollywood in the Information Age*.

8 Bluescreen is an optical effect technique whereby actors stand in front of a blank, blue-coloured screen which, because of the particular colour of blue used, does not register in the camera. This allows a separate image to be superimposed on the screen, making it look like the actors are actually occupying a different space.

9 Frank Biocca and Mark R. Levy, *Communication in the Age of Virtual Reality* (Hove and New Jersey: Lawrence Erlbaum Associates, 1995); Karen Carr and Rupert England, *Simulated and Virtual Realities: Elements of Perception* (London: Taylor & Francis Ltd, 1995); Bob Cotton and Richard Oliver, *Understanding Hypermedia: From Multimedia to Virtual Reality* (London: Phaidon, 1993); Terence Guthridge, 'Dr StrangeGlove, or how I learned to stop worrying and love virtual reality', *Metro*, no. 101 (1995); Stephen Jones, 'A sense of space: virtual reality, authenticity and the aural', *Critical Studies in Mass Communication*, vol. 10, no. 3 (1993); Joan Pennefather, 'From cinema to virtual reality', *Intermedia*, vol. 22, no. 5 (October–November 1994); Howard Rheingold, *Virtual Reality* (London: Secker & Warburg, 1991).

Chapter 8

Widescreen composition in the age of television

Steve Neale

As is well-known, a number of widescreen processes and formats were adopted by Hollywood during the course of the 1950s as a means of attempting to maintain the profitability and appeal of its films in the face of declining attendances at cinemas and increasing competition from television and from other leisure pursuits.[1] As is also well-known, increasing reciprocity between the film and television industries during the 1950s and 1960s resulted, among other things, in the screening of films, including widescreen films, on television.[2] Since then, with the conglomeration of the industry, and with the advent of cable, satellite, video and other 'windows' for the industry's product, this reciprocity has further increased, and with it the necessity to design the industry's films, its widescreen films included, with each of these windows in mind.[3]

Until the recent advent of widescreen television, itself a sign of the synergy that now exists between the film, television and video industries, the proportions of the television screen and of all widescreen formats were significantly different – which of course was one of the reasons for Hollywood's adoption of widescreen formats in the first place. What interests me here are the effects of the growing reciprocity between the film and television industries, of the existence of two very differently shaped and proportioned windows, on the visual composition of widescreen films, and hence on what we see in the windows themselves. Considerable attention has been paid to the compositional issues, opportunities and problems created by Hollywood's adoption of widescreen technology in the 1950s.[4] As we shall see, some attention has also been paid to the issues and problems involved in the screening on television of films composed in and for widescreen formats. But there has been very little discussion – even in the industry's journals – of the issues and problems involved in composing films for widescreen exhibition in cinemas *and* for subsequent television screenings, and even less of the compositional conventions, devices and effects that appear to have evolved as a result. Such writing as there has been on this topic – by Belton, for instance, and by Eidsvik[5] – has been surprisingly vague, and, as we shall see, surprisingly inaccurate in suggesting that directors and cinematographers now simply 'keep essential information away from the edges of screen'.[6] Designed more than anything to promote further research, much of what follows is exploratory, provisional and open even more than is usually the case to future revision.

One index of the growing reciprocity between the film and television industries in America in the 1950s had been the selling and renting of films to the television networks for television screenings. Initially, most of these films had been made prior to 1948, but in 1960, agreements were struck which enabled more recent films – including films made in widescreen formats – to be rented and shown. As part of a package provided by Twentieth Century Fox, *How to Marry A Millionaire* (1953) became the first widescreen film to be shown on television in America when it was broadcast in NBC's Saturday Night at the Movies slot on 21 September 1961. As John Belton has pointed out, this screening 'ushered in not only the era of the prime-time network feature film, but also that of the panned and scanned film'.[7] He goes on to explain:

> Filmed at the same time as *The Robe*, *Millionaire* was Twentieth Century Fox's second CinemasScope feature. Films in CinemaScope, which had an aspect ratio of either 2.5 or 2.35:1, posed problems for television broadcast, because the TV screen possessed only a 1.33:1 aspect ratio. If the full width of the widescreen image were to be shown on the TV screen, the top and bottom of the screen would be left with blank areas above and below the image. If the top and bottom of the screen were to be filled, then the sides of the image would have to be cropped by 50 percent or more. The major networks quickly 'resolved' the essential incompatibility between the widescreen and television formats by deciding to pan and scan (that is, to crop) films rather than to present them in what was subsequently referred to as the 'letterbox' format.[8]

Panning and scanning involves selecting portions of the widescreen image for presentation on the whole of the television screen. In moving from one portion of the widescreen image to another – during the course of a single shot, or while moving from one shot to another – panning and scanning entails either 'cutting' or 'panning' from one portion of the screen to another.[9] It thus re-composes films made in and for widescreen formats in at least three different ways: by reframing shots, by re-editing sequences and shots, and by altering the pattern of still and moving shots used in the original film. Michael Kerbel and John Belton both provide detailed examples of the effects panning and scanning has had on a number of films composed in and for widescreen formats. Kerbel discusses *The Graduate* (1967),[10] and Belton discusses, among others, *Rebel Without a Cause* (1955), *East of Eden* (1955), *It's Always Fair Weather* (1955) and *The Good, the Bad, and the Ugly* (1967).[11] I would like here to add just two further examples, from *Some Came Running* (1958) and from *Patton* (1970).

Dramatically, spatially, morally – and ironically – the figure of Ginny (Shirley MacLaine) comes in the end to occupy centre-stage in *Some Came Running*. The ironies involved are in part dependent on the peripheral position she initially occupies in the hearts, minds and lives of characters like Dave Hirsch (Frank Sinatra), who are structurally much more central, and who appear to command greater consideration, attention and sympathy. They are therefore in part dependent on the peripheral position she initially seems to occupy within the film as a whole. The framing of the first shot after the credits is thus of some significance. Dave is framed sitting upright in his seat on a greyhound bus. He occupies a prominent compositional position, foreground centre-right, and his face – the face of the film's major star – is fully visible for the first time in the film. Crucially, Ginny is also visible, though barely noticeable, lying face down in her seat in an apparently peripheral position on the extreme left-hand side of the widescreen frame. However, when panned and scanned, the composition fragments, the significance of the framing is lost – and the ironies unwittingly redouble. For Dave becomes even more prominent, and Ginny disappears altogether.

In *Patton*, Patton himself (George C. Scott) tends to be portrayed as a self-assured, self-confident maverick. Touched with the military genius he is convinced he possesses, sure of his own military judgement and devoted to his own military code, he is constantly flouting, or constantly tempted to flout, civilian and military authority, and hence constantly in danger of depriving himself of the role in world events for which he is convinced he is – or should be – destined. At a number of points in the film he is paired with General Bradley (Karl Malden). Unlike many of his fellow officers, Bradley is sympathetic to Patton. Aware of his virtues and strengths as well as his weaknesses, he is the closest thing Patton has to a confidante, adviser and friend. Bradley himself is much more practical, much more sensible, much more orthodox and much more down to earth. He thus complements Patton, tempering his excesses, his impatience, his arrogance and his incipient megalomania, and helping him exercise his talents and achieve his ambitions in constructive ways. In the scenes they share together, the complementary nature of their relationship – and of Bradley's role within it – finds articulation in a distinct and systematic pattern of editing and framing. For the most part they are framed together in two-shots. Their scenes together nearly always begin and end in this way. But as and when, during the course of these scenes, Patton's excesses come to the fore, the pattern of the framing changes. Two-shots give way to shots which separate the characters from one another by framing them singly. Either that, or two-shots of Patton and Bradley alternate with shots which frame Patton on his own. Either way, the relationship is disturbed, the balance upset, by the weight of

Patton's ego. And either way, because the two-shots that mark the balance in the first place occupy most of the widescreen frame, the pattern disappears altogether from panned and scanned versions of the film, the two-shots replaced, for the most part, by shots which frame the men singly throughout.

Patton was made in the late 1960s. Its patterns of framing alone suggest that it was composed principally, if not solely, for widescreen exhibition in cinemas. The same is true of a number of other late 1960s films, including those, like *The Graduate* and *The Good, the Bad, and the Ugly*, discussed by Kerbel and Belton. If so, there appears to be something of a lag or gap between principles and practice. For as Belton explains, only a year after NBC's screening of *How to Marry a Millionaire*,

> [t]he Research and Education Commitee of the American Society of Cinematographers devised a method of producing motion pictures for theatrical wide screen presentation so they may also be shown on television 'without impairment of the picture image'. To accomplish this seemingly impossible task, the committee established what it called a 'safe action area': 'that portion of the picture area inside the camera aperture borders within which all significant action should take place for "safe" or full reproduction on the majority of black-and-white and color home receivers'".[12]

Noting that 'Camera manufacturers began to produce viewfinders which indicated this area with a dotted line', Belton goes on to argue that 'directors of cinematography began to "protect" their compositions for television by keeping essential narrative and aesthetic elements within this frame-within-a-frame.'[13] He continues:

> Though many cinematographers deny that they compose for subsequent television release of their work, awareness of TV's 'safe action area' undoubtedly influences their approach to widescreen composition. In the 1950s, Zanuck instructed his directors and cameramen to spread the action out across the full width of the frame in an attempt to maximize the CinemaScope format. Today, with one or two notable exceptions, directors and cameramen, who realize that the majority of their audience will see their work on television rather than in the theater, take pains to insure their films against the potential damage that panning and scanning can inflict.[14]

Quite how cinematographers began to 'protect' their compositions, quite what is meant by 'essential narrative and aesthetic elements', and quite what is entailed in keeping these elements within the 'frame-within-a-frame' are questions I wish to return to in a moment. In the meantime, it is at least worth asking whether economic and industrial factors – such as the demand for films which were easier, quicker and cheaper to pan and scan – played a part in these developments. And it is at least worth posing the question as to when the compositional practices associated with the safe action area became the norm. Although I cannot as yet answer either question, my impression, based partly on the evidence of films like *Patton*, is that compositional practices began to change, not in the 1960s, but during the course of the 1970s – a period of initial recession, and of considerable aesthetic and industrial readjustment.[15] This point can be made, I think, by looking briefly at two 1970s films, *Pat Garrett and Billy the Kid* (1973) and *Chinatown* (1974).

Both films contain motifs which exploit the proportions of the widescreen frame. Throughout *Pat Garrett*, the actions and behaviour of Pat (James Coburn) and Billy (Kris Kristofferson) are constantly witnessed by groups of people – homesteaders, townsfolk, members of gangs, members of posses, the inhabitants of Fort Sumter, and so on. These groups frequently gather, as it were, on the edges of the widescreen frame. In consequence their presence and their impact tend to diminish when the film is panned and scanned.

Chinatown, meanwhile, is marked by a number of distinct but overlapping motifs. One centres on the capacities and limitations of vision, of visual representation, of the human eye, and of the means and devices used to extend its capabilities, counteract its flaws, and fix the appearances with which it is confronted. Another centres on biblical imagery in general, and Old Testament imagery in particular. And a third centres on water. Water is prominent as a narrative catalyst, as a motivating factor in the activities of a number of major and minor characters, and as an element central to the lives of those who live and work in LA and the farmland around it. In its visual forms, this motif is apparent in a number of sequences and scenes – most of the scenes in which Jake Gittes (Jack Nicholson) is seen trailing Hollis Mulwray (Darell Zwerling), the civic official responsible for Water and Power, the scene in which Gittes himself is nearly drowned, the scenes that take place on the coast, and the scenes by the pool in Mulwray's garden. And it is apparent whether or not the film has been panned and scanned. However, additional instances, instances located, for the most part, on the very edges of the widescreen frame, disappear altogether from panned and scanned versions of the film. These include the car immobilized by lack of water in the street outside the barber's shop, the water dispenser in Gittes' office, visible on the left-hand side of the frame in the shot in which the real Evelyn Mulwray (Faye Dunaway) makes her first appearance, the image of the fish on the wall in Hollis Mulwray's office, and the vase of flowers on the left-hand side of the desk in Mulwray's secretary's office.

Thus *Chinatown* and *Pat Garrett and Billy the Kid* seem to have been composed with widescreen exhibition in mind. What interests me about these instances, though, is the extent to which the principal characters and the narrative actions in which they are engaged are all visible on screen once the films have been panned and scanned. It appears, in other words, as though the proportions of the TV screen have been taken into account in staging and framing these shots and scenes, and as though the motifs in question have been used to fill what would otherwise be unused or unoccupied widescreen space. A similar strategy seems to have been used in later films like *Blade Runner* (1982). Here the edges of the widescreen film are frequently filled with images and objects relating to the film's concern with simulacra of one kind or another – toys, models, mannequins, photographs and so on. Once again these images and objects often disappear when the film is panned and scanned; once again, though, the configurations in which the principal characters and their actions have been placed remain intact.

Another compositional device used in all these films to occupy the width of the widescreen frame while enabling easy panning and scanning is a device I call 'the over-the-disposable-shoulder shot'. All three of these films involve two-way conversation scenes which are composed in alternating two-shots. Each shot is in each case framed so as to show the face of one of the characters in medium close-up on one side of the frame and the shoulder of his or her interlocutor on the other. When subject to panning and scanning, the patterns of alternation are preserved – there is no need for subsequent 'editing' – and all that disappears are the shoulders. A series of over-the-shoulder two-shots is replaced by a series of medium close-ups of each of the characters in turn framed in a manner compatible not only with the dimensions of the TV screen, but also with the conventions deployed in television for editing and framing conversation scenes in general. Unsurprisingly, none of these films even attempts to deploy widescreen composition or to construct patterns of widescreen framing in the way that *Some Came Running* and *Patton* do.

There are two additional characteristics of the framing of some of the shots and scenes in *Pat Garret*, *Chinatown* and *Blade Runner* which seem to me to indicate composition with the safe action area in mind. Both are ubiquitous in post-1960s widescreen films, and unlike the means and devices discussed so far, both result in large quantities of what I am tempted to call 'empty space'. One is the grouping of characters in one particular sector of the frame – a sector whose dimensions correspond precisely to those of the television screen, and which thus leaves the rest of the frame empty of anything other than inert background decor. The other is more distinctive, a real compositional hallmark of post-1960s widescreen films. It often occurs, once again, in conversation scenes, when a decision has been made to frame the characters singly rather than in two-shot. Instead of locating the characters at or near the centre of the widescreen frame, they are located at or near one of its edges. In addition, in cross-cutting between set-ups of each of the characters in turn, one will usually be located on the extreme left-hand side of the frame and the other on the right. The result is the generation of a symmetrical pattern or rhythm across a set of markedly asymmetrical components, and when viewed in the cinema is a bit like watching a tennis match. On television, however, the asymmetry is lost, and shots appear to be framed more conventionally.[16]

These examples all show that in acknowledging the existence of a safe action area and the dimensions of the TV screen, post-1960s widescreen films are marked by a variety of compositional strategies, devices and styles. The over-the-disposable-shoulder shot and the deployment of significant – but equally disposable – motifs on the edges of the widescreen frame show that the demands of the safe action area do not necessarily result in large quantities of empty or unoccupied space. And the sectoral grouping or zoning of characters and actions, and in particular the asymmetrical framing of characters in conversation scenes, show that a distinct and interesting compositional style is perfectly possible. However, in addition to the types of framing found in *Some Came Running* and *Patton*, what seems, if not impossible, then at least very rare in modern widescreen cinema is the use of the full width of the frame in staging central narrative actions, and in particular in blocking the positions, looks and movements of the characters involved. Compare two conversation scenes, one from a mid-1950s film *23 Paces to Baker Street* (1956), the other from an early 1990s film, *Unforgiven* (1992).

While by no means identical in content, both scenes involve a number of different characters united in a common purpose or cause, both are set indoors, and both contain little in the way of spectacular narrative action. The scene in *23 Paces to Baker Street* is brief and transitional (see Plate 8.1). It basically comprises a telephone call, a subsequent conversation, and a decision to leave the room – a police inspector's office – in search of the next piece of information in the hunt for an unknown killer. There are two shots in this scene. In the first, we see Inspector Grosvening (Maurice Denham) seated at a desk by the telephone, an unnamed assistant frame left, Philip Hannon (Van Johnson) seated foreground right, and Jean Lennox (Vera Miles) seated foreground centre-left. The action consists of a set of conversational exchanges among and between these various characters. It begins with Grosvening on the phone, the others all looking towards him from various points in the room and positions in the widescreen frame. He puts down the phone, addresses a comment to the man on his right, then a series of remarks to Philip. Philip then turns toward Jean. He addresses a series of remarks to her and she to him. She then turns to speak to Grosvening, who responds to her before turning, finally, to Philip, at which point, having rounded off this particular set of exchanges, we cut to the scene's second shot. The key points here are that all of the characters in the frame are involved in these exchanges at one stage or another; that each exchange is marked in and through a series of eyelines and adjustments to the head as they turn to address one another (and this despite the fact that one of these characters – Philip – is meant to be blind); that at various points these exhanges and eyelines traverse the width of the frame (this is especially apparent in the exchanges between Grosvening and Philip); and hence that the width of the screen has not just been 'filled' with people, it has also been articulated, on the one hand, and activated on the other, by each of the exchanges, movements, and eyelines that occur or are momentarily established during the course of the shot as a whole. A similar strategy marks the second shot, in which the characters gather by the door before departing for the next location.

The scene in *Unforgiven* is also fairly brief. The prostitutes who have hired William Munney (Clint Eastwood), the Schofield Kid (Jaimz Woolvett) and Ned Logan (Morgan Freeman) to enact revenge for the scarring of Delilah Fitzgerald (Anna Thompson) are gathered together in an upstairs room observing the reaction of a group of townsmen to the killing of one of the cowboys responsible. Having turned from the window, the camera pans right to include all six of the women present in the room in the frame. A conversation ensues. Unlike the conversation scene in *23 Paces to Baker Street*, the scene here is edited. But the set-ups in each case frame a number of the women together. Where the scenes really differ is in the blocking of the action and the handling of the eyelines. At no point in the scene from *Unforgiven* does the flow of the conversation, the movement of the characters or the articulation of their eyelines occupy or activate the width of the frame in the way that they do in *23 Paces to Baker Street*. They are either restricted to one particular sector of the frame (thus enabling easy cropping for TV) or they are directed out of frame and matched or picked up in a subsequent shot. The same is true of an earlier scene in which the prostitutes gather together to plan their revenge. In both cases figures may, from time to time, occupy the edges of the frame. But they either remain at that point uninvolved in the conversation and are hence compositionally dispensable, or else, if they are involved, the sector of the frame they don't themselves occupy is dispensable instead.

There is undoubtedly more to be said about widescreen composition in the 1970s, the 1980s and the 1990s. I would like to return, though, by way of conclusion, to the 1950s. It may seem as though I have painted a picture in which a stable set of compositional conventions was disrupted by the increasing importance of television as a site for the screening of films, as though compositional coherence, a hallmark of the 1950s (and 1960s), was eventually replaced by instability, variability and incoherence. While it remains true, I think, that the advent of television as an exhibition outlet had a decisive impact on the compositional practices and norms of Hollywood films, any impression of the 1950s as an era of compositional stability and coherence needs to be questioned. For one thing the introduction of processes such as Cinerama and CinemaScope itself disrupted established compositional practices and norms. As Belton points out, the compositional strategies used in early CinemaScope films 'differed markedly from the compositional paradigms employed in traditional narrow-screen 1.37:1

Figure 8.1 23 Paces to Baker Street (1956). Courtesy of Twentieth Century Fox

filmmaking'.[17] For another, these processes all differed one from another, and often underwent subsequent change and modification. Ratios varied from 2.77:1 (for Cinerama) to 2.55:1 (for the earliest CinemaScope films) to 2.35:1 (for CinemaScope films made after 1956). A third point is that in a number of cases at least films shot in standard academy ratio were masked in projection to produce what Belton calls an 'ersatz' widescreen image, while others, like *Invasion of the Body Snatchers* (1956), were shot in academy but cropped in processing to produce something more akin to a widescreen look.[18] In all these ways, the 1950s was a period, not of stability, but of instability, not of constancy ('classical' or otherwise), but of adaptability, variation and change. It would be fair to argue that for a time in the mid- to late 1950s and early 1960s directors and cinematographers were able to compose their films in the expectation that they would only be shown in cinemas, and in the knowledge that most cinemas in the US were equipped to show widescreen films. It would therefore be fair to argue that, whatever the format employed, most directors and cinematographers could gear their compositions to the format they used, and that this situation changed at some point during the course of the following decade as television screenings became an increasingly important industrial factor. Even here, though, care must be taken, especially when considering the use of formats like VistaVision.

VistaVision was pioneered by Paramount and introduced in 1954, when it was used to shoot films like *Strategic Air Command* and *White Christmas*. It was Paramount's response to Cinerama, CinemaScope and the general vogue for widescreen formats. Unlike CinemaScope and Cinerama, which used anamorphic lenses to squeeze the image in filming and to unsqueeze the image in projection, VistaVision involved masking the top and the bottom of the image in the aperture gate of the projector. It was thus designed to be flexible, to allow for variations in the aspect ratio of the image projected in cinemas, and hence for variations in the circumstances in which its films were shown: 'VistaVision offered theaters which, for economic or architectural reasons, were unable to convert to CinemaScope, a viable widescreen alternative, permitting them to project VistaVision pictures in aspect ratios ranging from 1.33:1 to 2:1, which it considered the maximum width that most medium-sized and small theaters in the country could employ.'[19] Composing shots for VistaVision was thus in many ways comparable to composing shots for all subsequent non-anamorphic widescreen formats (all of which involve masking the top and the bottom of the frame), and in some ways comparable to composing shots for anamorphic cinema projection and for subsequent television screenings. However, there is a difference. Non-anamorphic systems require that the top and the bottom of the image are rarely used for narrative or for compositional purposes. However, the width of the image *can* be used, because the ratios used in non-anamorphic formats are not as extreme as those used in anamorphic ones. As far as subsequent television screenings are concerned, this means that VistaVision films like *The Searchers* (1956), unlike CinemaScope films such as *Home from the Hill* (1960), require no panning and scanning, and are comparable in this respect to modern non-anamorphic widescreen films like *Raging Bull* (1980).

By way of conclusion, I would like to stress the need for further research on the impact of television, not just on widescreen composition, but on Hollywood aesthetics in general. The interplay between cinema and television is clearly complex, many-sided, and by no means one-way. The increasing use of zoom and telephoto lenses in Hollywood films after the mid-1950s is a case in point. If, as Richard Maltby and others have argued, the influence of television was crucial here,[20] it should be borne in mind that zooms were used in American films as early as 1926,[21] and that what were then called 'telephoto lenses' (lenses with focal lengths up to 150mm) were used as early as the turn of the century.[22] It should also be borne in mind that the use of zooms and telephoto lenses in films like *The Wild Bunch* (1969) and *The Long Goodbye* (1973) was often spectacular, and in that sense 'cinematic' – rather than 'televisual' – in its effect. The fact that both *The Wild Bunch* and *The Long Goodbye* were also shot in Panavision, an anamorphic widescreen process, that *The Long Goodbye* and other Altman films in particular have had a considerable impact on the style of American TV shows like *Hill Street Blues*, *NYPD Blue*, *ER* and *Homicide – Life on the Streets*, and that Altman and Peckinpah, the director of *The Wild Bunch*, both worked as directors in television in the 1950s and 1960s, merely adds to the complexity of the interplay. Whether the same complexity is apparent when it comes to cutting rates, the ratio of close-ups to medium-shots and long-shots, the relationship between the image and the soundtrack, the duration of segments and scenes (especially dialogue scenes), and the general avoidance of deep-staging, and in particular deep multi-plane staging, in post-1950s Hollywood films, remains to be seen.

Notes

1 See among others, Tino Balio (ed.), *The American Film Industry* (Madison: University of Wisconsin Press, 1985), pp. 427–33; Tino Balio (ed.), *Hollywood in the Age of Television* (Boston: Unwin Hyman, 1990), pp. 23–38; John Belton, *Widescreen Cinema* (Cambridge, Mass: Harvard University Press, 1992), pp. 69–210.

2 See Balio (ed.), *The American Film Industry*, pp. 437–8; Balio (ed.), *Hollywood in the Age of Television*, pp. 30–2 and 37–9; Belton, *Widescreen Cinema*, pp. 214–18; William Lafferty, 'Feature films on prime-time television', in Balio (ed.), *Hollywood in the Age of Television*, pp. 235–56.

3 See Balio (ed.), *Hollywood in the Age of Television*, pp. 39–40 and 262–93; Charles Eidsvik, 'Machines of the invisible: changes in film technology in the age of video', *Film Quarterly*, vol. 42, no. 2 (1988–9), pp. 18–24; Janet Wasko, *Hollywood in the Information Age, Beyond the Silver Screen* (Cambridge: Polity Press, 1994).

4 See among others, Charles Barr, 'CinemaScope: before and after', *Film Quarterly*,

vol. 16, no. 4 (1963), pp. 4–25; André Bazin, 'Three essays on widescreen film', *The Velvet Light Trap*, no. 21 (1985), pp. 8–16; Belton, *Widescreen Cinema*, pp. 183–203; David Bordwell, Janet Staiger and Kristin Thompson, *The Classical Hollywood Cinema, Film Style and Mode of Production to 1960* (London: Routledge, 1985), pp. 358–64; Barry Salt, *Film Style and Technology: History and Analysis* (London: Starword, 1992), pp. 246–8.

5 Belton, *Widescreen Cinema*, p. 225; Eidsvik, 'Machines of the invisible', p. 21.

6 Eidsvik, 'Machines of the invisible', p. 21.

7 Belton, *Widescreen Cinema*, p. 216.

8 Ibid.

9 Ibid., pp. 216–20; Michael Kerbel, 'Edited for television, 1: scanning', *Film Comment* vol. 13, no. 3 (1997), pp. 28–30; William Lafferty, 'Feature films on prime-time television', pp. 252–3.

10 Kerbel, 'Edited for television', pp. 29–30.

11 Belton, *Widescreen Cinema*, pp. 218–24.

12 Ibid., p. 225.

13 Ibid.

14 Ibid.

15 See among others, Balio (ed.), *Hollywood in the Age of Television*, pp. 259–63; Thomas Schatz, 'The new Hollywood', in Jim Collins, Hilary Radner and Ava Preacher Collins (eds), *Film Theory Goes to the Movies* (New York: Routledge, 1993), pp. 8–25.

16 It should be noted that even in the 1950s, as David Bordwell has pointed out, it was rare to place single figures at the centre of the widescreen frame. 'In framing a single figure in medium shot', he writes, 'the dominant widescreen practice is to avoid exact centering; the actor is positioned slightly off-center, leaving space for his or her gaze or for pertinent background material. . . . Using the lateral stretch in this way, the Hollywood filmmaker confirms our sense of the unity of profilmic space: the glance and the setting charge the empty arena with narrative meaning' (Bordwell, Staiger and Thompson, *The Classical Hollywood Cinema*, p. 362). The difference between common practice in the 1950s and common practice in the 1970s, the 1980s and the 1990s lies in the degree of off-centredness involved. It should also be noted that the 'tennis match' effect I am referring to here clearly differs from any comparable effect produced by placing the participants in a two-way conversation at the edges of a widescreen two-shot.

17 Belton, *Widescreen Cinema*, p. 198.

18 Ibid., pp. 116–17. On *Invasion of the Body Snatchers*, see Matthew Bernstein, *Walter Wanger, Hollywood Independent* (Berkeley: University of California Press, 1994), pp. 312–13, and Al LaValley, 'Invasion of the body snatchers', in Al LaValley (ed.), *Invasion of the Body Snatchers* (New Brunswick: Rutgers University Press, 1989), p. 26.

19 Belton, *Widescreen Cinema*, p. 125. See also Brad Chisholm, 'Widescreen technologies', *The Velvet Light Trap* no. 21 (1985), p. 71. Chisholm points out that in using VistaVision, 'shots had to be composed with all possible aspect ratios in mind'.

20 Richard Maltby, *Harmless Entertainment: Hollywood and the Ideology of Consensus* (Metuchen: Scarecrow Press, 1983), pp. 334–7. See also John Belton, 'The bionic eye: zoom esthetics', *Cineaste*, vol. 9, no. 1 (1980–1), pp. 20–7, and Paul Joannides, 'The aesthetics of the zoom lens', *Sight and Sound*, vol. 40, no. 1 (1970–1), pp. 40–2.

21 Salt, *Film Style and Technology*, pp. 185–6.

22 Ibid., p. 33.

Chapter 9

The classical film score forever?

Batman, Batman Returns and post-classical film music

K.J. Donnelly

Since the 1930s, music has not only been a significant component of narration in mainstream films but also has been organized as a coherent and discrete discourse within them. *Batman* (1989) and its first sequel *Batman Returns* (1992) highlight the ways post-classical Hollywood employs and orders music, both in terms of using classically inspired forms and more recent procedures. It is possible to see the musical strategies of contemporary films in the light both of continuity and of discontinuity with those of classical cinema. In what follows, I will investigate these two films, attending to the relationship between contemporary film music and the film music of classical cinema, noting the similarities but emphasizing the significant differences between the two.

Music was (and continues to be) an integral part of the multimedia phenomenon of the Batman films. Danny Elfman wrote the musical scores for *Batman* and *Batman Returns*, and they provide a continuity across the films along with director Tim Burton and Michael Keaton as Batman. Elfman's music had a significant impact and elevated his reputation for engaging and effective film scores. In some ways, these two Batman films are representative of the contemporary trends in expensively produced Hollywood blockbuster films – *Batman* was ranked in the Top Ten grossers of all time[1] – although both films also have interesting and unusual aesthetic strategies.

The past few years have seen a growth in the number of serious considerations of film music. Although this charting of undiscovered territory has to be welcomed, the focus of most writings upon the musical wealth of classical cinema means that more recent Hollywood film music has been largely ignored. Claudia Gorbman refers to 'classical film scoring' and Kathryn Kalinak to 'the classical film score' to describe the music of classical cinema.[2] For most classical feature films, an orchestral score would be specially written as a coherent piece of music, yet it would be comprised of fragments. It was an intermittent yet substantial, and almost continuous ('wall-to-wall') musical fabric, integrating itself with the film as secondary to the action. The assumption was that music should 'underscore' the visuals, creating emotional and dynamic effects, homologizing visual activity and providing information and atmosphere for the film's narrative development. Kathryn Kalinak, in *Settling the Score*, asserts that contemporary Hollywood film music proves the persistence of the musical blueprint established by classical cinema,[3] suggesting that the style and assumptions behind film music have changed little. Her declaration of the seeming permanence of Hollywood film music's form directly matches Bordwell, Staiger and Thompson's claim for the persistence of the classical mode of film production.[4] Kalinak points to the prevalence of pop songs as scores in the late 1960s and early 1970s as a sort of aberration, indeed an opposition to classical principles through which the process of 'classical scoring' has managed to endure.[5] Yet although many contemporary scores bear some resemblance to studio era film music, industrial imperatives and aesthetic concerns have not remained static, mitigating against the notion of a direct continuity between contemporary film music and that of classical cinema.

While films like *Easy Rider* (1969) and *American Graffiti* (1973) forewent especially written musical underscores in favour of a succession of pop songs, many contemporary Hollywood films use *both* in some way. In addition to this, instrumental forces changed. The sound of the romantic large-scale orchestra, which had been introduced to films from the classical concert hall and was ubiquitous from the early 1930s onwards, had declined in the 1960s and 1970s. There were more sparse scores, both in terms of the amount of music and the number of instruments used. Also evident was the use of a more discordant musical language imported from more recent concert music. Prime examples of these styles are Richard Rodney Bennett's score for *Figures in a Landscape* (1970), Jerry Fielding's music for *Straw Dogs* (1971) and Jerry Goldsmith's score for *Chinatown* (1974). In 1970, composer Ron Goodwin declared:

> I think there was once an attitude, very firmly adopted, that 'if it's film music, it's got to be big', but that has certainly changed in the last couple of years . . . the main thing [now] is that 'wall to wall' music isn't necessary. You must give the film room.[6]

Kalinak points out an explicit return to the style and sound of the classical film score in the wake of John Williams' music for George Lucas' *Star Wars* trilogy (*Star Wars* (1977), *The Empire Strikes Back* (1980) and *Return of the Jedi* (1983)). These films use a lot of music, and *Batman* and *Batman Returns* both have scores of more than an hour's duration, returning to the wall-to-wall *bravura* orchestral music that had seemingly drifted out of fashion.

Orchestral music in the two Batman films certainly draws on the classical Hollywood tradition, yet rather than being simply a return to the styles of studio era scores, it manifests explicit allusions to particular stylistic aspects of studio era film music. Kalinak's use of the term 'persistence' presupposes direct continuity – 'revival' might be a more appropriate description. After all, contemporary Hollywood films differ in many ways from those of the studio era.

In industrial terms, the mode of production for film music in contemporary cinema is very different from that of classical cinema. There are no longer any full-time employees and thus there is no more film music 'production line',[7] where there were rosters of composers, arrangers and musicians all under one roof. This has meant that there is undoubtedly less of the standardization that characterized the music of classical cinema. Now there are even a few film composer superstars with names known by the general public, figures like Ennio Morricone, John Barry, Jerry Goldsmith, and Vangelis. The last of these composers had a Number One single in Germany with the 1995 release of his music for *1492: Conquest of Paradise* (1992) and a UK Top 20 and a US Top 10 hit with his theme for *Chariots of Fire* (1981). Scores by solo synthesizer players such as these are now a relatively cheap and easy option, a process that is reminiscent of nothing so much as the cinema pianist of silent days. Most significantly, there are different imperatives, especially tied-in musical products – namely singles (45s) and soundtrack LPs of both orchestral scores and pop songs. There have been musical tie-ins with films since silent days, for example, 'Fats' Waller's 'The Sheik of Araby' was sold as a sheet music tie-in for the Rudolph Valentino film *The Son of the Sheik* (1926), while the development of the film musical gave great impetus to the sheet music industry. Yet since the late 1950s, with the advent of rock'n'roll and the saturation development of the record market, there has been a proliferation of tied-in songs in films.

Batman's high-profile release in 1989 was complemented by the release of two soundtrack LPs, Danny Elfman's large-scale orchestral score and Prince's song cycle. At this point, Elfman was a relatively minor name on the film composing circuit, having scored Tim Burton's previous films *Pee Wee's Big Adventure* (1985) and *Beetlejuice* (1988). Prince, on the other hand, had become one of the best-selling pop artists of the 1980s with LPs such as *Around the World in a Day* (1985) and *Sign 'O' the Times* (1987), as well as writing the music for and starring in the film *Purple Rain* (1984). *Batman* involves a cohabitation of Elfman's score with Prince's songs. Although the songs are marginalized and indeed much of Prince's LP does not grace the film, it manifests an *extension* of the text beyond its traditional boundaries to include intersecting aesthetic products.

During the 1980s, the term 'synergy' gained currency as a description of the simultaneous promotion of a 'franchise' product,[8] tying-in products from the music industry with the film industry to create a compound package. Thomas Schatz cites *Batman* as characteristic of the multimedia nature of contemporary film production.[9] The existence of two soundtrack LPs for *Batman*, indeed the existence of Prince's music tied to the film, is an example of the synergy of

Warner Brothers' recording and cinematic arms. *Batman*'s producer Jon Peters commented on the high-profile extensions of the film: 'The album and the film are two separate works . . . in two different media, complementing and supporting each other.'[10] It seems that Peters was instrumental in the release of Elfman's LP, the music of which was originally to appear only as a track or two on the Prince LP.[11]

Soundtrack LPs provide a space for the plenitude of music; what may have been a few seconds and hardly noticed in the film can be enjoyed as an aesthetic object in its own right, its own logic undiluted by the exigencies of the film. *Batman* was the first film to institute the release of two soundtrack LPs, a strategy that has become more common since, examples being *Dick Tracy* (1990) (three LPs), *Addams Family Values* (1993), *The Crow* (1994) and *Forrest Gump* (1994) (two LPs, one of them double). In each case, these soundtracks reveal a division of the films' music into orchestral score and song compilation. One reviewer commented about *Batman*'s dual soundtracks: 'both [LPs are] excellent accessories for the further enjoyment of the biggest movie of the year' and suggested, 'Buy the Prince album to get in the mood for the movie. Then go see it and whistle Elfman's haunting theme on your way back home to Prince.'[12]

Prince's LP forms an intersection with the film, aesthetically, commercially and in narrative terms. Prince's LP not only includes some dialogue from the film, but is bizarrely conceptualized as a coherent narrative with dialogue apparently sung between the characters. It comprises its own narrative of sorts, with Prince singing various character parts: Batman in 'The Future', Joker in 'Electric Chair', Vicki Vale and Bruce Wayne in 'Arms of Orion', Joker in 'Party Man', Bruce Wayne in 'Vicki Waiting', The Joker in 'Trust', Vicki Vale in 'Lemon Crush', Batman in 'Scandalous', and all characters in 'Batdance'. This final song is the culmination of the dynamics and the narrative of the LP. 'Batdance' comprises an 'operatic' interaction between Joker, an obscure character called 'Gemini', Vicki Vale, Bruce Wayne and Batman. While Joker and Batman interject samples of dialogue from the film (such as 'I'm Batman'), the sleeve notes also ascribe voices within this song to 'choir', 'Joker's Gang', 'Bat Dancers' and even 'Prince' himself.

'Batdance' was the scout single from the package, released before the film to precede it as an advertisement. It became Prince's equal most successful single in the UK and was the forerunner to two other UK Top 30 singles from his soundtrack ('Party Man' and 'Arms of Orion'), with the film seemingly having driven his LP's success.[13] 'Batdance' provides an interface with the past, announcing the new Batman film through referencing the chorus vocals from Neal Hefti's theme for the camp 1960s television show. This provided a musical bridge between the previous representation of the character and the oncoming film. *Batman* presents all the songs as diegetic music, that is, it grounds them all as appearing 'realistically' within the filmic world. 'Party Man' is foregrounded, played on a ghetto-blaster by Joker when he indulges in some art terrorism, while 'Trust' materializes at the carnival and some Prince songs appear as ambient music at Bruce Wayne's party ('The Future', 'Vicki Waiting', 'Electric Chair'). Thus the film ties the songs to the mundane everyday 'reality' of the film, while Elfman's more prominent non-diegetic orchestral score functions as the film's 'heavenly voice', appearing from nowhere. Despite the bipartite nature of the music in the film, there is one point of union between the two. The Prince song 'Scandalous' appears for a portion of the end credits while some of its music, rearranged by Elfman, appears earlier in the film, albeit fleetingly. Generally, Prince's music appears obtrusively but only occasionally, while Elfman's orchestral music is virtually continuous throughout the film. The music as a whole is constantly foregrounded in a non-classical fashion; as we will see, musical logic often overrides narrative logic.

Reviewers noted the film's musical strategy, that of Elfman's wall-to-wall studio era-styled score plus the foregrounding of Prince's music in the fringes of the film: 'Prince's songs, which interrupt an outstandingly old-fashioned score by Danny Elfman . . . only get gratuitously in the way during two scenes.'[14] Prince visited the set during production and was inspired. He reportedly said, 'I can hear the music.'[15] But sadly for him the final product turned out to have Danny Elfman's music rather than his own.

Elfman's orchestral score dominates, but is not as well integrated with the film as it initially appears. At times it is obscured by sound effects rather than taking them into account, and the internal musical logic of many pieces outweighs their logic in the filmic environment. For example, when Joker first sees a picture of Vicki Vale, the refrain of 'Beautiful Dreamer' appears, and dialogue continues, the music lacking any direct interface with the action. At this point, the music does not bow to the image track through matching the momentary dynamics of the action; rather its time scheme carries on regardless of the film. Much in the same way that pop songs often have in films, the music here retains its own full integrity rather than being forced to bend itself to fit the action. Songs usually have their own regular rhythmic and standardized temporal structure (set by tempo and repeating structures like verse and chorus), which means that when they are foregrounded, action must be cut to their requirements, unlike the flexible orchestral underscores which have traditionally been built around the require-ments of the processes of filmic narration.

Elfman's music distinctly resembles scores from classical Hollywood films. His score not only uses an extremely large orchestra, up to 110 instrumentalists, but also *leitmotifs*, musical themes associated with characters or other things, a central strategy of musical scores in classical cinema. There is the repeated Batman theme, while Joker has a foregrounded musical theme associated with him, the melody from the old Stephen Foster song 'Beautiful Dreamer'. In addition to these, a rearrangement of Prince's 'Scandalous' appears twice, associated with the love of Wayne and Vale. These themes interact at times, forming a direct union between musical and narrative processes. At the film's conclusion, for example, the Batman theme and the 'Scandalous' melody (the love theme) alternate in quick succession, suggesting a union of Batman and Wayne's love for Vale, the two halves of the protagonist's schizoid character. Yet the film's climactic triumphant fanfare, which owes more than a little to Richard Strauss' *Also Sprach Zarathustra*, immediately supersedes them and asserts the superhero himself as we then see Batman alone on the rooftops.

The theme for Batman himself codes the Gothic at its opening, with deep strings and brass, and then the martial, where it leads to a pounding march with snare drum and brass punctuation. It functions directly as a fanfare for Batman, announcing his presence while being associated solidly with both film and character. Consequently, along with the overall style of the film's music, it also works outside the film's context. It was prominent in the trailer for the film and reappeared in the first sequel, *Batman Returns* (1992). Despite the wide usage of the theme, *Batman Forever* (1995) and *Batman and Robin* (1997), in keeping with many other changes from the previous films, instituted a new theme for Batman, the musical score being written by Elliot Goldenthal rather than Elfman. Along the same lines, one-time Elfman orchestrator and conductor of the *Batman* score, Shirley Walker, wrote the music for the film derived from the animated television series, *Batman: Mask of the Phantasm* (1993), and declined to use Eltman's Batman theme. However, the distinct flavour of Elfman's music is so centrally associated with Batman that both Goldenthal's music for *Batman Forever* and Walker's for *Batman: Mark of the Phantasm* have retained its broad style.[16]

A key characteristic of Elfman's score is the use of massed and strident brass instruments. In this way, Elfman's music betrays an influence from key film composer Bernard Herrmann, who is most widely known for his scores for many of Hitchcock's films in the 1950s and 1960s. The non-diegetic score for *Batman* is characterized by parallel harmonies, chords that move up and down by a semitone, a staple of music in the horror genre. The music is also underlined consistently by a strong rhythmic impetus, a pulse or beat that is at the heart of many of the film's pieces of orchestral music. This beat gives the music a highly purposeful edge as well as propelling the action. For instance, when Batman with Vicki Vale drives the Batmobile to the Bat Cave, the music is portentous and compensates for the lack of dialogue. A vocal chorus provides stabbing rhythmic notes, reminiscent of Carl Orff's *Carmina Burana*. The choir keeps a regular rhythm in operation, which builds and paves the way from the Batman theme's climactic entrance, and while this provides an aural zenith for the sequence, it is surmounted by the visual *coup de grâce* of the Batmobile not slowing to enter a hatch in a sheer rock wall.

Elfman's music in *Batman* is pure Gothic melodrama, using a large, dark and

Wagnerian orchestral sound. Some reference points apart from Wagner might be Saint-Saëns' *Danse macabre* and horror film music that has formalized Gothic musical traits. Indeed, it signifies directly to the audience through the use of recognizable musical forms and styles. It uses the melody of 'Beautiful Dreamer' for its many extra-textual connotations of wistful nostalgia. The arrangements of the tune underline this, coding childlike innocence and having an air of ironic sincerity that counterposes Joker's real intentions with respect to Vale. The score is also replete with waltzes of all kinds, which are also associated with Joker. These include a circus-type waltz when Joker first reveals himself and kills crime boss Grissom and later a mock-Strauss waltz when he dances with Vale. Elfman's arrangements include some very distinct instrumental sounds, such as the celesta and the Ondes Martenot. The celesta's delicate bell-like sound is probably most widely known for its use in Tchaikovsky's *Dance of the Sugar Plum Fairy* from *The Nutcracker*, while the Ondes Martenot was an early electronic musical instrument used for its otherworldly sound in some film scores of the 1940s such as Miklos Rosza's for *Spellbound* (1945) and *The Lost Weekend* (1945). At the denouement in Gotham's deserted cathedral the score uses a *Phantom of the Opera*-style organ, a referential strategy that Elfman also followed in his score for *Darkman* (1990).

The Flugelheim art gallery sequence is explicit in its use of the audience's mental library of musical styles and genres. It contains in succession Mozart's *Eine kleine Nachtmusik* (a token of high art culture), Prince's 'Party Man' (pop song) and 'A Summer Place' (cheap Mantovani-style arrangement of a worn-out romance tune, originally a film theme). Audiences are more musically literate than in the past. They are familiar with a wide variety of musical styles through radio, television and the saturation marketing of the recording industry. The music in the film gears itself precisely towards this. Also, while Joker and his gang perform their art terrorism in the gallery, the foregrounded song 'Party Man' flaunts its self-consciousness through being explicitly about Joker and indirectly about Prince. ('All hail, new king in town. Young and old, gather round. Black and white, red and green, the funkiest man you've ever seen.')

In the 'Party Man' sequence, the beat of the music is the central temporal process, underlined by some cuts taking place on emphasized beats (the first beat of the bar). Joker and his gang's actions directly reflect the rhythmic impetus of the song through their dancing. Musical logic dominates visual and narrative logic. This bears out Kalinak's point about pop songs disregarding the dynamics of films,[17] yet in this case the song is articulating and creating the dynamics of the action in a way reminiscent of song sequences in film musicals. In any case the aesthetic evident in this sequence is certainly an anomaly in the dominant form of mainstream narrative cinema, where music regularly takes a back seat to other elements of the film, and traditionally is rarely foregrounded in this manner.

Prince's songs are notably associated with Joker, 'Party Man' at the Flugelheim and 'Trust' at the Gotham carnival. These and 'Beautiful Dreamer' tend to keep their integrity, their musical logic – one could almost say that Joker represents the triumph of musical logic over cinematic logic, while Batman represents the subordination of musical logic to cinematic logic, his image consistently invoking his musical theme.

If *Batman* demonstrates a situation where commercial logic has foregrounded aspects of the film's music, the first sequel displays a qualitatively different scenario – or at least a development from the musical strategy of the original film. *Batman Returns* has a similarly large-scale orchestral score using a language derived from classical cinema, while relegating pop music's role to some music at a party and the end titles song. It has one featured song, 'Face to Face' (performed by Siouxsie and the Banshees), although it briefly uses Rick James' 'Super Freak'. 'Face to Face' was co-written by Elfman and attains a degree of continuity with the orchestral score through using musical elements from the film's character themes (*Leitmotifs*). It appears for the end titles and as diegetic ambient music in the party sequence where, literally face to face, Bruce Wayne (Batman) and Selina Kyle (Catwoman) recognize each other's alter egos. *Batman Returns* certainly contains less in the way of pop music than its predecessor, with the film's LP consisting of Elfman's score and the one featured song. According to Elfman, 'Tim Burton was very clear that there wouldn't be Top 40 songs dropped in at random.'[18] The film expressly used the song sufficiently to justify its tied-in status while the promo for the single incorporated images from the film.

Batman Returns' preponderance of scored orchestral music demonstrates film logic dictating musical logic, following the modes of the prestige orchestral scores of the 1930s and 1940s. The music is tethered directly to the screen action. So the film's principal characters all elicit the appearance of their respective musical themes: Batman has his own heroic theme that survives from the first film, a four-note figure and a deep plodding melody represent The Penguin, while Catwoman has scratchy string *glissandi* and a full string melody. My rudimentary descriptions of the respective musical themes ('scratchy' like a cat, 'plodding' like a penguin) bear out the use of musical clichés. Elfman confirms this: 'whenever he walked on the stage, I saw the Penguin as an opera singer who was about to deliver an aria. I gave his melodies a grand, overblown quality.'[19] All three *Leitmotifs* appear in quick succession when Batman accosts The Penguin 'surveying the riot scene', which intercuts with Catwoman's acquisition of a whip in a department store. Here the music moves from one character theme to the next, subordinating itself to the film's action. Classical Hollywood composer Max Steiner said of his score for *The Informer* (1935): 'A blind man could have sat in a theatre and known when Gypo was on the screen.'[20] Steiner means that whenever the film's protagonist appeared, he was doubled by the appearance of his own *Leitmotif*, much like sections of *Batman Returns*. Elfman's orchestral score is, however, paradoxical in that it follows very precisely the modes of classical scores, using thematic techniques to build a wall-to-wall fabric in the same way that Steiner and Erich Wolfgang Korngold constructed their scores in the 1930s and 1940s. It is a paradox in that it copies explicitly the musical techniques of classical cinema, yet the effect is overblown and parodic. On the one hand this is due to Elfman's distension of classical principles, but on the other it should be accounted for by changes in the ways that we understand film music. For example, in my experience audiences now think *Now, Voyager*'s (1942) music and romance crass, as the codings that applied in the 1940s have shifted.[21]

How far can post-classical film music revive the musical modes of the studio system, where the industrial base is no longer in place? The *Batman* scores seem quite literally to be 'speaking in a dead language' to use Fredric Jameson's phrase.[22] Arguably the language of classical film scores was already a dated if not outmoded musical language in its studio system heyday, since nineteenth-century concert hall music provided the musical language of classical cinema. The Batman scores do not fully comply with Jameson's description of pastiche, which he distinguishes from parody. While parody uses and exaggerates language with an ulterior (often comic) motive, pastiche involves the neutral re-use of an antiquated or obsolete language.[23] Rather the *Batman* scores contain a degree of parody corresponding with the generally hyperbolic and self-conscious character of the films themselves. They take the techniques of the classical film score and elevate them to the level of cliché. The music is melodramatic, lacks subtlety and foregrounds clichés with which the audience is familiar, or rather over-familiar.

We could see the score's 'revivalism' in terms of the art music (and art history) concept of the neoclassical, where composers 'revived the balanced forms and clearly perceptible thematic processes of earlier styles . . . [while] the prefix of "neo-" often carries the implication of parody, or distortion, of truly Classical traits'.[24] The *Batman Returns* score is certainly excessive in comparison with the scores in classical cinema, despite its obvious referencing of that style. It uses the principles and form, the surface of studio era scores, yet these appear distorted by the music's distinctive character and its conspicuousness in the film. Elfman verifies this process: 'Though I try to reflect the spirit of Korngold and Rozsa when I write traditionally, the music still goes through some funny circus mirrors in my head. So it comes out far more twisted than those great old scores.'[25]

John Williams' film music is also an essential reference point (in fact the *Batman* music bears a passing resemblance to Williams' music for Brian De Palma's *The Fury* (1978)), yet Elfman's music is much more arch and based more upon exaggerating the tenets of musical style in classical cinema. However, both composers could to some degree be dubbed neoclassical in that they value the classical and use it as a model while also differentiating their music from it. The architectural resonance of the term neoclassical ties the music of the Batman films with the startling set designs of Anton Furst (*Batman*) and Bo Welch (*Batman Returns*). Both music and set design situate the film in what seems to be an alternative present, one projected to now from a 1940s past. This resonates with Jameson's description of earlier representations of the future having 'turned out to have been merely the future of one moment of our past'.[26] Elfman's music then, seems to be a future version of the Classical Hollywood film score, but one that has followed a different and more direct line of development, although perhaps not as direct as John Williams' music. While both composers' music could be characterized as neoclassical, John Williams' work is best described as a pastiche of classical film scoring, and Danny Elfman's music for the Batman films as a parody of the film music of the past.

It is striking that Thomas Schatz identifies *Jaws* (1975), the film that established John Williams as one of Hollywood's pre-eminent composers, as the film that heralded the New Hollywood.[27] While *Jaws* has a prominent musical score, the music in classical films more directly inspired Williams' music for *Star Wars*. Kalinak writes that 'Through Williams' example, the epic sound established in the thirties once again became a viable choice for composers in contemporary Hollywood.'[28] Williams' music for *Superman* (1978) and *Raiders of the Lost Ark* (1981) are characteristic of this style, as is Alan Silvestri's for *Back to the Future* (1985). The epic sound and style of the studio era classical score is clearly evident in *Batman Returns*. Elfman is plain about his admiration for the scores of classical cinema, particularly Hugo Friedhofer's score for *The Best Years of Our Lives* (1946), and decries modern film music. He said: 'To me, contemporary film scoring doesn't enhance the action, all it does is provide pretty wallpaper. Old-fashioned film scores were much more dynamic.'[29] Elfman's music is certainly dynamic, but while it exhibits massive variation in texture as well as temperament, much of the rise and fall of the music's intensity is dictated solely by the film's visual track.

In *Batman Returns*, the music is tailored directly to the film's momentary dynamics. At times it even 'mickeymouses' – mimics screen action – yet it is not pleonastic, it is a central component of the film's identity and of its narration. The music sounds like an overblown, impossibly large and prestigious classical symphonic score. It sounds rather like a spoof, a distortion of studio era film music, but this is due to the use of culturally coded (or, more precisely, overcoded) instrumental timbres and styles, like the use of deep Gothic brass, chiming celesta and *grand Guignol* organ. These are musical clichés, and Elfman's awareness of this means that it is foregrounded as an effect. This procedure is far more pronounced than in *Batman*, forcing the music explicitly into the realms of parody. The sheer volume of music, added to the world that the film creates, is reminiscent of the stylized world of the film musical, such as *The Pirate* (1948) and *Seven Brides for Seven Brothers* (1954), where design and music coalesce into a world of dazzling visuals and explosive musical sound. This style also relates to cartoons and, like cartoons, *Batman Returns* constructs its own world rather than directly copying our own, while the preponderance of 'mickeymousing' (which was named after cartoon music) can be accounted for with reference to the Batman films' cartoon qualities, inherited from their origin in comics. Elfman supplied the theme for the television cartoon series *The Simpsons*, and there is a correlation between his style and the dramatic and quick musical changes, quotation and parody established by cartoon composers such as Carl Stalling and Dick Bradley.

Elfman is highly conscious of his music being something more than simply a silence-filler: 'I would love some day to have people hear the two *Batman* scores while looking at the image, but without the sound effects.'[30] The relationship of music to image in *Batman Returns* often resembles that of a ballet, in the way that the continuity of the music interacts with, but is not necessarily subordinated to other elements. Film composer Dimitri Tiomkin wrote: 'There is a much closer affinity between ballet and movies than casual thought suggests. . . . Sometimes I think a good picture is really just a ballet with dialogue.'[31] This perspective, also verified by sound designer Walter Murch,[32] is at times explicitly borne out by *Batman Returns*. Its opening gives Elfman a showcase for his music, with the first five minutes of the film containing just two words of dialogue, thus allowing the music a major role in the articulation of action. The opening of the film resembles silent cinema music in that it is continuous and proceeds without the inconveniences of the spoken word or excessive sound effects. The music replaces both, asserting itself as a major component of the film and retaining its own internal logic despite its close marriage with the image and storytelling processes.

Batman Returns starts with a slow version of the *Batman* melody as snow falls over the Warner Bros. logo. As this changes to an urban exterior scene, a Gothic organ presents the short four-note musical figure associated with the Penguin throughout the film. The camera cranes upwards and across to a large Gothic house that has a light and shape at the window in a visual *hommage* to *Citizen Kane* (1941). Cut to the interior of the house and a birth offscreen. Next a caged infant attacks a cat as its parents look on, and the music here features the celesta and plays a short ballet-styled piece to counterpoint the comic violence. The next cut moves back outside, following the parents pushing their cage-like baby carriage through a snowy park, and culminating in them throwing it into the river. Here the music is a corruption of clichéd Christmas music featuring sleigh bells and a wordless choir singing Disney-style. Elfman's interim project, *Edward Scissorhands* (1990), was undoubtedly influential, with *Batman Returns* using beautiful and overwrought fantasy-invoking choirs more than *Batman*. This walk to doom features the first appearance of the full melody associated with the Penguin, anticipating the child's rebirth. Upon the baby carriage's impact in the water and disappearance down a drain, the music punctuates the seeming finality of the act with tubular bell toll. The camera then closely follows the baby carriage down the river, while the music starts a solid 4/4 rhythm and begins tentatively to offer excerpts from the *Batman* theme. Upon the appearance of the main title (with bats flying through it) the music reaches a climactic chord and then proceeds with the full *Batman* theme that it has been withholding from the audience. The thumping beat persists along with an arrangement of the *Batman* theme that has changed little since the first film, as the camera follows the baby carriage floating along the sewer finally to come to rest inside the Penguin house at the zoo. It is a highly melodramatic opening to a film, with massively telescoped action in temporal terms. This sequence is a rebirth sequence, the Penguin going from human birth to symbolic rebirth through the sewer into the zoo. Radical changes in the character of the music mark each step of the way. It involves direct mimicking of action ('mickeymousing'), articulates the changes in the image track, and provides narrative information (themes for Batman and the Penguin, the Christmas setting, the film's mixture of moral darkness and quirky humour). *Batman Returns*' opening sequence provides remarkable scope for Elfman's music, indeed an opportunity rarely available for composers in contemporary cinema.

In summary, the first two Batman films demonstrate two strata of contemporary Hollywood's musical strategies. *Batman* exhibits a cohabitation of orchestral score and tied-in pop songs, while *Batman Returns* uses only one tied-in song and has a large-scale score inspired more directly by the music of classical cinema. They both use classically inspired forms recast by more recent procedures.

The fragmenting of the Hollywood studio system had a significant effect upon the production of music for films, and there have also been important changes in film music due to cultural developments outside the cinema. With film production becoming a component of multimedia industries, films themselves have increasingly become vehicles for tied-in pop music, as can be verified by any visit to a CD shop. Musical tie-ins were important for film production during the studio era and they directly affected film form: they spawned the musical film. With the recession of the musical genre, this impetus has moved into dramatic films, as witnessed by the use of Prince in *Batman*.

Yet, tie-ins can equally include the film's orchestral score as well as songs. The mere existence of two soundtrack LPs suggests that music has a more important position in films than it had in the past. It is not unreasonable to suggest that the dual function of music – as both film element and object in its own right – has had an effect upon the character of the music itself. Music's status in films has become elevated[33] and this has removed the orchestral music from the alleged position of 'unobtrusiveness' which it occupied in classical cinema and into a more conspicuous position.

Although it initially seems to resemble the film music of the 1930s and 1940s, the orchestral music in the two films signifies in a fundamentally *different* way from classical film scores. Both of the films are premised upon the existence of a sophisticated cultural literacy among the audience. This assumes that the unprecedented access to images and narratives has supplied a knowledge of the Batman figure, Gothic imagery, and so forth, largely made available through contemporary audio-visual culture's principle of recycling. The music works in exactly the same way, relying on the audience's musical literacy for its significa- tion. Particularly in *Batman Returns*, the music goes beyond the generic music and forms used in classical cinema. It works through the use of archetypal sounds and musical styles, burlesquing certain musical forms under the umbrella of its parody of the classical film score.

The orchestral music in the *Batman* films matches the mixed construction of period in the films, blending both the historical (1940s design, the classical score) with parodic and contemporary aspects. Post-classical cinema seems to display a proliferation of music that is unified at the point of the film as both text *and* as commodity. Indeed, Tim Burton, director of the first two Batman films allegedly asked, 'Is there a movie here, or just something that goes along with the merchan- dising?'[34] Yet *Batman* and *Batman Returns* can hardly be accused of being fully determined by the requirements of tie-ins. The music in the films is testament not only to the pressure to use marketable pop music in films, but also to the ongoing significance of several aesthetic traditions and strategies which incorporate such music in a variety of ways.

Notes

1 *Variety*, All-time Top Ten grossing films at North American Box Office, 20–26 Febru- ary 1995, A54.
2 Claudia Gorbman, *Unheard Melodies: Narrative Film Music* (London: BFI, 1987), p. 70; Kathryn Kalinak, *Settling the Score: Music and the Classical Hollywood Film* (Madison: University of Wisconsin Press, 1992), pp. xv–xvi.
3 Kalinak, *Settling the Score*, p. 189.
4 David Bordwell, Janet Staiger and Kristin Thompson, *The Classical Hollywood Cinema: Style and Mode of Production to 1960* (London: Routledge, 1985), p. 368.
5 Kalinak, *Settling the Score*, p. 187.
6 Rod Cooper, 'Beating the drum for the music makers' (Interview with Ron Goodwin), *Kinematograph Weekly*, vol. 634, no. 3279 (15 August 1970), p. 3.
7 William Darby and Jack Dubois, *American Film Music: Major Composers. Techniques, Trends, 1915–90* (Washington, DC: MacFarland, 1982), p. 486.
8 R. Serge Denisoff and George Plasketes, 'Synergy in 1980s film and music: formula for success or industry mythology?' in *Film History*, vol. 4 (1990), p. 257.
9 Thomas Schatz, 'The New Hollywood', in Jim Collins, Hilary Radner and Ava Preacher Collins (eds), *Film Theory Goes to the Movies* (London: Routledge, 1993), p. 32.
10 R. Serge Denisoff and William D. Romanowski, *Risky Business: Rock in Film* (London/ New Brunswick: Transaction, 1991), p. 694.

11 Jon Burlingame, 'Danny Elfman on the move', *Soundtrack!* (September 1990), p. 21; Daniel Schweiger, 'Danny Elfman returns' (interview with Danny Elfman), *Soundtrack!* (September 1992), p. 19.

12 Barry McIlheny, review of Elfman and Prince soundtrack LPs, *Empire* (1990), p. 108.

13 Denisoff and Romanowski, *Risky Business*, p. 697.

14 Kim Newman, review of *Batman* in *Monthly Film Bulletin*, no. 56 (668) (September 1989), p. 269.

15 Denisoff and Romanowski, *Risky Business*, p. 693.

16 Although Eliot Goldenthal praises Danny Elfman's music, he asserts that his music never looks back to it: Michael Singer, *Batman, and Robin: The Making of the Movie* (London: Hamlyn, 1997), p. 125.

17 Kalinak, *Settling the Score*, p. 187.

18 Daniel Schweiger, 'Danny Elfman returns', p. 19.

19 Ibid., p. 18.

20 Roy M. Prendergast, *A Neglected Art: Film Music* (New York: New York University Press, 1977), p. 42.

21 Just as the use of the sentimental Victorian violin tune *Hearts and Flowers* on a film soundtrack is now a joke about the hackneyed use of music in silent cinema.

22 Fredric Jameson, 'Postmodernism, or the cultural logic of late capitalism', *New Left Review*, no. 146 (July/August 1984), p. 65.

23 Ibid. The term comes from 'Pasticcio', which was used to describe operas that consisted of arias from disparate sources and 'faked' bridging parts.

24 Arnold Whitall, entry in Stanley Sadie (ed.), *The New Grove Dictionary of Music and Musicians*, vol. 2 (London: Macmillan, 1984), p. 104.

25 Daniel Schweiger, 'Danny Elfman returns', p. 17.

26 Fredric Jameson, 'Progress versus utopia, or, can we imagine the future?' in Brian Wallis (ed.), *Art After Modernism: Rethinkng Representation* (New York: New Museum of Contemporary Art, 1984), p. 244.

27 Schatz, 'The New Hollywood', p. 17.

28 Kalinak, *Settling the Score*, p. 189.

29 Didier Deutsch, Interview with Danny Elfman in *Soundtrack!* (December 1993), p. 9.

30 Ibid.

31 Dimitri Tiomkin, 'Composing for the films' in James Limbacher (ed.), *From Violins to Video* (Metuchen, NJ: Scarecrow, 1974), p. 58.

32 Frank Paine, 'Sound mixing and *Apocalypse Now*: an interview with Walter Murch', in Elisabeth Weis and John Belton (eds), *Film Sound: Theory and Practice* (New York: Columbia University Press, 1985), p. 356.

33 Gorbman, *Unheard Melodies*, p. 162; K. J. Donnelly, 'Altered status: a review of music in postmodern cinema and culture', in Steven Earnshaw (ed.), *Postmodern Surroundings* (Amsterdam: Rodopi, 1994), p. 50.

34 Daniel Schweiger, 'Danny Elfman returns', p. 19.

Chapter 10

A cry in the dark

The role of post-classical film sound

Gianluca Sergi

The word 'sound' has always had several positive meanings. Indeed, expressions such as *sound* thinking, a *sound* person, and *sound* judgements belong to our everyday vocabulary. However, all this stops when we reach the realm of Film Studies. Here, sound seems like an obstacle in the way of the essence of cinema: the image. This bias against sound, generated mainly by early film scholars, was partly supported by the limitations that characterized Hollywood film production and reception prior to the mid-1970s, as we shall see. However, since then, a series of technological developments and changes in production and reception have ensued, and these have modified the ways in which film sound has been constructed, and the relationship between sound and image, audience and film. It is this period, which we may define as the 'Dolby era', upon which I wish to focus here. In exploring its characteristics I shall follow two distinct 'tracks', an aesthetic one and an economic one. It is in the interaction between them that one can perhaps begin to identify the parameters of what might be called 'post-classical' film sound.

The soundtrack: a misleading notion?

Before launching into any discussion of the role – or roles – of film sound, we need to confront a major problem: the lack of a proper vocabulary with which to articulate the complexity of the subject. Although this is true of other areas of film (production design and art direction come to mind), this particular lack is an acute one. There are several reasons for it. Film sound shares the same physical medium as music, that is, sound waves, and this has often helped to reinforce the use of musical terms in discussions of sound. This is particularly evident in the insistent use of terms like pitch, tone and timbre. These terms are relevant but insufficient. They are simply not flexible enough to articulate the complexities of contemporary soundtracks (for example, musical vocabularies are concerned with sound *per se*, while film sound works in symbiosis with the image). This problem is intensified by the disparity in critical attention given to popular music as compared to the cinema. Whereas in the UK at least there are a number of TV shows which set out to discuss or to analyse films (such as *Film 98* and *Moviewatch*), equivalent programmes on pop music simply present the product or performer without ever discussing their qualities or the ways in which they work (consider, for example, *Top of the Pops* and *The Chart Show*). In short, we have an inadequate vocabulary which is in any case rarely used in popular critical contexts. Perhaps we should attempt to side-step some of these problems by turning our attention to the soundtrack itself.

Rather than being conceived as a complex combination of different elements, the term 'soundtrack' has come principally to signify the music track of a film, dialogue being confined to another – 'superior' – realm, that of the screenwriter. This is a rather convenient way of arranging perception and appreciation. First, by singling out specific portions of a soundtrack, critics can praise the contributions of individual practitioners rather than focus on the much more complicated issue of what actually becomes of these contributions once they are recorded, mixed and reproduced not as independent elements, but as elements in a complex structure. Second, this type of approach betrays a certain attitude towards the more apparently 'ordinary' elements of the soundtrack, its everyday sounds: noise and silence. Critics seem to find it easier – and worthier – to focus on the art of the spoken word or the composed note than on the unsettling noise or the 'empty' silence. Yet it is precisely the relationships between all four elements – effects, music, dialogue and silence – that require investigation, and that mark the nature of the soundtrack itself. A soundtrack is like a cake. Each ingredient has its own distinctive flavour and makes its own individual contribution. However, once blended together they cannot and should not be separated one from another. Their contribution to the final product can only be considered by referring to the other ingredients and to the cake itself as a whole.

Pre-Dolby sound

Although production during the classical period did not present sound personnel with insurmountable technical and creative barriers, reproduction did, and damagingly so. The poor conditions of sound reproduction present in the vast majority of cinemas was a key factor. Quite simply, most film theatres were incapable of coping with complex soundtracks, and often produced distracting echoes and unwanted reverberations. Loudspeakers were capable of reproducing only a very limited frequency range (they were designed principally to reproduce audible speech), and powerful sounds were in general not a feasible option because of the risks (or certainties) of sound distortion. Moreover, the (mal)practice of exhibitors in 'pumping up the volume' in order that action films had maximum impact on spectators often had the effect of wiping out the more subtle dimensions of sound design. Given these limitations, filmmakers could only feasibly employ a limited number of tracks if they were to avoid a cacophony of sounds, and tended to give aural priority to music and the human voice.

This is not to underestimate the aesthetic efforts or the technological advances of the 1950s and 1960s. The differences between then and now lie largely in the combination of standards of production and reproduction. Where with a film like *Spartacus* (1960), full stereo sound reproduction was possible with only a handful of (extremely expensive) 70mm roadshow prints in a handful of first-run cinemas, the soundtrack on *Star Wars* (1977) could be reproduced to high standards in most theatres thanks to the cheaper and more flexible Dolby system. Thus where the costs of quality sound reproduction in the 1950s and 1960s and the concomitant lack of good sound facilities in most theatres tended to inhibit the development of a more positive approach to film sound, the availability of Dolby has inspired confidence, and a concomitant willingness to experiment.

In the pre-Dolby era of the 1950s and 1960s, movie soundtracks were produced in-house by the studios, limiting external influences and generating a reliance on standard practices, established techniques and old sound libraries. In order to gauge the magnitude of the problem, it is worth bearing in mind that this was a period of profound changes and developments in aural terms. The 1960s witnessed the sweeping away of established listening patterns and the introduction of increasingly sophisticated experiments in sound recording and sound reproduction in the music industry as well as a much more 'aggressive' type of sound. Rock concerts in particular, with their blend of powerfully amplified music and enhanced 'sensual' experience (literally, sex, drugs and rock 'n' roll) introduced a new type of leisure activity engaging the 'participant' (no longer merely a 'spectator') on more than just an intellectual level. In addition, squeaky transistor radios were being rapidly replaced by affordable hi-fi systems capable of reproducing good quality sound. Consumers, spectators and participants could now enjoy better quality sound at concerts and in their homes than in the vast majority of cinemas. Films and film theatres desperately lagged behind and seemed unable to respond to such changes.

The unexplored potential of the medium was embodied in the fact that sound, a three-dimensional phenomenon, the *only* three-dimensional phenomenon in the movies, was being deployed in a one-dimensional manner, and not merely in the sense that sound reproduction was generally monophonic. To put it simply, the agenda informing the use of sound was that it should fulfil one principal requirement: to match the image without attracting unwanted attention. Even when we look at one of the most obvious areas for potential aural innovation, the musical, we find further evidence of a conservative use of sound. Hugely successful films like *Gigi* (1958) and *My Fair Lady* (1964) never really threatened the established power of the characters to open their mouths and summon up rivers of melody. Contrast this with later films like *American Graffiti* (1973) and *Saturday Night Fever* (1977), where music and its sources (a pirate radio station in *Graffiti*, a discotheque in *Fever*) must be actively sought for, and where the sounds of car engines and of New York slang are given such status that they are able to interrupt the sound of the music.

However, as these examples demonstrate, the early 1970s saw some filmmakers trying to use sound in new and interesting ways despite the continuing limitations of technology and studio practice. Films like *The Conversation* (1974), *Jaws* (1975), and *Taxi Driver* (1976) all evinced a willingness to experiment with the soundtrack by choosing to foreground sound (as well as music) rather than using it solely as a backdrop to the image. Moreover, this time a willingness to experiment (especially on the part of the 'movie brats'[1]) intersected with the availability of a new and important technology.

Listen, here comes Dolby

The development of sound technology from the mid-1970s on has been extensively charted in the last few years, thanks to an increasing interest in the subject. (See the section on sound in Michael Allen's Chapter 7 in this volume.) Thus it will be sufficient here to highlight the three major changes central to an understanding of what follows. First, the mid-1970s saw the introduction of the *Dolby Stereo Sound System*. This was the first economically viable stereophonic system. Employing multi-channel technology, Dolby was able to reproduce a new range of sounds (thanks to its wider frequency range) and, most importantly, it provided improved conditions of reproduction in most theatres. Second, at the beginning of the 1980s, George Lucas and his collaborators developed the *THX Sound System*. Arguably the most ambitious sound project in film history, the THX system enables conditions of reproduction in cinemas equal to those of professional mixing stages. In principle at least, it therefore enables the standardization of sound reproduction as intended by those at the point of production.[2] Last, but by no means least, the late 1980s have seen the introduction of digital sound in three different systems: *DTS*, *Dolby Digital SR-D* and *SDDS*. This is the present and future of film sound, extending frequency range to maximum capacity and providing discrete multi-channel recording and reproduction.[3] It allows soundtracks to reproduce extremely powerful and detailed sound at virtually zero distortion, and has generated a number of dramatic innovations. The result of these changes is that the situation now with regard to sound production and reproduction is almost the reverse of the situation prior to the advent of Dolby. I should like now to explore some of these changes in more detail.

Multi-layered sound

The first major development was the introduction of multi-channel recording technology. The use of an analogy may help us to understand the relevance of this change. Let us imagine that a film theatre has only one access door and that it is designed to admit twenty people at any one time. Should more than twenty people be admitted, the result would be chaos. This is akin to the situation prior to the mid-1970s, with the dominance of monophonic sound and hence one channel or 'door'. The introduction of stereophonic technology meant the opening of new doors to the same auditorium, and helped remove the old limitations as to the number of tracks those who made films could employ. The result was the use of dozens of different tracks, which meant that filmmakers had to deal with an increasingly complex, and increasingly multi-layered, 'architecture of sound', an architecture requiring careful planning, coordination and control.

Multi-directional sound

One of the consequences of this development was that multi-channel sound was projected into the auditorium from a number of different directions. Pre-Dolby 'classical' sound was overwhelmingly one-directional, and originated for the most part from the centre of the screen.[4] This limited the potential of the soundtrack to unsettle the audience's reception of a film. Spectators knew exactly what to expect and where to expect it from. Contemporary Hollywood film sound is multi-directional. Thus filmmakers now are able to challenge audience assumptions as to the range, power and source of sound and sounds. Theorists like Mary Ann Doane have argued that the new sound technology has increased the capacity of the apparatus to 'hide' itself.[5] I would argue on the contrary that the introduction of multi-directional sound has displaced the reproduction of sound, at least physically, from the screen to any point in the auditorium, hence alerting the audience to its place in a constructed environment. In other words, if it is conventional to accept that a spaceship can move towards us frontally, on the screen, it takes a bigger leap of the imagination to accept that it is flying over our heads and into the auditorium from a point in the cinema lobby.[6]

Larger sound budgets and increasing numbers of sound personnel

The more complex soundtracks became, the higher the budgets devoted to sound could be. Aside from the cost implications, this meant that more people could be employed to work on the construction of a soundtrack. Gone is the solitary credit attributing sound to one individual department head. In has come the listing on credits of more and more people (over fifty in the case of *The Fugitive* (1993) and *Speed* (1994)), and more and more specialist functions: sound designer, supervising sound editor, sound editor, foley artist, sound recordist, sound mixer, and so on. Moreover, sound personnel are now often involved not just in production and post-production, but in pre-production and initial planning and design as well. Crucially, the waves of sound personnel who worked in Hollywood from the 1970s on came from a variety of sonic backgrounds. They brought an awareness of sound and the possibilities of sound, bridging established patterns and contemporary innovations in both technological and cultural terms, and thus helped to spur and to enable the technological and aesthetic innovations of the post-Dolby era.

The creation of new sounds

The combination of new technologies, larger budgets and new personnel had an important effect: the creation of 'new' sounds. In an era when soundtracks were mostly created in sound studios, this was an important and significant step. Indeed, it signalled a definitive break with the sound of the past. New sounds meant new styles, and in retrospect we can pinpoint two major styles or schools: the precise and detailed Bay Area sound, influenced by the electronic and esoteric stylizations of the 1960s, and the more gutsy New York Metropolitan sound, influenced, among other things, by rap and other forms of black music. Instances of the former can be found in Spielberg's films, from the sound of Indiana Jones' cracking whip in *Raiders of the Lost Ark* (1981) to the creaking of Schindler's jacket in *Schindler's List* (1993). Examples of the latter can be found in Scorsese's films, from Jake La Motta's punches in *Raging Bull* (1980) to the editing of the fast-talking dialogue and menacing sounds in *Goodfellas* (1990).[7]

Improved sound reproduction in cinemas

Following closely on developments such as these, the quality of sound reproduction in auditoria began to improve. Sound engineers designed new auditoria and helped adapt existing ones. Sound-absorbent material was used to minimize unwanted echo and reverberation; sound insulation was improved to muffle the noise produced by projectors and air conditioning equipment, and to prevent the sounds from adjacent auditoria interfering with one another. In this context, it is significant that Lucasfilm's THX Division developed not just a sound reproduction system, but a set of criteria for sound reproduction as a whole. These developments signalled a definitive shift away from the old sound hierarchies in which speech and music were accorded unconditional priority. New auditoria were built with all four elements of the soundtrack in mind.

New sounds, new pleasures: physical sound and heightened realism

During the course of the 1970s, Hollywood's use and conception of sound underwent a fundamental change. The possibilities of multi-channel technology, a wider frequency range and improved conditions of reproduction encouraged filmmakers to feel more confident about sound, and led them to rely more and more on the soundtrack. As a result, contemporary filmmakers have shown an increasing awareness of the 'physical', three-dimensional qualities of sound, and audiences are encouraged not just to listen to sounds but to 'feel' them – film-goers experience sound more sensually than ever before. The extensive use of deep bass sounds, a legacy of the new 'aggressive' sounds associated first with rock then with rap, is a mark of this new physical style. However, it is not just a matter of matching 'big' sounds with 'big' images; it is rather a matter of achieving a startling, communicative effect. Thus in the opening sequence of *Terminator 2: Judgment Day* (1991), Linda Hamilton's voice-over guides us through the devastating effects of the machines' revolt against the humans. The camera picks out a human skull. As it lingers for a moment, all sounds fade. Then as the voice-over ends, a mechanical foot appears and crushes the skull. The deep bass sound employed at this moment (a sound hardly close to the 'real' sound an action like this would produce) is used both to startle the audience and to convey the mightiness of the struggle awaiting the humans in their fight against the machines. In such cases, to use an expression dear to sound designers, the sound 'breaks through the screen' and takes centre stage.

Another development, and a further departure from classical sound, is the use of what might perhaps best be defined as 'heightened realism'. By highlighting particular sounds and softening others, filmmakers can enhance sound detail in such a way as to enable audiences to hear the unhearable. An example can be found in the opening sequence of *Indiana Jones and the Temple of Doom* (1984). Three villains try to outwit Dr Jones by tricking him into drinking a glass of poisoned champagne. They reveal the nature of what it is he has drunk by showing him a bottle containing the antidote. In the struggle that ensues, the bottle is flung across the dance floor amid scenes of chaos and confusion. Yet the sound of a bottle rolling on the floor is given prominence over all the other sounds we can hear.

Thus contemporary film sound, unlike the sound in classical Hollywood cinema, is significant not just in terms of its literal meaning, but also in terms of its weight, its power, its detail and its direction. Moreover, the complexities of the contemporary soundtrack alter the relationship between sound and image. No longer content to function merely as an aural backdrop, the soundtrack takes its place as a site of interest and experiment in its own right.

The economic dimension

The need to reconsider the role and the relevance of film sound in contemporary Hollywood is as much a function of economics as it is of aesthetics. This is not just a matter of production costs. Other economic factors are at stake as well.

Since the 1920s in particular, sound, and in particular musical sound, has been of great importance in the marketing of films, and as an ancillary commodity or off-shoot of the industry and its product. In the form of sheet music, of stars like Eddie Cantor and Al Jolson, and in the form of radio programmes and variety shows, the cinema, music and broadcasting industries have often been interlinked through the medium of sound, and sound itself used as a vehicle for attracting audiences to films. However, sound has never been such an important marketing force as it is today. Since the introduction of Dolby, the industry has enjoyed a slow but steady revival in terms of attendances, revenues and profits. Indeed, it is worth noting that the twenty biggest money spinners in Hollywood's history have been produced in the era of Dolby sound. Emphasis has often been placed on the visual aspects and attractions of these films. But it is at least worth noting the contribution that sound has made as well, as it is a vital element in the visceral aesthetic of the contemporary blockbuster.

One of the major factors here is the extent to which audiences were now able to enjoy sound of a quality that matched, and often surpassed, that of the sound they could enjoy at home. Producers were quick to exploit the qualities of sur-round sound, for instance, not just in the films, but also in trailers and advertise-ments.[8] Film exhibitors rose to the occasion and started to advertise their theatres as being equipped with 'true stereo sound', and today all major chains make a point of advertising those theatres equipped with THX or the latest digital system. In the last few years, the ever-expanding home video industry has elected and advertised surround sound as one of its principal commercial attractions. Mean-while the advent of a wealth of consumer magazines run by a generation of sound-sensitive media journalists has been decisive in spreading knowledge about – and an appetite for – high quality sound both at home and in the cinema.

All these developments have accompanied and been accompanied by con-glomeration, particularly in the multimedia field. Large media conglomerates have invested heavily in the sites of interaction between the film and music industries – it is no accident that as I write, the three biggest selling singles in the UK in the 1990s (after 'Candle in the Wind 97') were all showcased by films, and can all be found on their soundtracks.[9] Almost inevitably, interest – financial as well as intellectual – in the new sound technologies has spilled over into the computer industry, with Dolby developing Dolby Net, a surround sound system for the Internet.

In addition, one of the bloodiest corporate battles of the last few years has been waged over digital sound. All the major companies are involved in this battle, each having developed and marketed their own particular system. MCA–Matsushita (now MCA–Seargrave) has developed DTS,[10] CBS–Sony has responded with SDDS,[11] and Dolby has collaborated with Time Warner to produce Dolby Digital SR-D.[12] What has been impressive has been the pace of acquisition of what is still a relatively new technology. When Time Warner joined forces with Dolby to launch the Dolby Stereo Digital system in 1992, there were only a handful of theatres equipped to show *Batman Returns* (1992) in digital sound. Two years later, over 2,000 systems had been installed. Even more importantly, the availability of hardware has been increasingly matched by the availability of software. Most of the majors have now pledged to produce all their new features in one or more of the digital formats, and digital is now also available in the lucrative home video and TV markets.

Agendas for further research

Vast areas still remain to be researched. The relationship between sound and censorship is one. At present, there would appear to exist an unwritten rule that 'what you can't see can't hurt you', a rule which allows spectators to hear – but not necessarily see – crushing bones, searing flesh and record-breaking sexual activity. A further issue is the issue of pleasure. A great deal of attention has been paid to visual pleasure, but little to its aural equivalent. It is significant that we tend to think of production values in visual terms, not in aural ones, despite the fact that the sound of a screeching car tyre in an elaborate chase sequence can be just as important as the close-up of the tyre itself. Another issue worth exploring is the issue of genre. Genres have frequently been defined in visual terms – in terms, for instance, of iconography – but rarely in terms of what they sound like (the musical is the obvious exception). Yet in films like *Batman Returns* we are often confronted with images that are drawn from fantasy and sci-fi, juxtaposed with sounds reminiscent of those from a 1930s gangster film.

This is a long list of topics. What is at stake is the theoretical framework that we bring to the analysis of films. The place of sound in this framework has for too long been left in the dark.

Notes

1 See Lynda Myles and Michael Pye, *The Movie Brats, How the Film Generation took over Hollywood* (London: Faber, 1979).
2 However, as Stephen Handzo has pointed out, the concept of 'correct' sound reproduction is by no means straightforward. See 'The sound of sound', *Cineaste*, vol. 21, nos. 1–2 (1995), p. 68.
3 Six channels for DTS and Dolby SR-D, and up to eight for SDDS.

4 The only exception, as we have seen, being a handful of extremely expensive 70mm roadshow prints, prints whose soundtracks mostly – and conventionally – prioritized music and speech.

5 Mary Ann Doane, 'Ideology and the practice of sound editing and mixing', in Theresa de Lauretis and Stephen Heath (eds), *The Cinematic Apparatus* (New York: St Martin's Press, 1989), pp. 47–56.

6 One of the best-known examples of directional sound occurs in the opening sequence of *Star Wars*, in which a rebel fighter and an imperial destroyer are first 'heard' at the back of the auditorium before flying over the heads of the spectators and eventually appearing on the screen.

7 Although the directors mentioned may call the shots, it is important to remember that behind these examples are the names of some of the best sound designers in Hollywood: Ben Burtt, Skip Lievsay, Frank Warner, Walter Murch and a number of others.

8 Some of these, specifically filmed for trailer presentation, employed sound in a very aggressive fashion to win viewers' attention. The sound of the earth-rumbling thumps of a terminator or of the glass-shattering force of a twister will command the attention of even the most dedicated popcorn-munching audience.

9 These are: Bryan Adams' 'Everything I Do, I Do It for You', from *Robin Hood: Prince of Thieves* (1991), Whitney Houston's 'I Will Always Love You', from *The Bodyguard* (1992), and Wet, Wet, Wet's 'Love Is All Around', from *Four Weddings and a Funeral* (1994).

10 DTS stands for Digital Theatre Sound, a sound-on-disc system capable of providing six discrete channels. It was launched with *Jurassic Park* in 1993.

11 SDDS stands for Sony Dynamic Digital Sound, a sound-on-film system capable of providing up to eight discrete channels. It was launched with *The Last Action Hero* in 1993.

12 SR-D stands for Spectral Recording-Digital, a sound-on-film system capable of providing six discrete channels. It was launched with *Batman Returns* in 1992.

Chapter 11

A close encounter with *Raiders of the Lost Ark*

Notes on narrative aspects of the New Hollywood blockbuster

Warren Buckland

Discussing the rise of the blockbuster in the New Hollywood, Thomas Schatz writes that the

> mainstream hits are where stars, genres, and cinematic innovations invariably are established, where the 'grammar' of cinema is most likely to be refined, and where the essential qualities of the medium – its popular and commercial character – are most evident. These blockbuster hits are, for better or worse, what the New Hollywood is about, and thus are the necessary starting point for any analysis of contemporary American cinema.[1]

Because popularity is commonly equated with escapism and triviality, blockbusters have either been shunned or dismissed by most academic film scholars as calculated exercises in profit-making. This is in contrast to the work of an auteur like Orson Welles, who receives an enormous amount of critical attention but whose films were commercial failures. However, those who dismiss blockbusters as exercises in profit-making fail to understand the New Hollywood's mode of production. Rather than the assembly-line production of the Old Hollywood, where stars, directors and technicians were tied to long-term contracts, in the New Hollywood talent is hired on a film-by-film basis. As a result, power has shifted to the deal-makers (the agents), who can attract and package talent around individual projects and films. The shift from assembly-line production to deal-making has had another effect: more and more money goes into the making of fewer and fewer films. Consequently, the films that are produced need to make enormous amounts of money in order to recoup their costs.[2]

So, expensive blockbusters are central to the output of modern Hollywood. But what, aside from costs, are their dominant characteristics? How are they able to attract, engage and entertain millions of people? One dominant characteristic of the blockbuster is its mode of address. As Timothy Corrigan has pointed out, the blockbuster, in contrast to the small-scale independent feature, is aimed at an undifferentiated popular audience rather than at any particular sector of the view-ing population.[3] It addresses this audience by means of a mix of genres – often combining action-adventure with comedy, drama, romance, science-fiction and the like – and by means of a remodelling of character and plot. Many critics argue that, in comparison with Old Hollywood, New Hollywood films are not struc-tured in terms of a psychologically motivated cause–effect narrative logic, but in terms of loosely linked, self-sustaining action sequences often built around spec-tacular stunts, stars and special effects. Complex character traits and character development, they argue, have been replaced by one-dimensional stereotypes, and plot-lines are now devised almost solely to link one action sequence to the next. Narrative complexity is sacrificed on the altar of spectacle. Narration is geared solely to the effective presentation of expensive effects.

In my view, this argument has been overstated, and my aim in the rest of this chapter is to reverse its emphasis by focusing on aspects of narrative and narration in a seminal early modern blockbuster, Steven Spielberg's *Raiders of the Lost Ark* (1981). As we shall see, even where the argument carries some weight, as in its description of the blockbuster in terms of a chain of relatively self-contained sequences and scenes, it is unable – or unwilling – to recognize the aesthetic possibilities of what is in effect an episodic narrative form, just as it is unable or unwilling to recognize its provenance in Old – or classical – Hollywood forms. Faced with what is in my view an unhelpful and hostile evaluative stance, it is best in my opinion to suspend aesthetic judgements, and to adopt an analytical and descriptive approach to these films. The foundations of such an approach are to be found in what David Bordwell and Kristin Thompson have dubbed 'historical poetics'. Historical poetics concerns itself with the analysis of those principles, norms and conventions dominant at any one point in time and their role in the construction of individual works. More formally, following the terminology of R. S. Crane, Bordwell has divided historical poetics into the following three domains:[4]

1   precompositional factors (sources, influences, received forms);
2   compositional factors (normalized principles of composition);
3   postcompositional factors (the varying responses to a film, including its evalua-tion and theorization).

For my purposes here, I shall only concentrate on the second domain. 'At this moment', writes Bordwell, 'I believe that the most promising avenues for poetic analysis are those opening onto compositional processes of form and style.'[5] The poetician begins from all the standardized compositional norms available at a given historical moment and analyses the actual choices made by filmmakers, through a close analysis of individual films. It thus helps to pinpoint the features and systems unique to a work, as well as those it shares with others.[6]

In an article in *Approaches to Popular Film*, Henry Jenkins makes the case for this approach and suggests its relevance to New Hollywood films. He points out that historical poetics is one of the few approaches to take 'popular cinema seriously *as an aesthetic practice*', and he goes on to suggest that 'To map the aesthetics of an otherwise neglected form . . . constitutes a political act, helping to question the naturalness of the aesthetic norms separating high and low culture (and with them, the social distinctions they express and repress)'.[7] Jenkins then notes that the deal-making system in which contemporary directors work, being contracted on a film-by-film basis, places emphasis on the director's particular treatment of theme and style – that is, on the poetics of their work:

> By treating film-makers as independent contractors, the new production system places particular emphasis on the development of an idiosyncratic style which helps to increase the market value of individual directors rather than treating them as interchangeable parts. Directors such as Steven Spielberg, David Lynch, Brian DePalma and David Cronenberg develop distinctive ways of structuring narratives, moving their camera, or cutting scenes which become known to film-goers and studio executives alike.[8]

New Hollywood directors develop their own recognizable style because it increases their market value. So an emphasis on the poetics of the New Hollywood does not present itself as just one approach among many, but sets itself up at the approach that can explain the specificity of the New Hollywood film.[9]

In his essay 'History and timelessness in films and theory' Dudley Andrew attempts to explain the widespread appeal of classic films, such as Marcel Carné's *Les Enfants du Paradis* (1945). He suggests it is hardly surprising that film scholars who attempt to explain the power of movies in general should concentrate on exemplary films, simply because the widespread appeal of such films illustrates what cinema in general is capable of achieving. Andrew begins by identifying the primary 'objects' of film theory: 'Both the immediate appeal of [a film] and the highly mediated systems that can be shown to determine it (structural, semiotic, psychoanalytic, etc.) are the direct objects of film theory.'[10] Here I wish to borrow Andrew's distinction between the immediate and the mediate to analyse the immediate, widespread appeal of Spielberg's films by studying the highly mediated systems that determine them. This links with historical poetics because 'poetics' analyses those basic and fundamental norms of composition that confer a sense of 'timelessness' on a classic film, while the historical can help us emphasize the 'timeliness' of a film, rather than simply its timelessness.

Andrew notes a number of reasons for the popularity of *Les Enfants du Paradis*: its articulation of the universal human need for stories of loss as manifest in melodrama, its explicit replaying of familiar, unavoidable and obsessive moral situations, and the spectator's primary identification with the narration as such and submission to the paternal authority of the storyteller.[11] But Andrew argues that it takes more than these timeless structures to explain the film's appeal and popularity – one must also consider what he calls its *inventiveness*, or response to its historical moment. Here, the film is seen, not merely as the manifestation of universal rules, but in terms of its individuality, including its response to its historical moment, in which style and composition respond to the historical questions posed in the culture in which the film is made. Andrew puts forward this notion of a film's inventiveness in opposition to essentialist and determinist theories of the cinema. Following the hermeneutic approach of Paul Ricoeur, Andrew looks at films as potential sources of new meanings rather than as mere vehicles of universal laws. Andrew writes that: 'Essentialism follows when theory aims to explain the power of cinema through such effectively timeless factors as technology, biology, psychology, logical structure, or language.'[12] By concentrating on the composition of single films, historical poetics can overcome this essentialism and go some way to explaining the popularity of individual films, particularly the blockbuster. It is in this spirit, and within this ambit of approaches and concerns, that the following notes on *Raiders* have been assembled.

Textual analysis with a vengeance

For directors of New Hollywood films, a variety of compositional norms exists for exploitation. These include: the selective quotation of Old Hollywood films, the visual rhetoric of comic books, the norms of television aesthetics, and the compositional norms of European art film and the avant garde. One aim of a historical poetics is to determine what norms dominate the composition of each particular film. In *Raiders of the Lost Ark*, one can find references to Old Hollywood films. Indeed, Omar Calibrese argues that 350 references to other films can be detected in *Raiders*.[13] As I point out below (see p. 171–2), *Raiders* is structured according to the serial format of the B-movie adventure stories, and we can also detect the influence of comic books, particularly in the storyboarded action sequences. Finally, elements of a television aesthetics are present (and it is important to remember that Spielberg worked in television from 1969–72).

Jerzy Toeplitz has argued that 'characteristically the directors who have come to film from television, regard montage as a much more important part of their skills than did the filmmakers of the 1930s and 1940s. . . . They seem closer to the tradition of the silent screen'.[14] Richard Maltby has suggested why editing and montage are fundamental to TV aesthetics.[15] He argues that, due to the small size of its screen and its lack of resolution, television has little use for complex, deep focus shots. Instead, it is dominated by close-ups (showing single objects in isolation), rapid cutting (since the close-up requires less time for its content to be exhausted), a highly mobile camera (for the same reason as rapid cutting), and a shallow, lateral space, partly created by the use of telephoto lenses.

For many critics, the consequence of television's aesthetics is that it foregrounds or overemphasizes action and divorces style and technique from narrative. Mark Crispin Miller has graphically illustrated the result of Hollywood's adoption of television aesthetics (as found in TV adverts and music videos in particular): 'Each shot [in contemporary Hollywood films] presents a content closed and unified, like a fist, and makes the point right in your face: big gun, big car, nice ass, full moon, a chase (great shoes!), big crash (blood, glass), a lobby (doorman), sarcasm, drinks, a tonguey, pugilistic kiss (nice sheets!), and so on.'[16] For Maltby, Miller and others, this aesthetic is created through an overemphasis on techniques such as saturated colours, strong backlighting, rapid editing or constant camera mobility, sound effects and special effects that directly assault the spectator's senses and nervous system. The result, according to these critics, is that style in the New Hollywood film becomes self-sufficient and autonomous, rather than being subordinated to a film's themes and narrative.

There are scenes in *Raiders* which would seem to support such an argument. The fight which ensues when Jones returns to Marion's bar provides an example of an action sequence that is structured according to television and comic book aesthetics.[17] The sequence lasts two minutes forty-four seconds, and consists of ninety shots. This makes for an average shot length of (or a cut every) 1.8 seconds. Moreover, one-third of the shots are close-ups (including medium close-ups). Although they don't appear to have been shot with a telephoto lens, many of the close-ups have a very simple, graphic composition and shallow space, since the characters are filmed against simple backgrounds such as walls. Moreover, there is no extensive use of camera movement, since the frenetic effect of the scene is created by the rapid cutting and by movement within the image. The overall effect of these stylistic choices is indeed to foreground the action and assault the senses and nervous system of the spectator.

But this is not, as it were, the end of the story as regards sequences such as these or the film as a whole. To begin with, it is worth noting that Spielberg himself has emphasized the importance of narrative, not least in terms of its commercial appeal. 'You need good story-telling to offset the amount of . . . spectacle the audiences demand before they'll leave their television sets. And I think people will leave their television sets for a good story before anything else. Before fire and skyscrapers and floods, plane crashes, laser fire and spaceships, they want good stories.'[18] In addition, Peter Biskind has argued that both Spielberg and Lucas initially set out to re-establish traditional – causal and linear – narrative values in the New Hollywood context in which they found themselves.

Biskind himself goes on to suggest that their attempts backfired, because they each tended to over-emphasize the plastic, formal and sensual qualities of sound and image. The 'attempt to restore traditional narration had an unintended effect – the creation of spectacle that annihilated story. The attempt to escape television by creating outsized spectacle backfired, and led to television's presentational aesthetic.'[19] Whatever the merits of Biskind's argument, it is clear that Spielberg was – and is – committed to narrative. It is also clear that *Raiders* itself tells a story, a story which is structured according to the principles of the serial format that operated in B-movie adventure films in the 1930s and 1940s – a style or mode of storytelling suppressed or dismissed as marginal in most accounts of 'classical' Hollywood narrative.[20] It can thus be divided into six distinct episodes, each of which is relatively self-contained, and each of which ends in a series of rapid dramatic actions and/or in an unresolved cliff-hanging sequence:

1   The first episode depicts Indiana Jones' (Harrison Ford) adventures in the South American jungle. He successfully retrieves a golden idol from a cave, only to have it taken away by Belloq (Paul Freeman). Belloq tries to kill Jones, but Jones escapes.

2   In the second episode we see the reverse side of Jones' character as he teaches a class of students. He is now presented as an eccentric professor. In a long expositional scene he explains the significance of the Ark of the Covenant to two government representatives. Jones is then asked to retrieve the ark before the Nazis get hold of it. This involves a detour to Nepal and a visit to Jones' former partner, Marion (Karen Allen), who possesses the headpiece to the staff of Ra that helps indicate where the ark is located. But the Nazis follow Jones to Nepal, burn down Marion's bar, and try to kill both Marion and Jones. Jones and Marion escape, and Marion decides to join Jones on his quest.

3   In Cairo, Jones and Marion are again pursued by the Nazis. Marion is kidnapped and appears to die in an explosion. Jones has the headpiece interpreted, and only just escapes being poisoned.

4   Jones locates the ark and discovers that Marion is alive but being held by Belloq. In an act of symbolic exchange, Belloq and the Nazis steal the ark from Jones, but in return give him Marion. Both Marion and Jones are then sealed inside a tomb.

5   Jones and Marion escape from their incarceration, blow up a plane, and retrieve the ark after a long struggle. Marion and Jones sail away with the ark, only to be stopped by a Nazi submarine. The Nazis take Marion and the ark, but Jones succeeds in escaping.

6   On a remote island, Belloq opens the ark to devastating consequences: all who witness its contents are killed. Only Jones and Marion, who close their

eyes, are spared. In an epilogue, the American government takes possession
of the ark, and Jones and Marion mark their status as a couple.

As is the case in most serial narratives, causal motivation appears at times to be
suspended: it is unclear, for instance, precisely how Jones escapes from the Nazi
submarine at the end of episode 5. However, a single plot-line linked to the search
for the ark of the covenant, and an antagonistic relationship between the hero,
Jones, and the villain, Belloq, link each of these sequences together. Moreover, in
contrast to the casual nature with which causal motivation is sometimes treated,
and as is common in Spielberg's films, an unseen or off-screen presence or agent is
used systematically to generate suspense and surprise at the level of each individual sequence. As these sequences accumulate, they generate an overarching
pattern that reaches its resolution in episode 6. The point to make here is that this
pattern transcends individual episodes, and is dependent for its very existence on
the presence of a feature-length story. It fits very well with Tom Gunning's
suggestion that we think of narrative as a 'process of integration' in which smaller
units, like episodes and scenes, are absorbed into, and generate, larger patterns of
precisely this kind.[21]

   The off-screen presence is an external norm to the extent that it dominates a
large number of contemporary films, and is consistently used to structure Spielberg's films. For example, in *Duel* (1971), *Jaws* (1975) and *Close Encounters of the
Third Kind* (1977), the off-screen presence remains off-screen or at least unseen
for most or all of the film. Similarly, in *Hook* (1991), during the kidnapping of
Peter's children from Wendy's house, Hook remains a menacing off-screen presence throughout the whole of the scene. In *Raiders*, this off-screen presence has a
fluctuating identity. The credit sequence shows Jones and his team searching for a
cave in a South American jungle. Some of the shots in this sequence can be read as
unattributed point-of-view shots, since the proximity of the foliage to the camera
suggests that the camera may be representing the visual experience of an unseen
agent. And the existence of an off-screen presence is confirmed when Jones later
discovers a poisonous arrow. At this point in the film, restricted narration is
employed: the provision of narrative information is filtered through Jones and his
helpers; we find out what they find out. It is only when Jones leaves the cave with
the idol that the off-screen presences – the Indians and Belloq – are shown on
screen. In passing, we can note that an unidentified causal agent appears to be at
work in the cave, for no natural motivation is provided for the sudden appearance
of the rolling boulder. Thus emphasis is placed in various ways on off-screen
agents and off-screen space. But the agents or presences themselves are not
necessarily fixed. And this is highlighted during the sequence at Marion's bar,
where at one point Jones himself becomes an off-screen agent.

   During the course of this sequence, Jones and Marion have an argument, and

Jones leaves – or appears to leave – the bar. As he walks away, he leaves the camera's field of vision, while the camera itself remains in the bar in order to show us what happens next. We are thus led to believe that Jones has left, and that the narration itself is omniscient – it has shown Jones' departure and is about to show us the next piece of narrative action. As Marion closes the bar, Toht (Wolf Kahler), who has followed Jones to Nepal, arrives and threatens her when she refuses to relinquish the headpiece. However, at the moment at which he is about to scar her with a red hot poker, we hear Jones' whip as it knocks the poker to the floor. We are thus suddenly and unexpectedly informed of his presence. He is now revealed to have been not absent but present off-screen, thus taking his place alongside others – like Toht himself – who have occupied a position that by now has become both marked and significant.

Jones' sudden reappearance is pleasurable to the spectator, not simply because of the narrative events (he saves Marion), but also because of the structure of narration employed. In effect, the film sets up in the spectator the belief that the narration is omniscient over Jones, but then negates this belief by showing that Jones knows as much as the spectators – only the spectators didn't realize this. Jones' sudden reappearance makes the spectator retrospectively reinterpret the scene, negating its previously omniscient nature. Unknown to the spectator, the film has negated the hierarchy of knowledge it initially set up: the spectator assumes that he has been privileged by the narration and thus knows more than Jones does, whereas in fact Jones knows as much as the spectator.

During the course of this scene, there are in fact one or two ambiguous textual clues suggesting Jones' continuing presence – off-screen – in the bar. As he leaves, Marion says 'See you tomorrow, Indiana.' But he pauses at the exit. And his backward glance and a second pause suggest that perhaps he does not intend to go anywhere. In addition, there are two possible unattributed point-of-view shots a little later on, shots which suggest that Jones – or some other character – may be hiding behind a pillar. Like similar shots in the opening sequence, these shots remain unattributed and hence ambiguous. In so far as they can be attributed to Jones, they can be seen as providing motivation for Jones' later appearance.[22] But they figure principally in the patterns of suggestion of an off-screen presence established early on in the film. And they figure in the condensation and combination of the norms and figures of serial narration that occur during the course of the sequence – and the film – as a whole, as Marion is threatened then rescued at the last possible moment, as an action sequence leads to the (temporary) defeat of the villains, as Marion's bar is burned down in spectacular fashion, as the central couple are united, divided, then united again, as Jones himself appears, disappears and reappears to thwart the villains and to rescue the heroine, and as two events central to portions of the story that follow are clearly established: Toht's hand is branded by the headpiece; and Marion joins Jones on his quest for the ark. It will be apparent, then, that in spite of – or rather in addition to – the spectacular rendering of the fight, the scene is replete with narrative interest and significance.

I shall demonstrate the use in *Raiders* of the figure or device of an off-screen presence in one more shot, a shot which occurs near the beginning of the scene in which Jones has the headpiece interpreted. Jones is shown peering out of a lattice doorway. He then leaves the doorway and exits into off-screen space. As he leaves, an Arab who has been following Jones enters the doorway and poisons some dates. Only then do we cut to Jones, providing us with a second shot of the film's principal protagonist, a shot we might have expected earlier on, immediately after he leaves the doorway, immediately prior to the entry of the poisoner, and hence immediately prior to the shift in significance and status of the shot of the doorway itself. This shot of Jones, the doorway and the poisoner is ambiguous from a narratological point of view. First, we see Jones stare out of the doorway. The shot appears to be objective, and it appears to be focused on Jones. However, as he leaves the frame the camera remains static; it has disengaged itself from Jones and is now focused on the doorway. Is it now an unattributed point-of-view shot? Does it now suggest an off-screen presence? Once Jones has left, the poisoner enters the frame. The camera now focuses on him as he engages in a significant piece of narrative action, the poisoning of the dates. The shot thus appears to centre on Jones but in retrospect it actually – or finally – centres on the Arab. In addition it initially appears insignificant, a linking or transitional shot of some kind, but it actually serves to provide us with important narrative information, information which of course isn't shared by Jones himself. Again, we can argue that this *process of reinterpretation* creates filmic pleasure. After the dates have been poisoned, only then do we cut to Jones, the shot we 'expected' as soon as he exited screen space. The moment of omniscient narration, showing us the Arab poisoning the dates, has therefore 'interrupted' the action, but for good reason. It also serves to generate suspense. What will happen now? Will Jones find out in time? As is typical of Spielberg, he only finds out at the last possible moment. As is also typical, the combination of purposes and functions served by what initially appears to be a single, simple shot seems clearly designed to engage the spectator in the narrative in as many different ways as is possible.

The fluctuations in audience knowledge that occur during the course of these sequences, combined with the generic figures and devices of serial adventure and the patterns of off-screen (and on-screen) presence, point to the need to consider narrative and narration, as well as spectacle, as sources of pleasure and appeal in a film like *Raiders*. They also suggest the need for close formal analysis. These elements are played, replayed and varied from scene to scene, sequence to sequence, episode to episode. In addition to the play with off-screen presences, two motifs in particular stand out: the last-minute rescue (or the last-second rescue), and an escape scenario, in which the hero has to escape from a seemingly impossible situation.[23] They culminate – in typically condensed form – in the scene in which the ark is finally opened. This is a scene of spectacle and special effects, but it is also a scene which combines suspense with surprise, and in which the ultimate off-screen presence is unleashed on the Nazis, serving both to vanquish the villains and to rescue heroine and hero alike. It thus highlights the extent to which narrative condensation and narrative economy – as well as spectacle and special effects – are hallmarks of this particular New Hollywood blockbuster, and perhaps constitute one of the features – or norms – of this particular type of New Hollywood film.

Left unanalysed, it would be easy to account for the popularity of a film like *Raiders of the Lost Ark* by referring to the presence of Spielberg's creative and expressive personality, or by simply referring to the annihilation of narrative in favour of special effects and action sequences. By contrast, poetics begins from the compositional structure of a film, the options available to the filmmaker and the actual choices s/he makes, including the specific way s/he combines compositional devices. This emphasis only marks the beginning of a comprehensive analysis of Spielberg's films: it would be foolish, of course, to suggest that they are only about spatial relationships. The next stage of analysis is to consider the relationship between the composition of *Raiders* and its themes, which would involve discussing it as 'Reaganite entertainment', and to specify and evaluate its inventiveness (in Andrew's sense of the term). And in addition to further work on narrative, Spielberg's films and action-adventure blockbusters in general would reward further research on the roles of sound and music (touched on elsewhere in this book by K.J. Donnelly and Gianluca Sergi: see chapters 9 and 10), on the constituents of spectacle, on the positive – as well as negative – influence of television, and on the impact of comic books on visual design. If everything else in this chapter has fallen on deaf ears, I hope at least to have shown that Spielberg's popular blockbusters have their own complex structure, and that their popularity does not preclude them from being considered as serious objects worthy of study. It is perhaps time to stop condemning the New Hollywood blockbuster and to start, instead, to understand it.

Notes

1 Thomas Schatz, 'The New Hollywood', in Jim Collins, Hilary Radner and Ava Preacher Collins (eds), *Film Theory Goes to the Movies* (New York: Routledge, 1993), pp. 10–11.
2 For an excellent account of the business strategies in the New Hollywood, see Mark Litwak, *Reel Power: The Struggle for Influence and Success in the New Hollywood* (Los Angeles: Silman-James Press, 1994).
3 Timothy Corrigan, *A Cinema Without Walls, Movies and Culture After Vietnam* (London: Routledge, 1991), pp. 21–4.

4 David Bordwell, 'Historical poetics of cinema', in R. Barton Palmer (ed.), *The Cinematic Text* (New York: AMS Press, 1989), p. 376. See also Kristin Thompson, *Breaking the Glass Armour, Neoformalist Film Analysis* (Princeton: Princeton University Press, 1988).

5 David Bordwell, *Making Meaning: Inference and Rhetoric in the Interpretation of Cinema* (Cambridge, Mass.: Harvard University Press, 1989), pp. 270–1.

6 Just as Christian Metz argued in his monumental book *Language and Cinema*, trans. Donna Jean Umika-Sebeok (Mouton: The Hague, 1974) that filmic specificity is defined in terms of a specific combination of codes, rather than in terms of a single specific code, so here I shall argue that the popularity of Spielberg's films can be defined in terms of a specific combination of compositional norms, rather than in terms of one single specific compositional norm. So it is not sufficient merely to list the compositional norms Spielberg uses, but to outline the specific way they are combined and used in each film.

7 Henry Jenkins, 'Historical poetics', in Joanne Hollows and Mark Jancovich (eds), *Approaches to Popular Film* (Manchester: Manchester University Press, 1995), p. 111.

8 Jenkins, 'Historical poetics', p. 115.

9 Note that this is not a return to the auteurism of *Cahiers du Cinéma, Movie* or Andrew Sarris, since the individuality of films is located, not in the testimony of a unique personal vision, but in a set of compositional norms from which a director can transgress, conform to, or develop in unforeseen ways. The specificity of a director's work can then be characterized according to the choices of both external and internal norms available to directors to adopt and manipulate within a particular historical moment and historical context.

10 Dudley Andrew, 'History and timelessness in films and theory', in David E. Klemm and William Schweiker (eds), *Meaning in Texts and Actions: Questioning Paul Ricoeur* (Charlottesville: University Press of Virginia, 1993), p. 117.

11 Andrew, 'History and timelessness in films and theory', pp. 117–20.

12 Ibid., p. 120.

13 Omar Calabrese, *Neo-Baroque: A Sign of the Times*, trans. Charles Lambert (Princeton: Princeton University Press, 1992), p. 173.

14 Jerzy Toeplitz, *Hollywood and After: The Changing Face of Movies in America*, trans. Boleslaw Sulik (Chicago: Henry Regnery Co., 1975), p. 92.

15 See Richard Maltby, *Harmless Entertainment: Hollywood and the Ideology of Consensus* (Metuchen, NJ and London: Scarecrow Press, 1983), Chapter 10.

16 Mark Crispin Miller, 'Advertising: end of story', in Mark Crispin Miller (ed.), *Seeing Through Movies* (New York: Pantheon Books, 1990), p. 205.

17 The influence of comic books is partly determined by Spielberg's extensive use of storyboards. The final shooting script is broken down into images that represent the composition of a particular shot. Each image on the storyboard usually contains camera angles, direction, camera movement and character movement.

18 Steven Spielberg, quoted in Peter Biskind, 'Blockbuster: the last crusade', in Mark Crispin Miller (ed.), *Seeing Through Movies* (New York: Pantheon Books, 1990), pp. 145–6.

19 Biskind, 'Blockbuster', p. 147.

20 Serials are only mentioned in passing in David Bordwell, Janet Staiger and Kristin Thompson, *The Classical Hollywood Cinema. Film Style and Mode of Production to 1960* (London: Routledge, 1985). They tend to be viewed as sites in the 1910s of a narrative

aesthetic discarded once the feature film and 'well-made' narrative values came to the fore. Their presence as an integral component in Hollywood's output in the 1920s, the 1930s and the 1940s is referred to only once, on p. 144.

21 Tom Gunning, 'Response to "Pie and Chase"', in Kristine Brunovska Karnick and Henry Jenkins (eds), *Classical Hollywood Comedy* (New York: Routledge, 1995), p. 121.

22 These shots remain ambiguous because they are unattributed to any character. However, it is not the task of a historical poetics to resolve these ambiguities, but to determine what aesthetic purpose they serve. As mentioned above, these two shots are textual clues that retrospectively seem to attest to the off-screen presence of Jones in the bar. On first viewing, it may appear that the film is constructing Jones as a superhero, or a supernatural causal agent, who simply knows everything, and can turn up at the right place at the right time. But these two unattributed point-of-view shots construct Jones as a conventional, human causal agent. All of this suggests that Jones' last-minute return to the bar is causally motivated, and foreshadowed in the textual structure of the film. Pleasure is generated by these ambiguous shots and by the fact that Jones returns at the last possible moment.

23 Jones not only rescues Marion at the last possible moment in the bar, but also rescues her from a plane seconds before it blows up. But Jones is also saved at the last possible moment on two occasions – when Marion shoots a Nazi in her bar, and when Sallah's children surround him in a bar in Cairo, just as Arabs are about to shoot him. Moreover, many scenes end on highly orchestrated and violent actions consisting of Jones and Marion escaping from seemingly impossible situations.

Chapter 12

Storytelling

Classical Hollywood cinema and classical narrative

Elizabeth Cowie

This chapter looks at the relation of notions of classical Hollywood cinema and classical narrative in Bordwell, Staiger and Thompson's account of classical Hollywood cinema. The initial and principal focus of discussion here will be classical Hollywood in terms of the studios as industrial/financial organizations, and as a mode of storytelling. It will be argued that classical narrative is only one aspect of, and is not synonymous with, classical Hollywood. Rather, classical Hollywood included forms of storytelling which lack the 'well-made' qualities associated with classical narrative form.

The transformations in the economic conditions in Hollywood and implications of these transformations for film production suggest that we should now refer to post-studio Hollywood production, while the extent to which post-studio production continues the imperatives for film making established in the classical system needs to be examined as such in order to understand its requirements for modes of narrative and narration. Unhooking classical narrative and classical Hollywood as equivalent is, I suggest, an important step in enabling the differences between 'classical' and 'post-classical' American cinema to be properly assessed.

Paradoxically, I suggest, in two of the most sustained accounts of classical Hollywood, *The Classical Hollywood Cinema: Film Style and Mode of Production to 1960* (*CHC*) by David Bordwell, Janet Staiger and Kristin Thompson, and David Bordwell's subsequent study, *Narration in the Fiction Film*, the Hollywood film becomes increasingly indistinct because it appears undifferentiated, at least narratively, as a result of the inclusiveness of the definition of classical narrative as it emerges in these two texts. A dominant mode of narration – classical Hollywood narrative – is defined, but its very definition includes, it seems, virtually all possible deviations, so that every exception therefore proves the rule. The church is so broad that heresy is impossible.

The hegemonic account of classical narrative in *The Classical Hollywood Cinema* arises as a result of the functionalist approach adopted there. As Dirk Eitzen shows in his discussion 'Evolution, functionalism, and the study of American cinema', its

> basic historical argument . . . is that every element in that system was more or less constrained to serve both the function of storytelling and the function of profit maximization. Innovations that performed better in both these roles than their functional alternatives tended to become incorporated into the system as norms or as standard practice.[1]

This approach, as Eitzen emphasizes, has value: it has produced a much clearer account of the Hollywood film industry both at the level of the description of specific practices – it contains a great deal of valuable information – and at the level of explanation: it avoids simplistic intentionalist accounts of history. Eitzen argues that *The Classical Hollywood Cinema* underrates or ignores 'other important impulses',[2] such as a non-narrative, melodramatic impulse, and the role of spectacle. But its limitations are not the effect of its restriction to just two pivotal functions – narrative and profit. The additional impulses Eitzen mentions cannot be added to the functionalist schema of the book without undermining it, for its limitations are the result of the assumptions framing its two determining functions.

The profit function is framed by the authors of *The Classical Hollywood Cinema* in terms of definitions of 'capitalism', and in terms of industry-generated definitions of profit. But it is qualified, they argue, by the ideological/signifying practices which arose in Hollywood, such that 'In the balance between economical production and a presumed effect on the film, the latter won out.'[3] Profit maximization was not determining; rather additional costs were accepted in order to preserve a mode of practice. This is explained as the result of the prioritization of classical narrative, for

> in a capitalist society there is no opposition of business and art: most artists make art to make money. And one could make movies more cheaply if one did not recognize conventions of narrative construction, spectacle, verisimilitude, continuity and so on.
>
> (*CHC*, p. 367)

The function of storytelling is bracketed as 'classical Hollywood narration', and all innovations, developments and changes are seen as functional for this form of narrative. Eitzen suggests, moreover, that those which cannot be related to this definition are seen as functioning for the profit motive. This is undoubtedly correct, but it is not quite the argument of *The Classical Hollywood Cinema*.[4] Instead there are two distinct strategies used in the book to negotiate the relation of these two functions, and these, I argue, are in the end in contradiction with one another.

First, in the discussion in 'The Hollywood mode of production: its conditions of existence', a neo-Marxist frame of analysis is adopted, drawing both on the work of Harry Braverman and, less directly, on the rereading of Marx by Louis Althusser. It is argued that 'While in the last instance economic practices may have been determinant, this part [Chapter 8] will stress that ideological/signifying practices continually influenced the necessity to divide labour and to divide it in its particular configuration' (*CHC*, p. 89). What in Althusser is argued as the relative autonomy of ideological practices becomes here the relative determination of the economic by the ideological.[5] *The Classical Hollywood Cinema* then attempts to shift away from a functionalist account and draws instead upon approaches influenced by Michel Foucault's work, emphasizing a field of competing discourses in which the economic is not simply determining.[6]

In the second strategy, however, the two functions come to be identified as the same, for in Chapter 30, 'Since 1960: the persistence of a mode of film practice', the assumption that Hollywood makes money, not art, is qualified: 'Hollywood makes *classical* movies to make money' (*CHC*, p. 367). This is a compromise which attempts to resolve the tension in the book between economism and the emphasis on the dominance of the ideological norms of Hollywood film practice, of a 'group style', and of classical narrative. What the authors seek here is to show the tensions and contradictions between the economic and the discursive field of signifying practices in the socio/political formation, implying a process of multiple determinations. This has been enormously helpful in demonstrating the discursive determinations of the ideological/signifying practices in distinction from the simple profit-function. As a result, the history of the process of their interaction can be studied. But, in contrast, the competing determinations in relation to the signifying practices *are* held to be resolved, producing a hierarchy in the 'group style' of realism and verisimilitude, causal coherence, continuity, spectacle, stars and genre, under the 'primacy of narrative', understood as 'classical narrative', which is in fact defined as all of these elements under the control of 'conventions of narrative construction' (*CHC*, p. 367). The problem here is not, or not only, that this is a circular argument, rather it is that we cannot study Hollywood production practices historically. For after 1917 no innovations produce change in the mode of practice, only accommodations; there is no 'resistance' in the system. Here the explanatory value of functionalism is considerably reduced.[7] Meanwhile this account, though explicitly qualifying it, still assumes profit as the determining function.

What, then, is the relation of storytelling and profit? For the Hollywood studios narrative or storytelling is secondary to the aim of profit; all films were made to make a profit but 'story' films made the most profit, hence they became synonymous with profit. The profitability of story-films is not inherent, but the result of specific exhibition practices in relation to the creation of a market (a middle-class audience) and a product for that market.[8] What emerges in the early years of cinema is not, simply, the narrative film – 'Hollywood's very definition of a movie' – but a profitable commodity, which can be produced through regular and controlled manufacturing processes (*CHC*, p. 367). The story-film could be produced within a fixed site under careful production control. The detailed division of labour which arose in film production facilitated not just the skills and practices of film production, but also the managerial supervision whereby economies in costs could be achieved through maximum use of labour time.[9]

What is critical for a manufacturer of luxury goods – as forms of entertainment such as films may be termed – is not simply the cost (which can, within limits, be passed on to the customer), but the predictability of cost so that advance sales can be planned and future returns on investment calculated. Thus 'factory' production, which began with the streamlined output of cheap one-reel films, was adopted throughout the industry. This produced not only a standardization of product but also standards of product, of qualities in films which themselves, as 'high production values', were (and are) an important component in profitability, defined in terms both of the quality of stars, costume, sets and locations, but also in terms of costs. Standards of narration in film were maintained through the continuity system of editing. The impetus to high standards in production requires determinate criteria, and it is here that the ideological and signifying practices which established the 'norms' of classical Hollywood arise, as Bordwell, Staiger and Thompson show.

These ideological and signifying practices are not, therefore, autonomous (even relatively), but solicited and supported by the firms. Moreover, that the pursuit of certain norms was costly was not necessarily in conflict with the function for profit. For capitalism as a mode of production the maximization of profit is not a simple calculation of what will make the most money, but a question of choices within a determinate economic context. In Hollywood, for example, the transition to sound in the late 1920s was undertaken under the new conditions of oligopoly in which the five studios which were vertically integrated with production, distribution and exhibition now functioned together with the three smaller producer/distributors to limit and delimit forms of competition between themselves. In this market it was possible for the studios to pursue the maintenance of established production procedures in the transition even where these would produce considerable costs, since they could be recouped at the box office and, more importantly, passed on to exhibitors. That the studios did so is not simply the consequence of the influence of ideological/signifying practices.

In the vertically integrated industry of Hollywood after 1924, profitability depended not on the unit-cost of individual films in relation to their returns but on the saleability of cinema as a whole – on the mass market for films in general –

and for this a system of regular and predictable production of films of determinate standards and quality was central. The role of monopolistic practices modifies the playing-field of competition and redefines the scope and means for profit-making. Eitzen claims that *The Classical Hollywood Cinema* presumes a continuous competition in the system between functional alternatives, for example, between studios, stylistic options and sound technology. But this was not the case, for not only were the five studios dependent as exhibitors on each other's product, but the history of the introduction of sound technology is the story of monolistic practices in the electrical communications industry as well as in Hollywood.[10] Thus Eitzen's summary could be rephrased, for there are not two functions but only one, profit, which nevertheless is subordinated in *The Classical Hollywood Cinema* to the function of classical narrative.

The emphasis I am placing here on profit in Hollywood is not an attempt to assert its simple primacy but to show, as Eitzen has pointed out, that certain elements in the 'group style' of classical Hollywood, notably genre and stars, but also spectacle and spectacular effects, were important not for narrative but as touchstones for the profitable film. Rather than classical narrative, I suggest that it is the notion of the 'package' which was key for the Hollywood studios. The story is part of the package but the studios wanted multiple guarantees. These would be provided – it was hoped – through the other elements of the package, notably stars and high production values, but also sensational and spectacular elements, involving set features such as battles or chases or spectacular settings and events in nature. John Ford's *The Iron Horse* (1924) typifies this package approach. According to Tag Gallagher, Ford

> commanded . . . 5,000 extras; construction of two whole towns; 100 cooks to feed the crew; 2,000 rail layers; a cavalry regiment; 800 Indians; 1,300 buffalo; 2,000 horses; 10,000 cattle; 50,000 properties; the original 'Jupiter' and '116' locomotives that had met at Promontory Point May 10, 1869; Wild Bill Hickcock's derringer; and . . . the original stagecoach used by Horace Greeley.[11]

The film had no scenario, only a short synopsis, and according to Gallagher, Ford kept making it up as the weeks went on – ten in all, rising from a budgeted four weeks. The film was among the top grossers for the decade, and against costs of $280,000 it returned over $2 million.

It (1927), by contrast, is a realistic romantic comedy with a contemporary setting involving sales girls in a department store, but it also functions as a package of story, spectacle and voyeurism, featuring not only its star – Clara Bow – but also the department store itself as a palace of consumerism. These were all recognizable elements in the film package for 1920s audiences. For *The Classical*

Hollywood Cinema, these elements are motivated by the generic identification of the film as comedy. Indeed by categorizing both key elements of the classical Hollywood 'group style' – genre and stars – as forms of motivation, each are brought into service for the norm of classical narrative. Motivation enables the viewer to understand why characters act as they do, or why an element is in the film: 'Motivation is the process by which a narrative justifies its story material and the plot's presentation of that story material' (*CHC*, p. 19). But, unlike motivation involving plot and characters – 'compositional motivation' (*CHC*, p. 19) – both stars and genre present extratextual references, functioning *intertextually*. These references are part of audience expectations for the genre or for the star and constitute an extratextual narrative image which is brought into play, varied and adapted within any particular film. As a result, it is argued, as viewers we are not at all disturbed when Judy Garland bursts into song, since we expect her to sing in films; audiences read such elements in relation to the star-image and/or generic conventions. Nor is the unity of the film disrupted, it is claimed, since it is premised on the inclusion of such elements. Such elements do, however, disrupt classical narrative since, as intertextual elements, they pose the narrative as a construct, disturbing the suspension of disbelief as audiences draw on their know-ledge of other films to understand the elements in this film. Nevertheless, while such elements do produce narrative disruption it is argued that they are motivated generically, within the classical narrative and as a result, 'in such instances the typical multiple motivation of the classical text simply gives way to a more linear series: a scene motivated compositionally, then a song or gag motivated generic-ally then another scene, and so forth' (*CHC*, p. 71). There is narrative disruption, since the structure of causality is interrupted and the film becomes discontinuous, but this is motivated generically. This is the achievement of classical Hollywood, but it is not, I suggest, classical narrative.

There are two different accounts of narrative motivation here. One emphasizes the notion of psychological and causal motivation, while the other poses the notion of 'unity'. 'Understanding classical story causality takes us toward grasping how a classical film unifies itself. Generally speaking this unity is a matter of *motivation*' (*CHC*, p. 19). While generic motivation does 'unify' an otherwise heterogeneous text, it does so in a way antithetical to classical narrative, since psychological and narrative causality are broken. The conflict here is recognized but dismissed on the grounds that

> On the whole, generic motivation co-operates with causal, or com-positional, unity. Genres are in one respect certain kinds of stories, endowed with their own particular logic that does not contest psycho-logical causality or goal-orientation.
>
> (*CHC*, p. 20)

This is true for narrative genres such as the detective story, and the gangster film, but not for the musical films and for comedies. However, strongly marked narrative genres, such as the horror film and detective film, were rarely 'A' pictures in classical Hollywood, at least before 1940. Musicals and comedies, both of which were regularly produced as 'A' pictures, were therefore important elements in classical Hollywood but were not confused with 'proper' story-films.

Genre reappears at the end of *The Classical Hollywood Cinema* to subvert the notion of a post-classical or non-classical cinema: 'Classical film style and codified genres swallow up art-film borrowings, taming the (already limited) disruptiveness of the art cinema' (*CHC*, p. 375). Thus Coppola's *The Conversation* (1974) 'exemplifies how the New Hollywood has absorbed narrational strategies of the art cinema while controlling them within a coherent genre framework' (*CHC*, p. 377). Genre, however, is not classical narrative.

The history of melodrama as a film genre exemplifies some of the problems of genre and classical narrative as well as the role of profit in classical Hollywood. While the story-film enabled economies of production, the profitability of the story-film arose with the shift to the middle-class audience and the higher admission prices that could be charged. At the same time that the turn to the middle classes offered respectability, and relief from the censorship and approbrium of reformers, it also opened up the possibility of creating a new mass audience. Tom Gunning has argued that to effect this shift appropriate narratives and forms of narration were adopted, and film's narrative role had to replace its role as fairground novelty. It was to respectable theatre and literature that film producers turned for stories and storytelling. Nevertheless the new narrator system he describes arising in the work of Griffith, and its more complex narrative form, 'derives more from the melodramatic stage than respectable classics'.[12]

Director Frank Borzage's comment in 1922 that 'Today in the pictures we have the old melodramatic situations fitted out decently with true characterizations' (cited in *CHC*, p. 14), points to this complex inheritance which is not yet, I think, fully understood or placed in relation to classical Hollywood and classical narrative. Indeed Borzage's own films specifically break the canons of classical narrative, not only in *Seventh Heaven* (1927) with its unmotivated ending, but also the later *Strange Cargo* (1940) which is on the one hand a standard star vehicle for Joan Crawford and Clark Gable and on the other hand presents a story of miraculous redemption which does not square with the rationalist motivation of classical narrative. The ending of *The Public Enemy* (1931) is pure theatrical melodrama. Suspense is created through the characters' lack of knowledge contrasting with the audience's partial knowledge and the forewarning given the spectator by the contrast of the music – with cross-cutting characteristic of D.W. Griffith and silent cinema melodrama. The sequence ends with a shot of Tom Powers' morally upright brother Mike stepping away from Tom's corpse and looming forward in frame, holding his fist in what might seem a gesture of revengeful anger, contradicting his earlier character and implying a new narrative. The ending is clearly not a closure. Rather a hesitation is introduced, and the death of Cagney as the Tom Powers character is presented as regrettable through our alignment with both his mother and brother, while the closing titles refer audiences to the general issue – and fears – of organized crime.[13] The ending suspends us, therefore, in a similar way to the ending of *Thelma & Louise* (1991).[14]

At the same time non-linear, episodic narrative, in which a series of narrative scenes are presented which are causally self-contained or only weakly causally connected, remained acceptable in Hollywood. *The Iron Horse* is one example, while Ford's later *Four Sons* (1928) only partially conforms to Bordwell's outline – the son who leaves for America fulfils the criteria of a goal-oriented hero, but he does not bring about the story's events. In the 1930s, and staying with Ford as exemplar, *Steamboat Round the Bend* (1935), a highly successful Will Rogers vehicle, is not a story in which events are causally prepared for.[15] All the key actions are given off-screen and reported by characters, including the killing and Duke's subsequent trial, as well as his appeal against his conviction and sentence to death. These, moreover, are displaced by the set pieces such as the wedding, and the confrontation with the local community leaders who are won over to the 'educational' travelling show. The rivalry of the steamboat captains is set up with the bet on the race, and then abandoned as a narrative goal, for although Captain John does enter the race and succeeds in beating Captain Eli, he does so in order to reach Duke before he is hung.

The Classical Hollywood Cinema, however, argues that the narration which arises with the films of narrative integration has wholly adopted the norms of bourgeois theatre and literature, and it is this that it terms classical. A 1920 manual for aspiring scriptwriters is cited as a typical account, 'Plot is a careful and logical working out of the laws of cause and effect. The emphasis must be laid upon causality and the action and the reaction of the human will.' The authors add that 'Here in brief is the premise of Hollywood story construction: causality, consequence, psychological motivations, the drive toward overcoming obstacles and achieving goals. Character-centered – ie personal or psychological – causality is the armature of the classical story' (*CHC*, p. 13). A similar account is given over forty years later by Irwin R. Blacker in *The Elements of Screen-writing*.[16] This seems to support the case made in *The Classical Hollywood Cinema* for the continuing hegemony of classical narrative, but it may more simply attest to a continuity in assumptions about the norms of screenwriting which writers assert. What is presented here is a discourse of screenwriting which, even in 1986, bases itself on the priority of Aristotelian principles. Blacker, for example, notes that 'All plots are contrived, but they must not appear to be so', hence too much coincidence must be avoided.[17] Similarly 'story holes' or an unexplained piece of story create gaps which can 'shatter the willing suspension of disbelief and leave the audience unsatisfied'. It is just such a 'story hole' which John Ford introduces in *The Searchers* (1956) when Ethan Edwards, instead of shooting Debbie as he had sworn to do, sweeps her up into his arms and embraces her.

Blacker's guide, while drawing in the main on a much later repertoire of film references, remains closely within the terms set out by Frances Marion in 1937.[18] But films are not equivalent to their screenplays, and an aspect of such manuals, at least in the period of classical Hollywood, was the assertion of the craft and art of scriptwriting against the barbarism of the producer's (and, with Ford, the director's) cuts. Blacker notes that the demands of the industry are at variance with good scriptwriting:

> In the film industry, the lead character is very important: producers will ask about the character before the story because of the star factor in financing and distribution. And film critics tend to praise character portrayal more than plot because the audience identifies with the characters. This is not the natural way to work on a screenplay, and it creates distortions.

Rather, citing Paddy Chayafsky, Blacker argues that the writer starts with the incidents and then develops characters to execute those incidents, 'so that the characters take shape in order to make the story true'.[19]

What is presented in these accounts is a version of the 'well-made play', in contrast to the melodrama of the nineteenth century. Namely, the centring of a few or one protagonist, with causally connected incidents, motivation, and psychologically developed characters. As Barry Salt has noted, the innovation of American cinema here – drawing on theatrical norms – is the inclusion of comic incident as contrast.[20] In the accounts of the screenwriting guides, melodrama is eschewed. As a result, as noted earlier, the heritage of stage melodrama and its role for cinema has been obscured – it is both a source for classical Hollywood,[21] and the form against which classical narrative in Hollywood defines itself, rejecting the stereotypes, the use of spectacular staging and effects, and the subordination of dialogue, acting, and indeed narrative, to the pictorial, all of which were seen as characteristic elements of theatrical melodrama at the turn of the century. For A. Nicholas Vardac, melodrama is the precursor of silent cinema,[22] but screenwriters such as Frances Marion rejected it:

> Melodrama bears somewhat the same relation to tragedy as farce does to comedy. It requires sensational situations with exaggerated power to affect the plot actors and it also needs acute conflict. The plot is more important than the characterization because the plot controls the

characters. The action, the events, are stressed and chance or fortune is the motivating factor. The weakness of melodrama lies in the use of plot for plot's sake.[23]

Blacker similarly asserts that 'Plot is more than a pattern of events: it is the ordering of emotions. If the plot is all action and little emotion, it is melodrama'.[24]

Narratives require a cinematic discourse in order to become film stories – to be narrated in cinema. Film form in Hollywood, the particular deployment of cinematic techniques, is characterized in *CHC* by its unobtrusiveness. The 'continuity style' of Hollywood emphasized imperceptible editing, while camera movement, angle and shot scale served the dramatic action. It is a styleless style. Classical narrative, for Bordwell, Staiger and Thompson, is the subordination of form to narrative (*CHC*, p. 50). Stylistic features are placed in the service of the narrative, conveying information, helping the spectator to construct a coherent – causal and logical – time and space. David Bordwell sees classical Hollywood as drawing on a limited paradigm of stylistic and technical devices which offers a codified system recognizable by the spectator. This allows him to argue that the classical system always codifies, or contains, any excessive stylistic element, any feature which deviates from the norm of psychological motivation.[25]

While norms of cinematic narration, such as the 180° rule, were characteristic of the studio-system in Hollywood, these were not necessarily used in an unobtrusive way. *Detective Burton's Triumph* (1914), cited as an example of the subtle use of eyeline matches (*CHC*, p. 209), appears quite self-conscious in its use of shot-reverse shot between the characters looking and the object of their looks. The film *displays* the eyeline match, just as it displays the visual procedure of investigation by the Pinkerton detective, and preparation of and for the crime. The film is less incipient classical narrative than a precursor to the documentary drama of a film like *Call Northside 777* (1948).

Such norms, moreover, were not always accompanied by the kind of classical story *The Classical Hollywood Cinema* outlines. Howard Hawks' *The Big Sleep* (1946) is wholly classical in its style, unfolding action and space coherently. This clarity does not support a similarly straightforward narrative, however. Of course, as a detective mystery, the unfolding of the narrative involves keeping the spectator in the dark – the film is characterized by quite extreme retardation of narrative information, restricting us to Marlowe's knowledge but without any access to his understanding or analysis of the events and actions until the end. Here the film is clearly generic, but, while remaining formally a detective story, it fails to deliver as a whodunit. Although the film does supply causes for all its events (despite Hawks' claim to the contrary), these are highly convoluted. For example, Geiger's death and Carmen's involvement arise independently, but appear in the film at first as causally linked. The problem is not, or not just that, as Bordwell notes, causal information about the crime is rarely given more than once, rather it is that the film does not make it clear how the crime-detection is being pursued in the actions and events we are shown. The key to the story is Carmen, it is she who is the cause of the events in the film. She killed Regan, leading Vivienne to seek Eddie Marr's help in covering it up, opening her to his blackmail, and it is Carmen's drug habits which give rise to demands for money which prompt General Sternwood to engage Marlowe's services. All of this is not the central story, rather it is a *mise-en-scène* for the love story which develops between Marlowe and Vivienne. Structurally, all the murders function much in the same way as the leopard in *Bringing Up Baby* (1938), that is, as devices.[26] Bordwell suggests that '*The Big Sleep* is a detective film in which the interest of constructing the investigation *fabula* takes precedence over the construction of a coherent crime *fabula*'. I would suggest, however, that both of these are displaced by our interest in the interaction of characters. As a result the lack of 'proper' motivation in relation to why and how is not disturbing. Nevertheless while *The Big Sleep* is classical cinema, it deviates from the definition of classical narrative in *The Classical Hollywood Cinema*

My aim here has been to find a way to challenge the hegemony of this account of classical narrative. For the 'flexibility' claimed for it becomes so elastic that there can never be a post-classical that is not absorbable by the classical system. Contemporary American cinema is marked by the disappearance of the studio system and by new forms of competition and organization 'for profit' in the context not merely of television, but of cable, satellite and video. Its aims, as a narrative cinema, cannot be seen as unified as was possible under the old oligopoly. Stylistic norms have changed, and perhaps no longer exist as a consistent group of norms. The relation of contemporary American cinema to classical Hollywood and its narrative forms remains to be investigated.

Notes

1 Dirk Eitzen, 'Evolution, functionalism, and the study of the American cinema', in *The Velvet Light Trap*, no. 28 (Fall 1991), p. 75. Eitzen refers to two systems and functions, but then suggests that every element must serve both of these, implying in fact only one system and one function.

2 Eitzen, 'Study of American cinema', p. 80.

3 David Bordwell, Janet Staiger and Kristin Thompson, *The Classical Hollywood Cinema: Film Style and Mode of Production to 1960* (London: Routledge & Kegan Paul, 1985), p. 89. Hereafter cited in the text as *CHC*.

4 Eitzen writes, 'Musical production numbers that do not advance the storyline of a movie are regarded as vestiges of a past system, namely vaudeville, that have been preserved in the system because of their close links with successful traits, particularly sound'(p. 80). The page-citation given, however (*CHC*, p. 71) refers to the absorption of such disruption through generic and other motivation.

5 Louis Althusser, *Lenin and Philosophy and other Essays*, trans. Ben Brewster (London: New Left Books, 1971); Harry Braverman, *Labor and Monopoly Capital: The Degradation of Work in the Twentieth Century* (New York: Monthly Review Press, 1974).

6 For example, Paul Hirst, *Law and Ideology* (London: Macmillan, 1979), Chapter 3; Barry Hindess and Paul Q. Hirst, *Pre-Capitalist Modes of Production* (London: Routledge & Kegan Paul, 1975); Antony Cutler, Barry Hindess, Paul Hirst and Athar Hussain, *Marx's Capital and Capitalism Today* (London: Routledge & Kegan Paul, 1975).

7 This is true for all functionalist explanations, since they depend on showing how processes and practices 'fit' and function for the system. Thus Eitzen argues that 'In this way, despite constant innovation and change, the underlying system perpetuated itself' (Eitzen, 'Study of American cinema', p. 75).

8 Eitzen seems to give an autonomy to the function of narrative when he refers to the 'regularities of the environment', arguing that 'narrative movies exist because even before they existed people were predisposed toward narrative forms of entertainment' (Eitzen, 'Study of American cinema', p. 81).

9 Analysed by Janet Staiger in 'Dividing labour for production control: Thomas Ince and the rise of the studio system', *Cinema Journal*, vol. 18, no. 2 (Spring 1979), pp. 16–25.

10 Douglas Gomery, 'The coming of sound', in Elizabeth Weis and John Belton (eds), *Film Sound: Theory and Practice* (New York: Columbia University Press, 1985).

11 Tag Gallagher, *John Ford: The Man and His Films* (Berkeley: University of California, 1986), p. 31.

12 Tom Gunning, *D. W. Griffith and the Origins of American Narrative Film: The Early Years at Biograph* (Urbana: University of Illinois, 1991), p. 95.

13 The film was also read generically; the *New York Times*' reviewer André D. Sennwald called it 'just another gangster film, weaker than most in its story, stronger than most in its acting' 24 April 1931, p. 27, cited by Garth Jowett in 'Bullets, beer and the Hays office: *Public Enemy*', in P. Davies and B. Neve (eds), *Cinema, Politics and Society in America* (Manchester: Manchester University Press, 1981).

14 Richard Maltby's discussion of *Casablanca* (1943) shows the deliberate inclusion of shots which produce two mutually conflicting readings of the scene when Ilsa (Ingrid Bergman) first seeks Rick's (Humphrey Bogart) help, and passport, to escape Casablanca; Richard Maltby, '"A brief romantic interlude": Dick and Jane go to 3½ seconds of the classical Hollywood cinema', in David Bordwell and Noël Carroll, *Post-Theory: Reconstructing Film Studies* (Madison University of Wisconsin, 1996), pp. 434–59.

15 The film was co-written by Lamar Trotti whose work as a censor with the Studio Relations Committee Production in the late 1920s, as well as a screenwriter when he joined Fox in 1932, clearly shows his grasp of 'classical narration' in the sense of the well-made play.

16 Irwin R. Blacker, *The Elements of Screen-Writing: A Guide for Film and Television Writers* (New York: Collier Books, 1986). Blacker taught at the University of Southern California where his students included the writers of *American Graffiti*, *Apocalypse Now* and *Star Wars*, as well as Bob Gale, writer of *Back to the Future*.

17 Blacker, *The Elements of Screen-Writing*, p. 32.

18 Frances Marion, *How to Write and Sell Film Stories* (New York: Colvici Friede, 1937).

19 Blacker, *The Elements of Screen-Writing*, p. 36. A player's star-image in classical Hollywood always took precedence over plot, sometimes disrupting storylines, as *The Classical Hollywood Cinema* emphasizes. Thus Cary Grant cannot be a murderer

in Hitchcock's *Suspicion* (1941), while the casting of Rita Hayworth in *Gilda* (1946) requires a happy end which is insufficiently motivated given the earlier plot. In *Dead Reckoning* (1947), where Hayworth was replaced by Lizbeth Scott, very similar plot elements are recycled but the different star, and star image, meant that the film could kill her off. The story of *Mildred Pierce* (1945) was changed not only in order to satisfy the Production Code but also in order to produce an appropriate vehicle for Joan Crawford.

20 Barry Salt, *Film Style and Technology: History and Analysis*, 2nd edition (London: Starword, 1992) p. 113. Salt cites here Aldred Hennequin's *The Art of Playwriting*, published in 1890. Salt gives as an example the films of Mary Pickford where she was her own producer, such as *Poor Little Rich Girl* (1917), in which she insisted on comedy scenes despite director Maurice Tourneur's resistance.

21 'It is probable that such casual splendors [in *Casbah* (1948)] offered by the Hollywood film owe a great deal to its mixed parentage in vaudeville, melodrama, and other spectacle-centred entertainments.' (*CHC*, p. 21).

22 A. Nicholas Vardac, *Stage to Screen: Theatrical Origins of Early Film – David Garrick to D. W. Griffith* (New York: Da Capo Press, 1987).

23 Marion, *Film Stories*, p. 141.

24 Blacker, *The Elements of Screen-Writing*, p. 20.

25 Bordwell, *Narration in the Fiction Film*, p. 188.

26 For Raymond Bellour the 'high classicism' of *The Big Sleep* lies in its filmic mode of narration, i.e. in its deployment of the codes of cinema, editing, shot scale, length of shot, etc., in a characteristic structure of repetition and difference through symmetry and dissymmetry. He uses the term 'classic narrative film', in order to focus on the classicism of the Hollywood narrative film, not the classical narrative of the Hollywood film. See Raymond Bellour, 'The obvious and the code', *Screen*, vol 15, no. 4 (Winter 1974/5).

Chapter 13

Specularity and engulfment

Francis Ford Coppola and *Bram Stoker's Dracula*

Thomas Elsaesser

New Hollywood

When looking to define post-classical Hollywood, one could do worse than take the current American cinema's most maverick of charismatic producer-director-auteurs as example, and among his varied *oeuvre*, pick one of the more hybrid films. Francis Ford Coppola's *Bram Stoker's Dracula* (1992) was allegedly a 'commercial' and therefore less 'personal' project (in the language of auteurism), helping to restore the director's battered industry reputation after the collapse of Zoetrope and the disaster of *One from the Heart* (1982).[1] But it could also be regarded as a professionally confident, shrewdly calculated and supremely self-reflexive piece of filmmaking, fully aware that it stands at the crossroads of major changes in the art and industry of Hollywood: looking back as well as forward, while staking out a ground all its own.

Post-classical filmmaking of the kind represented by *Bram Stoker's Dracula* is unthinkable without the 'New Hollywood', a label referring, above all, to the economic revival of Hollywood filmmaking since the mid-1970s.[2] Its beginning dates back to the worldwide success of Steven Spielberg's *Jaws* (1975), George Lucas' *Star Wars* (1977) and Coppola's *The Godfather* (1972).[3] Three elements make up the 'New Hollywood': first, a *new generation of directors* (sometimes called the 'Movie Brats'),[4] second, *new marketing strategies* (centred on the blockbuster as a distribution and exhibition concept),[5] and third, *new media ownership and management styles* in the film industry.[6] One could add *new technologies of sound and image reproduction*, ranging from digitized special effects to Dolby sound, and *new delivery systems*, but it seems that the second – the new marketing strategies, also known as 'High Concept'[7] filmmaking – was in many ways the most crucial. If the cinema was to survive, so common wisdom has it, it needed to attract audiences brought up on television and popular music, audiences who identified with the broader attitudes and values of 'youth-culture' (non-conformism, rebelliousness, sexual freedom, fashion-consciousness and conspicuous consumption). The signs, images and sounds of this youth-culture have, since the mid-1950s, dominated much of domestic and public space in the USA, before taking over the urban landscape of the everyday in the rest of the developed and developing world. Hence the argument that the New Hollywood's greatest challenge was the industry's uncertainty about an identifiable audience.[8] Even before the arrival and rapid diffusion of new consumer-oriented delivery systems like satellite broadcasting and the home VCR, the one commodity classical Hollywood could be sure of – the family audience – had begun to regroup around television. But with the cable-satellite-videotape revolution granting viewers a hitherto unknown freedom over the uses of the audio-visual product, it made even this audience 'invisible' to the statistical targeting which formed the basis of the film and TV industry's traditional marketing strategies. Timothy Corrigan, borrowing a term first used by Robin Wood,[9] went so far as to claim that this made for 'illegible texts'.[10]

That it was Hollywood and moviemaking which appeared to 'resolve' this crisis, rather than television (still grappling with the implications of 'desperately seeking the audience'),[11] is one of the more startling features of the 1990s. In order to understand at least some of the factors, one has to cast one's eye sideways as well as backwards and include, along with these technological and demographic changes, the renaissance and international marketability of at first European (the *nouvelle vague* in France, the New German Cinema) and more recently Asian national art and/or cult cinemas (Taiwanese, Hong Kong and New Chinese cinemas) whose critical reputations seem invariably built around star directors. Taking its cue from these diverse trends in popular culture, Hollywood, too, began promoting 'name' directors as superstars, often film-school graduates with a cult movie or a surprise success to their credit. After the roller-coaster years of box-office failure for costly auteur projects in the late 1970s – the most notorious being Michael Cimino's western epic *Heaven's Gate* (1980) – but also record profits earned by outright commercial productions in the wake of *Jaws* (1975), the major Hollywood companies oscillated between giving new talent a chance and backing more conservative ventures. But the significance of the new breed of filmmaker (the line runs from Martin Scorsese, Paul Schrader, Brian De Palma to David Lynch, Quentin Tarantino, Abel Ferrara) rests also on the influence that the European cinema and its critical traditions (such as the 'auteur theory') have had on the American cinema's own understanding of itself. For instance, the mixing of genres, the mania for citation and self-referencing so typical of contemporary cinema can be traced to the French *nouvelle vague*'s admiration for the Hollywood of the 1940s and 1950s, and the use of film citation in the works of François Truffaut, Jean Luc Godard, Jacques Rivette or Claude Chabrol.

Yet this 'vanguard' role of Europe is complex and ambiguous. Ever since the European cinema came of age in the 1920s, and again after 1945, it was in fact

Hollywood that provided the implicit reference point of European national cinemas, whether commercial in orientation or *art-et-essai*. Rival to some, the Hollywood film was the admired model to others. In both cases, since much of any European nation's film culture is implicitly 'Hollywood' (because this is what most people see when they go to the cinema), none of the relations of rivalry and emulation can be seen as purely positive terms, just as Hollywood itself is hardly a monolithic entity.[12] The 'New Hollywood' of Coppola, Scorsese or Altman: is it 'new' in opposition to 'old' Hollywood (the different as same: Coppola playing at being a reclusive mogul like Howard Hughes and an 'auteur maudit' like Orson Welles), or is it 'new' in relation to Hollywood assimilating its own opposite (the same as different): Arthur Penn borrowing from Truffaut, Altman's films influenced by Godard, Woody Allen's by Ingmar Bergman and Fellini, Schrader by Dreyer and Bresson, while Scorsese, avowed admirer of Godard and Truffaut has also championed Michael Powell and Jerry Lewis, the latter possessing an auteur's reputation only in Europe?

Thus, in order to account for the play with quotations, with genre parody, clichés and pastiche in post-classical cinema (and by extension, to point to the complex hopscotch logic of Europe's evaluation of American cinema/New York's evaluation of Europe/Hollywood's response to New York), we need to go beyond 'influence'. A number of paradigms offer themselves for these different love-hate relationships, including that of 'self-colonization' and 'elective paternity'.[13] Noël Carroll has proposed the term 'allusionism',[14] basing his thesis on the premise that filmmakers and audiences grew up together, sharing a common film experience which shaped their social experience. Robert Ray offers a differently angled picture, partly to explain why the New Hollywood is successful even though its primary audiences seem both younger and more diverse. For him, success has to do with a double inscription of audiences, where the viewer is simultaneously addressed as a naive and an ironic spectator, as an innocent and a knowing one.[15]

This double register has many names: Fredric Jameson, in a different context, has called it 'blank irony', that is, unmarked, deadpan or neutral.[16] It can be related to the pervasive cultural feeling of nostalgia, itself a constitutive element for a sensibility which in the words of Gore Vidal 'remembers the future and dreams the past'. Such a definition of nostalgia makes it the simultaneous co-presence of the desire for the myth and a cynicism about its efficacy. Sociologically, one could say that blank irony is merely the broadest common denominator among diverse audiences, reconstructed as subjects capable of being in two places at once.

The extraordinary economic rallying of Hollywood around the late 1970s can therefore be seen in terms of subjectivity as well as demography, against a common background of an attunement of the culture to youth audiences of whatever age, 'sophisticated naivety' giving a focus to the infusion of talent. It provided the industry with exceptional growth potential as well as bequeathing to it a nerve-racking volatility, while the introduction of so many new technologies called for a different managerial and financing logic (what has been called the move from 'industry' to 'business').[17] After the near-bankruptcy of all the major film studios, Hollywood appeared once more full of life, having mutated and shape-shifted out of all recognition. Curiously de-centred and re-centred by the series of studio acquisitions on the part of multinational corporations, the balance of power had shifted, making movies a minor element of the global entertainment industry, and the entertainment industry itself merely one part of multinational corporate planning, focused on oil, transport, car-parks and property dealing.[18]

Citizen Coppola

In such changing contexts of entrepreneurship, technological innovation and the culture of youth and nostalgia, the career of Coppola occupies a symptomatic space. His gifts, his successes, but also his tragic mistakes shed light on more than his own work, making the man and his myth a particularly striking example of the different options between classical and post-classical Hollywood, as well as between modernist and postmodern authorship. As a film director, Coppola sees himself clearly in the American tradition, comparable to D.W. Griffith or John Ford, but this does not prevent him from identifying with Orson Welles, the great outsider of the American cinema *par excellence*, and the opposite of classical Hollywood's studio directors.[19] However American he is, though, Coppola also belongs to America's 'European' heritage, being a second-generation Italian immigrant, with strong emotional and family roots to Southern Europe, and a keen sense of a past either real or 'dreamt about', and of futures either possible or 'remembered'.

Coppola's ambition has always been of Shakespearean proportions. Famous and wealthy at an early age (after the success of *The Godfather*), he built up his own studio, Zoetrope, and wanted to make it in every way the prototype for filmmaking in the twenty-first century.[20] The shape and thematics of Orson Welles' *Citizen Kane* (1941) are everywhere in Coppola's films: from the Brando character in *The Godfather*, and the Brando figure in *Apocalypse Now* (1979) to the more recent *Bram Stoker's Dracula* and *Mary Shelley's Frankenstein* (1994). Beverle Houston, referring to Welles' heroes, once called them 'power-babies': men obsessed with control, and highly skilled in the devious ways of wielding it, but in some sense crippled by an immaturity, a thirst and a craving for attention reaching back to childhood, intemperate, insatiable and unmeasured.[21] These configurations in Coppola's fictional characters have coloured the myth of his person: hence his reputation as an overreacher and a gambler, a man who takes immoderate risks, leaving a trail of destruction as likely as fabulous success and spectacular achievements.

New Hollywood when embodied by Coppola is rewriting the 'old' as the 'new' in another sense too. The very classicism we now associate with Hollywood and its golden age, its canonical directors and masterpieces, were mostly named and defined not in the USA but by the *nouvelle vague*, precisely by the generation of critics-filmmakers like Godard, Truffaut, Chabrol, Rohmer, who in turn became a double influence on the American cinema by telling a new generation of Americans what and who was important in their own cinema, and by inspiring them to be innovative in style, storytelling and sensibility. Yet by the 1980s, it was Coppola who rendered an inverse service to a younger generation in Europe, most notably from the New German Cinema. His Zoetrope Studio imported Wim Wenders (who made *Hammett* (1983) there), and Coppola made possible the distribution of Werner Herzog's films, as well as of Syberberg's *Hitler: A Film From Germany* (1977). Fitting into the pattern, too, was Coppola's decision to bring to the States Kevin Brownlow's magnificent restoration of Abel Gance's *Napoleon* (1927), for which he asked none other than his father, Carmine Coppola, to compose a score and conduct it with a live orchestra. Aguirre, Hitler, Napoleon – European overreachers, failed world conquerors, studied with nonchalant but hardly casual interest by an American movie mogul, building up media power that seemed poised to take on the world, yet sufficiently European to be also fatally in love with this ambition's failure: elements of a mythology perhaps too potent to resist. Does this not suggest an ironically self-referential relation of Coppola also to Dracula, and across the myth, to history as a horror film?

Typical of the New Hollywood is a self-conscious use of old mythologies, genre stereotypes, and the history of the cinema itself. But even more striking is the revival of genres which – in the 1950s – were regarded as 'B-movies': the sci-fi film, the 'creature-feature' or monster film, and the many other variations on the horror film. B-picture conventions, when taken up in the 1980s and 1990s, introduced into mainstream cinema the sort of ruptures in realism (understood as narrative coherence, unified characters, goal-directed story structure) that European filmmakers had brought in the 1960s to their own modernist art cinema practice. Unlike the full-blown (literary) modernism of Alain Resnais or Michelangelo Antonioni, however, the sources and techniques that split open the new Hollywood narratives came mostly from the American cinema itself, its minor genres and debased modes. The horror film especially permitted deviations and transgressions of the representational norm. In contrast to maintaining a coherent diegetic world and the rule of narrative causality, horror films almost by definition disrupt the cause and effect patterns of such classical devices as shot/countershot, continuity and reverse field editing in order to create a sense of mystery, of the unexpected, of surprise, incongruity and horror, misleading the viewer by withholding information or keeping the causal agent, the monster, off-screen for as long as possible.

In this play with spatial relationships around what is and what is not visually present, sound has always played a particularly important role. But while in classical continuity cinema the sound–image synchronization perfectly reproduces the question/answer pattern of linear narrative, because the viewer identifies a sound by picturing its source, the horror film emphasizes the presence of sound in order that the absence of its source becomes localized by the mind more vividly – and more like a fantasm.[22] Thus, the horror film's generic device of breaking the neat synchronization of sound and image by keeping the sources of sound invisible and off-screen also helps destabilize the primacy of the diegetic story world over the extra-diegetic or non-diegetic world. Without resorting to supernatural forces or extra-terrestrial beings, the skilful use of sound can draw sharp attention to the characters' as well as the viewers' limited and partial perspectives. It is as if the formal resources of sound in the horror film as genre signal all kinds of other social or political 'horrors', yet the starting point would not be ideological or mimetic: senseless slaughter, social injustice or human evil, calling for the horror film genre as its most appropriate 'reflection' or adequate 'representation'. Rather, it may be better pictured the other way round: in Vietnam films, for instance, the jungle becomes the epitome of the horrible not because reluctant G.I. conscripts face a determined and ruthless enemy. Instead, it is because the films draw on the familiar horror genre trope of the 'monster in the swamp' – nowhere to be seen, but when heard, effective action comes too late – that they succeed so well in 'rendering' the bodily sensations of danger in the face of the Vietcong.[23] In other words, with the horror genre, we are no longer in the episteme of 'realism' or 'reflection', but encounter the cinema experience as first and foremost a bodily one, and thus an end in itself, rather than a means to an end, political, represen-tational or otherwise. Many of these cinematic techniques, adopted from the horror genre and explicitly drawing upon visual disorientation and the loss of temporal certainties figure prominently in Coppola's *Apocalypse Now*,[24] but also in the visual and sound effects of *Bram Stoker's Dracula*: in what could be called a *trompe-l'œil* effect for hearing, as when Jonathan Harker, while exploring the Count's labyrinthine chambers, hears the sound of liquid splashing upwards before he is raped by a gang of female Draculas.

Rewriting and self-reference, palimpsest and *mise-en-abyme*

The reasons for choosing *Bram Stoker's Dracula* to examine the classical/post-classical divide are thus partly based on considerations of genre, and the curious reversal that seems to have taken place between technology and referent, motiva-tion and technique. In addition, if New Hollywood in the economic sense (the revival of the fortunes of the US film business discussed above) and the post-classical in the textual sense (a high-concept visual impact movie, preferably in the thriller mode)[25] share the vigorous refiguring of the text and its limits, of the product and its market, we might define the new (postmodern) episteme as one which joins economic with textual excess. Consequently, a 1990s film about Dracula, figure of excess *par excellence*, as well as boundary-creature and boundary-crosser, invariably alerts one to the possibility of different forms of audience engagement, different ways of being inside and outside when it comes to identification and participation. Riding on the new audience demographics with their split mode of address is a 'post-classical' treatment of often very classical narratives, a new treatment of sound and of the image, or at any rate, of the hierarchies between them. My argument would be that Coppola's *Bram Stoker's Dracula* is symptomatic because in it the classical, the post-classical and the postmodern find distinct articulations. Indeed, part of the ambiguity of response or irritation this has generated among the critics[26] seems negatively to confirm the slippery, self-referential and self-mocking pose the film strikes in respect to its own place in movie history. Yet this overdetermined hybridity evidently appealed to the volatile audiences Hollywood is chasing, perhaps not least because the film features an agelessly youthful hero who remembers a future, while living in a past which is yet to happen. What Pierre Sorlin has suggested about film history in general – namely that since there can be no history without singularity or absence, films do not have a history, given that they are fully 'present' every time they are screened[27] – thus refers quite accurately not only to Count Dracula, but to our 'postmodern' position *vis-à-vis* classical cinema: because of its undead nature, the cinema perhaps does not have a history (of periods, styles, modes). It can only have fans, clans and believers, forever gathering to revive a fantasm or a trauma, a memory and an anticipation.

This last point is pertinent to *Bram Stoker's Dracula* in another respect as well. In the press release and in interviews, Coppola made much of his faithfulness to the novel, but the script is actually based on a book by Leonard Wolf, *The Annotated Dracula*.[28] Even the sources, then, confront one with a commentary on a commentary, whose *mise-en-abyme* structure can be celebrated as the film's particular authenticity, itself only heightened when one realizes how replete with citations to other films Coppola's adaptation of Bram Stoker's novel is: at the last count, no less than sixty titles. Besides the thirty-odd Dracula films, this still leaves a dense intertextuality, though perhaps not as eruditely pedantic as Stanley Kubrick's *Barry Lyndon* (1975), where Omar Calabrese confidently identified 271 individual paintings.[29] To name a few of the films in *Bram Stoker's Dracula*: Louis Lumière's *Arrival of a Train* (1895), Jean Epstein's *The Fall of the House of Usher* (1928), Jean Cocteau's *La Belle et La Bête* (1945), Akira Kurosawa's *Throne of Blood* (1957), Walter Hill's *The Long Riders* (1979), Werner Herzog's *Heart of Glass* (1976), and also Herzog's *Nosferatu* (1979), itself a remake of Murnau's famous film. We are thus offered a highly self-referencing text in relation to movie history, but also with respect to technology, in particular, the technologies of recording, visualization and reproduction: diaries, phonographs, dictaphones, peep shows, the *cinématographe* all play prominent and narratively important parts.

Allusions to paintings, too, are almost as conspicuous as films and recording instruments: for instance, the Count's portrait pointed out by him to Harker as a picture of his ancestor Vlad is, as we know, a portrait of himself. In the posture of the figure and the composition, it alludes to Albrecht Dürer's famous self-portrait, which was itself a *Self Portrait as the Young Christ*, making the portrait in Dracula's castle a citation, as well as a *mise-en-abyme* of this citation around the trope of 'the self as other'. Also present is one of the most famous paintings in the Western canon, the *Mona Lisa*, precisely invoked in the scene with Mina/Elzbieta over absinthe in the café: as Mina 'remembers' Transylvania, the sylvan landscape of da Vinci opens up behind her, hinting at the film's pastiche of a painterly 'classicism', in the service of a postmodern subjectivity of 'colonized memory' and 'trauma', while – as so often in this film – drawing attention to the signifier, with a visual/verbal pun on the word 'Transylvania' [beyond the woods].

Altogether, the film poses as a kind of palimpsest of a hundred years of movie history: the year Dracula comes to London is 1897, and the reason he gives for his trip (to the hapless Mina) is that he had heard about a new marvel of science: the cinematograph. What more fitting, then, than the idea that Dracula should seduce Mina at the movies, illustrating how a vampire film today qualifies as at once prototypical for movie history and for postmodernity. The theme of repetition and seriality, of cliché and stereotype, of reworking and re-turning applies materially to both the vampire myth and its perennially favourite status as a movie subject at least since F. W. Murnau's *Nosferatu* from 1922. In so far as Dracula is almost another word for an ambiguous nostalgia, it remains the archetypal movie motif, for the very theme of the undead lies at the heart of the cinema's power and cultural presence. One only has to think of old stars still alive, interviewed on television, looking at their earlier selves on the silver screen. Is not each his or her own Dracula, trying to reincarnate themselves, charm once more, and unable to rest quietly in their retirement graves, become the ghost at the feast of yet another retrospective? The very peculiar tragedy of photography and the cinema – that they appear to be defying time – is as deeply embedded in Dracula as it belongs to the literary thematic of, say, Oscar Wilde's *The Picture of Dorian Gray* and Edgar Allan Poe's *The Oval Portrait*.

If the word 'palimpsest' seems a rather literary term when applied to film, risking to remain a mere metaphor, it is none the less appropriate in ways which I hope will provide a novel perspective on how to reread the 'classical' and the mythological in *Bram Stoker's Dracula* within its 'post-classical' circulation of modes of address, media-forms and merchandised commodities. The changes, for instance, that Coppola and his scriptwriter introduced, notably with respect to Van Helsing's presence both inside the narrative as Dracula's nemesis and out-side the narrative as the omniscient narrator/framer of the tale — his double function only marked by the recognizable voice of Anthony Hopkins, and thus another aural pun, so to speak — hint at a de-centring not only of body and voice, but of 'text', 'subtext' and 'intertext', preparing the 'merger' of Mina and Elzbieta, on which Coppola's narrative turns, in order to unite Dracula with his ultimate love, the one that has always been his. Literally remembering the future, his errance across the centuries has no other goal than to recapture what he had already had, when a single, fatal moment of 'bad timing' deprived him of its possession.

Fin-de-siècle cinema: classical, post-classical or postmodern

The echoes of Oscar Wilde and Edgar Allan Poe in the basic theme of the undead bring one back to Bram Stoker as a writer of his time. It suggests that the term postmodern is not altogether that remote from the pre-modernist: for what one can identify in the cluster of motifs with which this pot-boiler seduces the reader might more properly be called 'decadence', or '*fin-de-siècle*'. And if we look at *Bram Stoker's Dracula* — mindful of its intertextuality with respect to painting — we do indeed recognize in the figural work of Coppola's *mise-en-scène* a filmic equiva-lent of meandering motifs à la Aubrey Beardsley, or the monsters of Gustave Moreau, surging forward in the female vampires who are Gorgons and Medusas, snake women with writhing heads and dilating eyes. Mina herself, in the end decapitating Dracula, is reminiscent of Salomé, one of the quintessential motifs of French and European decadence: if the 1890s knew all about sexual ambigu-ity, then they share with the 1990s the uncertainty of gender and representation. Coppola seems to have taken his date of 1897 rather seriously, and we can reflect on the peculiar contiguity of *fin-de-siècle* painting and the birth of the cinema, which he brings together in Mina's seduction, where the scene shifts to the typical chambre separé of the 'naughty nineties'. Yet instead of Moulin Rouge dancers, one can recognize a movie show of the Lumière London Polytechnic programme across the frosted windows.

The point to make, however, concerns less the self-conscious citations of period detail, lending yet another layer of 'authentic' movie patina to Bram Stoker literary *décadence*. Rather, such references as there are to pre-Raphaelite pictorialism in *Bram Stoker's Dracula* can also be understood as giving the director a historically secured vantage point for something altogether more tentative: to put into play several distinct systems of representation, whose coexistence and frictions in the film help to define what might — in retrospect, so to speak — have been at stake aesthetically, as well as for media technology and audiences in the shift from classical to post-classical. Here the notion of the palimpsest seems also apposite, for in *Bram Stoker's Dracula*, the classical is preserved in its very over-writing, just as other oppositions, such as Hollywood/Europe, are sustained in a non-binary way. In this sense, the film conducts a kind of deconstruction of the linear narrative/monocular perspective system of representation which film studies has identified with the classical. Dominated by a 'character-centred causality', this model of narrative, faithful to broadly Aristotelian principles (unity of time, space and action) is organized according to a clear cause and effect chain which relentlessly motivates the action, and displays a high degree of 'character consistency' (meaning that the protagonists normally do not do things out of character, unless the genre permits it, and they do not change physical shape or appearance other than in tales of magic and the fantastic).

By contrast, post-classical cinema could be said to have introduced two major changes: in many mainstream or popular productions of the 1990s, the narrative progression has become quite involuted, with complex temporal schemes binding the segments – many time-travel films such as *Back to the Future* (1985), *Peggy Sue Got Married* (1986), *Twelve Monkeys* (1995), or multi-strand narratives as in *Pulp Fiction* (1994) and *Short Cuts* (1993) come to mind. The second change concerns 'character consistency'; here, too, contemporary films can be quite radical: one thinks of John Malkovitch in *In the Line of Fire* (1993), of Arnold Schwarzenegger and his antagonist in *Terminator 2* (1991) and *Total Recall* (1990), the alien in *Alien* (1979), the play with dual personalities in Lynch's *Twin Peaks* (1989–90) and *Lost Highway* (1997), or the undecidability of who is replicant and who human in *Blade Runner* (1982). Similar 'deviations' are present in *Bram Stoker's Dracula*: the temporality, while apparently linear, jumps some four hundred years after the opening, and – as already indicated – is internally quite complexly interwoven via the different levels of recollection and memory in Mina, and the count's omnipresence and undeadness. In addition, Dracula manifests himself in a startling multiplicity of guises, only few of which are anchored in the myth itself. Instead of character consistency, post-classical cinema confronts the viewer with shape-shifting serial killers, voraciously vigorous vampires or time-travelling terminators, while still trying to negotiate the concepts of identity, person, agency. This may have been another reason why critics did not like *Bram Stoker's Dracula*, complaining that the plot was confusing, the allusions gratuitous, or arguing that at a deeper level the film had destroyed the potency of the myth, with Coppola driving a final stake through all the Dracula films.[30]

The combined impact of these changes in chronological time schemes and character identity can be observed in the fate of another feature of the classical cinema, the double plot structure, where an adventure plot and a romance plot are at once distinct from and intertwined with each other. The first is often a quest, an investigation, the pursuit of a goal, while the second is always centred on the formation of the heterosexual couple, with the latter strand (the formation of the couple) usually providing the terms of closure. The post-classical plot is able to take greater liberties and 'get away with it'. For instance, endings in post-classical films are often so open, so ambiguous (see also *Basic Instinct* (1992), *Twelve Monkeys*, *Total Recall*) that one cannot really speak of the 'formation' of a hetero-sexual couple, and even where the final situation is not ambiguous, it is positively menacing (as in *The Silence of the Lambs* (1990)) and open-ended enough to allow for a sequel. *Bram Stoker's Dracula* is in this respect also a symptomatic example, in that it deconstructs the classical by excessively instantiating it. The plot involves the formation of two couples: the Jonathan Harker/Mina couple and the Dracula/Mina couple are at once superimposed and displaced in relation to each other, thanks to the time shift that allows the characters to exist in two temporalities at once. Character consistency, faithfully observed in the classical mode, can – as indicated – be transgressed in the classical model's minor genres, such as horror, science-fiction and fantasy. Here, too, the post-classical does not oppose the classical, but emphatically re-centres it, precisely by making the marginal genres the dominant ones, pulling an unusual time structure, a novel sound practice or an expressive visual style into focus and dead centre, without thereby neutralizing their unsettling aberrance. As for narrative-visual closure, *Bram Stoker's Dracula* provides a particular bold example of the classical 'to excess': its ending is already embedded in and enfolds itself into the opening in the most startling manner.

One will recall that this opening – added by Coppola – is set in 1497, after the fall of Constantinople. Going into battle for Christendom, Count Vlad defeats the Ottomans, but loses his bride Elzbieta, who commits suicide after receiving a false message of the Count's death. Cursing God, the Count vows himself to the quest for Elzbieta, thus condemning himself to the unnatural, non-human existence arrested between life and death. Coppola thus gives his Dracula a quite unambigu-ously 'classical' motivation, but he does so in a visual configuration that suspends the narrative's trajectory. For the sequence ends with the establishment of a double absence: that of Elzbieta's inert body, and of an unmatched shot of Dracula looking upwards. The gap here opened up is only filled in the final scene, once more in the chapel of Dracula's castle, when in the place of Elzbieta's prostrate body we now see the dying Dracula, about to be released into mortality, and eyes cast heavenwards. As Mina/Elzbieta cuts off Dracula's head, we are allowed to see what Dracula is/had been looking at: the dome of the chapel with the painted ceiling, showing Dracula and Elzbieta united. With it, the point of view shot of the opening is sutured, allowing for a perfect visual rhyme, though not in the mode of 'repetition/resolution',[31] but by way of an elaborate relay of gazes across the delay not only of the film's narrative completion, but of the viewer's realization that the opening scene had been seen from the point of view of the ceiling picture, inscribing the formation of the couple, Dracula's gaze and desire, as well as the viewers' point of view. Thus, the specularity of the opening scene commands its own temporality and memory, constructed in the mode of a future anterior of 'what will have been', giving/withholding the fulfilment before the promise, while catching our look in the gaze of an Other.

Such a baroque spatio-temporal-specular bracket around the film forcibly draws attention to the status of perspectival space in the post-classical cinema. Euclidian geometry and Renaissance vision, or rather, the resulting architecture of looks (between the characters, between spectator and screen, between camera and characters) is said to constitute the visual regime of the classical paradigm, and holds – as psycho-semiology has taught us – the subject 'in place' by way of voyeurism and specular identification. It is this regime that the scene just quoted seems to be putting into infinite regress, as it deconstructs the cinema's specularity by highlighting it so dramatically via the missing reverse shot and the optative realized in its temporal delay. *Bram Stoker's Dracula* subsequently does not abandon the familiar geometry of representation and its implied 'play of gaze and glance',[32] rather, the specular becomes the surplus and the supplement of another mode, grounded in a different kind of image. Often, for instance, there seems no frame to an image, nor does one always know exactly where and how a shot ends and another begins (cf. the steadicam tracking shot that indicates Dracula's presence, which suddenly seems to explode as a gunshot 'blows' away Quincy, the Texan). At other times, space contracts and expands, as in the scene where Dracula visits Mina, and suddenly Van Helsing bursts in: an intimate bedroom has become a vast baronial hall, and Dracula, at first a bat-gargoyle hanging from the ceiling, becomes a huge looming figure in a carapace and armour.

The term to which I therefore want to contrast 'specularity' is 'engulfment', in order to indicate how such a non-specular, body-based pliability of the image might modify the terms of the viewer's subject position. For what we seem to be witnessing is the 'decomposition' of the image as representation and the screen as a bounded frame, in which case the representational mode of post-classical cinema would indeed resituate both classical painting and photography. It would also explain why Coppola invests instead in the pictorialism and representational codes that are the precursors of abstract art, namely symbolist painting, expressionist colour schemes, art nouveau ornament.

The key technical means or figural trope used in order to achieve this end is superimposition. There is superimposition in classical cinema, too, but it is mainly used to indicate either a shift in time and/or space, or to signal interiority, that is, the character's thoughts. But in a post-classical film such as *Bram Stoker's Dracula*, superimposition is freed from these connotations, no longer functioning as boundary marker. A key example is the parting scene between Jonathan Harker and Mina, with the couple in the garden placed in the foreground so as to create an exaggerated perspective to the rose garden and the fountain at the far end. All of a sudden, a peacock's feather forecloses our view of the lovers' kiss, until the 'eye' of the feather opens up like an iris shot in an early film, though in fact transforming itself into the tunnel through which speeds the train that is already taking Jonathan away from Mina. What makes these metamorphoses partake in the new solidity and material consistency of the image are, paradoxically, the sound effects of the scene, with the cry of the peacock modulating into the whistle of the train before becoming the plaintive voice of Mina reading the letter Jonathan has written to her on that train.

This new material density of the non-perspectival, figurative image is, however, itself an illusion, for its consistency is guaranteed less by any tactility of perception, and more by the semantic-cognitive effects put into play, illustrated by the visual and aural puns, such as the peacock's eye or the train's whistle. Another instance would be the pun on AB(SIN)THE in the seduction scene between Dracula and Mina, which starts with a close-up of the drink being poured, forming a vortex that shapes into an eye, not unlike the bathwater/plughole/eye transformation in the shower scene of *Psycho* (1960). Coppola plays on eye, glass, drink and bottle: startling changes of perspective put the mind on high alert, for the attack on vision and perception in these scenes inevitably reminds one of the even more ferocious assault on the eye in Luis Buñuel's *Un Chien Andalou* (1928). Coppola repeats the effect later in the scene, when the ring with diamonds which Dracula is offering to Mina/Elzbieta seems to 'graze' her eye, here building up, however, to the romance cluster of associations that lead from eye to stars to diamonds to tears, for Dracula, having gathered Mina's tears from her cheeks, can now, with a magician's gesture, open his palm and reveal that they have turned into precious stones.

Engulfment: beyond narration and perspectivism?

With all these visual puns and *double entendres*, some of which are gross or grotesque, such as the fade that makes the slicing of a red side of beef by Van Helsing rhyme with his decapitation of Lucy, one is unsure of how 'Coppola' (i.e. the narrating instance) wants to be 'read': does he mock the viewer or does he mock his characters? Is it irony (blank or red-blooded), parody or pastiche? Is it deadpan humour, sick humour or black humour? What is the mode of engagement, what is the interpersonal tone and address, or is it a kind of queasy complicity that here substitutes for voyeurism and fetishization, the classical model's modes of 'identification'? This is part of the irritation that the film provokes, because its tone is unreadable in 'classical' terms. What from the point of view of cinematic modernism or European art cinema might be a 'foregrounding of the device' would from the vantage point of 'classical cinema' appear merely as a gratuitous 'showing off', the 'bad taste' of B-movies, or even confusing the viewer by obstructing narrative progress and transparency. Yet from another vantage point, such gyrations of tenor and tone invoke an altogether different viewing experience and viewing habit: not of the cinema, nor even television, but the viewing experience of the screen as a monitor, as a flat surface, upon which, in a visual-video overlay, any number of elements can be called up simultaneously: graphics, images, script, text, sound, voice, in other words, a whole array of media signals. What Coppola (now perhaps less as auteur and cinematic heir to the traditions of Ford or Hawks, but as founder-owner of Zoetrope studios and erstwhile recipient of research and development funds from the Sony Corporation) seems to be examining is the multimedia viewing experience, now writ large, though – if we believe the publicity department's assertion that the film contains no digital special effects – done as an 'authentic pastiche' of the thrusting enthusiasm and craftsmanlike pride associated with the early cinema's inventor-bricoleur-pioneers.[33]

Just as the cinema of the first decades developed sophisticated spatial arrangements, favouring subtler forms of spectator participation, sometimes at the expense of narrative, so Coppola's film can be seen to suspend narrative in favour of spatial play or aural perspectivism, though these moments of pseudo-primitivism are themselves elaborate semantic puzzles, crafted in order to engage narrative on its own terrain by deconstructing its logic of agency, motivation, temporality and the causal chain. Yet *Bram Stoker's Dracula*, despite its shock effects, does not thereby treat the viewer to the video game emplotment of 'shoot them, kill them, chase them, thrill them'. Its own mode proposes a kind of articulation where consequence, motive and implication are still vital, but where none the less a different form of participation and engagement obtains. Engulfment thus is meant to indicate a distinct mode of consequence, of implication and interrelation, signifying at once an attenuated kind of causality, but also something more dangerous, because no longer capable of being kept at the sort of distance that engagement via the eye and mind assures. Instead of the bounded image, the mode of engulfment works with the ambient image, in which it is sound that now 'locates', 'cues' and even 'narrates' the image, producing a more corporeal set of perceptions; instead of voyeurism and fetishistic fixation, there is spatial disorientation; instead of the logic of the 'scene', it is semantic clusters, mental maps, spatial metaphors that organize comprehension and narrative transformation.

Finally, the term 'engulfment' also signals changes to the way one might think about narrative and causality in a social or political context. Against the basically agonistic/antagonistic principle of Aristotelian poetics, or even the structuralist model of binary oppositions and logical transformation (Lévi-Strauss or Greimas), the more 'embodied' nexus of the post-classical implies power-gradients and feedback loops that can encompass relations of 'contamination', but also those of involuntary attraction: of memory and trauma, of anticipation and the *après-coup*, of dependence and interdependence, of addiction, of the host and the parasite, and all of them suspending and yet sublating the Hegelian master–slave dialectic with which the Dracula myth is often associated.

In light of this, one can understand how the myth of Dracula does double duty for Coppola: not only in so far as it allows a reversal of the classical paradigm (where the story's transparency makes the technology invisible and inaudible) in favour of a re-materialization of the filmic signifiers via techniques that are often adapted in *Bram Stoker's Dracula* from early cinema and 'decadent' visual culture. Where other postmodern directors might fetishize the 'new' technologies, and in their films 'test-drive' the recent developments in sound (Dolby), frame (special video-effects of overlay and morphing) and image (steadicam), Coppola seems more ironically detached, perhaps melancholically conscious of haunting the present by having been a pioneering godfather in almost all of these fields. Second, the Dracula myth already literalizes this different causality of contamination and interdependence, as well as the 'causality' of media events or, more specifically, the blockbuster phenomenon. The pervasiveness of these media epidemics at all stages of the body politic and the public sphere, with their peculiar absorption of the past into the present and their virus-like multiplications, seems to have become emblematic for the instabilities of the post-binary, post-antagonistic, post-Cold War world (dis-)order.

Against this, one might hold the irritation that Coppola has betrayed the myth by appending a frame tale which trades a deeper truth for the politically correct move of unambiguously identifying Dracula with the historical figure of Vlad the Impaler, thereby thematizing the so-called 'clash of civilizations' when Orthodox Christianity 'saved' the West from Islam and the Turks. Similarly, one might accuse him of having turned Dracula's sexuality from one of indiscriminate poly-morphously perverse lust into the dimensions of a romance story about star-crossed destinies, unnecessary suicides and a 'love that never dies', when the vampire ought to stand for a lust that never dies. Anything else, it is said, emascu-lates the potency of the very notion of the undead, sacrificing the psychic economy of eros and thanatos on the paltry altar of a heterosexual *Liebestod*.

Yet such differences cannot be settled without the considerations that have informed this chapter: namely, that the film proposes various paradigms, leaving it up to the viewer whether to be engaged as (already) a post-classical viewer within the classical mode, or (still) as the classical viewer within the post-classical mode. One conclusion might be that the perspectival metaphor which has dominated film studies for so long will have to give way to a different metaphoric cluster: the one suggested for *Bram Stoker's Dracula*, not surprisingly, has alluded to 'trauma' and 'contamination', but it might equally well be some other 'figurative' space, like that of the 'visceral' and 'body horror'. It is precisely because a film like *Bram Stoker's Dracula* offers itself not only to very different readings, but is able to combine the viewing experience of the big screen and the small screen, the monitor and the video-arcade that it belongs to the New Hollywood, to the history of the cinema and to this history's afterlife. In this respect at least, *Bram Stoker's Dracula* is an authentic enactment of the myth: the true Dracula of cinema – once more risen from the grave of the (much debated) 'death of cinema' and the (box-office) 'death of Coppola' to haunt us all – hopefully for quite some time yet, because who does not want the cinema to be the love that never dies?

Notes

1 Jon Lewis, *Whom God Wishes to Destroy* (London: The Athlone Press, 1995), p. 160.

2 The subtitle of *Whom God Wishes to Destroy* is *Francis Coppola and the New Hollywood*. See also James Monaco, *American Film Now* (New York: Oxford University Press, 1979).

3 Thomas Schatz, 'The New Hollywood', in J. Collins, H. Radner and A. Preacher Collins (eds), *Film Theory Goes to the Movies* (London: Routledge, 1993), pp. 8–36.

4 Michael Pye and Lynda Myles, *The Movie Brats* (London: Studio Vista, 1985).

5 Schatz, 'The New Hollywood', pp. 26–8.

6 Tino Balio (ed.), *Hollywood in the Age of Television* (Cambridge, Mass.: Unwyn Hyman, 1990).

7 Justin Wyatt, *High Concept: Movies and Marketing in Hollywood* (Austin: University of Texas Press, 1994).

8 Tim Corrigan, *A Cinema Without Walls: Movies and Culture After Vietnam* (New York/ London: Routledge, 1991).

9 Robin Wood, *Hollywood from Vietnam to Reagan* (New York: Columbia University Press, 1986).

10 'Since the mid-seventies, the international film industry has been defined by more economic and productive contention and alteration than coherence. . . . This . . . follows clearly from the uncertainty and instability about the reception of a product that has too many audiences or too vague an audience: an audience that can only be designated, in the jargon of Hollywood producers today, as "fly-overs," a mass of undifferentiated desires that lives below planes moving between Los Angeles and New York City.' Tim Corrigan, *A Cinema Without Walls*, pp. 22–3.

11 See Ien Ang, *Desperately Seeking the Audience* (London: Routledge, 1995).

12 Thomas Elsaesser, 'National cinema: the competition with Hollywood', *Skrien*, no. 186 (1992), pp. 50–3.

13 Thomas Elsaesser, 'German postwar cinema and Hollywood', in D. Ellwood and R. Kroes (eds), *Hollywood and Europe* (Amsterdam: Vrije Universiteit, 1994), pp. 283–302.

14 'The boom of allusionism is a legacy of American auteurism, a term that . . . denotes the frenzy for film that seized this country in the 60s and early 70s. Armed with lists from Andrew Sarris and compatible aesthetic theories from Eisenstein, Bazin, Godard and McLuhan, a significant part of the generation raised in the 50s went movie mad and attacked film history. They passionately sought out films they had missed, returned obsessively to old favourites, and tried to classify them all. Among those engaged in this discovery of film history – particularly American film history – were some people who would become filmmakers.' Noël Carroll, 'The future of an allusion', *October*, no. 21 (1982), p. 54.

15 Ray sees here the effect of television, purveying a certain kind of film culture: 'Television, with its indiscriminate recycling and baroque deployment of the American cinema's basic paradigms . . . has perpetuated the most conservative incarnation of those codes. As a result, we may be on the verge of witnessing the creation of mass audiences with a truly double system of consciousness, by turns (or simultaneously) straight and ironic.' Robert Ray, *A Certain Tendency of the Hollywood Cinema* (Princeton: Princeton University Press, 1985), p. 244.

16 Fredric Jameson, *The Political Unconscious* (London: Methuen, 1981), p. 207.

17 Chris Hugo, 'The economic background', parts I and II, *Movie*, nos. 27/28 (1984), pp. 43–9, and nos. 31/32 (1986), pp. 84–8.

18 Another round of acquisitions began in the early 1990s: the media mergers continue to make headlines, involving Time Warner, Disney, Turner Broadcasting, Viacom, and in 1995 the foundation of a new studio was announced, KSG Dreamworks, headed by Jerry Katzenberg, Steven Spielberg and David Geffen. In the post-studio system period each film has become a media event, exploiting different star qualities or spectacle attractions, whether a mechanical shark in *Jaws*, a musical score (the *Star Wars* theme), or an ingeniously designed logo in *Batman*. Borrowing the formal features of 'shareability' (merchandizing, spin-offs, sequels) from the music and advertisement industries, the blockbuster movie is based on a very quick cycle of commercial exploitation, the high visibility ensuring that its initial cinema release is followed by a saturation of even more profitable secondary markets like video releases and computer games. Producers are thus looking for ways not so much of targeting different audiences, but of targeting audiences differently.

19 'I would give anything to have a life like Orson Welles' (quoted in Peter Cowie, *Coppola* (London: Faber, 1990), p. 222).

20 Cowie, *Coppola*, pp. 43–58.

21 Beverle Houston, 'Power and dis-integration in the films of Orson Welles', *Film Quarterly*, vol. 35, no. 4 (Summer 1982), p. 2.

22 Michel Chion, *Audiovision: Sound on Screen* (New York: Columbia University Press, 1994).

23 In *Apocalypse Now*, both times the patrol boat is attacked by Vietcong guerrillas, their presence is first indicated by the sound of their guns and arrows, and when they are finally visually located in the image (and noticed by the American soldiers), it is too late to escape: both times a soldier loses his life.

24 Thomas Elsaesser and Michael Wedel, 'The hollow heart of Hollywood: sound space in *Apocalypse Now*', in Gene Moore (ed.), *Conrad on Film* (Oxford: Oxford University Press, 1997). Some of the material used here is taken from this essay and I gratefully acknowledge Michael Wedel's contribution.

25 Post-classical cinema is associated with East Coast directors like Scorsese, de Palma, Schrader, David Lynch and West Coast directors like Spielberg, Lucas, Coppola (from USC and UCLA film schools). But post-classical films are also directed by Adrian Lyne and Alan Parker, Ridley Scott and Paul Verhoeven, and more recently by Wolfgang Petersen, with Michael Ballhaus, the cameraman on *Bram Stoker's Dracula* a conspicuous presence: there is thus not only an input from advertising (in which the British excel), but also from continental European cinema talent.

26 See Richard Dyer, 'Dracula and desire', *Sight and Sound*, vol. 3, no. 1 (January 1993), pp. 8–12.

27 Pierre Sorlin, 'Ist es möglich, eine Geschichte des Kinos zu schreiben?', *Montage a/v*, vol. 5, no. 1 (1996), p. 27.

28 See Steve Biodrowski, 'Coppola's Dracula', *Cinefantastique*, vol. 23, no. 4 (1992), p. 24.

29 Omar Calabrese, 'I Replicanti', paper given at the Semiotics Conference 1986 in Urbino.

30 See special issue of *Sight and Sound*, vol. 3, no. 1 (January 1993), especially the review essays of Ian Sinclair (p. 15) and Richard Dyer (pp. 8–12).

31 The terms used by Raymond Bellour to describe the functioning of the classical cinema's visual-narrative economy. See R. Bellour, 'The obvious and the code', in Phil Rosen (ed.), *Narrative, Apparatus, Ideology* (New York: Columbia University Press, 1986), pp. 93–101.

32 'In order to have an image you need to have a scene, a certain distance without which there can be no looking, no play of glances, and it is that play that makes things appear or disappear. It is in this sense that I find television obscene, because there is no stage, no depth, no place for a possible glance and therefore no place either for a possible seduction.' Jean Baudrillard, *Baudrillard Live* (London: Verso, 1989), p. 69.

33 This ironic-indulgent stance *vis-à-vis* film history itself seems to me one difference between Coppola and other practitioners of the multimedia mode in cinema today, such as Peter Greenaway in his experiments with video (e.g. *Prospero's Books* (1991)) or his recent cinema films, such as *The Pillow Book* (1997). There, one senses rather more the director's conviction that the whole tradition of classical Hollywood is an irrelevance in the real business of cinema developing as an art form.

Part IV

Audience, address and ideology

Chapter 14

Hollywood and independent black cinema

Tommy L. Lott

The development of black cinema over the past generation is reflected in a grow-ing number of book-length commentaries.[1] Among the contributions to this rap-idly growing body of literature are Manthia Diawara's anthology *Black American Cinema* and Ed Guerrero's *Framing Blackness*.[2] Diawara brings together essays by a host of prominent literary and film scholars, whereas Guerrero employs a histor-ical survey format to analyse the black film image. There seems to be a consensus among black film scholars that contemporary black cinema encompasses films produced both in and out of Hollywood. Nevertheless, several themes pertaining to the history and theory of black cinema can be identified in black film commen-taries which suggest a specific role or function for independent black cinema. By focusing on these themes I want to examine more closely the concept of con-temporary black cinema implicit in recent criticism.

Most commentators agree that the more radical aesthetic and political orienta-tion of many independent black films is largely a function of counter hegemonic practices, yet they have not given sufficient attention to some of the important questions that arise from the recent merger of these practices with studio produc-tion. The aim of the black independent movement was to resist the image of black people presented in Hollywood films. In the absence of this oppositional role the function of independent black cinema is no longer clear. My reflections on recent commentaries will show that notions of contemporary black cinema that rely on too rigid a dichotomy between independent and studio films are unable to accommodate recent developments in the film industry.[3] Commentators who want to maintain this dichotomy can no longer ignore the fact that in the closing years of this century there is less disparity between the film practices of black independents and black filmmaking in Hollywood.[4]

Blaxploitation era filmmaking and black independents

One of the earliest independent black films was *Birth of a Race* (1918). As in the case of Oscar Micheaux's *Within Our Gates* (1919), Emmett J. Scott (Booker T. Washington's former secretary) was politically motivated to make this film in order to counter the racism in D.W. Griffith's *Birth of a Nation* (1915). Although early black filmmaking practices, at their inception, were defined in terms of an oppositional relation to Hollywood, they were also dominated by Hollywood's influence on black audiences. On occasion even Micheaux was induced by competition with the studios to include scenes of blackface minstrels for entertainment value. But if even the most negative aspects of the Hollywood image of black people are sometimes reproduced by black filmmakers in an effort to attract black audiences, the opposition of black independents to Hollywood films seems amenable to compromise. Such compromise is crucial to understanding the three-stage historical scheme Guerrero posits in discussing the black image in Hollywood cinema. According to Guerrero there was a pre-blaxploitation era, during which a mainstream image of black accommodationism and submissiveness prevailed. This was followed by a blaxploitation era of resistance and co-optation dominated by black action films employing strategic reversals of mainstream ideology. After more than a decade of ideological recuperation by Hollywood studios, the filmmaking practices of both black independents and blaxploitation era filmmakers slowly merged into the present era of the new black cinema.

Guerrero's exploration of Hollywood's treatment of the topic of slavery traces the evolution of the plantation genre, which reached its peak just prior to the Second World War with the release of films such as *Jezebel* (1938) and *Gone With the Wind* (1939). After the Civil Rights movement of the 1960s the plantation mythology began to collapse and the genre's ideology was momentarily reversed in blaxploitation era films such as *Slaves* (1969) and *Mandingo* (1975). Gordon Parks attempted in *Solomon Northup's Odyssey* (1984) to move in the direction of deepening and refining this reversed perspective on slavery, but other conscientious projects, such as the filmed version of Shirley Anne Williams' *Dessa Rose* were cancelled. Less obvious remnants of the plantation genre continued to resonate as allegorical themes in a wide range of contemporary films including John Sayles' independently produced *The Brother From Another Planet* (1984), as well as Steven Spielberg's glossy studio production, *The Color Purple* (1985).

Certain aspects of Guerrero's assessment seem misguided, mainly because his historical survey of the plantation genre ends before the release of Haile Gerima's *Sankofa* (1994), a powerful independent black film that deliberately aims to destroy the Hollywood image of slavery. Gerima's film is closer to the Cuban films of Tomás Gutiérrez Alea (*The Last Supper*, 1976) and Sergio Giral (*The Other Francisco*,

Figure 14.1 Sankofa (1994). James (Jim Faircloth), the overseer, has whipped Kuta (Alditz
McKenzie), a pregnant slave, to death. Courtesy of Mypheduh Films

1974). Giral's *Francisco* is the earliest film about slavery that consciously deconstructs the plantation genre. Similarly, the theatrical distribution of an independently made film about American slavery that does not renege on the question of
collective resistance represents a milestone in independent black filmmaking. Had
Guerrero given some attention to the alternative paradigm offered by Third
Cinema, perhaps he would have shown less pessimism.[5] His chapter on slavery
ends with the remark that 'The film industry and the consumer imagination are
not ready for any cinematic tale of slavery that strays too far from the framing
confines of Hollywood's crude fantasies and exploitative strategies.'[6] The fact that
this claim is no longer true counts as a major achievement of the independent
black cinema movement of the 1970s. The large number of African-Americans
who responded to word-of-mouth promotion of Gerima's film was a major factor
in getting it into theatrical distribution.

The term 'independent black cinema' applies to several different filmmaking
practices in America. In addition to the Hollywood studios, there was public
television, as well as the film school at UCLA, all providing overlapping arenas for
black filmmaking in the late 1960s and early 1970s. The studios had produced
films using atheletes such as Jim Brown and Fred Williamson as early as the

mid-1960s, beginning a trend of black audience films that gradually accelerated with the release of *100 Rifles* (1969), *The Learning Tree* (1969), *Cotton Comes to Harlem* (1970) and *Watermelon Man* (1970). But it was the success of Melvin Van Peebles' *Sweet Sweetback's Baadasssss Song* (1971) at a time of financial exigency that fuelled a deluge of formulaic studio productions, from the macho heroes in *Shaft* (1971) and *Superfly* (1972) to their female counterparts in *Cleopatra Jones* (1973) and *Foxy Brown* (1974). Some of the black Hollywood filmmakers (e.g. Michael Shultz) and actors (e.g. Fred Williamson) of this period have continued making films well into the 1990s. None the less, by January 1974 the black film explosion of the early 1970s was officially declared by *Variety* as 'a thing of the past'.[7]

The recruitment of black film talent into black television programmes was a factor influencing the decline of blaxploitation films. Television was also a site of resistance for black filmmakers. In addition to those black writers, directors, actors and technicians who worked on programmes for commercial television, there was a group of politically conscious documentary filmmakers who were producing black-oriented films for public television on WNET's *Black Journal*. The Executive Director of this one-hour monthly television news series was William Greaves, a Canadian trained African-American filmmaker who had acquired solid technical skills making films abroad. *Black Journal* was a direct outcome of the black power movement and the massive uprisings of the late 1960s. Following the assassination of Martin Luther King, Jr, network executives were urged by the Kerner Commission to give the black community a voice in mass media by providing a television format for presenting issues relevant to the black community.[8] Greaves' *cinéma vérité* style of documentary filmmaking was well-suited to carry out this mandate. This award winning programme helped establish early on the reputation of independent black filmmakers such as Madeline Anderson (*Children's Television Workshop, Malcolm X*, 1969), St Claire Borne (*Let the Church Say Amen*, 1973) and Charles Hobson (*The Africans*, 1986).

Winning a Grammy following a first-year nomination attests to the talents of the filmmakers who worked on *Black Journal*. Their technical achievement is important to acknowledge because of the tendency of some critics to associate amateur technical skills with independent black filmmaking.[9] Even with regard to Third Cinema practices this tendency must be viewed with suspicion, given that many of the independent black filmmakers in the 1970s studied film at UCLA.[10] Ntongela Masilela outlines the emergence of this group.[11] He describes the key events which helped to shape its development, citing the Civil Rights Movement, the Women's Movement, the anti-war movement, and national liberation struggles in Africa, Asia and Latin America as major influences. The collective endeavor of this group (under the mentorship of Teshome Gabriel) to develop an alternative cinema has been called 'The LA Rebellion' by Clyde Taylor.[12]

Rejecting the traditional Hollywood 'production values' they were being taught to emulate, the filmmakers at UCLA instead aligned themselves with the alternative styles of filmmakers such as Sembene Ousmane from Africa, Sergio Giral and Pastor Vega from Cuba, Glauber Rocha, Nelson Pereira dos Santos and Ruy Guerra from Brazil and Octavio Getino and Fernando Solanas from Argentina. Julio Garcia Espinosa's classic essay, 'For an imperfect cinema' (the manifesto of the Third Cinema movement), provided an ideological framework within which filmmakers such as Haile Gerima (*Bush Mama*, 1972), Larry Clark (*Passing Through*, 1977), Charles Burnett (*Killer of Sheep*, 1977) and later Julie Dash (*Illusions*, 1982), Ali Sharon Larkin (*A Different Image*, 1982) and Billy Woodbury (*Bless Their Little Hearts*, 1984), produced politically conscious films that contest the aesthetic codes of Hollywood cinema. Whatever fault detractors may find with the 'production values' with which these filmmakers operate, the charge of technical incompetence is misplaced, for it amounts to a denial of agency to a group of insurgent black filmmakers who have mastered film technique and have chosen not to emulate Hollywood filmmaking.[13] The alternative style of filmmaking practiced by the Los Angeles School aimed to politicize the question of technical competence.

Masilela questions whether the acquisition of technical competence is sufficient to carry out the ideological and aesthetic tasks of the black independent movement.[14] He praises Jamaa Fanaka's 'solid grasp of film language', but criticizes his films (*Penitentiary*, 1979; *Emma Mae*, 1976 and *Street Wars*, 1991) for their lack of political consciousness. Masilela uses Fanaka to illustrate the fact that a fundamental tenet of the Los Angeles School, namely its opposition to Hollywood, was not a unanimously held view. The implication of this acknowledgement is that some black independents are seeking to make movies in Hollywood. It is important to clarify that the opposition of black independents to Hollywood-style filmmaking need not be taken to mean that a black filmmaker must seek complete economic self-reliance. Some commentators seem overly worried that unless black filmmakers are completely independent from Hollywood's financial resources they will lose control.[15]

Although he recognizes the oppositional function of independent black cinema, Guerrero has taken a much more accommodationist position on the relation between Hollywood and black independents. For the new generation of black filmmakers since the late 1970s the use of guerrilla tactics to finance a film has been primarily a means of getting a deal with the Hollywood studios. Spike Lee's notion of 'guerrilla cinema', which Guerrero seems to have adopted, contrasts sharply with the notion advanced by Toni Cade Bambara.[16] Bambara constructs her notion of guerrilla cinema around the subversive achievements of Bill Gunn, a blaxploitation era filmmaker. Gunn was hired by the Hollywood studios to make a black horror film, but he instead made two socially conscious films, *Ganja and Hess* (1973) and *Stop!* (1975) that were never released, but have been widely shown at film festivals and museum events. *Ganja and Hess* is a Hollywood studio production (albeit a subversive one) that is closer to the Los Angeles School's Third Cinema aesthetic orientation than the independent productions of Spike Lee and Robert Townsend. Bambara appeals to this important aesthetic difference to distinguish between commerical filmmakers and 'conscious Black cinematistes'. Spike Lee is excluded from the latter because he represents the new generation of black filmmakers 'who regard the contemporary independent sphere as a training ground or stepping-stone to the industry, rather than as a space for contestation, a liberated zone in which to build a cinema for social change'.[17] In the light of what happened to black filmmakers such as Bill Gunn, Bambara cautions against Hollywood-made black films. She raises the question of whether former black independents who work in Hollywood have been co-opted by commercial influences.

The dialectic of co-optation

Bambara seems to treat as irrelevant the fact that some of the new generation of independent black filmmakers take themselves to be socially conscious. Lee and Townsend, for instance, believe that they can make socially conscious films that will meet the box-office demands of a commercial industry. Bambara refers to this mass appeal factor as 'crossover' in order to distinguish Julie Dash's *Daughters of the Dust* (1991) from crossover films by other black independents. But the fact that Julie Dash, along with Haile Gerima and Charles Burnett (all from the Third Cinema wing of the Los Angeles School), have succeeded in placing their films into theatrical distribution suggests that the former apartheid relationship between black independents and Hollywood has changed. Unlike Bambara, Guerrero's accommodationist view is more amenable to the crossover aspirations of black independents. With an eye to the problem independent films have had attracting black audiences, he argues that since the most liberating films will have little social impact without a black audience, the bottom line that any black filmmaker must recognize is that 'narrative cinema is a capital-intensive, mass-audience-driven social practice'.[18]

Diawara's position is closer to the more radical stance against Hollywood-produced films taken by critics such as Toni Cade Bambara and Mark Reid. He defines independent black cinema as 'any Black-produced film outside the con-straints of the major studios'.[19] But some of Bambara's ideological and aesthetic concerns regarding independent black filmmaking practice cannot be resolved on wholly definitional grounds. The meaning of independent black cinema cannot be limited to films made outside of the Hollywood studio system, given that the two icons of independent black cinema Diawara canonizes, Melvin Van Peebles and Bill Gunn, worked in Hollywood as a means of financing films that were counter-hegemonic. Their status as black independents who worked both in and out of Hollywood fails to support Diawara's conception of the relationship between black independents who work outside of the studios and black filmmakers who seek to challenge the aesthetic codes of the studios from the inside.

This flaw in Diawara's concept of black independent cinema parallels a similar flaw in Guerrero's concept of blaxploitation cinema. In addition to the reversed images in the blaxploitation action genre Guerrero identifies a category of positive image films, such as *Melinda*, *Sounder* and *Buck and the Preacher*, that were produced in 1972. He notes that, during the black film boom between 1970–3 only forty-seven of the ninety-one films were modelled on the blaxploitation formula. The tendency among commentators to identify blaxploitation era filmmaking largely with the action/crime genre must be drawn into question if there were just as many 'positive image' films in other genres.[20] There were some black films, such as *Melinda* (1972), *Five On The Black Hand Side* (1972) and *The Spook Who Sat By The Door* (1973), released at the height of the blaxploitation era that were produced, written and directed by socially conscious African-Americans who assumed a 'burden of representation'.[21]

Michael Shultz was among this group of socially conscious black filmmakers. His film *Car Wash* (1976) is very carefully explored by Richard Dyer to determine its status as a musical.[22] Although Dyer concludes that it is not a musical, he is more concerned with the political ideology displayed in certain blaxploitation era films, a question he raises by focusing on the implications of the form of *Car Wash*. He notes a relation between narration and music fashioned in a manner similar to what can be observed in many black-audience films from *St Louis Blues* (1958) to *House Party* (1990). By reference to James Snead's much celebrated notion of repetition as a figure of black culture, Dyer distinguishes the active use of music by characters in *Car Wash* and other black films, including Isaac Julian's *A Passion of Remembrance* (1986) and Spike Lee's *Do the Right Thing* (1989), from the typical Hollywood representations of 'black musicality as an emanation of the Black personality, a given of the Black psyche'.[23] In black-audience films there is an important difference in what the numbers signify in the course of the narrative, as well as a difference in how they figure in the lives of the characters. In white musicals the musical numbers are usually diegetically motivated. Only one scene in *Car Wash*, Daddy Rich's (Richard Pryor) visit, is like a musical in this sense. Instead, as in *St Louis Blues*, *House Party* and *Do the Right Thing*, 'the music is always there, not as background but as the thing that is there for the film to pick up'.[24] In these black films music is picked up not only by the characters in the film, but also by the narration itself.

Dyer argues that *Car Wash* is more like *Do the Right Thing* than *The Sound of Music* (1965) because, unlike the latter film, there is no 'utopia of transformation' signified by the music. Rather the repetitional use of music in black cinema suggests that things are constantly changing, being made and remade, hence, in the face of this, music functions as a coping mechanism. In white musicals narration and music combine to yield a form for enjoying the vision of change taking place, whereas in black films music offers a way of 'celebrating the recurrent resources for survival and change'.[25] Dyer raises the question of whether this coping strategy suggests an accommodationism that does not argue for change by drawing attention to the similarity of this function of music and narration with the way camp functions to keep gay men going while keeping them in their place. Like Dyer, Guerrero is generally sceptical, but wisely avoids the commonly held view that blaxploitation era films always succumbed to the Hollywood ideology. In a superb political economic analysis of the blaxploitation formula Guerrero spells out a process of co-optation in terms of the tandem workings of ideology and economics. It seems inconsistent, however, for Guerrero to extend this analysis to black cinema practice in the 1990s without raising the same political concerns.

In 1971 the Hollywood studios faced an economic crisis. Profits went down to 15.5 million dollars from an earlier high of 90 million annually. The new management shifted from making blockbuster pictures to contracting to distribute independently produced features.[26] This opened up opportunities for black Hollywood filmmakers such as Gordon Parks, Jr and Sr and Michael Schultz, as well as independents such as Melvin Van Peebles and Bill Gunn. The post-Civil Rights political climate, a major factor influencing the production of blaxploitation films, was a defining element. According to Guerrero, these two factors were linked. He tells us, 'the accelerating appearance of black-oriented pictures (yearly production tripling from six features in 1969 to eighteen in 1971) was largely fueled by the overdetermining pressures of a disastrous downturn in studio profits and the steadily rising tide of black political activism'.[27] The industry was under pressure from the NAACP regarding its discriminatory policies on and off the screen. Blaxploitation films met this demand and also provided a vehicle for getting a younger black audience into the theatres.

It is somewhat ironic that the blaxploitation formula adopted by Hollywood was supplied by an independent black filmmaker who meant to challenge the Hollywood codes. How could one of the icons of independent black cinema provide a formula so well-suited for Hollywood? In a colloquy on *Sweetback* that included St Clair Bourne, Haile Gerima and Pearl Bowser, Van Peebles responded to criticism of his Hollywood orientation by denouncing the manifesto of the Third Cinema movement. He insisted that the aesthetic codes of Hollywood are the most effective strategy to reach an otherwise unreachable black audience.[28] He defended his intention to subvert the Hollywood entertainment codes with a politically conscious message, in spite of the effectiveness of studio co-optation of *Sweetback's* political statement by the subsequent rash of macho action films.

The black action genre and black spectatorship

There do not appear to be any clear criteria by which to distinguish between 'ghettocentric' films that use the criminal as a heroic figure of resistance and those that merely exploit this image for profit. Guerrero's tendency to side with critics of *Sweetback* is inconsistent with his claim that Spike Lee's 'epic' film *Malcolm X* is 'the outstanding achievement of black film-making in the nineties'.[29] Diawara has argued that the conversion narrative in the second part of Malcolm X's autobiography is dominated by the story about his life of crime in the first part. Indeed, the reason Malcolm X is so popular among black youth is that they 'see a mirror image of their own lives in the experience of Detroit Red'.[30] Less dramatic conversion narratives were employed in *Sweetback* and *Superfly*. The charge of exploitation arises in cases where the conversion theme of films of this sort is dominated by a socially unredeeming 'bad nigga' narrative that fundamentally denies community.[31] But if this is the charge then *Superfly* seems no worse than many of its recent descendants, including *New Jack City* (1991) and *Boyz N the Hood* (1991) which are also dominated by their 'bad nigga' narratives. The idea that the 'bad nigga' narratives of 'ghettocentric' films (including Spike Lee's *Malcolm X*) often dominate the political themes they incorporate is also supported by Diawara's account of black spectatorship.

Diawara identifies themes of caring for the community in 'ghettocentric' films such as *Boyz N the Hood*, *Juice* (1992), *Straight Out of Brooklyn* (1991) and *Deep Cover* (1992).[32] To what extent, however, can such themes coexist with the neo-blaxploitation aspects of these films? Guerrero tells us that the male-focused action/crime black films are the biggest moneymakers. Singleton's film *Boyz N the Hood* satisfied Hollywood's low-budget, high-profit blaxploitation formula 'beyond the industry's wildest expectations'.[33] Singleton admits to having intentionally deceived black youth into coming to see his film. He fashioned trailers which suggested a film about gang violence, whereas, as Guerrero notes, the film itself reverts to a 'melodramatic devotion to the cult of the enterprising individual'.[34] Singleton understood that the theme of caring for the community would not have any special appeal to black youth. He deliberately employed the figure of the gang member (Ice Cube) and not the father (Larry Fishburne) to attract a black youth audience. This narrative strategy is at odds with Singleton's neo-conservative thesis that the future of all the young males in the film turns on the absence or presence of the father.[35] The attempt to smuggle these conservative values into a film that is constructed around Ice Cube's forceful portrayal of the 'bad nigga' character generated a political contradiction in the film. The film suggests a remedy for the pathology of black male adolescents that requires a nuclear family prescription. But it fails to show any women capable of filling it. Although Guerrero notices that the film's insider depiction of gang culture occasionally contradicts Singleton's anti-violence message, he does not comment on the 'bitches and ho's' image of women.[36] The negative portrayal of women in *Boyz N the Hood* is inconsistent with any claim to advocate social change that is grounded on a notion of community.

Unlike *Boyz N the Hood*, the nihilism of some of the classic 'bad nigga' narratives operates with a much less disguised misogyny that is not amenable to a melo-dramatic treatment. Themes about caring for the community were frequently incorporated into 'ghettocentric' blaxploitation era films, but their reading by black audiences remained the strongest factor determining whether a film was judged to be exploitative. Hollywood films had always required 'bad niggas' to be punished. For the first time on a theatre screen *Sweetback* showed a 'bad nigga' beating the system after undergoing a transformation in political consciousness. Since the 'bad niggas' in black folklore are typically committed only to an arbi-trary existential freedom of action, conversion themes are always negotiated in terms of the black male spectator's knowledge of this more traditional representation.

The attempt to incorporate themes about caring for the community into the blaxploitation formula of the 'bad nigga' beating the system required a number of modifications of the traditional folkloric renderings of this character. In *Sweetback*, Van Peebles transformed the 'bad nigga' into a revolutionary, where-as, in the *Shaft* series, the 'bad nigga' figure was recoded as an ally of the white power structure. Hollywood further capitalized on the appeal of the 'bad nigga' figure by later extending it to include a role for women. St Clair Bourne claimed that the inclusion of a female version of the 'bad nigga' with a badge was the ultimate move to 'de-sex' and co-opt the revolutionary aspect of *Sweetback*.[37]

Bourne's point regarding Hollywood's shift towards a de-sexed 'bad nigga' figure cannot be taken, plausibly, to mean that the black female protagonists in *Cleopatra Jones* and *Foxy Brown* were not portrayed as sex objects. Rather, I think Bourne wanted to draw attention to the attempt by Hollywood to contain the image of black male sexuality that had been suddenly unleashed on the screen in *Sweetback* and its numerous blaxploitation sequels. Nevertheless, films in which the 'bad nigga' figure is recoded as a female cop, or undercover agent, do not seem to square with the claim that 'bad nigga' narratives are anti-women because of their inherent nihilism. By comparison with the use of such narratives in black folklore, it seems that the use of women in *Cleopatra Jones* and *Foxy Brown* ought to count as an egalitarian act on the part of the studios to include women. There is, of course, another reading that can be given of these films in terms of their ideological function. In keeping with Guerrero's account of how the ideological component of the blaxploitation formula serves to co-opt radical political views, we can understand the ideological function of a re-gendered figure of the 'bad nigga' to be co-optation of both the blaxploitation macho image and the rising tide of feminist consciousness.

Representing politics, gender and sexuality

Often black filmmakers are expected to address the concerns of spectators from a variety of standpoints ranging across lines of class, gender and sexual orientation. Spike Lee has a legion of black critics, including feminists, gays and political radicals all vying for attention to their specific issues. But what about the right of an artist to view the world from a particular standpoint?[38] A theory of black cinema that reduces the perspective of each spectator and filmmaker to a specific standpoint is very limited. Conversely, the supposition that a filmmaker's perspective must accommodate the standpoint of every black person is far too demanding. We must be wary of criticism that imposes this burden of representation on black filmmakers.

Questions regarding the representation of politics are raised by Amiri Baraka and Houston Baker, who offer two divergent readings of Spike Lee films. Baraka connects Lee with what he calls a 'retrograde trend' of younger generation filmmakers dismissing the political struggle in favour of an economic struggle.[39] He accuses Lee of becoming a caricaturist of black revolutionary politics, pointing out Dyer's worry that in *School Daze* (1988), for instance, the light-skinned/dark-skinned conflict eschews actual class analysis, and is dealt with as 'a number'.[40] Similarly, in *Do the Right Thing*, the protest over the lack of black photos in the pizza parlour, as well as the killing of Rahim over a loud radio, trivialize the black liberation movement. Unlike Baraka, Baker finds a great deal of merit in Lee's films.[41] Baker interprets Lee's focus on economics as a political ideology. With regard to *Joe's Bed-Stuy Barbershop: We Cut Heads* (1983) he tells us that Lee 'has managed to extrapolate, from the deteriorating, grainy, muffled landscapes of a Bed-Stuy that doesn't look like it is "going to make it," the possibility of a Black artistic reinstitutionalization of Black commerce and culture'.[42] Baker takes *She's Gotta Have It* (1986) to be a 'filmic equivalent' of Zora Neale Hurston's *Their Eyes Were Watching God*.[43] He draws a parallel between several features of Hurston's story and Lee's film. By citing Love Daddy's injunction to the neighborhood in *Do the Right Thing* to register to vote (against Mayor Koch), Baker urges us to recognize Lee's engagement with New York City politics as an important element in this film. Although critics such as Baraka may choose to question Lee's political orientation from a more radical perspective, Baker makes clear why it is a mistake to deny altogether that Lee's films are political.

Most critics, including Baker and Baraka, seem to agree that Lee's treatment of women characters in his films falls short of the mark. Concerned with the image of black women Jacquie Jones critically examines the various mechanisms used by both black and white male filmmakers to deny the human dimensions of black sexuality.[44] Although her criticism focuses on representations of the sexual behaviour of black heterosexual men primarily in relation to white men and black women, she claims that Marlon Riggs' film *Tongues Untied* (1989) is 'possibly the most powerful examination of Black sexual identity ever produced'.[45] Her rationale for this claim is that Riggs' film integrates the sexual with the political and social. It is far from clear, however, whether Riggs' critique of heterosexism in *Tongues* cuts into Jones' own thesis regarding the 'normalization' of black sexual characterization.

With Riggs' documentary treatment of black gay sexuality in mind, Jones criticizes Spike Lee's portrayal of women by pointing out that the central female characters in several of his films are powerless and abused. She appeals to Jessica Benjamin's Hegelian analysis of sexual domination to explain how the powerlessness of women in Lee's films creates a situation in which 'sexual activity in the films functions as a kind of symbolic rape rather than cooperative process'.[46] The problem is that, if we accept Hegel's argument (not Benjamin's), sexual pleasure derived through the practice of domination is normal. Jones argues further that Spike Lee suffers from 'an overidentification with White maleness and the systems of sexual oppression in the society at large'.[47] But, if the norm is being sought, then Lee's representation of sexuality is right on the mark. Her proposal regarding the 'normalization' of black sexual representation (although I am not sure what this means) could be strengthened by considering, in addition to Riggs' gay critique of heterosexual norms, alternatives offered, perhaps, by black women writers and filmmakers.

Issues pertaining to the representation of sexuality and gender have been at the centre of several interesting debates regarding black spectatorship. Henry Louis Gates, Jr examines Isaac Julien's critique of the 'malign sexual politics' inherited from black nationalism.[48] According to Gates, Julien's film *Looking for Langston* (1989) is as much about contemporary black London as it is about New York at the time of the Harlem Renaissance. He emphasizes the fact that the Harlem Renaissance 'was surely as gay as it was Black, not that it was exclusively either of these things'.[49] Hence, Julien's meditation on this movement provides an impassioned rebuttal to the homophobia expressed by Eldridge Cleaver, the early Baraka, Sonia Sanchez and other policemen of black male sexuality. Gates cites an epidemic of physical violence against gays as a direct social consequence of this homophobia. The political dilemma this creates for the black gay community had been faced by the Harlem Renaissance writers as well. In both cases black gay men were expected to foster and to transcend the identity politics of nationalism.

Gates refers to a scene in Julien's film that uses Mapplethorpe's photos to represent racial issues among black and white gays. He interprets the scene to be a critique of Mapplethorpe's 'Primitivist evocations'. But other readings of this

Figure 14.2 John Wilson, Matthew Baidoo and Ben Ellison in *Looking for Langston* (1989).
Courtesy of Sunil Gupta and Sankofa Film and Video

scene are possible. Realizing that Mapplethorpe's images engendered ambivalence in him, Kobena Mercer offered an alternative reading based on a more complex black gay perspective.[50] Mercer acknowledged his own feelings of envy and rivalry – that on the one hand he resisted identification with the black men depicted as sex objects for white fantasy, while on the other he shared the same desire to look. Mercer's self-disclosure must be well taken, for a theory of black spectatorship has to account for more complex readings of film texts to accommodate cases such as this.

The difficulty is that reflection on cases in which a black spectator inhabits two or more contradictory standpoints at the same time has led some commentators to assert that a rupture has occurred, while others maintain that identification has occurred. With regard to the representation of black women, Michelle Wallace reports that she identified with both the Rita Hayworths and Lana Turners as well as with the Butterfly McQueens and Hattie McDaniels in Hollywood films of the 1940s, whereas bell hooks maintains that black female spectators turned away as a gesture of resistance to such images of black women.[51] Unfortunately, the accounts of spectatorship given by these scholars do not provide any means of ascertaining the relative strength of their opposing claims.

The future of independent black cinema

Guerrero considers it an achievement for a crossover black independent such as Spike Lee to make the epic Hollywood film *Malcolm X*. When the ideological frame of the Hollywood epic is taken into account, however, Guerrero's assessment must be reconsidered. There can be no doubt that Lee's representation of Malcolm X was influenced by the box-office demand for his film to have a 'crossover' appeal. Bambara's criticism of crossover films by black independents must be well taken given that one of the underlying assumptions of Lee's film practice since *Do the Right Thing* is that no Third Cinema styled film will cross over, whereas in the making of earlier films such as *Joe's Bed-Stuy Barbershop* and *She's Gotta Have It* his assumption seems to have been that the Hollywood aesthetic must be challenged.[52] Although I want to question Bambara's anti-Hollywood stance, her general position can be distinguished from her particular concern regarding the potential for co-optation of the political views of black independents entering the studios.

In addition to this worry about political co-optation, the notion of crossover is further nuanced by the fact that, recently, the alternative cinema of independent black filmmakers such as Julie Dash and Charles Burnett has entered the space in the commercial market created by white independents. Lee's crossover success has expanded this specialized market by attracting the black filmgoer, estimated by *Variety* to be about 30 per cent of the mainstream market.[53] For this reason Guerrero prefers to distinguish between the different outlooks of black independent and mainstream cinema without oversimplifying the complexity of these overlapping practices.

> The line of feature films spanning the work of Micheaux in the 1930s; Van Peebles, Parks, and Poitier in the 1970s; Woodberry and Burnett in the early '80s; and Lee, Singleton, Duke, Dash, and Palcy, among many others, in the 1990s is more tangled than such terms imply.[54]

The crossover independents from the 1970s and 1980s, such as Spike Lee and Warrington Hudlin, are now joined in Hollywood by Matty Rich, who epitomizes the independent impulse in the new wave of black directors in the 1990s, and John Singleton who is prominent among the directors working within the mainstream. Guerrero speculates that the future of independent black cinema may develop from the hybrid styles of 'black-oriented projects that achieve a subtle mix of independent and mainstream qualities.'[55] In this mixed category he includes Matty Rich's *Straight Out of Brooklyn*, Joseph Vasquez's *Hanging with the Homeboys* (1991), Mira Nair's *Mississippi Masala* (1991) and Wendell Harris's *Chameleon Street* (1989).

Diawara prefers to emphasize the 'interactive relations' between black independent and Hollywood cinema. On Diawara's model, despite the hegemony of studio films, independent black filmmakers have managed to exert an influence on them. He describes a two-way exchange in terms of the dominant influence of Hollywood's master narrative on the work of black filmmakers, but he also speaks of the latter's 'surreptitious infiltration of the film industry, changing the complexion of Hollywood cinema in the process'.[56] According to Diawara,

> [A] look at the relations between Oscar Micheaux and the Hollywood 'race films,' Melvin Van Peebles and the Blaxploitation films, Charles Burnett (*Killer of Sheep*), Haile Gerima (*Bush Mama*), and Spike Lee and the rethematization of urban life in such films as *City of Hope*, *Grand Canyon*, *Boyz N the Hood*, and *Straight Out of Brooklyn* reveals that mainstream cinema constantly feeds on independent cinema and appropriates its themes and narrative forms.[57]

The insight that underlies Diawara's comment must be heeded, although he suggests a mutually autonomous relationship between black independent and Hollywood cinema that is difficult to maintain with respect to some of the films of Spike Lee and Matty Rich.

Diawara distinguishes between realist and symbolic narratives in a fashion that situates contemporary black filmmaking practices on a political spectrum. Realist films such as *Sweetback* and *Boyz N the Hood* have more in common with the classical Hollywood narrative, whereas symbolic films such as *Ganja and Hess* and *Daughters of the Dust* have more in common with black expressive forms. With an eye to audience reception, Diawara points out that independent black cinema has remained marginal until now because its language is 'metafilmic, often nationalistic, and not "pleasurable"' to black audiences conditioned by Hollywood movies. He suggests that the real challenge to 'the formulaic verisimilitude of Hollywood' will come from independent black filmmakers. In keeping with Diawara's view of the traditional educational role of independent black filmmaking, Guerrero welcomes the new access to studio distribution as a means of enhancing contact between black independents and black audiences. Whether this new development will in fact help or hinder the ideological objectives of the earlier Third Cinema movement remains to be seen.

Notes

1 For a listing of this recent work see the bibliography compiled by Stephen Best in Manthia Diawara (ed.), *Black American Cinema* (New York: Routledge, 1993), pp. 303–10.
2 Ed Guerrero, *Framing Blackness* (Philadelphia: Temple University Press, 1993).

3 Some of my remarks here repeat parts of my discussion of this issue in my essay 'Aesthetics and politics in contemporary black film theory', in Richard Allen and Murray Smith (eds), *Film Theory and Philosophy* (Oxford: Oxford University Press, 1997), pp. 282–302.

4 See, for example, Mark A. Reid, *Redefining Black Film* (Berkeley: University of California Press, 1993). Reid maintains that a film must be completely controlled by black people from production to distribution to count as a black film. See note 15.

5 I follow Kobena Mercer's use of 'Third Cinema' as a 'flexible and open-ended term for independent film practices in the geo-political spaces of the Third World and its metropolitan diaspora(s)'. Kobena Mercer, 'Third cinema at Edinburgh', *Screen*, vol. 27, no. 6 (November–December 1986), p. 95.

6 Guerrero, *Framing Blackness*, p. 40.

7 Cited in Guerrero, *Framing Blackness*, p. 105. See also Jim Pines and Paul Willemen (eds), *Questions of Third Cinema* (London: BFI Publishing, 1989).

8 See *Report of the National Advisory Commission on Civil Disorders* (New York: Bantam Books, 1968). I discuss the Kerner Commission mandate in my article, 'Documenting social issues: *Black Journal*, 1968–70', in Janet Cutler and Philis R. Klotman, (eds), *Struggles for Representation: African American Documentary, 1943–1993* (Bloomington: Indiana University Press, forthcoming).

9 See the debate between J. Ronald Green and Thomas Cripps over the question of agency in some of Oscar Micheaux's extant films, in Diawara (ed.), *Black American Cinema*, pp. 26–48 and 71–9.

10 See, for example, David Nicholson, 'Voices', *Wide Angle*, vol. 13, nos. 3 and 4 (July–October 1991), pp. 120–5.

11 'The Los Angeles School of black filmmakers', in Diawara (ed.), *Black American Cinema*, pp. 107–17.

12 Clyde Taylor, 'The LA rebellion: a turning point in black cinema', Circular for *The New American Filmmakers Series*, 26 (New York Whitney Museum of American Art, 3–19 January 1986).

13 The former editor of *Black Film Review*, David Nicholson held this view. 'If Black filmmakers want their productions to be viable in an increasingly competitive market, their films must be far better than the worst Hollywood has to offer.' *Wide Angle*, vol. 13, nos. 3 and 4 (July–October 1991), p. 124.

14 Masilela, 'The Los Angeles School of black filmmakers', p. 115.

15 Mark Reid, for example, was led by this worry to embrace a concept of independent black cinema that rigidly excludes films by Oscar Micheaux and Melvin Van Peebles because they were either financed, or distributed, by whites. Reid, *Redefining Black Film*, p. 17.

16 Bambara, 'Reading the signs, empowering the eye: *Daughters of the Dust* and the black independent cinema movement', in Diawara (ed.), *Black American Cinema*, pp. 118–44.

17 Bambara, 'Reading the signs', p. 137.

18 Guerrero, *Framing Blackness*, p. 182.

19 Diawara, 'Black American cinema: the new realism', in Diawara (ed.), *Black American Cinema*, p. 7.

20 See, for instance, Thomas Cripps, *Black Film as Genre* (Bloomington: Indiana University Press, 1979), Chapter 8.

21 See Kobena Mercer, 'Black art and the burden of representation', in his *Welcome to the Jungle* (New York: Routledge, 1994), pp. 233–58.

22 Dyer, 'Is *Car Wash* a black musical?', in Diawara (ed.), *Black American Cinema*, pp. 93–106.

23 Ibid., p. 98.

24 Ibid., p. 104.

25 Ibid., p. 105.

26 Guerrero, *Framing Blackness*, p. 83.

27 Ibid., p. 82.

28 Gladstone Yearwood (ed.), *Black Cinema Aesthetics* (Athens, Ohio: Ohio University Press, 1982). See my discussion of this issue in 'Aesthetics and politics', pp. 291–4.

29 Guerrero, *Framing Blackness*, p. 197.

30 Manthia Diawara, 'Malcolm X and the black public sphere: conversionists versus culturalists', *Public Culture*, vol. 7, no. 1 (1994), p. 35.

31 For a discussion of 'bad nigga' narratives see Daryl Cumber Dance, *Shuckin' and Jivin': Folklore from Contemporary Black Americans* (Bloomington: Indiana University Press, 1978), pp. 224–46, and H. Nigel Thomas, *From Folklore to Fiction: A Study of Folk Heroes and Rituals in the Black American Novel* (New York: Greenwood Press, 1988), pp. 71–9. I discuss this issue in 'Aesthetics and politics', pp. 290–1.

32 'Black spectatorship: problems of identification and resistance', in Diawara (ed.), *Black American Cinema*, pp. 211–20.

33 Guerrero, *Framing Blackness*, p. 182.

34 Ibid., p. 186.

35 Guerrero mentions the fact that Singleton's film was recommended as a prescription for social change by Governor Pete Wilson following the 1992 uprising in Los Angeles.

36 See Jacquie Jones, 'The new ghetto aesthetic', *Wide Angle*, vol. 13, nos. 3 and 4 (July–October 1991), pp. 38–41.

37 Yearwood, *Black Cinema Aesthetics*, p. 55.

38 After citing a pattern of negative images of women in his films, Pearl Bowser makes this concession to Van Peebles. See Yearwood, *Black Cinema Aesthetics*, p. 65.

39 'Spike Lee at the movies', in Diawara (ed.), *Black American Cinema*, pp. 145–53.

40 Diawara, *Black American Cinema*, p. 148.

41 'Spike Lee and the commerce of culture', in Diawara (ed.), *Black American Cinema*, pp. 154–76.

42 Baker, 'Spike Lee and the commerce of culture', p. 160.

43 Zora Neale Hurston, *Their Eyes Were Watching God* (Philadelphia: Lippincott, 1937).

44 'The construction of black sexuality: towards normalizing the black cinematic experience', in Diawara (ed.), *Black American Cinema*, pp. 247–56.

45 Ibid., p. 256.

46 Ibid., p. 255. We are left to wonder how this criticism would apply to black gay films that depict sexual domination, for example, Isaac Julien's short film, *The Attendant* (1994).

47 Ibid., p. 254.

48 Gates, 'Looking for modernism', in Diawara (ed.), *Black American Cinema*, pp. 200–11.

49 Ibid., p. 202.

50 *Welcome to the Jungle* (New York: Routledge, 1994), pp 171–219.

51 'Race, gender and psychoanalysis in forties film: *Lost Boundaries, Home of the Brave* and *The Quiet One*', in Diawara (ed.), *Black American Cinema*, p. 264, and 'The oppositional

gaze: black female spectators', in Diawara (ed.), *Black American Cinema*, p. 293. For a discussion of this issue see my 'Aesthetics and politics', pp. 292–5.

52 See his criticisms of other black filmmakers and actors in Spike Lee, *Spike Lee's Gotta Have It: Inside Guerrilla Filmmaking* (New York: Fireside Press, 1987), pp. 20–62.

53 See Jacqueline Bobo, '"The subject is money": reconsidering the black film audience as a theoretical paradigm', *Black American Literature Forum*, vol. 25, no. 2 (Summer 1991), pp. 421–32.

54 Guerrero, *Framing Blackness*, pp. 167–8.

55 Ibid., p. 177.

56 Manthia Diawara, 'Preface', in Diawara (ed.), *Black American Cinema*, p. ix.

57 Diawara, *Black American Cinema*, p. 4. Diawara does not explain his inclusion of Matty Rich's *Straight Out of Brooklyn* here, although this was a low-budget independent production.

Chapter 15

No fixed address

The women's picture from *Outrage* to *Blue Steel*

Pam Cook

The women's picture has played a major role in the development of feminist film criticism over the last fifteen years or so – partly in response to a certain tendency in some 1970s feminist film theory to prioritize 'the male spectator', and partly as a strategic move to reassess a critically devalued and neglected genre. This debate, which has centred on questions of female spectatorial pleasure and address, has produced some remarkable textual analyses and trenchant critiques of the ways in which classical Hollywood cinema both represents and positions women, opening up issues such as narrative structure, masochism and consumerism. Despite the revisionist impulse motivating much of this work, it has tended to locate itself within a more general critique, inherited from 1970s film theory, which perceives classical Hollywood as inherently bourgeois and patriarchal, and therefore inimical to feminist interests. My own article, 'Melodrama and the women's picture', written in 1983, while attempting to account for the genre's popular appeal, betrays a deep suspicion of the whole idea of the woman's picture.

> One question insists: why does the women's picture exist? There is no such thing as 'the men's picture', specifically addressed to men; there is only 'cinema', and 'the women's picture', a sub-group or category specially for women, excluding men; a separate, private space designed for more than half the population, relegating them to the margins of cinema proper. The existence of the women's picture both recognises the importance of women, and marginalises them. By constructing this different space for women (Haskell's 'wet, wasted afternoons'), it performs a vital function in society's ordering of sexual difference.[1]

There is more than a hint of conspiracy theory in this formulation, which implies that the category of the women's picture exists in order to dupe female spectators into believing that they are important, while subtly marginalizing and disempowering them. This is an intellectual position that echoes through much feminist writing on the Hollywood woman's picture. More recent work in the area of audience response has suggested that through identification with stars and emulation of their image, female spectators may feel empowered and act out that feeling in their everyday lives.[2] Although I still consider that feminist discussion of the women's picture has been enormously productive, I no longer believe that popular texts necessarily operate in the way I suggest in the above quote, that is, to marginalize and disempower female spectators. However, nor do I think that a simple reversal of that position, which looks at the women's picture in terms of the way it offers pleasures of female empowerment, gets us much closer to understanding the complexities of audience engagement with popular films.

My concern here will be to trace, selectively, some of the shifts that have occurred in the way that the women's picture has been discussed by feminist writers, in order to ask some preliminary questions about genre and gendered address. At the same time, I shall explore the differences and continuities between a specific manifestation of the classical woman's film and some post-classical developments, with the aim of assessing what, if anything, has changed in Hollywood cinema since the 1950s with respect to women filmmakers and audiences. First, a couple of caveats. Since the relationship of the woman's film to classical Hollywood cinema is often uneasy, to say the least, it is somewhat misleading to refer to 'the classical women's picture'.[3] Moreover, if the transition to what is known as 'post-classical' or 'new' Hollywood can be seen as spanning the period between the 1948 Paramount decrees and the completion of divorcement at the end of the 1950s, then the 'classical' status of films produced in the late 1940s, and the designation of 1950s Hollywood cinema as 'post-classical', are clearly both problematic.

While recognizing the difficulties inherent in the terms 'classical' and 'post-classical', particularly when used to impose definitive formal or temporal boundaries, I employ them here to indicate a process of transformation of the Hollywood industry and its products rather than a strict demarcation between two distinct phases of production. The Hollywood film industry, like any other, is always in the process of transition; indeed, it has been argued that since the classical studio system has been reorganized rather than dismantled, new Hollywood and its products are not that different from the old.[4] Nevertheless, the changes following the Second World War, such as the reorganization of the studio system, the relaxation of censorship, the expansion of low-budget independent production, the trend towards high-concept blockbusters, and the growth of new production and exhibition sites such as drive-in cinemas, theme parks, television and video, seem to have initiated a profound shift in the way cinema is produced and consumed.[5] One of the characteristics that quite clearly differentiates post-classical from classical cinema is the move towards greater visibility of sex and violence, and it is this development that partly concerns me here.

The dissolution of boundaries – between different modes of production such as television, video and cinema, and between different generic forms – has also been identified as a distinctive post-classical characteristic.[6] The permeability of boundaries is central to my discussion of genre and gendered address. Approaches to classical generic categories have traditionally assumed a gender-specific address. Thus the woman's film is perceived in terms of a primary address to female spectators, an assumption supported by reference to textual strategies such as narrative and *mise-en-scène*, to extratextual discourses such as promotional material and fan magazines and to historical evidence of industry policy. Though it is sometimes accepted that women's pictures are also addressed to male spectators, these are perceived as secondary audiences and have received little or no critical attention. Most other genres – even those such as musicals and musical comedies which do not appear to be clearly gender specific – are discussed in terms of their address to the ubiquitous male spectator. The western, the gangster movie or the horror film, which appear to feature central male protagonists and secondary female characters, are perceived as 'masculine' genres.

I do not need to labour the point that, with the exception of feminist work on melodrama and the woman's film, film studies has overwhelmingly privileged male spectatorship, and has thereby contributed to the consensus that cinema is primarily addressed, and belongs to men. Yet while teaching a course on John Ford and the western recently, I was struck by the similarity of many classical western narratives, with their emphasis on circularity, digression and delay, to the structure of classical women's pictures. The choices facing the western hero, between love and duty, family life and a wanderer's existence are not that different from those encountered by women's picture heroines. In several of Ford's classical westerns, the expressive use of music and *mise-en-scène* to heighten emotional affect can only be described as melodramatic – indeed, I would suggest that a comparative analysis of *My Darling Clementine* (1944) and *Written on the Wind* (1957) would produce interesting results in terms of generic cross-fertilization. It's interesting that, in his study of *Stagecoach* (1939), Edward Buscombe examines the way that the film was marketed using Claire Trevor's costume and hairstyle, one of the strategies employed in promoting women's pictures.[7]

Of course, the idea that genres are mixed is not new, nor am I the first, by any means, to suggest that we cannot make easy assumptions about genre and gendered address. Broadly speaking, in discussion of such issues, a tension can be discerned between approaches that identify a single, gender-specific mode of address, and those that posit multiple address, whether in terms of gender duality, or spreading the net more widely to include groups defined by class, race and ethnicity, age and sexual preference. In what follows, I shall navigate a path through some of this writing, following a particular course. Since it is the increased visibility of sexual violence in the post-classical period that has inspired a number of critiques, feminist and otherwise, I shall look at a certain tendency in the woman's film which concerns itself with sexual violence. This route will take me from the 1940s Gothic influenced paranoid woman's film analysed by Mary Ann Doane, via its transformation in 1950s family melodrama, 1970s and 1980s low-budget rape-revenge and 1990s sci-fi blockbusters.

In her introductory chapter to *The Desire to Desire*, Doane outlines the ways in which psychoanalytic film theory's account of the cinematic apparatus has overwhelmingly privileged male subjectivity. One of her reasons for choosing the 1940s cycle of woman's films was to open up questions of female subject-ivity in one of the few genres to put a feminine sensibility at the centre. In contrast to the voyeurism and fetishism associated with the male spectator, Doane sees femininity in cinema defined in terms of masochism, paranoia and hysteria. As she says:

> These scenarios of female subjectivity have generally *not* been instru-mental in delineating the cinematic apparatus. Nevertheless, they are fully compatible with the scenarios of the woman's film as a genre, particularly when they concern themselves with masochism. For in films addressed to women, spectatorial pleasure is often indissociable from pain.[8]

She proceeds to examine a number of woman's films for the ways in which they narrativize masochistic and/or paranoid scenarios – such as *Rebecca* (1940), *Possessed* (1947) and *Secret Beyond the Door* (1948) – in which the heroines' assump-tion of active investigative and heterosexually desiring roles is turned around on them to reveal and confirm their destiny as victims.

Doane claims that it is through such scenarios of victimization and suffering that the 1940s woman's films address a specifically female spectator. She is careful to assert on numerous occasions that audience address and spectator positioning are not at all the same thing:

> Women spectators oscillate or alternate between masculine and feminine positions . . . and men are capable of this alternation as well. This is simply to emphasise once again that feminine and masculine positions are not fully coincident with actual men and women.[9]

She goes on to qualify this statement:

> Nevertheless, men and women enter the movie theatre as social subjects who have been compelled to align themselves in some way with respect to one of the reigning binary oppositions (that of sexual difference)

which order the social field. Men will be more likely to occupy the positions delineated as masculine, women those specified as feminine.[10]

It is the slippage between the first and the second proposition that interests me. It would surely have been as easy, and as convincing, to reverse the second assertion: social subjects who have been compelled to align themselves with binary oppositions of sexual difference are quite likely to occupy other, opposing positions in the movie theatre. But what is significant is that there is no evidence to support either proposition. While the oscillations or multiple identifications offered by fictional texts may be defended, in theory, by recourse to psycho-analysis, there is no way, beyond the anecdotal, of knowing what happens when real spectators enter the cinema. I shall return to the question of audience address, response and evidence later. For the moment, I want to stay with the relationship between actual spectators and the films they go to see.

In her overview of recent developments in theories of spectatorship, Judith Mayne takes issue with the way many film theorists have over-simplified identifica-tion in the cinema, in that they assume both that identification takes place between spectators and characters, and that spectators identify with those characters that correspond most directly with their own identity. She sees this assumption as contravening the psychoanalytical theories on which much of this work was based, which questions the very idea of stable identities:

> There is something too literal about a notion of identification whereby I, as a woman or a US citizen or a middle-class academic, necessarily and supposedly unproblematically 'identify' with whatever I see on screen that most approximates my identity. . . . Identification understood as a position – and more properly as a series of shifting positions – assumes that cinematic identification is as fragile and unstable as identity itself.[11]

Mayne discerns a shift in notions of identification that has taken place with the emergence of reception studies, which takes spectators rather than the cinematic institution as the point of departure. This shift has opened up a gap between what is perceived as the homogenizing impulse of the institution and the potentially multiple, conflicting responses to it, and a space between address and reception. Thus the implied spectator positions offered by popular Hollywood texts are not necessarily inhabited by real audience members, who may experience such films in ways that go against the ideological grain. Later in her discussion, Mayne develops one of the implications of the idea of the gap between texts and spectators:

> Film theory has been so bound by the heterosexual symmetry that

supposedly governs Hollywood cinema that it has ignored the possibility, for instance, that one of the distinct pleasures of the cinema may well be a 'safe zone' in which homosexual as well as heterosexual desires can be fantasized and acted out. I am not speaking here of an innate capacity to 'read against the grain', but rather of the way in which desire and pleasure in the cinema may well function to problematize the categories of heterosexual versus homosexual.[12]

One could take this suggestion further by arguing that, contrary to the claims made by much film theory that 'the cinematic institution' works to endorse and sustain dominant ideology, popular cinema problematizes all social categories – of class, race and ethnicity, national identity, gender, sexuality, age and so forth. The invitation to the cinema is based on the promise that spectators may experience the thrill of reinventing themselves rather than simply having their social identities or positions bolstered.

Despite the loosening of the bonds between spectators and cinematic texts in revisionist film theory, the implications of this 'gap' or 'safety zone' idea have not generally been embraced with enthusiasm, presumably because it opens up a hornet's nest of further problems. It challenges a number of film theory's underlying assumptions. For example, by positing that popular cinema is more ideologically open, and processes of identification more fluid than has previously been imagined, it suggests that opportunities for resistance are more available than the opposition between 'dominant cinema' and 'counter cinema' would allow. And, of course, the proposition accepted by so much feminist film theory, that Hollywood cinema works to exclude, marginalize and victimize women, whether as fictional characters, filmmakers or spectators, is radically questioned by the idea that all spectators may redefine themselves in relation to the dominant social categories, not only in the darkened space of the cinema, but outside it too.

My feeling is that these cracks appearing in the surface of film theory are the result of a change in perception of popular cinema and its ideological operations. The self-fulfilling prophecy whereby women are perceived as the dupes and victims of a patriarchal Hollywood machine is gradually giving way to a more historical sense of the relationship of women to cinema, one which could reveal their role as more significant and central than has so far been argued. But this is jumping the gun. To follow the trajectory of this shift, I shall return to my discussion of Mary Ann Doane's work on the 1940s woman's film. Doane's account is particularly useful because it limits itself to specific overlapping categories accessible to psychoanalytical interpretation, such as maternal melodramas, films with physically or psychologically afflicted female characters, and the Gothic paranoid cycle. All of these, she argues, dramatize female emotional over-investment, the despecularization of the female body (that is, the woman is often the object of a curious rather than an erotic male gaze) and the textual difficulties inherent in putting female subjectivity at the centre of the narrative.

I do not wish to reduce Doane's analysis, which is impressively detailed and elaborate in its mobilization of psychoanalytic theory. However, in the space available here I can only pick up on a few of her points. In particular, I'd like to explore her notion, outlined above, that the woman's film addresses female spectators as masochistic victims. While I do not deny the masochistic pleasures offered by the woman's film, Doane's assumption that these pleasures are gender specific seems too limited. Moreover, her adherence to a negative notion of female masochism, defined in terms of passive suffering, ignores the extent to which many of the films she discusses have as their backstories dramas of male masochism. That is, titles such as *Rebecca*, *Secret Beyond the Door*, *Jane Eyre* (1943) and even, perhaps, *Now Voyager* (1942) feature damaged male characters who in the past have been punished and/or abused by dominant, powerful women who continue to exert a hold over them. In these films, then, the hero is not the only sexual aggressor, and he is also a victim. Thus, in the course of the woman's picture narrative the heroine confronts not only her own victimization, but that of the hero as well (and sometimes that of subsidiary characters). In the Gothic influenced films in particular, female pathology is matched and often outdone by male psychosis in a kind of overlapping of male and female desire.

There are two significant points here: one is that these multiple masochistic scenarios bear a striking resemblance to those identified by Carol J. Clover in *Men, Women and Chainsaws*, discussed on pp. 239–41, as being at work in the modern American horror film, where psychologically damaged and sexually impaired men turn their aggression against female characters. There are, however, two major differences – the 1940s heroines do not usually turn the tables on their aggressors in the same way as their 1970s counterparts (indeed, they often end up in an uneasy and haunted couple relationship with them), and the sexual violence is implied in the 1940s cycle rather than graphically depicted.

The other point is that the multiplication of masochistic scenarios in the 1940s woman's films implies a dual address to male and female spectators. This suggests that we should look again at the widely accepted notion that the woman's film is primarily addressed to female spectators. For example, a notable feature of the 1940s films discussed by Doane is their deferral of gratification. The possibilities of happiness and fulfilment offered by heterosexual romance and marriage are constantly postponed by the failure of both male and female characters to resolve their Oedipal problems. The much vaunted textual openness of the melodramatic narrative can partly be put down to this playing out of masochistic scenarios of postponement and deferral. Needless to say, this problematizing of heterosexual romance and deferral of consummation is not confined to melodrama and the women's picture, and the pleasures offered by such narratives are presumably available to all spectators.

I have lingered on Doane's analysis because her psychoanalytic textual approach illuminates the problems inherent in the idea of a woman's film dependent on a gender-specific address. In the 1940s films in question, not only is the female masochistic scenario reciprocated by that of the male, but the scene set by the Gothic paranoid films in particular is one of total victimization in which everyone suffers. Gender boundaries are blurred by the reciprocation of the characters' fantasies. A theatrical space — usually in the localized arena of a large house — is opened up where both men and women act out fantasies of victimization in which the roles of victim and aggressor are often interchangeable. If male and female characters are more alike than different in these films, it might make more sense to talk, in textual terms at least, of an ungendered address. As I suggested earlier, the appeal of such movies may lie precisely in the way they offer the lure of the abandonment of socialized gender and other positions. Another significant feature of the Gothic paranoid cycle is that the stories are highly localized and rarely look outside the family for the causes of psycho-sexual disturbance. The family and home are defamiliarized, serving as external projections of psychic trauma and pain. In 1950s melodrama, this defamiliarization process, together with the scenarios of sexual violence and psychological damage, do not disappear. Rather, the personal takes on an added dimension, shifting on to social and national levels. I shall discuss Ida Lupino's *Outrage* (1950) as a key transitional film in this respect. For the moment, I want to return to questions of address.

Barbara Klinger's work on the studio promotion of 1950s family melodramas such as *Written on the Wind* offers historical evidence of address to audiences defined in gender terms. In a chapter titled 'Selling melodrama' in her book on Douglas Sirk, *Melodrama and Meaning*, Klinger takes issue with the idea put forward by 1970s film theorists that the melodramas directed by Sirk, Minnelli and Ray articulated a subversive critique of 1950s repressive, consumerist America, particularly through their visual style. Instead, she argues, the visual excess characteristic of these 'sophisticated' melodramas participated in and was sustained by ideological discourses of sexuality and affluence prevalent at the time. I do not have space to do justice to Klinger's argument about the place of 1950s melodrama in relation to what she terms 'the adult film'. I want to focus on her attempt to establish, through a contextual approach which examines the promotion, reception and other discourses surrounding the movies themselves, multiple, often conflicting forms of address, and a dual gendered address to spectators. For Klinger, the liberalization of discourses around sexuality in the post-war period privileged heterosexuality at the expense of others, such as homosexuality and African-American sexuality, that were demarcated as deviant. In addition, the increase in explicit representations of sexual display was, she argues, often focused on the nude or scantily clad female body. Magazines such as *Playboy*, launched in 1953, were devoted to a philosophy of extra-marital male sexual freedom, while exposé journals such as *Confidential*, directed at women readers, luridly revealed the private lives of celebrities in articles devoted to such questions as Robert Wagner's problems in the bedroom.[13]

The promotion of adult melodramas during this period mobilized both discourses – that of female sexual display directed at presumably heterosexual men and that of sexual scandal directed at women. It is interesting that Klinger also identifies a discourse of sexual violence against women in the promotional campaigns, associated with a double language that exploited the films' adult, sensational content as well as their serious, realistic approach. At the same time, advertising foregrounded spectacular *mise-en-scène* devoted to displays of affluence in order to appeal to the upwardly mobile aspirations of audiences, thus introducing a class address. Since women were key figures in the shift to a post-war consumer economy, these discourses, according to Klinger, were primarily addressed to them. Thus sexual display was not only a source of erotic fascination, it was intimately linked to acquisitiveness. The images of sexual and material excess in 1950s melodramas were, in Klinger's account, embroiled in current strategies of capitalism and patriarchy, and there is reason to suppose that audiences would enter the cinema expecting to enjoy them in voyeuristic and consumerist terms.

Klinger's analysis of the promotional discourses employed by Universal suggests that both generic identity and audience address must be considered historically rather than via the attribution of transcendental, unchanging formal characteristics. It also implies that ideological meanings cannot be accounted for simply by authorial intention. However, Klinger is not concerned with displacing authorial interpretation only to replace it with another, institutional one:

> Examples of social readings like those geared towards voyeurism and consumption are particularly important to consider in relation to assessments of the film/ideology relationship. They do not necessarily produce a unified text with a coherent ideology, but suggest that institutional and social forces can act to produce a heterogeneous text offering a variety of viewing pleasures – grounded in various kinds of social ideologies – to its audience.
>
> From such a perspective, we cannot consider the family melodrama of the 1950s as necessarily subversive to the repressive regimes of the decade. Rather . . . such films often helped realize the heightened sexual depictions and affluent ideologies that marked the culture.[14]

Convincing though Klinger's argument about multiple address in the studio's promotional material for *Written on the Wind* is, her assertion that 1950s audiences may have enjoyed the adult melodramas in the terms set up by the surrounding discourses without 'getting' the subversive critique of US society is on the level of speculation. Her contextual approach suggests that the potential shifts of identity offered by multiple modes of address are consonant with marketing strategies that tie spectators in to prevailing ideologies of consumerism, sexuality and class rather than loosen ideological and social bonds – but in the absence of historical evidence of audience response, the question of what actually happened to spectators in the cinema remains obscure. Nevertheless, her investigation does make it clear that although the 1950s melodramas, like the 1940s woman's films, were addressed to women, they were certainly not just addressed to women, nor were women the primary audience addressed in all cases.

Klinger's emphasis on the conflicting discourses in play during the 1950s, and her identification of multiple modes of address in and around the adult melo-dramas, usefully provide the context for *Outrage* (1950), directed and co-scripted by Ida Lupino – a film that occupies an interesting position in relation to the transformation of the Hollywood industry at this time, and to the big-studio, sophisticated melodramas that have dominated discussion. It was independently produced for RKO by The Filmakers, a company formed by Ida Lupino and Collier Young in the wake of the dissolution of the contract system which tied stars to specific studios. Many other stars took the same route during this period. As producer/writer/director, and occasionally actress too, Lupino can be seen as an early example of the hyphenate phenomenon characteristic of modern Hollywood. *Outrage* is typical of the low-budget, black and white social issue melodramas produced by The Filmakers company in the 1950s. Its story, which deals with the traumatic rape of a young woman by a psychologically damaged war veteran, quite clearly participates in liberal discourses prevalent at the time – for example, in the social message delivered by minister Bruce Ferguson to the court about the need for compassion towards all of society's victims. Many of the The Filmakers' films contained similar scenes of liberal pleading.

In the space it gives to the perspectives of different characters, *Outrage* is a particularly good example of multiple, conflicting textual address. Indeed, this multiplicity tends to obliterate the predicament of the rape victim, which has proved difficult for some present-day viewers expecting a recognizable feminist agenda. It is not my intention to rehabilitate *Outrage* as a feminist text. In fact, as I have argued elsewhere, I believe the film's resistance to present-day feminist analysis to be a strength, since it demands to be seen in historical context.[15] It is worth noting in this respect that at the time of their release in the UK, The Filmakers' films were often praised by critics for their feminist take on social issues relevant to women. Lupino herself was a key factor in both promotion and reception.

In the context of my present discussion, what interests me about *Outrage* is its symptomatic status. It occupies a position between different production contexts and between genres. It is a hybrid: part studio production (evident in the early city scenes, shot in *noir* style), part documentary (the exterior Calforina sequences and the sections featuring the orange ranch); a mix of *film noir*, melodrama, social problem movie, teen pic and exploitation movie. Its emphasis on sexual violence and its relentless victimization scenario, in which almost everyone is perceived as damaged in some way, recall the 1940s Gothic paranoid cycle, while its comparatively explicit depiction of the causes and consequences of rape looks forward to later adult melodramas. The narrative structure of flight and pursuit prefigures 1960s serial television narratives such as *The Fugitive* (1963–4), for which Lupino directed three episodes, while the post-war rehabilitation theme emulates bigger-budget post-war reconstruction movies such as *The Best Years of Our Lives* (1946), also independently produced for RKO. Thus, in looking backwards and forwards at the same time, *Outrage* appears to occupy a place on the boundary between classicism and post-classicism itself. Indeed, it seems to embody the fluctuating, unsettled nature of that boundary.

Outrage is also partly a rape-revenge story, though the revenge element is somewhat obscured by the narrative drive to pathologize the rape victim. As already remarked, its representation of sexual violence is relatively explicit when compared to the 1940s woman's films, and it belongs with the 1950s adult melodramas in this respect. But it can also be linked to low-budget exploitation movies, and to 1970s and 1980s rape-revenge, not least in the way it connects the personal trauma of sexual assault with wider moral and social issues. However, in the twenty or so years separating Lupino's rape movie from its 1970s sisters, quite a lot happened. Most obviously, in *Outrage* the rape discreetly takes place off-screen, while in 1970s rape-revenge the brutality of rape and sexual assault is represented in graphic detail, albeit mostly from the point of view of the victims rather than the perpetrators. Rape-revenge is usually associated with the modern American horror film rather than with melodrama, though we would do well to remember the Gothic roots of both – we are back in the realms of generic inbreeding.

Arguably, it is in post-classical horror and associated cycles such as slasher films and rape-revenge that sensationalized displays of sexual violence reach their apotheosis, a factor which has provoked critiques from a number of directions. Many of these antagonistic responses, feminist and otherwise, have focused on the *visibility* of sexual violence, claiming that such spectacularization is both morally offensive and socially undesirable, in so far as it panders to sadistic, voyeuristic male fantasies. In her chapter on rape-revenge in *Men, Women and Chainsaws*, Carol J. Clover challenges this received wisdom, arguing that the focus of such films on the perspective of the female victim-turned-avenger may actually place viewers in a masochistic position – doubly so, in that they are invited to identify not only

Figure 15.1 Outrage (1950). Courtesy of the Kobal Collection

with the rape victim, but also with her male victims as she goes about killing, maiming and castrating those who have harmed her. Clover detects a shift – which she suggests may have something to do with the influence of 1970s feminism – from the male-centred rape films of the early 1970s such as *Straw Dogs* (1971) and *Frenzy* (1972), in which spectators are encouraged to collude with the rapist's sadism, to female-centred rape-revenge films such as *I Spit on Your Grave* (1977) and *Ms .45* (1980), where the female rape victim's perspective, and her quest for bloody revenge in kind, move to centre-stage:

> Ironically, it may be the feminist account of rape in the last two decades that has both authorized a film like *I Spit on Your Grave* and has shaped its politics. The redefinition of rape as an offense on a par with murder, together with the well-publicized testimonials on the part of terrified and angry victims, must be centrally responsible for lodging rape as a crime deserving of the level of punishment on which revenge narratives are predicated.[16]

A similar argument is made by Linda Williams in *Hard Core* about changes in the depiction of rape in pornography in the early 1980s. Williams claims that due to a number of factors, including the heightened acceptance of the feminist critique of male sexual violence, enjoyment-of-rape scenarios became increasingly unaccept-able in an industry trying to expand its viewership.[17] It is interesting in this respect that the mainstream blockbuster *Basic Instinct* (1992) – that least politically correct of films – contains a rape scene presented as 'bad sex' which, although its focus is on the psychologically disturbed Nick Curran character, also registers the pain and anger of the rape victim, albeit rather weakly. Clover seems to regard the rape-revenge cycle as an appropriation of, rather than an active engagement with, feminist politics. Despite the gender implications of her arguments about feminist influence and the female victim heroes and final girl survivors, and her problem-atization of male spectatorial pleasure, she adheres to the commonly held opinion that viewers of low-budget horror are predominantly young men, and considers that the films are addressed to them, though she offers very little hard evidence in support of her claim. In her brief discussion of horror audiences at the beginning of her book, she glosses over the question of privatized video viewing and the lack of reliable statistics for the composition of horror film audiences in favour of the accepted notion of the younger male as 'majority viewer'.[18] Yet, as with the woman's film, the masochistic scenarios she identifies are surely not so gender specific in their address as her argument suggests. Nor should the greater visibility of young men as horror viewers lead us to assume that they are always the genre's primary audience.

Evidence that audiences for horror are not confined to men is offered by Linda Williams in an article about the exhibition context of *Psycho* (1960). The article includes frame stills from a cinema managers' training film which show a line of ticket holders waiting outside the DeMille Theatre in New York for a matinee screening. They are all women, mostly middle-aged. Other photographs taken with infra-red cameras during a screening at the Plaza in London show audience members, men and women, reacting to what they see and hear. Williams interprets these images as performative responses to the unresolved gender disturbances at the heart of *Psycho*, suggesting that some gender destabilization took place in the cinema audience as well as on screen. From the photographs it appears that some women were adopting contained, stoical ways of looking associated with masculinity, while some men reacted with anxious gestures closer to the histrionic performance of fear associated with femininity. Taken at the time of viewing, these photographs are perhaps the most convincing evidence so far of the potential fluidity of gender identification among the cinema audience, and of the cinema experience as offering a 'safe zone' for the enjoyment of such adventures in masquerade.

I find the notion of the performative nature of the viewing process explored by Williams intriguing. She links the gender performance in the film (Norman Bates' masquerade as his mother) with what takes place in the movie theatre, arguing that the exaggerated poses adopted by audience members suggest 'a pleasurable and self-conscious performance'.[19] Although Williams considers that such performative responses were initiated by *Psycho*, which she sees as inaugurating the 'thrill-producing visual "attractions" that would become fundamental to the New Hollywood',[20] some of the arguments that I have considered so far imply that this destabilization of gender and other social categories in the cinema is more common than we are prepared to admit, and cannot be limited to a classical/post-classical division. Nor, I would suggest, can the performative response be limited to what takes place in the movie theatre itself, since people may adopt disguises outside the cinema too. I have discussed elsewhere a particular example of gender masquerade in the critical reception of Scorsese's *Cape Fear* (1991), in which some male writers reacted to the film's disturbing gender reversals by adopting the mantle of femininity.[21] This clearly has implications for studies of audience response that rely on the evidence of people recalling their experiences.

We should be wary of identifying a single film as a historical benchmark, and many of the elements identified by Williams as specific to the *Psycho* experience can be found earlier, in 1950s Hollywood cinema. Nevertheless, in some ways, *Psycho*, like *Outrage* ten years before, does seem to stand at a frontier of cinema history. In the shower sequence, Hitchcock created, through editing and sound, an illusion of graphic sexual violence. In fact, the audience had seen very little. Even so, a border had been crossed. Nudity and graphic sex and violence became more visible. This situation intensified with the move of low-budget exploitation into the mainstream as the major studios began to penetrate new markets in the 1970s and 1980s, and with the expanded availability of video. As I have already mentioned, the increased visibility of sex and violence in post-classical Hollywood cinema has been the subject of extensive feminist critique. The graphic representation of rape and sexual assault against women in exploitation genres has been vociferously contested by those concerned that such scenarios perpetuate misogynist attitudes and encourage men to perform real acts of sexual abuse. As we have seen, such critiques have had a powerful effect on what it is considered permissible to show.[22]

In the wake of such critiques, to an extent, the representation of rape and the viewing of such representations have become associated with the act of rape itself. Those who enjoy watching sexual violence on screen, particularly in its 'low' manifestations, are highly suspect. If they are men, they are potential rapists, if they are women, they are potential rape victims. The revisionist work by feminist critics such as Clover on low-budget horror and Williams on pornography has demonstrated that the situation is more complex. The gender reversals character-istic of these 'low' genres allow for the empowerment of female victims and the disempowerment of male aggressors. Although we still cannot be absolutely sure what is taking place here, particularly with the proliferation of exhibition sites, the potential for multiple, shifting identifications seems to be there. It is important to note, of course, that this fluid situation is not necessarily in the interests of feminism. It is interesting, for example, that *Disclosure* (1994), in which a happily married businessman, played by Michael Douglas, is 'raped' by his female boss (Demi Moore), reverses the pattern of female victim/male aggressor in what can only be construed as a highly anxious response to the power of women in the workplace. However, it should also be pointed out that the film highlights with startling clarity the fact that its motivating fantasy of sexual submission and dominance is not gender specific.

This brings me back to genre and audience address – in the light of the above discussion, the assumption that genres employ a single gender address can no longer be taken for granted. Nor can the potentially fluid situation of multiple address and plural identifications at work in popular cinema be associated simply with post-classical Hollywood. By the same token, the idea that certain genres are, or ever have been, more 'suitable' for women as either viewers or as filmmakers has come under pressure. This is Kathryn Bigelow, quoted in Jim Hillier's book *The New Hollywood*:

> Conventionally, hardware pictures, action oriented, have been male dominated, and more emotional material has been women's domain. That's breaking down. This notion that there's a women's aesthetic, a woman's eye, is really debilitating. It ghettoises women. The fact that so many women are working as directors now . . . across the spectrum, from comedy to horror to action . . . is incredibly positive. . . . You're asking the [Hollywood] community to reprogramme their thinking.[23]

Bigelow perhaps overestimates the numbers of women directors who have moved into contemporary Hollywood, and it is well known that those who have made that difficult transition rarely make the 'A' list. Without diminishing the real problems faced by women working in Hollywood, it is possible to argue that the focus on marginalization and exclusion that has preoccupied feminist criticism for more than twenty years needs to be rethought, and the historical contribution of women to cinema across the board recognized. This involves a shift in perception – away from counting the relatively small numbers of female directors towards a more historical and contextual analysis of different points of entry into the industry by women, in what is, after all, a collaborative medium. The influence of female audiences, and the considerable impact of feminism – or should I say feminisms – across the full range of production have scarcely begun to be addressed.

It is tempting to conclude, as Bigelow seems to suggest in the above quote, that the post-classical period has seen an opening up of opportunities for women filmmakers. Although there is an absence of statistical information, one nevertheless gets a sense of the presence of women in all aspects of the production process – as stars, producers, directors, technical and creative personnel – and in all genres. Bigelow herself is a high-profile example of a cross-over phenomenon – a woman director who works with traditionally male action genres, who collaborates with male filmmakers and whose work cannot easily be assimilated in gender terms. Her films *Near Dark* (1987) and *Blue Steel* (1990), both generic hybrids, confront head-on difficult questions of violence and sexuality, while the bigger-budget *Point Break* (1991) and *Strange Days* (1995) both handle the technical problems of blockbuster action filmmaking with masterly style and verve.

Like Ida Lupino almost fifty years before, Bigelow is a writer and producer as well as director, and interesting comparisons could be drawn between their production contexts and their work, particularly between Lupino's rape film *Outrage* and Bigelow's cop movie *Blue Steel*, which includes a rape-revenge scenario. Such a comparison might suggest that the conjunction of post-1970s feminism and the entry of women filmmakers at all levels of the industry with the greater visibility of graphic sex and violence, deplored by many, has had some beneficial effects for women, in that it has allowed feminism to move into a wider arena. Women filmmakers can, it seems, now use sexually explicit and violent material to confront issues of representation before much larger audiences.

It also appears as though the concerns of the paranoid woman's film have moved from the localized, domestic arena they occupied in the 1940s on to the global stage in the 1980s and 1990s. It is interesting to note, for example, that in the *Alien* series of films, a paranoid woman saves the world, while in *Terminator 2: Judgment Day* (1993) a paranoid woman changes the course of history. Thus the question I raised in my 1983 article, echoed in Kathryn Bigelow's comments above, about the ghettoizing effect of a woman's film defined in terms of an exclusive address to female spectators, appears to have come full circle, and to have been answered, at least partially, by the increased gender fluidity and genre hybridity characteristic of the new Hollywood. However, I do not think we can make any assumptions about 'progress', in feminist terms at least, based on a classical/post-classical divide.

If it is true that there are greater numbers of women working in contemporary Hollywood, the nature of the impact of the presence of women as producers, directors and writers remains unclear. How, for feminist purposes, do we weigh up the value of Jonathan Demme's feminist influenced *The Silence of the Lambs* (1990) against Kathryn Bigelow's *Strange Days*? Is it the case, perhaps, that female audiences have at times exerted greater control over Hollywood production than those working inside the industry? As I have already suggested, only a historical investigation of the contribution of women to all aspects of cinema can assess the significance or otherwise of that contribution at specific conjunctures.[24] I would anticipate that such an investigation will produce a more complex map of the role of women in Hollywood cinema than models defined by exclusion and marginalization. After all, the conclusions we draw from historical enquiry and evidence depend to some extent on what we are looking for in the first place. The agendas and methodologies adopted by historians are just as much subject to social and cultural forces as the objects chosen for study.

Notes

1 Pam Cook, 'Melodrama and the women's picture', in S. Aspinall and R. Murphy (eds), *BFI Dossier 18: Gainsborough Melodrama* (London: BFI Publishing, 1983), p. 17.

2 See, for example, Jackie Stacey's study of the interaction of female audiences with star figures in *Star Gazing: Hollywood Cinema and Female Spectatorship* (London and New York: Routledge, 1994).

3 In *The Desire to Desire: The Woman's Film of the 1940s* (Basingstoke: Macmillan, 1987), Mary Ann Doane identifies an ironic approach to classical Hollywood narrative conventions as a characteristic of women's pictures.

4 See David Bordwell and Janet Staiger, 'Since 1960: the persistence of a mode of film practice', in D. Bordwell, J. Staiger and K Thompson, *The Classical Hollywood Cinema: Film Style and Mode of Production to 1960* (New York: Columbia University Press, 1985).

5 An argument put forward by, for example, Jim Collins, 'Genericity in the nineties: eclectic irony and the new sincerity', in J. Collins, H. Radner and A. Preacher Collins (eds), *Film Theory Goes to the Movies* (New York: Routledge, 1993).

6 See Timothy Corrigan, *A Cinema Without Walls: Movies and Culture After Vietnam* (New York: Routledge, 1991).

7 Edward Buscombe, *Stagecoach* (London: BFI Publishing, 1993).

8 Doane, *The Desire to Desire*, p. 16.

9 Ibid., p. 8.

10 Ibid., p. 8.

11 Judith Mayne, *Cinema and Spectatorship* (New York and London: Routledge, 1993), p. 27.

12 Ibid., p. 97.

13 Barbara Klinger, *Melodrama and Meaning: History, Culture and the Films of Douglas Sirk* (Bloomington and Indianapolis: Indiana University Press, 1994), p. 54.

14 Ibid., p. 68.

15 Pam Cook, '*Outrage*', in A. Kuhn (ed.), *Queen of the 'B's: Ida Lupino Behind the Camera* (London: Flicks Books, 1995).

16 Carol J. Clover, *Men, Women and Chainsaws: Gender in the Modern Horror Film* (London: BFI Publishing, 1992), p. 153.

17 Linda Williams, *Hard Core: Power, Pleasure and the 'Frenzy of the Visible'* (London: Pandora, 1991), p. 166.

18 Clover, *Men, Women and Chainsaws*, pp. 6–7.

19 Linda Williams, 'Learning to scream', *Sight and Sound* (NS) vol. 4, no. 12 (December 1994), p. 17.

20 Ibid., p. 17.

21 Pam Cook, '*Cape Fear* and femininity as destructive power', in P. Cook and P. Dodd (eds), *Women and Film: A Sight and Sound Reader* (London: Scarlet Press, 1993).

22 1 am referring here to approaches to representation inspired by, for example, Catharine MacKinnon and Andrea Dworkin's radical feminist critique of pornography, cited by Linda Williams in *Hard Core*, pp. 17–18.

23 Jim Hillier, *The New Hollywood* (London: Studio Vista, 1993), p. 127.

24 This work has already begun – see, for example, Lizzie Francke, *Script Girls: Women Screenwriters in Hollywood* (London: BFI Publishing, 1994); Jackie Stacey, *Star Gazing*; and Miriam Hansen on Rudolph Valentino and female audiences in *Babel and Babylon: Spectatorship in American Silent Film* (Cambridge, Mass.: Harvard University Press, 1991).

Chapter 16

New Hollywood's new women
Murder in mind – Sarah and Margie

Hilary Radner

> What am I doing here? (Laughter) Especially considering the extraordinary group of women with whom I was nominated. We five women were fortunate to have the choice – not just the opportunity but the choice – to play such rich complex female characters and I congratulate producers like 'Working Title' and 'Polygram' . . . for allowing directors to make autonomous casting decisions based on qualifications and not just market value. And I encourage, I encourage writers and directors to keep these really interesting female roles coming and while you're at it you can throw in a few for the men as well.
>
> Frances McDormand, Academy Awards, Oscar for
> Best Actress, 1996

Frances McDormand cut a strikingly anomalous figure at the 1996 Oscar Awards (March 1997) – an anomaly underlined by the contrast between her and Juliette Binoche, who won the Oscar for Best Supporting Actress that year. Binoche oozed glamour, glided across the stage, and was appropriately distraught. She managed to insult veteran Hollywood star Lauren Bacall in her attempt to pay homage. McDormand was clothed in a very simple blue dress, severe by Hollywood standards in comparison to Binoche's elaborate opulent gown. McDormand awkwardly climbed the stairs, looking pale, 'unmade up', her bare back muscular rather than erotic. She strutted across the stage, a displaced 'butch' in a 'femme' role. Though obviously moved, she retained enough composure to attribute dignity rather than pathos to her fellow nominees. As the camera lingered on each in turn, McDormand's refusal of her role as Hollywood star was further emphasized. The traditional series of close-ups of the 'losers' seemed designed to frame the luscious lips, bejewelled necks and elaborate coiffures that characterized the four other nominees, often in stark contrast to the roles that they had played. Frances McDormand, notwithstanding the Oscar grasped in her hands, was out of place.

Feminists might decry her uxorious devotion to her writer-director husband –
who she claimed in her acceptance speech 'made a woman' of her. She also
ironically comments in the production notes: 'It's the first time in twelve years of
sleeping with the director that I got the job, no questions asked.'[1] In many ways
her story fits the Hollywood prototype.[2] And yet if her story seems all too
familiar, her image remains out of place. New Hollywood's New Women often
hold paradoxical positions, in which their stories, while confirming the dominant
model, 'catch' at some moment or another, unravelling this narrative, if only
sporadically and temporarily. However, these moments of *aporia* open the narrative to the possibility of other narratives, other stories about femininity. What is
the significance of these moments? Have there been changes wrought within a
system of representation that Raymond Bellour characterized again and again as a
machine based on the reciprocity between state and family designed to produce
the heterosexual couple?[3]

The popularity of the 'psychofemme', to quote the title of an article appearing
in *Mirabella*, a women's magazine directed towards an upscale readership, suggests
a general anxiety about the state of the couple in contemporary culture.[4] Glenn
Close and Sharon Stone excel in the portrayal of the traditional *femme fatale* of
classical Hollywood gone 'psycho', no longer even nominally under the control of
men. The magazine emphasizes her importance as a figure of heterosexuality gone
awry. Is the 'psychofemme' the expression of the lunacy of women crazed by
heterosexuality? Is heterosexuality indelibly marked as insane? Or, is she the sane
response to the initial and more fundamental lunacy of men? Stanley Cavell
comments that certain types of films within the classical Hollywood paradigm
revolve around 'the idea of maleness itself as villainous, say sadistic'. Cavell
suggests that within classical Hollywood cinema the 'male gender . . . is tainted
with villainy'.[5] The films of the studio era that Cavell examines seek to contain
this 'taint' through sacrifice on the part of woman (melodrama), or through her
acceptance of the trauma of man's villainy, her 'education' as Cavell would have
us believe (comedies of remarriage). The 'psychofemme' refuses these alternatives, these programmes of containment that fail to rock the boat of heterosexuality. She seems to ask: how then might a woman react once she recognizes this
villainy as the defining characteristic of man within heterosexuality, once she sees
his inevitable lunacy within the history of Hollywood cinema?

In response, so to speak, to this question, Hollywood has produced a new
generation of *femmes fatales*, of pyschofemmes – of women who refuse the violence
of men. Two of its more formidable examples are found in two contemporary
Hollywood films, *Terminator 2: Judgment Day* (1991) and *Fargo* (1996). These films
have in common that they take up the problems of the lunatic violence of men,
and of death, more specifically, of murder. *Terminator 2* pushes the rationale of the
'psychofemme' to its logical (and extreme) conclusion in which only the maniacal

(violent) pursuit of the ethical imperative offers an adequate response to the lunacy of men. *Fargo* similarly constructs a cosmology in which only a woman animated by an ethical imperative so overwhelming that it verges on lunacy can withstand the chaos produced by the violence of men. The ethical imperative that clearly governs the actions of the female protagonists sets these heroines apart from the traditional *femme fatale*. These narratives themselves offer symptomatic articulations of the larger problematic of feminine culture and its relationship to the violence of men.[6] The issues of femininity and its response to masculine violence are articulated within popular culture in a number of significant ways. Perhaps most palpably this response manifests itself in terms of the representation of the body as that upon which masculine violence is most visibly enacted and of the repossession of that body by the woman as a site of struggle and empowerment. This concern with the body marks out one of the major areas of crisis for contemporary women in their attempt to forge a feminine identity, and certainly occupies the foreground of feminine culture as a whole. Thus, it is no coincidence that the narrative of a high-concept film such as *Terminator 2*, which revolves around a woman's attempt to save humanity from man's violence in the form of his machines, is inflected with a set of paradoxes generated around the literal body of the woman.

Scholarly analysis of the Cameron films has tended to emphasize the role of the cyborg's transformation from murderer to father.[7] In contrast, popular culture and women audiences in general seized upon the changes wrought upon the body of the female star, Linda Hamilton. In *The Terminator* (1984), to which *Terminator 2* serves as a sequel, Hamilton's body is clearly offered up within a heterosexual context: the camera lingers over its curves – fragile, rounded and fecund – in the film's only sex scene. This single encounter, as if to prove her nubility, her currency as that which can be exchanged between men, results improbably in pregnancy. In the film's final scene we are left with the image of pregnancy as an inflation, an awkwardness of the female body – the sign of its vulnerability – but also the source of its strength. This strength is evidenced in the new determination and decisiveness of the protagonist as she competently conducts her four-wheel drive vehicle into the wilds of Mexico there to meet her exceptional fate. This fate marks her as outside an economy of exchange, as occupying a position of incommensurability, which is the result of her pregnancy. This destiny is informed by a murder that may have already taken place in the future, of which her son-to-be is the victim. This unborn son, ordained to save mankind, sends his father back into the past in order to ensure the future he now inhabits by impregnating his mother. The son thus gives her the child that he already is.

The twisted logic of this narrative in *Terminator 2* is a manifestation of the hyper-rationality that characterizes Sarah Connor (the character played by Hamilton) and her insanity. The lunacy of men results in the insanity of a machine-dominated future. Only the rationality of woman, delineating the limit of rationality itself, can save 'man'kind. We witness then a reversal of the traditional conceptions of masculine and feminine, in which the masculine is associated with the rational, the feminine with the irrational. Certainly within the film, men appear to operate rationally. Even Connor's son is initially convinced of her lunacy. Yet the rationality of men is the logic of endless profit, in which the possibility of profitable enterprise, without thought of consequence, becomes the terms of sanity. In her attempt to assert another set of concerns, Sarah Connor is incarcerated in a lunatic asylum, from which she must escape to save her son (and humanity) from the future.

This figure of paradoxical femininity recalls Jacques Lacan's description of Antigone as the inscription of the limit between that which is not human and that which is human. 'Antigone appears . . . as a pure and simple relationship of the human being to that of which he miraculously happens to be the bearer, namely, the signifying cut that confers on him the indomitable power of being what he is in the face of everything that may oppose him.'[8] The English translation displaces the gender of the original pronouns.[9] 'She' – Antigone – becomes 'he' who has the 'power'.[10] This displacement points to the transformation wrought upon the body of Sarah Connor, initially transformed through pregnancy, ultimately through an act of will that causes the body to signify agency.[11] In other words, it is only her lunatic devotion to absolute rationality, to the ethical imperative to save humanity, that preserves humanity as such. This lunacy as her 'indomitable' will is written out upon a body that inevitably becomes something other than itself, thus a sign at the limit of signification – an affirmation of nature (as maternity) through the production of a denaturalized body. The body of the woman thus undergoes a number of transformations beginning with that of pregnancy.

The fact that this is an unreal – a fictional – transformation does not detract from the power of this image. The transformations of pregnancy are familiar if not necessarily reassuring facts of human reproductive biology.[12] Connor/Hamilton gives birth to a child but also to a new 'self in the form of a new body – hardened, honed, small breasted and taut. This body defies a stereotypical image of the woman after childbirth in which her body is often seen as weakened and softened by the ordeal of pregnancy. Connor/Hamilton's arms are sinewy and tough, emphasized by her sleeveless T-shirts ('wife beaters'), which she wears in all weathers, baring her arms rather than her breasts for an admiring viewer's gaze. This body was a frequent object of discussion by the press circulating its reconstruction as a significant element of the narrative.

Us magazine asked in September 1991: 'So how did the 34-year old actress, who had a child less than a year before shooting began get her body to look like a cyborg? . . . Hamilton says her new look is the result of three months of intensive training: running, cycling and workouts under the supervision of personal trainer Anthony Cortes.'[13] The changes that Hamilton, with the help of her trainer, inscribes in her very musculature, subsequent to her actual pregnancy, are significant precisely because the viewer knows that these are 'real'. This new musculature is the verifiable sign of her mastery over the terrain of her body. It is the physical symbol of her ability to control not only her fate, but also ultimately the fate of the human race. This body positions itself at the limit of erotic fascination, a gesture that reworks the status of that body as the limit between that which is human and that which is machine.

This limit between human and machine is one that the *Terminator* films play through again and again on different terrains, most strikingly through the bodies of its stars. If at times, as the film notes again and again, her cyborg ally (Arnold Schwarzenegger) seems more human than Sarah Connor, as a human machine it is she who embodies the ethical imperative necessary to the salvation of humanity. Her maniacal obsession produces the lunacy that defines the possibility of sanity. The rationality of the machine as the insanity of man can only be defeated by the lunatic rationality of a woman, which she imparts to a machine, the cyborg (Schwarzenegger) whom she 'humanizes' by teaching him the necessity of self-sacrifice. She and her son make a mother of him. At the film's end the cyborg must destroy himself to ensure the survival of mankind. This sacrifice is made possible, made meaningful, through the sacrifice of her own sanity already made by Sarah Connor.

Figure 16.1 Arnold Schwarzenegger, Linda Hamilton and Edward Furlong in *Terminator 2: Judgment Day* (1991). Courtesy of Guild and the Kobal Collection

Not surprisingly, film scholar Susan Jeffords describes this transformation as a horrific erasure of femininity-as-maternity:

> Sarah Connor's character is repeated and inverted in the second film. In the first she was uncertain, frightened and weak; in her rebirth she is tough-minded, fearless, and strong. . . . The 'new' Sarah Connor looks like the mercenary she has trained to be through all the intervening years. She wears fatigues, totes heavy weapons, and has a mission to perform. As final proof of her new hard character, she even forgets to love her son.[14]

The 'unnaturalness' of a maternity that gives priority to the survival of the human race over sentimental attachment to childhood was also underlined by the press. Hamilton herself confesses to *Village View* that 'another difficult part was holding back her normal maternal instincts with Eddie Furlong, who portrays her screen son John Connor'.[15] In spite of, or perhaps because of, this erasure of a specific femininity, women viewers commented endlessly and enviously on this remarkable new body. Their responses echoed the position of a contemporary article in *Shape* (a women's magazine that focuses on exercise and health) which claims: 'When you've got biceps and triceps, who need diamonds?'[16] It is as though woman must abandon the obvious conspicuous signs of maternity, marriage, femininity (diamonds) in order to assume maternity as a form of agency. It is her task, again in Lacan's words, 'to represent the radical limit that affirms the unique value of his being'[17] – that of her brother in the case of Antigone, that of her son in the case of Sarah Connor – ultimately that of humanity itself within the cosmology of *Terminator 2*.

Antigone's implacability is never explained. In contrast, the two films delineate a process whereby Sarah Connor moves from 'ordinary' femininity to 'extraordinary' femininity. From mother to 'macha killerette'.[18] She becomes Lacan's Antigone, pushed to her limits by the insanity of men, showing 'neither fear nor pity'.[19] This is the body of a killer – but also a killer body. In *Terminator 2* this new body emerges as if in response to Sarah's dream in which she witnesses the death of humanity, a 'holocaust' with which the film begins. It is a peculiarity of film that dream and experience are syntactically confounded; retrospectively we as viewers realize that we have seen a dream, Connor's nightmare. This nightmare, however, takes on the status of truth within the narrative, the truth of a death that will have already happened in the future if Connor fails to transform the present.

Once Connor succeeds in transforming the present, just as she has transformed her body, aspects of the narrative move the viewer back to an ideal of maternity and femininity that understands but does not condone the monstrosity of Connor. At the film's conclusion, her sacrifice enacted for her by the cyborg, Sarah returns to 'motherhood'. She and her son drive off companionably into a now unknown future, in which he effectively becomes the child he never was. He is no longer the saviour of mankind, but a child whose future cannot be predicted. Hamilton also planned to make her body become more feminine. '. . . [N]ow that *T2* is done, she's working with Cortes to maintain, yet modify, her form. "I need to feminize my body a bit," she explained. . . .'[20] However, this new 'feminine' also emphasizes the body as a site of transformation, which remains a significant association that is intertextually defined.

The particular story of Linda Hamilton's transformation and its overdetermined relationship to femininity and the body is superseded and augmented by other such stories, that of Demi Moore for example. Her pregnancy and 'refiguration' were publicly documented by *Vanity Fair* – in August of 1991 she appeared on the cover of the magazine, her naked stomach indicating her condition, photographed by Annie Leibovitz – an image that was considered scandalous. Less scandalous but equally 'talked about' was her August 1992 cover photo (again for *Vanity Fair*), in which a 'suit' is painted on to her now refigured eroticized sleek body, recovered and reformulated after its previous distension, the ordeal of pregnancy. This refiguration differs from that of Hamilton in that it emphasizes a voluptuous body that controls itself for the public gaze, rather than a body ready for action (as was that of Hamilton). Paradoxically to be ready for action in the film actor's world is to be ready for the camera gaze, as Moore's subsequent activity in her chosen field has amply proven. Though Moore has been amply rewarded for her body, it is the disembodied McDormand who, in 1997, her body 'shaped' by a 'pregnancy pad' rather than her will, receives the Oscar for Best Actress of 1996.

In producing a heroine so 'out of place' in Hollywood, *Fargo* speaks most eloquently to the transformation that Hollywood's New Woman has undergone – one that clearly demarcates a reformulation of the body. The transformation of this body from *Terminator* to *Terminator 2* might be said to represent a move within dominant feminine culture to repossess the female body as a site of realization and agency outside heterosexuality through the articulation of specific technologies of the self. *Fargo* represents another move away from the body of the *femme fatale* as the object of a voyeuristic gaze, but in a different direction. Hamilton's body engages the viewer at the limits of eroticism; this eroticism is denied and effaced within the context of *Fargo*. Margie (Frances McDormand), *Fargo*'s heroine, refuses to perform the role of the fetishized body. She refuses to become the object of cinematic fetishistic scopophilia – the role that Laura Mulvey pointed out was historically assigned to 'woman', the role that defined her as such, within the classical Hollywood cinema.[21]

The fetishized body is a body that is misrecognized – a body that is the product of disavowal on the part of the masculine subject who believes (and yet knows that this is not the case) that the woman is not castrated, that the mother is all powerful. To persist in a fascination with the *femme fatale* as the phallic woman is inevitably, in Stanley Cavell's words, 'death dealing'. Death may be deferred but the subject is none the less caught in an economy of death.[22] *Fargo* in its departure from the known must begin with a moment of indeterminacy, marking out the limits of knowledge. 'Fargo' itself is hardly even a 'place' within the film, whose narrative travels, on the road between Brainerd, Minneapolis and elsewhere – that is to say nowhere.

Popular critic David Denby writes: 'In the dead of winter, a car drives towards us through white fields and white air, a whiteness so enveloping that we cannot tell where ground and air meet.'[23] In a memorable opening, two lights, which the viewer recognizes belatedly as the headlights of a car, move painfully slowly through the literal 'snow' of the screen towards the camera. A form emerges, which can be understood, but this understanding, this knowledge marks the limits of that which can be understood and known. As the narrative unfolds, it becomes clear that these limits are those of the body and the possibility it offers as the site of identity. The body, however, that emerges is not the fetishized body of classic Hollywood. This is a body that defies fetishism; it fascinates through a voyeuristic investigation of what this new body might be.

The central figure of *Fargo* is a female policewoman: Margie, Chief Marge Gunderson, a detective, whose job it is to track down a killer. She is not the woman unworthy of the camera gaze; however she is strangely disembodied – 'pithed' – without the fetishistic core that defines the feminine as such within Hollywood iconography. She is not disembodied because she lacks something but because of an excess of 'body', represented through her obvious pregnancy, to which she refers throughout the film. Her body makes demands – she constantly eats – she vomits – she sleeps – she dresses; this body is obtrusive and conspicuous. It impedes the heroine's movement, intruding between her and the objects that surround her. None the less, it itself is not an object offered up to the viewer's voyeuristic gaze. Her body is rather discreetly covered – yet not veiled. Here the body's power derives from its monumental failure to arouse our erotic interest. This pregnant cop, a new *femme fatale* whose fatality remains indecipherable, does not kill, though she always gets her man. She arrests killers who fail to recognize her for what she is. She is unreadable like the landscape she inhabits, which comes to define her as Monument Valley defined John Wayne.

As a policewoman, Marge Gunderson represents the law rather than desire, though as the law it is more remarkable for its persistence than its monumentality. She is the 'Chief' who solves the triple murder that besmirches the white snows of her town, of her 'beautiful day', which we must not fail to recall presents us with an interminable blizzard. Her 'implacability', which she places in the service of the law, is the only force that can arrest, literally, the lunacy of men. Among men, desire flows freely seemingly without hindrance from any laws, except the logic of

Figure 16.2 Frances McDormand as Margie in *Fargo* (1996). Courtesy of
PolyGram/Pictorial Press

profit, the logic that in *Terminator 2* threatens humanity, that Connor must counter
with her other rationality. 'I just need the money', claims Jerry Lundegaard
(William H. Macy) as he attempts to explain to two thugs, Carl Showalter (Steve
Buscemi) and Gaer Grimsrud (Peter Stormare) that he wants them to kidnap his
wife. Though the thugs are not convinced of the 'sense' of his plan they agree
because, perhaps, they too just need the money. Death, always accompanied by a
horrible mutilation of the body, occurs similarly without reason – the result
seemingly of pure moments of abreaction – of psychic discharge through which
the body as agent and object loses its specificity as 'human'.

This irrational body (the body defined through abreaction) constitutes itself as
male. Its symptom as the moment of murder is transferred from one man to
another. Showalter greets the first murder committed by the mute Grimsrud with
pain and astonishment. 'Oh Daddy', is all he can say, as though evoking some
parody of a lost patriarchal order; however, he too comes to kill unthinkingly,
adding an innocent parking lot attendant without afterthought to the growing list
of the dead. Murder like a hysterical symptom is passed from one lunatic to
another – all men. Wade Gustafson, the kidnapped wife's father, is infected –
Showalter merely shoots first. The intent to kill taints all the men in the film, even,
as we shall see, Marge's husband Norm.

In contrast, the women of the film – the wife who is kidnapped and murdered
– the prostitutes – all attempt to create 'sense' within the limited means available
to them. If they are damned, it is through stupidity rather than violence. They are
wives, and prostitutes, without means of their own – they are thus unable to

overthrow the lunacy of men. They are often victims. They sometimes escape. But they are not the agents of violence. If there are men that also fall into this category, this merely serves to illustrate the indecipherability of gender as a function of the body within the context of narrative. A man may escape the taint of his gender by submitting to the intelligence of woman. The men of Brainerd, beginning with Norm, submit themselves to the intelligence of woman, of a woman, and thus at least temporarily escape their fate.

Women, however, suffer from a different set of limitations. These limitations are most clearly articulated through Wade's wife, Jean (Kristin Rudrud). Tied and blindfolded by her husband's hired thugs, she is literally deprived of agency and thus falls victim to the senselessness of her captors. The question that haunts her fate: why did she marry Jerry in the first place? The answer lies perhaps in her father, who, as the patriarch of the family, the successful self-made man, incarnates the violence of money in his incomprehensible desire to accumulate 'more'. He even attempts to bargain with his wife's kidnappers. Jerry must remind him: 'We're not horse trading here, Wade.' Of course, Jerry's lunacy consists of the fact that he is doing precisely that which he claims he is not or rather that which he hopes Wade will not do. He is 'horse trading' – only instead of a horse, it is his wife on whom he is trying to trade.

The irrationality of masculine desire and the role of woman plays itself out in a scene in which Marge encounters a former high-school classmate, Mike Yanagita (Steve Park), who is clearly obsessed with her. His passion is aroused when he sees her on television. He thus sees her in the improbable position as 'image', improbable in so far as McDormand systematically refuses that role. It is, however,

Figure 16.3 William H. Macy as Jerry in *Fargo* (1996). Courtesy of PolyGram/ Pictorial Press

Margie as Chief of Police, Chief Gunderson (an image that paradoxically signifies the power to act) that mesmerizes him, her power as the agent of narrative rather than as image that compels him. She appears, then, to incarnate that possibility of restoring order to the disorder, the insanity, of his life. They meet in Minneapolis, which Marge visits in the course of investigating the murder of three people, accidentally killed by the two thugs while transporting the kidnapped wife to their hideout. Mike's obsession with Marge is clear to everyone but Marge. Less clear is the life that he fabricates for himself – the 'true' story he accords himself in which he is married to a dead woman – perhaps signifying the 'taint' of the man who fails to find his Antigone and submit himself to her harsh rule.

The 'insanity' of Marge's sensibility also reveals itself in this scene. She fails again and again to recognize the signs of Mike's instability. Almost, it would seem, by sheer force of will, she imposes her perception of the situation upon him. It is this stubbornness, this implacability, that ties her to Antigone, to Sarah Connor. Marge pursues Grimsrud with the same intensity, and with the same lack of affect with which he pursues the inadvertent witnesses of his first murder. Marge's stolid observance of convention enables her to reconstruct an order out of the disorder created by men. She effects this transformation through a dogged, persistent, and finally irrational pursuit of the rational, breaking down the conventional easy categories of logic and the logical. Like Antigone and Sarah Connor, Marge claims a position that confounds any clear-cut opposition between the rational and the irrational, defying a traditional association of the masculine with the former and the feminine with the latter.

And in the end she gets her man[24] – caught in the act of feeding his partner's body to the wood chipper. She shoots him deliberately and without haste as he attempts to flee across a white expanse of snow. As she drives him to the station, she ponders the relationship between money and death, a seeming commensurability in the world of men. The 'more' of more money is an assumption upon which the narrative is predicated but which has no meaning for her. Marge queries Grimsrud: 'And for what? For a little bit of money. There's more to life than a little money you know. Don't you know that? And here you are, and it's a beautitul day. Well. I just don't understand it.' Grimsrud, always a man of few words, has no answer for her, if he even listens. As she speaks, he turns to give a parting glance to the statue of Paul Bunyan, axe in hand, at the town limits.

Here again we must question Marge's sanity. Her beautiful day is an interminable blizzard; Paul Bunyan, a folk hero of the frontier, noted for his ability to chop down trees, appears to have more in common with Grimsrud than with Marge. Denby comments: 'She discovers a modern Paul Bunyan and she takes him into custody.'[25] Marge refutes the myth of the frontier – she takes the legend into custody in order to institute the law of women. But what does she offer in place of the frontier, its endless promises of desire and death, of more? What is the 'more' to life on which Marge is willing to stake her own life?

If there is a redemptive relationship in the film it is that of Marge and Norm, her husband. Their bedroom returns again and again to the screen, a place of warmth and comfort in contrast with the stark world outside. At the same time the bedroom is strangely connected through camera movement, point of view and editing, to this world of violence.

We first see Marge and Norm immediately after Grimsrud kills his two witnesses. A fade to black concludes Grimsrud's senseless triple murder. We fade in on Norm's studio, as the camera slowly moves across his paints and 'stuffed' ducks: the traces of a now aestheticized wilderness. Death as violence, immobilized through the techniques of taxidermy, none the less demarcates the territory of man, distinguishing it from the 'bed' as the site of domesticity and the terrain of woman. The camera continues its slow movement, without a break, stopping at the peaceful sleeping couple, whose slumber will be momentarily disturbed by the news of events we, as viewers, have just witnessed. Later in the film, Showalter turns on a faulty television and the camera cuts to an image which could be the one he finally receives but is (we discover retrospectively) the set in Marge's and Norm's bedroom. It is Marge's point of view, rather than Carl's, that is retrospectively defined through the conventions of editing; however, there is one moment in which the two coincide, in a confusion of spaces. The spaces and 'looks' of the two characters are connected through the tropes of editing, suggesting the precariousness of the marital refuge.

The film's conclusion similarly produces a permeable space in which criminality and domesticity coincide. The police apprehend Jerry in a hotel room, pinning him down on a double bed and cuffing him as he whimpers inchoately. The camera cuts to the Gundersons' double bed, in which Norm is seated alone, screen right like Jerry, prone on the double bed of the hotel room. Norm is watching television; the light flickers across his face. What is the difference between Norm and Jerry, except perhaps Marge?

If the film ends with Marge and Norm safely at home in bed, there is also something vaguely disquieting about their stability. This uneasiness refuses the viewer the sentimentality that such an image of connubial happiness conventionally conveys in a Hollywood film. Ethan Coen comments:

> [W]hile Marge and Norm's marriage is good, it's also dull; they're happy with all that routine. Usually in Hollywood films, happiness is shown as something sentimental and dramatic, whereas the happy stuff in this film is *grindingly* dull. At the same time the marriage is happy and stable, and Marge is a better person, less conflicted, than the main characters in most of our movies, so in that sense, multiple murders aside, it is our warmest movie.[26]

Given that we are willing to leave 'multiple murders aside', murders that have invaded the bedroom, it is perhaps the fact that Marge herself is 'grindingly dull' that disturbs us. Do we secretly long for the violent release of death? The myth of the frontier as characterized by Richard Slotkin depends upon a belief in (a nostalgia for) 'regeneration through violence'.[27] The new frontiers of domesticity and of cloistered interiors governed by the law of the feminine offer no place for violence. The film even refuses us the aesthetic release of the grandiose panoramic landscape, the sublime images that compensate for the fact that our lunatic hero, our Shane, our Ethan Edwards, inexorably moves towards death. Marge chooses life, such that it is. Here her pregnancy plays a crucial role in defining that choice. And it is in that choice and that willingness to accept and even to take pleasure in 'the little things' that reside in her heroism and her insanity. Her heroism depends upon the triumph of the inadequate, of the less.

It is perhaps an attribute of film as a medium that it always testifies to the inadequacy of language. Within classical Hollywood conventions, film offers the image as a compensatory moment, as the moment of hallucinatory fantasy, a fetishist compensation within Mulvey's terms. In *Fargo*, language is inadequate. Marge and Norm can only repeat 'I love you' in a monotone. Marge greets death with 'Aw Jeez.' However, there is no image, no phantasmatic moment of compensation, perhaps as a direct result of McDormand's refusal of the fetishistic gaze. There is only less, and less. Snow and more snow. Norm escapes the taint of his gender only to the extent that he is willing to accept the ethics of less, of order, proposed by Marge.

Norm must dedicate the little things of his life to Marge, who in turn consecrates and renders them meaningful, to the degree that meaning is possible within the constraints of the 'grindingly dull'. As Marge climbs into bed, having solved her multiple murders, Norm offers her his little triumph: his painting of a mallard has been chosen to adorn a three-cent stamp. Marge is properly appreciative – though it is not clear to what extent her tone differs from that which she uses in coaxing a willing but somewhat dense witness. 'Whenever they raise the postage, people need the little stamps. . . . When they're stuck with a bunch of the old ones.' She stills Norm's fears that somehow a three-cent stamp is without value by pointing out that nothing, not even stamps, has a fixed value. The cost of sending a letter will always rise, is inherently unstable – thus the necessity for the little lunacy, the three-cent stamp that men bring to the rational system of women. She tells him 'Heck, Norm, we're doing pretty good', knowing that this is the best that one can expect. Norm of course will always want more. Yet in this final moment Marge's 'pretty good' seems no more rational than Norm's 'more'. Marge's pregnancy, the new life within her, speaks a 'more' that depends upon the little things of domesticity, outside the instability of money and of an arena in which the price of things will always go up.

In the last instance the law of woman is as incomprehensible as the lunacy of men – but it is the limit inscribed by woman, incomprehensible in and of itself, that permits a story that will eventually make sense of itself. Men, who always want more, are without limits – and thus produce only senselessness – within the logic of *Fargo*. Certainly the film confirms heterosexuality as the only relationship capable of providing equilibrium (though only moderately reliable) within a world gone awry. This is a curiously de-eroticized heterosexuality predicated on maternity – an alliance in the face of an economy governed by unpredictable moments of abreaction – an economy that requires constant vigilance on the part of those that refuse its logic of desire and death. In a similar vein, one might point out that Hollywood tends by and large to reproduce the social structures facilely described as heterosexuality and patriarchy. Perhaps of equal interest are the occasions, the exceptions rather than the rule, in which Hollywood produces something else. Marge and Sarah are perhaps the most visible and the most obvious of Hollywood's gender paradoxes but they are not without sisters, cousins and aunts.

It is not my intention here to legitimate New Hollywood as the authentic expression of a popular feminism or as a politically correct moment in the evolution of heterosexuality. Rather I point to these heroines because their personae suggest that it would be a mistake to see heterosexuality as a monolithic category caught in the binaries of homosexuality/heterosexuality. These films testify to the permeability, the mutability and the instability of heterosexuality – itself in a continual process of transforming – a 'becoming' (to borrow a term from Judith Butler) rather than something one 'becomes' – in which '[policing] the social appearance of gender' must ultimately fail.[28] And perhaps this is Marge's greatest triumph: she offers not so much a solution, but a fantasy of happiness outside the insanity and delirium that as a rule fuels Hollywood fiction. It is not a monumental happiness. But as happiness it is worth the insanity she suffers in order to police the lunatic violence of men.

Sarah and Margie defy the Hollywood machinery that all too often reduces femininity to her image, the flattened body that functions as a projection of masculine desire. None the less these figures maintain the convention of an opposition between masculinity and femininity in which maternity and its representation remains a founding characteristic of woman – variously deconstructed and reconstructed. The bodies of women remain within the territory of the feminine while multiplying the sites of identity that femininity might claim as such. A crucial question that both these figures pose, then, is that of the persistence of gender in spite of the increasing plasticity and indeterminacy of the body that defines that terrain. This is an issue that both Hollywood and feminist scholarship will continue to rework as part of the struggle to assert the dream of human agency as the grounds of a future that has not already been condemned by the irrationality of man.[29]

Notes

1 'Fargo Production Notes', gift of Jay Kugelman, Academy of Motion Picture Arts and Sciences Library, Beverly Hills, California.

2 *Fargo* itself might be considered 'un-Hollywood' in terms of its production history. It is not a major Hollywood studio production; yet it cannot simply be categorized as an independent production. This 'hybridity' might be considered another attribute of contemporary Hollywood; for a more industrial and institutional perspective on this question, see the chapters by Tino Balio, Justin Wyatt and James Schamus in this volume.

3 See in particular Raymond Bellour, 'Symboliques', in R. Bellour (ed.), *Le Cinéma américain: analyse de films* (Paris: Flammarion, 1980), pp. 173–99.

4 Karen Durbin, 'Psychofemmes', *Mirabella* (June 1992), pp. 44–8. For a discussion of the *femme fatale* in Hollywood cinema, see Mary Anne Doane, *Femmes Fatales: Feminism, Film Theory, Psychoanalysis* (London: Routledge, 1991).

5 Stanley Cavell, 'Psychoanalysis and cinema: the melodrama of the unknown woman', in Françoise Meltzer (ed.), *The Trial(s) of Psychoanalysis* (Chicago: University of Chicago Press, 1987), p. 231.

6 The choice of the object of analysis is always to a degree arbitrary and idiosyncratic. This is not an exhaustive survey of current Hollywood film; the analysis points out moments of interruption in the otherwise smooth functioning of the Hollywood machine.

7 See, for example, Forest Pyle's excellent analysis of the films' deconstruction of the opposition human/machine. Forest Pyle, 'Making cyborgs, making humans: of terminators and blade runners', in Jim Collins, Hilary Radner and Ava Preacher Collins (eds), *Film Theory Goes to the Movies* (New York: Routledge, 1993), pp. 227–41. See also Doran Larson, 'Machine as Messiah: cyborgs, morphs, and the American body politic', *Cinema Journal*, vol. 36, no. 4 (1997), pp. 57–75.

8 Jacques Lacan, *The Seminar of Jacques Lacan: Book VII, The Ethics of Psychoanalysis 1959–1960*, ed. J.-A. Miller, trans. D. Porter (New York: Norton, 1992), p. 282.

9 In French, the use of the masculine pronoun has a purely grammatical function and is divorced from the actual gender of the referent. Thus 'professeur' is masculine whether the individual professor is a woman or a man because grammatically the word functions as masculine. In English the pronoun designates the gender of the referent rather than grammatical category. In referring to the human as 'he', the translator makes a choice to attribute the masculine gender to the human. In French there is no choice and thus the use of the pronoun does not carry the same connotations.

10 '*Pur et simple rapport de l'être humain, avec ce dont il se trouve être miraculeusement porteur*' (Jacques Lacan, *L'Éthique de la psychanalyse*, 1959–1960 (Paris: Editions du Seuil, 1986), p. 328).

11 By referring to Lacan, I wish to acknowledge a debt to psychoanalysis in the sense that its discourse has been fundamental in producing a historical context that makes possible the interrogation of gender. *Seminar VII* in particular suggests the complexity of the Lacanian conceptualization of gender as an affective and social category.

12 Though Hamilton did have a child between the two movies, at the end of *The Terminator* she wears a 'pregnancy pad', as does Frances McDormand in *Fargo*.

13 Jean Oppenheimer, 'Judgment days', *Village View*, 5–11 July 1991, p. 20.

14 Susan Jeffords, *Hard Bodies: Hollywood Masculinity in the Reagan Era* (New Brunswick, NJ: Rutgers University Press, 1994), p. 160.

15 Oppenheimer, 'Judgment days', p. 20.
16 Scott Roberts, 'Five simple moves for a sleek, strong upper body', *Shape*, December 1992, p. 88.
17 Lacan, *The Seminar of Jacques Lacan*, p. 279.
18 James Bowman, 'The child is father to the man', *The American Spectator*, September 1991, p. 33.
19 Lacan, *The Seminar of Jacques Lacan*, p. 273.
20 Mark Morrison, 'She's back', *Us*, August 1991, p.73.
21 Laura Mulvey, 'Visual pleasure and narrative cinema', in Constance Penley (ed.), *Feminism and Film Theory* (New York: Routledge, 1995), pp. 57–68.
22 See S. Cavell, 'Psychoanalysis and cinema: the melodrama of the unknown woman', p. 227. See Jean Laplance, *Life and Death in Psychoanalysis* (Baltimore: Johns Hopkins University Press, 1976) for a full account of this paradigm.
23 David Denby, *New York*, 18 March 1996, p. 50.
24 Ironically, the tip that leads the Brainerd police to the kidnappers' hideout comes from a man who fails to realize the significance of the information he holds until his wife points it out to him.
25 Denby, *New York*, p. 52.
26 Geoff Andrew, 'Pros and coens', *Time Out*, 15–22 May 1996, p. 24.
27 Richard Slotkin, *Regeneration Through Violence: The Mythology of the American Frontier* (Middletown, Conn.: Wesleyan University Press, 1973).
28 Judith Butler, *Gender Trouble: Feminism and the Subversion of Identity* (New York: Routledge, 1990), p. 33.
29 I wish to thank the many people who helped me and who would no doubt have done a better job as author than I have: Michael Friend for his invaluable assistance in drawing my attention to *Fargo*, underlining its importance, and letting me raid the resources of the Library of the American Academy of Motion Picture Arts; Kathy Psomiades for her seemingly inexhaustible interest in feminist scholarship; Susan White for her sense of the implications of feminist theory and her thoughtful reading of this text; the Philosophy and Literature Concentration at the University of Notre Dame for focusing my attention on the work of Stanley Cavell; Ewa and Krzysz Ziarek for their support in the face of my endless fascination with 'low-brow' culture; Steve Neale and Murray Smith for their patience and encouragement.

Chapter 17

Censorship and narrative indeterminacy in *Basic Instinct*

'You won't learn anything from me I don't want you to know'

Steven Cohan

Some of the most salient textual characteristics of 1940s *film noir* (for example, the displacement of sexuality into dialogue, the moody *mise-en-scène,* the enigmatic *femme fatale*, the convoluted plots, even the coded use of cigarette smoking) resulted from restrictions imposed by the Production Code Administration (PCA), which regulated what films could and could not represent. Annette Kuhn's analysis of institutional as well as ideological censorship in Howard Hawks' 1946 version of Raymond Chandler's *The Big Sleep* shows how the PCA functioned, in effect if not in intention, as a productive rather than repressive force upon the representation of sexual difference in *film noir*. 'Censorship', Kuhn explains, 'may be seen both as an unconscious operation which structures the film text, and also as the textual effect or residue of a set of institutions and practices operating at the level of the film's material production. . . . It is evident that at both levels censorship is a *productive* operation, rather than, as it is commonly conceived, a process of excision, of cutting things out.'[1] In the case of *The Big Sleep*, she demonstrates, both institutional and ideological interventions resulted in protracted censorship of the narrative; consequently what the narrative itself can no longer specify exactly – 'the menacing riddle of female sexuality' – is directed elsewhere, into the film's *mise-en-scène*, which 'bears the traces of the unrepresentable'.[2]

The abandonment of the original Production Code and its replacement by a rating system in 1968, itself revised several times since its inception, brought about what was then – and continues to be – perceived as a 'liberation' of mainstream American cinema, allowing for a franker representation of sexuality, and laying the ground for a revival of *film noir* that, with the licence afforded by the new R-rating, supposedly 'corrected' the omissions and silences of 1940s thrillers like *The Big Sleep*. The rating system, however, is in its own way still a means of regulating cinematic representation. Paul Verhoeven's *Basic Instinct* (1992), perhaps the most notorious example of sexual explicitness in the '*faux noir*' revival, offers an illuminating parallel to *The Big Sleep* because it, too, was censored for theatrical release in the United States. *Basic Instinct*, in fact, re-enacts the censoring activities of 1940s *film noir* that Kuhn analyses, only in reverse. The *mise-en-scène* of *Basic Instinct*, not its thriller narrative, manifests the collusion of institutional and ideological censorship in producing a text whose purpose is to contain transgressive sexuality, and the thriller narrative bears symptomatic traces, in its indeterminacy, of what the *mise-en-scène* represses: the dangerous, dysfunctional male sexuality of the film's hero, Nick Curran (Michael Douglas), nicknamed 'Shooter'. In support, I read the film against an 'official' auteurist interpretation offered by director Paul Verhoeven in a lengthy interview entitled 'The secrets of *Basic Instinct*' and his running scene-by-scene commentary. Both are included on the laser disc release of the unrated director's cut of the film and for this reason can be considered part of the 'authentic', 'uncensored' text in the United States.

Censored *Instincts*

The notoriety surrounding *Basic Instinct* centred around two controversies, its explicit imagery of sex and violence, which required cutting in the US to avoid receiving an NC-17 rating from the Motion Picture Association of America (MPAA), and its bisexual killer, which prompted picketing by gay and lesbian activist groups during the film's production in San Francisco and then again later, when it premièred in big cities. The question of the film's censorship focused on the explicitness of the *mise-en-scène* in the first instance and on the representation of sexuality by the narrative in the second.

Interviewed for the home video release of the director's cut, Verhoeven explains that he added the graphic sex to the Joe Eszterhas script, which had indicated a more elliptical and discrete handling of what the scenes were actually to show, in order to push the limits of US censorship, thereby positioning his film at the very cutting edge of explicit representation. 'I thought it would really be interesting to see how far I could go in the United States and how far I could go with a well-known actor like Michael Douglas', Verhoeven comments on the laser disc. 'And I thought there was a real challenge to find out if I could push the limits as much as possible . . . I think it's fun to be offending, provocative. It keeps you alive.'[3]

Reports of the film's sexual explicitness during its production were consistent with references to Verhoeven's 'interest in showing male nudity in sex scenes; in the past he has told associates that he wants to make sex on screen as explicit as the violence in his movies'.[4] 'He's willing to be very graphic', Polly Platt said of Verhoeven. 'He's willing to show a man naked.'[5] His intention to be visually explicit caused a rupture between Verhoeven and Eszterhas. The writer publicly objected to Verhoeven's 'plans to make the steamy thriller even more sexually explicit' and left the project two months later, once Douglas sided with the director. 'My intention when I wrote the script,' Eszterhas stated at the time, 'was that it be a psychological mystery with the love scenes subtly done. Every love scene in my script begins with the words: "It is dark; we can't see clearly".'[6] Then, when he saw that Verhoeven's additions to his script 'were just some visual changes that Paul brought to it', Eszterhas just as publicly reconciled with the director in April 1991, while the film was shooting in San Francisco.[7] As gay and lesbian activists protested the film's storyline and tried to disrupt the shoot, at some point, in response to the charges of homophobia and misogyny, Eszterhas 'proposed changes to a number of scenes and to all of the central characters, as well as the use of a disclaimer to remind viewers the movie is fiction'.[8] However, Verhoeven and Carolco, the production company, held fast, issuing a press release that stated, 'Censorship by street action will not be tolerated',[9] and the writer left the project once again, not viewing the film until it opened commercially nearly a year later (when he paid for his own ticket). Ever the backslider it appears, Eszterhas told the *Los Angeles Times* that the finished film was '99% mine', and that he was 'happy' that Verhoeven had 'had the wisdom to turn down my suggestions'.[10]

The MPAA was not quite as happy that audiences could see the sex more clearly than the screenplay had first envisaged, but it had more institutional clout than either Eszterhas or the protesters. The *Los Angeles Times* reported that the question of *Basic Instinct*'s rating came at a particularly inopportune time for the MPAA, since Cardinal Mahony of Los Angeles 'was publicly calling on Hollywood to voluntarily adopt an updated Hays Code. . . . The last thing the ratings board wanted to see was this movie. They just didn't want to deal with it'. According to the *Times*, 'after much soul-searching and viewing the film, or portions of it, seven times', the MPAA's ratings board demanded cuts, to which Verhoeven and Carolco had to agree in order to deliver an R-rated print to TriStar according to their contract.[11]

The MPAA objected to the explicitness of three scenes: the murder of Johnny Boz, Nick Curran's 'date rape' of Beth Garner (Jeanne Tripplehorn), and his first sexual encounter with Catherine Tramell (Sharon Stone). In the murder scene, Verhoeven had to reduce shots of the killer's breasts, primarily so as not to show their movement, and eliminate long shots of the bodies, first shown grinding in sex, then writhing spasmodically in the killing. The two sex scenes had to be recut in order to obscure what Nick does sexually, taking Beth from behind in the first instance and going down on Catherine in the second. With the substitution of shots, the difference between the NC-17 and R versions amounted to just over forty seconds of running time. What is notable about these cuts is that, in all three scenes, the boundary of permissible representation had to do with the spectacle of explicit violence and eroticism as brought to bear upon the male body. Female nudity was not eliminated from the murder scene, nor was it cut from either of the two sex scenes. Rather, the violence with which Johnny Boz's body is repeatedly penetrated by the ice pick was censored, as were shots that clearly identified Nick Curran's 'deviant' sexual practices in the two sex scenes. The cuts in those two scenes effaced how the original version more directly incorporates Michael Douglas's nude body in the camera's sexual objectification of his female co-stars, which the censorship did not change.

However, for all the director's desire for sexual explicitness even in his original cut, in another form of institutional censorship acting upon *Basic Instinct*, Douglas's contract clearly defined the limits to which Verhoeven could go with his star since it reportedly included a 'penis clause' preventing the actor's genitals from being shown.[12] Douglas's exposed buttocks, in contrast to the flaccid penis of the murdered Johnny Boz, which equates male sexuality with vulnerability, eroticizes the star's body to a degree, but, much as in body-building exhibitions, 'as a non-intimidating symbol of passivity associated with infancy or childhood'.[13] The penis, by contrast, as Richard Dyer observes, 'isn't a patch on the phallus. The penis can never live up to the mystique implied by the phallus'.[14] In *Basic Instinct*, the defensive laughter shared by the detectives when they examine Johnny Boz's endowment – 'Very impressive', Nick notes, and his partner, Gus (George Dzundza), then jokes, 'he got off before he got offed' – makes the same point. The censorship of Douglas's body thus reinscribes in the film's *mise-en-scène* the asymmetry of the male/female sexual relation around the display of genitalia. In both the R- and NC-17 rated versions of the film, Douglas is shown nude from the rear after Nick has sex with Catherine; and his cocky stride after passively experiencing what he calls 'the fuck of the century', with its ambiguous, potentially dangerous restaging of Johnny Boz's murder, means to restore his phallic power as he walks into the bathroom, where he verbally puts down his rival, Catherine's other lover, Roxy (Leilani Sarelle).

The controversy generated by its troubles with the ratings board and the protests by gay and lesbian activists guaranteed *Basic Instinct* an opening weekend of $15 million (and an eventual US gross in excess of $100 million) because it established the film's credentials as an erotic thriller. Explained one anonymous marketing executive in the *Times*: 'The thing that helped *Basic Instinct* more than anything else was that the studio let people know they were going to see sex like they haven't seen on screen in a long time. . . . I think the rest of it was almost entirely irrelevant.'[15] But not entirely. Brushing aside its cutting of the film to meet MPAA requirements, the studio continued to trumpet its victory in having successfully resisted censorship of the script, and this tactic determined the strategies of activists once the film premièred. When *Basic Instinct* opened in the US on March 20 1992, gay and lesbian protesters had to refute the charge that they themselves were taking a 'censorious approach', violating moviegoers' 'First Amendment right to see whatever they wanted'.[16] As well as passing out leaflets protesting at the film's misogyny and homophobia, the protesters now brandished signs pronouncing 'Catherine did it!' as a means of spoiling the ending for prospective audiences.[17] The media made the picketing an event, disseminating the news around the country on television and in the press. So despite their inability to intervene in the script during the film's production or to drive away moviegoers after its release, from the perspective of publicizing their complaints, the demonstrators made their point all the same, helping to determine its reception. Chris Holmlund points out, 'Although not successful in altering the film, the demonstrators received so much coverage that mainstream and alternative critics alike found themselves responding to activist charges' in their reviews.[18] Actual and theatened censorship from various sites thus appeared to end up confirming the selling value of Verhoeven's explicit *mise-en-scène* as the ultimate guarantee of *Basic Instinct*'s 'cutting-edge' representation of sexuality.

'Catherine did it!'

> It was written precisely this way by Joe. We start feeling that something is wrong, and that she has a hidden agenda. . . . Something hidden, something she's going to pick up – well, of course it's an ice pick. I think everybody knows that something is there. She probably dropped it on the floor again and just decided not to kill him. And then this fade out/fade in is just a trick of course like in a Brian de Palma movie that's saying, 'it's over, no, no, it's not over, because – look!' – and we find at the end, that the ice pick is there anyhow. And it's the steel-handled ice pick proving that it's her ice pick. . . . Throughout this whole last scene she has been really tempted to kill him, but ultimately she decides that it would be stupid. She would be caught because the police would reopen the case, and wouldn't believe anymore that it was Beth who did it. So, she doesn't do it. She waits. She'll wait a couple of months or half a year and then she'll do it anyhow. Nick is doomed. Her behavior only makes sense when you really assume that she's the devil. Of course, a normal person would never have been able to foreseen [*sic*] all the things that she foresaw and planned. So, Catherine Tramell is the devil.
>
> (Verhoeven's commentary on the final scene of *Basic Instinct*)

My own response to reports of the demonstrations after I saw the film some time later was initially wonderment at the confidence with which the picketers could so easily determine Catherine's guilt as the ice-pick killer. For the film tries to have it both ways, depending on whether one follows its narrative, which establishes Beth Gamer as the killer, or its *mise-en-scène*, which, as Verhoeven claims, identifies Catherine Tramell as the culprit through her metonymic association with the deadly ice pick in the final shot. The official resolution of the narrative painstakingly adds detail upon detail to build a clear-cut case against Beth – the blonde wig, police department raincoat, and bloody ice pick in the hallway; the hidden revolver in Beth's apartment, along with signs of her obsessive fixation on Catherine; Beth's proximity to Johnny Boz through his psychiatrist, who shares an office with her and a year before had introduced her to the victim. 'We are proving to the audience that Beth is the killer and that Catherine is innocent,' Verhoeven explains at this point in his running commentary. Several minutes later, his description of the closure's postmodemist trickery – it is over, no it is not, and here is the ice pick to prove that Catherine is guilty, Beth innocent – makes it seem as if the narrative may actually be proposing two different endings for the diegesis, marked out by the fade to black between them, much in the manner of 'a Brian de Palma movie'.

Overdetermining the official resolution of the various murders that satisfies the police department and Nick, the doubled closure pushes *Basic Instinct* to a point of narrative excess which, as Verhoeven's resorting to a supernatural explanation evinces, defies the logic of realistic, psychological plotting and its corollary in the thriller genre: the place of motive as evidence in determining guilt. Instead, Verhoeven's explanation rests entirely on the shot of the steel-handled ice pick on the floor under Nick's bed. But this account of the film's closure begs many questions. Why, if she were the killer and now intended to murder Nick, would Catherine even think of using her own ice pick on him when she has not used it as a weapon in the past? This ice pick has the identifiable steel handle that marks it as hers, as opposed to the one used in the other ice-pick killings; a cheap anonymous instrument with a wooden handle, it is available for a few dollars at any K-Mart. For that matter, why does she even need to bring her ice pick over to Nick's when there is already one like the others in his apartment, purchased at a K-Mart? Rather than intending to use her ice pick to kill Nick, it's just as likely that Catherine could be bringing it with her as a kind of sex toy, just as she had earlier brought out the white silk Hermes scarf to tie up Nick when they first have sex, restaging the Johnny Boz murder to incorporate male masochism into their love-making as a form of sex play that she knew would turn him on, as it indeed does. In the same vein, the *mise-en-scène* appears to convict Catherine of Gus's murder, because – Verhoeven explains – a scene from her novel announces what will happen to Gus; but while this detail, shown to the audience in close-up as Nick scans the printout, may later inspire him to draw the connection, deduce the set-up and rush to his partner's aid, it still does not explain why Nick should then conclude that Beth is guilty and shoot *her* – Beth didn't write the novel that predicts Gus's murder, Catherine did.

The point of the final shot of the ice pick, it seems to me, is less to identify Catherine as the murderer pure and simple than it is to confirm what we have seen a few moments before the camera looks under the bed: the juxtaposition of Nick's bare 'vulnerable' back (as Verhoeven describes it) and Catherine's capability of sticking a literal or symbolic knife in it after he has 'gotten off'. As Verhoeven's phrasing suggests, she has a 'hidden agenda', which the director sees materialized in the deadly, emasculating weapon. But Catherine's agenda could as easily be construed as resistance rather than murder. As they lie in bed, she asks, 'What do we do now?' And Nick says, picking up a remark made earlier by Gus, 'fuck like minks, raise rug rats, and live happily ever after.' As her arm moves under the bed, Catherine states, 'I hate rug rats,' so Nick replies they can forget them, and still 'live happily ever after'. In making this concession he conceivably takes away her motive for killing him, that is, if we situate her murderous desire in the context of the other instances of irrational violence against men (not only Johnny Boz, but also Hazel Dobkins' husband, Roxy's brothers, Beth Gamer's husband) that occur in the narrative, the eruption of which implies a pervasive, haunting and unresolveable presence of female anger at the oppression of women under patriarchy. The suicide of Nick's wife, which Catherine links to his drug use and violence, implies the same sort of rage, only turned inward.

It is significant that *Basic Instinct* cannot bring itself to name Catherine as the murderer in its narrative, only in its *mise-en-scène* and a supplementary commentary that continues to surround the film, first with the protesters' pickets, then, more authoritatively if defensively, with the director's auteurist account on the laser disc. For as Lynda Hart suggests, '*Basic Instinct*'s real interest lies in the fear of ambiguity, the inability to detect which woman might be the real offender.'[19] It does not matter whether Beth or Catherine did it, exactly, since the two women, fashioned after the conventional light/dark heroines of *film noir*, are made reversible in the narrative but not in the *mise-en-scène*. Which is the copycat blonde and which is the original? 'When we ask the film to tell us who *did* it,' Hart concludes, 'the only answer it can give us is that *women* did it.'[20] Whether interpreted as a bonding or a rivalry, the copycat relation between the two women that began when they attended University of California-Berkeley motivates a narrative of female desire not regulated by men, occurring beyond the ken of the male detective and so outside the film's *mise-en-scène*. It is possible that their relationship has continued all these years, that one woman is using the murders as a way of courting the other, indeed even that there may be more than one killer since there is more than one type of weapon used in the various killings.

The script of *Basic Instinct* recognizes the reversibility of Catherine and Beth in a moment of pronoun slippage after the murder of Nielson. Putting him on suspension, Lieutenant Walker (Denis Arndt) orders Nick to keep in touch with Dr Garner: 'It will help in the investigation.' Nick replies, 'She killed him, Phil.' 'Beth?' Walker asks incredulously. 'Now you got Beth killing people?' 'Catherine Tramell', Nick corrects him. 'It's part of her game.' The equivalence of these two bisexual women, the blonde matched with the brunette, makes them both appear antagonistic to the male, regardless of which one is innocent. Yet despite the apparent reversibility of Catherine and Beth, as far as concerns the *mise-en-scène*, it *does* matter that the more indecipherable of these two women is the blonde.

The blonde leading the blind

The much discussed shot of Sharon Stone uncrossing her legs to reveal her vagina in the interrogation scene visualizes both *Basic Instinct*'s claim to be representing female sexuality in the most explicit way imaginable and the opacity of that representation. The extreme visibility of the female body appears to subject it fully to the investigative eye of many male gazes. This 'money shot' reveals that Catherine is, after all, the one natural blonde in contrast to all the bleached blondes who mirror her in the diegesis, implying the equation between visibility and authenticity that grounds the male's faith in the power of the male gaze and the heterosexuality it appears to confirm. Furthermore, Catherine's body supplies the ocular proof that she murdered Johnny Boz, since Verhoeven confirms that, though her face is not shown and her identity not determined by the narrative with any finality, the actress in the opening scene is 'always Sharon Stone'. In short, the treatment of the female body in the *mise-en-scène*, particularly with regard to its nudity, which the MPAA did not censor, is the ultimate guarantee of what the narrative refuses to determine. The exposed female body at once stands for the absence of institutional and ideological censorship while marking its impact.

Verhoeven says he added the nudity to the interrogation scene because 'it has a lot to do with control and how she brings all these people to her knees, basically, you know.' When Catherine brings the male spectators in the interrogation room 'to her knees', what she reveals is the indeterminacy of the narrative, its refusal, like hers, to lay bare 'the secrets of *Basic Instinct*'. 'I have nothing *to* hide', she defiantly announces, when asked why she has not brought a lawyer with her to the police station, and to prove it, she shows all the men that she does not wear underwear. Later, as Nick drives her back to her mansion, he mentions that she knows an awful lot about him, and she counters by saying the same thing about him. 'I don't know anything that's not police business', he states, and she replies, 'You know I don't wear underwear, don't you Nick?' After she and Nick make love, and he boasts that he is still going to nail her, she warns him not to mistake their intimacy for revelation: 'I'm not going to confess my secrets, Nick, just because I have an orgasm. You won't learn anything from me I don't want you to know.'

The interrogation scene poses the epistemological stake of Catherine's body for *Basic Instinct*. It should expose her secrets, but functions instead to mark out – and I quote this in full recognition of the phallocentric pun that the loaded phrase calls to mind – what Mary Anne Doane refers to as 'a hole in the visible', which explains 'the seductive power attributed to the figure of the *femme fatale* in *film noir* [as it] exemplifies the disparity between seeming and being, the deception, instability, and unpredictability associated with women.'[21] Particularly in close-ups, Doane continues, the figure of the woman is conventionally 'masked, barred, shadowed, or veiled, introducing a supplementary surface between the camera or spectator and the contents of the image', producing, in effect, 'a second screen'.[22]

In *Basic Instinct* Catherine's blondness functions as such a second screen, which does not reveal or mediate the truth of the visible but instead reflects the troubled masculine imago of the gazing heterosexual male. Indeed, it is striking to notice how closely Verhoeven's account of his direction of *Basic Instinct* mirrors all the evidence he mounts to prove, through the logic of metonymy governing his *mise-en-scène*, that Catherine is the ice-pick killer. For instance, he explains that she kills 'because she likes it, and to see if she can get away with it', and he says much the same about his wanting to push the limits of US censorship. He blames Catherine for Gus's murder by pointing out that what happens in the elevator conforms in detail to what Nick reads in her novel: it is 'a very clear clue that Catherine did it . . . . She knew that it was going to happen, so she wrote that scene before it happened'. At the same time, Verhoeven acknowledges how that scene was staged and photographed in imitation of the murder of Angie Dickinson in De Palma's 1980 release *Dressed to Kill*. Verhoeven sees Catherine as an agent working behind the scenes of the narrative to control Nick's behaviour, and he discusses how he actually switched back and forth between studio and location shooting of certain scenes – like the one of Catherine and Nick in the car after the interrogation – to maximize his control of shooting conditions. Perhaps most interestingly, he talks about Catherine's passive manipulation of the male gaze in the interrogation scene, and he describes his manipulation of the steadicam in the same terms:

> It seems, of course, that the camera is always following the actors. But what I did was to move the actors in a way that the camera, by following them, would reveal everything that I wanted to show. So it's more that the actors are really, uh, dragging the camera, pushing the camera towards the angles that I wanted the audience to see. It's never coinci-dental, you know, it's always choreographed.

Metacinematically, what Catherine enacts in the narrative as she challenges the epistemology of the visible is the cinema's own problematic relation to what Verhoeven calls, whenever he talks about moving his camera outside a studio, 'reality'.

When *Basic Instinct* follows *film noir* convention in identifying a dark-haired killer, but singles out the 'true' blonde as the culprit in its *mise-en-scène*, it registers the ideological disturbance that Catherine's blondeness produces. Her being blonde condenses the preoccupation of white masculinity with the construction of desirable femininity out of blondeness to signify 'racial, not just sexual, superiority'[23] – and to efface the constructedness of white masculinity itself out of a system of symbolic differences that justify its empowerment. The impenetrable blonde of this film brings men to her knees as they gaze at her body when placing it under interrogation, and her power to destabilize the ground of masculinity is epitomized by the film's insistence on her opacity as a bisexual body, just as it is inflected, in turn, by Verhoeven's conviction that her ability to blind the detective's investigative eye must mean that Catherine is 'the devil'.

Poor Nick

Actually, any solution to the film's mystery successfully works to contain Catherine's transgressive sexuality, which disturbs the phallocentric premise of heterosexual masculinity since her desire, focused on a woman as easily as a man, is aimed at but never fully invested in men. Answering the question 'who did it?' ends up describing how Catherine functions to absorb all responsibility for Nick's own culpability as a male 'shooter' who is, as Internal Affairs charges, 'out of control'. If she did *not* do it, then Catherine and Nick can 'fuck like minks' and live happily every after. If she *did* do it, then she cannot kill Nick without losing her alibi, as Verhoeven points out, a factor which effectively contains her sexuality too: they can *still* 'fuck like minks' and live happily ever after – at least, until the time comes to make *Basic Instinct II*. Either way, Nick is 'doomed', as Verhoeven says, doomed to a repressive heterosexuality that reinforces his masculinity while profoundly endangering it. The ambiguity of Catherine's guilt in the narrative epitomizes the discomfiting position of masculinity that the *mise-en-scène* effectively censors; and the only way that Verhoeven himself can account for the narrative's indeterminacy and attribute it to Catherine is by demonizing her.

In his running commentary on the laser disc, as Verhoeven tries to make sense of the narrative's many blanks, gaps and inconsistencies, he appeals to the same logic of metonymy determining his *mise-en-scène*. Thus, at the same time that his commentary reveals the plot's incoherence, it glides past what the indeterminacy of the narrative manifests. Verhoeven charges Catherine with guilt by association: 'Because Catherine has dangerous friends, and Catherine might be dangerous herself. Both Hazel Dobkins and Roxy are killers, so why should not Catherine be a killer?' Regarding Gus's murder, as already indicated, Verhoeven points to the incriminating evidence of Catherine's novel. Likewise, her intentions about framing Beth go way back: 'But even eight years ago, she was already preparing for what's going to happen now, so of course she's the devil.' After explaining how Catherine manipulates Nick to set him up for Gus's death and to shoot Beth himself, Verhoeven states: 'Ultimately Catherine succeeds in having Nick kill the only nice person in his life – Beth. That's basically her plan and Catherine, of course, is the devil.' Listening to such goofy reasoning, my head spins; but it nevertheless cannot be ignored out of hand, because what Verhoeven says aptly summarizes the difficulty that Catherine poses to the film's representation of sexual difference.

In the director's account of *Basic Instinct*, Nick and Catherine occupy the conventional gender positions of 1940s *film noir*, the male detective investigating the enigma of the *femme fatale*, but their characterizations invert the customary masculine and feminine traits that stabilize this positioning according to the conventional asymmetry of the Hollywood couple. She, not the male, is active, empowered to take charge of the narrative because of her intelligence, whereas he, not the female, is passive, victimized by her in the narrative because of his passion. Viewing the script from this perspective, Verhoeven confesses that he originally had difficulty finding a coherent interpretation of Catherine's character that could take her power into account without sacrificing her femininity. At first he was attracted to the project because of its likeness to the strong 'fatal' women in 1930s and 1940s films, which he mistakenly claims had been absent from the screen for the past twenty years. 'Joe Eszterhas wrote a script about a woman that was really in control. And that was not a victim of men. In fact, it's more reversed, isn't it?' At the same time, her control greatly perplexed him because it summarized the character's complexity, more an effect of the indeterminate narrative than of realistic character psychology: 'When I [read] the script for the first time,' Verhoeven recalls, 'I thought that all the characters were realistic to a certain degree but that the character of Catherine Tramell was artificial, that it was something constructed. I couldn't imagine that a woman could be so manipulative, so strong and so vulnerable at the same time.'

Nick, on the other hand, offered the director easier access to the script because the detective's masculinity recuperates Catherine's artifice through male sentiment and pathos. 'Nick is much more of an emotional guy, you know', Verhoeven comments. 'He's living on the edge but it's not like he's planning to live there. . . . Michael's character Nick is a guy who's kind of emotional, and so he grabs a gun and he shoots or he takes cocaine and kills a couple of tourists. You know, it's not somebody who plans to kill, it's just somebody who's so, uh, so less in control of himself, so little in control of himself, that he makes those big mistakes. And is hurting people.' By contrast, Verhoeven continues, 'Catherine Tramell is planning to live on the edge. . . . She's planning to be dangerous and to be hurting people. Catherine Tramell really wants to hurt people. If you really analyse the script, you can see that everything that's happening is manipulated, foreseen, and let's say, constructed by Catherine Tramell, mostly to cause harm.' In Verhoeven's account of the narrative, then, Nick is taken in completely by this deceitful, harmful woman; and as the contrast to Catherine suggests, the detective's victimization essentializes his masculinity as emotionality, which discounts the harm he causes as a 'shooter'. Catherine sends Nick away after completing her novel, Verhoeven explains, because 'she wants to bring him out of balance again. She wants to set him up in an emotional mood [so] that he loses control and will become the person that he is when he is trigger happy. She wants to bring him to that emotional level so that he's not controlling himself any more . . . so that he will not use his brains any more and kill Beth.'

Nevertheless, we also cannot forget the question that Catherine herself puts to Nick: 'Four shootings in five years? All accidents?' For Catherine, as one used to say of Freud, there are no accidents. When Verhoeven reads Nick as Catherine's opposite, juxtaposing the man's vulnerability to the woman's manipulation, his accidents to her premeditation, his impotence to her control, it has the effect of rewriting Nick's dangerous 'trigger happy' past, conforming it to Michael Douglas's star persona as 'the heroic, resentful, white-guy, white-collar, heterosexual victim'.[24] A female studio executive quoted in the *Times* after the film's big opening weekend put Douglas's persona in more commercial terms. More than the sex, 'a lot of [its financial success] had to do with the star power of Michael Douglas. . . . The fact that he's in this has given the film a rubber stamp of authenticity that might not have happened from another actor.'[25]

Reading Nick through Douglas's authenticating persona, Verhoeven all too easily conflates the two in his commentary, as when he refers to the character as 'Michael', allowing the director to overlay upon the detective's psyche a romanticized, sentimental view of the sexual relation that Catherine (never 'Sharon') challenges. 'I wasn't dating him', she says when interrogated about Johnny Boz, 'I was fucking him.' 'More of an emotional guy', Nick believes in Catherine's innocence, Verhoeven maintains, because he wants to be sure 'that making love to her is not dangerous but wonderful.' Catherine has the power to send Nick 'to the edge', so that he ceases to think with his brains but instead acts with his gun, simply by stopping their affair. When he returns to his apartment, in the set-up for the double closure, Nick, Verhoeven comments in a soft undertone, is 'really suffering. So vulnerable . . . and he really believes her.' This sentimental view of Nick ignores how the narrative of *Basic Instinct* doubles him with Catherine, suggesting that they both harm people or, conversely, as she says early on in the film in reference to their each having successfully passed a polygraph test, that they both are innocent. The more he is drawn to Catherine, the more Nick becomes like her, as the second interrogation scene – which puts him in her place, the parallelism causing him even to repeat her lines – makes evident. As well as suggesting his attempt to outwit her by mastering her at her own game, their doubling as another pair of copycats intimates the bisexuality Catherine and Nick have in common, which he represses and she flaunts.

Verhoeven mentions that the cryptic reference to Johnny Boz's 'special relation' to the mayor may imply some homosexual connection between those men, but it is 'a smoke curtain'. 'It doesn't mean anything', he insists, because it is narrative information that does not add to the resolution of the mystery. A 'smoke curtain', perhaps, but one that raises a suggestion of the homoerotic undercurrent of Nick's 'special relation' to Gus. Nick's one and only friend, Gus likes to play 'cowboy' to Nick's 'hoss'. Exploding – with what? jealousy? – when he guesses that Nick has slept with Catherine, Gus exclaims: 'You think I'm getting any? Sure, I can get laid by goddam blue-haired women. I don't like them.' If Catherine is the killer, she eliminates her two rivals for Nick's affections – Beth *and* Gus – in one fell swoop. This action underscores the parallel between the same-sex pairings of Catherine and Roxy, and Nick and Gus, and the death of a same-sex partner in each case, tit for tat. When Nick returns to his apartment in the final moments of the film, he is suffering, 'so vulnerable', grieving because Catherine has rejected him, certainly, but also because Gus has been killed.

The intimation of male as well as female bisexuality that arises from the narrative's doubling of Nick and Catherine has the effect of cutting through the veil of sentimentality and emotionalism that characterize his masculinity as the principal means of differentiating male from female. For with her own staging of 'the fuck of the century' as a performance that incorporates Nick as an actor, not a spectator, and that instead implies a lesbian spectator, Roxy, who *is* watching, Catherine marks a vantage point of resistance to the 'official' heterosexual text of *Basic Instinct*. Bisexuality, Marjorie Garber comments, is a state 'of being all-desiring and all desired', producing a 'heightened performative state. . . . It is not only the "performer," but also the "performance," which can be bisexual.'[26] Catherine's bisexuality does not negate sexual difference, but unmoors its fixity, just as the disruptive force of her doubling with Nick arises from the resulting implication that their sexuality is equally performative.

Sharon Stone's star persona, which *Basic Instinct* crystallized for her after years of acting in second-rate films, invites an audience to follow Catherine in taking up this queer perspective on the film. During the opening weekend, an interview with the *Los Angeles Times* promoted Stone's 'brazen instincts' in surviving the controversies accompanying the film's debut while reinventing herself as a sex star with, in her words, 'a vagina and a point-of-view . . . a deadly combination'. In the process, the interview also blithely gave away the film's mystery since it mentions her personal difficulty in shooting the ice-pick murder of Johnny Boz, which caused her to keep passing out from the agitating effect of miming the stabbing. 'I'd do it and the blood stuff would come out and they'd have to bring the paramedics in and lie me on the floor and give me oxygen. My best friend, Mimi (Craven), who always comes with me when I have to do the scary parts was there, lying next to me telling jokes and I'm breathing oxygen and laughing my ass off. We had to loop the whole thing later.' While the article reports Verhoeven's wonder that 'she identified with the scene so much', Stone's own account emphasizes the scene's performative value for her – this is acting, not identification – and brings to it a disruptive bisexual dimension. The disclosure triangulates the scene's heterosexual violence, puncturing its misogynist paranoia with the revelation that her best friend, 'who resembles Stone so closely they have been mistaken for twins', was there right beside her at the filming, watching like Catherine's double, Roxy, and causing Stone to double up with laughter.[27]

Conclusion: queer *Instincts*?

Catherine's avowal of her bisexuality marks out her erotic disengagement from a phallocentric fantasm of the female that underwrites male heterosexuality through the gaze. She disrupts that gaze through her performativity – not only in the interrogation scene but also in her manipulation of the narrative, which, in Verhoeven's view, grants her an incomprehensible agency superior to Nick's, one that openly affronts the heterosexual regulation of desire according to the binary that polarizes 'straight' against 'queer'. This is perhaps why the character's commanding performativity, not to say Stone's, has turned out to be so attractive to queer audiences of both genders, in much the same way that critics such as Andrea Weiss and Ellis Hanson remark about the popularity of lesbian vampire movies for gay and lesbian viewers.[28] From this perspective, perhaps Verhoeven is right after all: underneath its '*faux noir*' trappings and investigative narrative, *Basic Instinct* may well be a supernatural erotic thriller.

For Donald Morton, who uses *Basic Instinct* to exemplify the ahistoricism of contemporary queer theory's concentration on the performativity of desire as a mode of resistance, Catherine is a devil, but of another sort: 'a ludic (post) modern subject . . . [for] whom desire *is* relatively autonomous . . . for whom historical reality is only virtual.' Morton equates both Catherine's mastery of a 'virtual reality' in the diegesis and her motive of 'relatively autonomous desire' with an ideology projected by the entire film that, in many respects, parallels Verhoeven's account, albeit glossing it through considerably different political priorities. According to Morton, Nick functions as a nostalgic echo of modernism set against Catherine's postmodernity; the detective's *need* (to work for money) contrasts with the writer's *desire*, 'which seems to have escaped mere need' because of her enormous wealth and so 'occlude[s] the connections of gender and sexuality to need (class)'. 'The film's [explicit] sexual content,' Morton argues, is 'a calculated transgression of bourgeois values for shock effect' that denies history altogether, specifically, 'a transition in bourgeois consciousness' under 'late, multinational capitalism' that has collapsed 'the space of civil behavior into the private space of instinctual reaction.' Just as Verhoeven comments that the film's closure is 'just a trick of course, like in a Brian de Palma movie', Morton concludes that *Basic Instinct* 'is an investigation of the principles that history is nothing more than a text and that the text's meaning is undecidable.'[29]

Far from being 'undecidable' in its meaning, the indeterminate narrative of *Basic Instinct* does not erase history but, on the contrary, manifests its evidence through marks of institutional and ideological censorship that regulated the film's explicit *mise-en-scène*. For by equating female resistance with the irrational murders of men, *Basic Instinct* articulates apprehension about emergent historical shifts in the culture's sexual, racial and social composition that, while not seriously reshaping the hegemony of white, middle-class, heterosexual masculinity, have nevertheless challenged its presumption of hegemony. It does not seem accidental that the narrative takes place in San Francisco, the Californian city most associated with queer sexualities and racial heterogeneity, particularly given that state's recent conservative backlash in public referenda aimed against illegal immigration and Affirmative Action entitlements. Disavowed by the film's explicit *mise-en-scène* and the institutional and ideological controversies surrounding it, a perceived threat to the sovereignty of normative straight white masculinity makes itself evident in both the indeterminate narrative *and* the 'indecipherable' (which is really to say, bisexual) figure of Catherine Tramell. It is important to remember that Catherine does not occupy an ahistoricized position in the diegesis. Wealth may liberate her from the claims of a middle-class morality, but she is also the one character in the film linked to women of other classes – that is, Roxy and Hazel – just as their shared blondeness indirectly alludes to race, by making its relative absence from the diegesis all the more pronounced as another, censored historical factor in female oppression.

Reducible neither to the demonic nor to postmodern historical disengagement, Catherine's 'incomprehensibility' as the bisexual killer, like the *mise-en-scène* of *Basic Instinct*, condenses multiple levels of censorship operating from within the film and from without. The resulting collusion of institutional and ideological priorities exerts a censoring force comparable to that of 1940s *film noir*, but operating in reverse. Regulation of the film's representation of sexuality focused on the explicitness of its *mise-en-scène*, and, with the release of the unrated cut on home video, continues to do so, concentrating attention on *Basic Instinct*'s ability to titillate, shock or offend. The indeterminacy of the narrative, on the other hand, which the censorship never called into question – and, in the case of the controversy brought to the film by gay and lesbian activists, did not appear to fully recognize, since they assumed that 'Catherine did it!' – may fail to solve 'the secrets of *Basic Instinct*', but it does disclose what ideological concerns that censorship is responding to. More to my point, it prevents audiences from viewing the film in quite the way that Verhoeven and company originally intended. How appropriate, therefore, that the very first scenes of *Basic Instinct* were shot in San Francisco in a gay country-western bar that the film crew 'converted into a heterosexual nightclub'.[30] This substitituton of 'straight' for 'queer' is what galvanized the activists' protests to begin with, and it is fittingly emblematic of the unstable position of 'sexuality' in the film's indeterminate narrative.

Notes

For US newspapers standard MLA citation is used, e.g. F-1 denotes the section and page number within that section, and + indicates that the article runs for more than a single page.

1 Annette Kuhn, *The Power of the Image: Essays on Representation and Sexuality* (London: Routledge, 1985), p. 79.
2 Kuhn, *The Power of the Image*, pp. 93–4.
3 All quotations from *Basic Instinct* (1992, dir. Paul Verhoeven) and the director's commentary and interview are my own transcription of the Pioneer Special Edition laser disc issue of the unrated version of the film with supplementary materials.
4 Nina J. Easton, 'Eszterhas vs. Verhoeven', *Los Angeles Times* (23 August 1990): Home Edition, F-1 +, *Los Angeles Times* archives online.
5 Quoted in Easton, 'Eszterhaus vs. Verhoeven', p. F-1 +.
6 Easton, 'Eszterhaus vs. Verhoeven', p. F-1 +.
7 Nina J. Easton, Verhoeven, Eszterhas make amends', *Los Angeles Times* (1 April 1991): Home Edition, F-1 +, *Los Angeles Times* archives online.
8 David J. Fox, '*Instinct* sizzles at the box-office', *Los Angeles Times* (23 March 1992): Home Edition, F-1 +, *Los Angeles Times* archives online. See also David J. Fox and Donna Rosenthal, 'Gays bashing *Basic Instinct*', *Los Angeles Times* (29 April 1991): Home Edition, F-1 +, *Los Angeles Times* archives online; David J. Fox and Donna Rosenthal, 'Eszterhas presses for *Basic Instinct* script changes', *Los Angeles Times* (1 May 1991): Home Edition, F-4 +, *Los Angeles Times* archives online; and Charles Lyons, *The New Censors: Movies and the Culture Wars* (Philadelphia: Temple University Press, 1997), pp. 128–9.
9 Quoted in Lyons, *The New Censors*, p. 129.
10 Fox, '*Instinct* sizzles at the box-office', p. F-1 +.
11 Robert W. Welkos, 'Director trims *Basic Instinct* to get R rating', *Los Angeles Times* (11 February 1992): Home Edition, F-1 +, *Los Angeles Times* archives online.
12 Chris Holmlund, ' "Cruisin' for a bruisin' " ': Hollywood's deadly (lesbian) dolls', *Cinema Journal* 34 (Fall 1994): 48n.
13 Kenneth R. Dutton, *The Perfectible Body: The Western Ideal of Male Development* (New York: Continuum, 1995), p. 312.
14 Richard Dyer, 'Don't look now: the male pin-up' (1982); rpt. *The Sexual Subject: A Screen Reader in Sexuality*, London: Routledge, 1992, p. 274.
15 Andy Marx, 'A look inside Hollywood and the movies: pretty basic; sex, violence or Douglas? well, nobody left a Stone unturned', *Los Angeles Times* (29 March 1992): Home Edition, 35 +, *Los Angeles Times* archives online.
16 Lyons, *The New Censors*, p. 141.
17 For a fuller account of the protests when the film opened, see Lyons, *The New Censors*, pp. 132–45.
18 Holmlund, ' "Crusin' for a bruisin' " ', p. 35.
19 Lynda Hart, *Fatal Women: Lesbian Sexuality and the Mark of Aggression* (Princeton: Princeton University Press, 1994), p. 128.
20 Hart, *Fatal Women*, p. 132.
21 Mary Ann Doane, *Femmes Fatales: Feminism, Film Theory, Psychoanalysis* (New York: Routledge, 1991), pp. 45–6.
22 Doane, *Femmes Fatales*, pp. 48–9.

23 Holmlund, ' "Crusin' for a bruisin' " ', p. 39.

24 J. Hoberman, 'Victim victorious: well-fed yuppie Michael Douglas leads the charge for resentful white men', *Village Voice*, 7 March 1995, p. 29.

25 Marx, 'A look inside Hollywood', p. 35 +.

26 Marjorie Garber, *Vice Versa: Bisexuality and the Eroticism of Everyday Life* (New York: Simon & Schuster, 1995), pp. 140, 142.

27 Hilary de Vries, 'The brazen instincts of Sharon Stone', *Los Angeles Times* (15 March 1992): Home Edition, Calendar 3 +, *Los Angeles Times* archives online.

28 See Andrea Weiss, *Vampires and Violets: Lesbians in Film* (New York: Penguin 1993), pp. 84–108; and Ellis Hanson, 'Lesbians who bite', in Ellis Hanson (ed.), *Out Takes: Queer Theory and Film* (Durham: Duke University Press, forthcoming 1998).

29 Donald Morton, 'Birth of the cyberqueer', *PMLA*, no. 110 (1995), pp. 378–9.

30 Lyons, *The New Censors*, p. 107.

Chapter 18

Rich and strange

The yuppie horror film

Barry Keith Grant

In this chapter, I shall discuss a group of recent American films that presents a distinct variation of the horror film I call 'yuppie horror'. This group includes, among others, *After Hours* (1985), *Desperately Seeking Susan* (1985), *Something Wild* (1986), *Fatal Attraction* (1987), *Bad Influence* (1991), *Pacific Heights* (1990), *The Hand that Rocks the Cradle* (1992), *Poison Ivy* (1992), *Single White Female* (1992) and *The Temp* (1993). Some of these films, to be sure, reveal affinities to other genres: both *Something Wild* and *Desperately Seeking Susan*, for example, possess elements of screwball comedy – a genre, it is worth noting, that shares with horror the irruption of the irrational into the workaday world. Yet, to a significant extent, all these films retain much of the style and syntax of the horror genre, while substituting a new set of semantic elements. And although it may be argued that some of these movies exhibit only a minimal relation to the horror film, together they form a distinct generic cycle that, instead of expressing the repression and contradictions of bourgeois society generally, as many critics agree is central to the ideology of the genre,[1] specifically addresses the anxieties of an affluent culture in an era of prolonged recession.

The term 'yuppie' was coined in 1983 to describe an emergent and seemingly distinct class of young urban professionals, transcending categories of both race and gender, that embraced values of conspicuous consumption and technology as unambiguously positive.[2] Yuppiedom thus combined the 'me-generation' philosophy of the Carter era with Reaganomics, becoming a convenient image of the era's *Zeitgeist*.

More precisely, according to Marisa Piesman and Marilee Hartley in *The Yuppie Handbook*, the term

> would include a person of either gender who meets the following criteria: (1) resides in or near one of the major cities; (2) claims to be between the ages of 25 and 45; and (3) lives on aspirations of glory, prestige, recognition, fame, social status, power, money or any and all combinations of the above.[3]

These values coalesced into a lifestyle, a veritable *Weltanschauung*, that embraced what one observer has called a 'religion of Transcendental Acquisitions'.[4] This is nicely expressed in *Bad Influence* when the yuppie Michael, asked whether he needs his elaborate new video system, replies 'That's not the point.' Michael Douglas's Gordon Gekko in *Wall Street* (1987), with his hair slicked back and braces on his trousers, was the perfect icon of the high-powered businessman, and the patron saint of yuppies, for whom 'greed is good' because 'money means choices'.[5] The term caught hold of the popular imagination, generating much media hype and spawning a gaggle of other demographic acronyms. In short order there were, among others, DINKs (Double Income No Kids), WOOFs (Well Off Older Folks), and SWELLs (Single Women Earning Lots and Lots).[6]

Commercial cinema, with its antennae sharply attuned to popular taste, mobilized the tested appeal and contemporary popularity of the horror film in the late 1970s and early 1980s to address this new cultural force with money to spend in the 1990s. Further, yuppies had infiltrated the movie industry itself, which beckoned with the lure of high-powered deals. 'You can work on your screenplay/ I'll update my c.v.', David Frishberg sings in his satiric song 'Quality Time'. Indeed, both *The Player* (1992) and *Swimming with Sharks* (1994) showed yuppie monsters as Hollywood producers. With typical self-absorption, yuppie filmmakers may have assumed that their own preoccupations were generically marketable. Thus the fears and anxieties of the yuppie subculture, which has been estimated to include anywhere from four to twenty million people,[7] encourage the transformation of 'evil' in these movies from the classic horror film's otherworldly supernatural to the material and economic pressures of this world that is too much with us. This change strikes me as marking a generic change as profound as, say, the shifting antinomies of the contemporary western.

Defining yuppie horror

Yuppie horror is a subgenre that employs – but modifies – the codes and conventions of the classic horror film. 'A good horror film', notes Bruce Kawin, 'takes you down into the depths and shows you something about the landscape; it might be compared to Charon, and the horror experience to a visit to the land of the dead'.[8] In *After Hours*, Paul's taxi ride to the different, Bohemian world of Soho in lower Manhattan is shot in fast motion – a joke about New York taxi drivers, to be sure, but also a suggestion of crossing over into another place, like Jonathan Harker's coach ride through the Borgo Pass in Murnau's classic *Nosferatu* (1922). Other instances of the use of this narrative convention of the genre include Michael's descent into the underground bar in *Bad Influence*, site of alternative sexual practices (the passwords include 'gay white male' and 'fun loving couple'), and the movement in *Desperately Seeking Susan* from the rational materialism of Fort Lee, New Jersey to the dark and magical world of Manhattan, as if New York were across the river Styx rather than the more mundane (but perhaps equally dead) Hudson.

In an economy characterized by increasing economic polarization and spreading poverty, these scenes of crossing into the nether world of urban decay 'exude the Manichaean, middle-class paranoia . . . that once you leave bourgeois life, you're immediately prey to crime, madness, squalor, poverty.'[9] Hence in *Bonfire of the Vanities* (1990) wannabe Gecko Sherman McCoy quickly plummets from being a self-described 'master of the universe' with a '6 million dollar apartment' to the dark underpass of a highway ramp in the Fort Apache wilderness of the South Bronx. So, too, in *Pacific Heights* the reddish lightbulbs of the 'Loan' sign behind Patty Parker flash as if in warning to abandon all hope ye who enter here.

This fear informs the premise of the descent by middle-class characters into the hell of the inner city, as in both *Trespass* and *Judgment Night* (both 1993) – the latter employing the metaphor of the mobile home to represent lack of bourgeois stability, an idea earlier used in the supernatural horror film *Race With the Devil* (1975). Like the return of the oppressed, this nightmarish world threatens always to erupt, as in *Grand Canyon* (1991), when Steve Martin's yuppie entrepreneur is hospitalized after a mugger takes his Rolex. To use the terms of another of these movies, one must always be on guard against the temp who aspires to become permanent.

Within this dark underworld of bankruptcy and property divestiture, several of the films offer upscale variations on the horror film's old dark house, what Robin Wood calls the terrible house and Carol J. Clover the terrible place, making them into Gothic, horrifying 'workspaces' or 'living spaces'.[10] Indeed, the eponymous upscale high rise in *Sliver* (1993) is explicitly referred to several times by some of its inhabitants as a 'haunted house'. The New York apartment building in which the two women live in *Single White Female* is visually reminiscent of the spooky Dakota in *Rosemary's Baby* (1968) – a deliberately resonant reference, as Polanski's film may be seen as an early instance of yuppie horror in which Satan's manifestation functions as the unrepressed return of Guy's real desire to further his career over commitment to raising a family.[11] In *Unlawful Entry* (1992) the installation of the warning system and the periodic spotlight from the police car put the white family in the position of South Central LA blacks, making their home seem more like a prison, a horrifying vision of the couple's anxiety about whether they can afford their house. Michael's place in *Bad Influence* becomes frightening mostly after Alex has stripped it clean of all the yuppie toys – an ironic inversion of the conventionally cluttered Gothic mansion.

This seeming oxymoron of the terrible luxury home is explicitly the subject of

Pacific Heights. The plot concerns a couple's efforts to gentrify an old Victorian house, a popular yuppie pastime.[12] Initially, the yuppie couple, Patty Parker and Drake Goodman, conceive of their home as little more than a profitable investment, as a financial arrangement not unlike their cohabitational agreement. But the home soaks up renovation money like an insatiable sponge, a money pit – a scenario presented in a manner not like the blithe spirit of *Mr Blandings Builds His Dream House* (1948) but with the ominous foreboding of *Amityville Horror* (1979), perhaps the first real estate horror film. Stephen King perceptively described this film as the generic 'horror movie as economic nightmare'.[13] Drake and Patty inexorably fall from the beatific heights of potential profit to the lower depths of looming insolvency.

An essential visual difference between horror and science-fiction films is one of vision. In science-fiction, vision – of the characters, the text and the spectator – is characteristically bright and directed upward and out, while in horror, by contrast, it is directed down and inward, darkened and obscured.[14] A similar visual design tends to inform yuppie horror films. In *Poison Ivy*, for example, both the mother and the deadly outsider contemplate plummeting downward into the big sleep of reason, creating a vertiginous gloom that pervades the entire film from the opening giddy bird's-eye shots of Drew Barrymore swinging out over a steep cliff. The sleek black car driven by Carter Hayes in *Pacific Heights* appears ominously over the crests of hilly San Francisco streets as if surfacing from the underworld. Carter, Peyton in *The Hand That Rocks the Cradle*, and the deadly roommate Ellen in *Single White Female* are all associated with the basement and darkness. *Pacific Heights* uses a swirling 360 degree camera movement at crucial moments in Patty and Drake's crumbling finances, both to visualize their sinking deeper and deeper into debt and to lend their descent into the maelstrom metaphysical weight, as if their very worldview had been pulled out from under them, *à la Vertigo* (1958). Not coincidentally, this Hitchcock film is one among several referred to diegetically on the television in the smartly intertextual *Single White Female*.

Monstrous others and material fears

An essential element of the horror film is the presence of a monster. In yuppie horror films the villains are commonly coded as such. Alex's face in *Bad Influence* is frequently streaked by the noirish shadows of trendy Levelor blinds, and the killer's face in *Desperately Seeking Susan* is often bathed in a hellish red light. When Carter Hayes successfully installs himself in the apartment of the yuppie couple's home, he is said by their lawyer to have 'taken possession'; in the climax, Carter is impaled, a fitting demise for a blood-sucking vampire, financially speaking. In the climaxes of *Fatal Attraction* and *Something Wild*, both Alex and Ray seem implausibly unstoppable, like their supernatural counterparts Jason, Michael Meyers and Freddy Krueger. And in *The Hand That Rocks the Cradle*, the tension established between the seeming girlish innocence of the evil nanny Peyton (Rebecca De Mornay) and her fiendish malevolence is firmly rooted in the tradition of such 'possessed child' horror films as *The Exorcist* (1973) and *The Omen* (1976), and further back, *The Bad Seed* (1956).

Furthermore, much like the traditional monsters, the evil characters in yuppie horror movies function as the Other, as an external, disavowed projection of something repressed or denied within the individual psyche or collective culture. These films tend to depict the monstrous Other as the protagonist's *doppelganger*, a convention Wood calls 'the privileged form' of the horror film.[15] Roland Barthes writes that 'The petit-bourgeois is a man unable to imagine the Other' and so makes him over into the image of himself,[16] a point that would seem especially true for yuppies, who, according to sociologist Jerry Savells, '*assume* control of their lives and their fate, without question'.[17] Pam Cook has suggested, for example, that Max Cady in Scorsese's remake of *Cape Fear* (1992) offers a 'distorted picture' of the Bowden family's 'own rage and pain, and of their desire for revenge', called forth from within the family by the daughter Danielle; Cook argues that the film has to be understood as Danielle's subjective vision, what Bruce Kawin would call her 'mindscreen', because it is marked by her voice-over in the form of recollection.[18]

Cook's reading may be applied equally to several other of these films, among them *Pacific Heights*, *Bad Influence* and *Poison Ivy*. In the latter, for example, the bad girl who seduces the father is clearly the incarnation of the rebellious daughter who considers herself to be unfeminine and unloved. The film's narrative, as in *Cape Fear*, is framed by the daughter's voice-over recollection. In Michael Cimino's remake of *Desperate Hours* (1991), the fleeing criminal Michael Bosworth, threatening the upscale family he has taken hostage in their home, suggests that he represents a 'reproach' to what he refers to as the 'mendacity' of the family patriarch, who is having an extra-marital affair, as if he were the return of the man's repressed self – the Father confronted by Big Daddy, as it were – a relation wholly absent from the original drama.

Similarly, in *Something Wild*, Charlie begins as what Lulu calls a 'closet rebel', but the 'something wild' within him is brought out by his passion for Lulu/ Audrey and his struggle against Ray Sinclair. During the climax, Charlie and Ray seem to embrace even as they fight, like twin Stanley Kowalskis in their T-shirts. Lulu says to Charlie in the end, 'What are you going to do now that you've seen how the other half lives . . . the other half of you?' A similar reading is invited by *Desperately Seeking Susan*, in which the bland Roberta learns to be more assured sexually, like the extroverted Susan whom she encounters, significantly, through the personal want ads. In *Single White Female*, in a way the inverse of *Poison Ivy*,

Ellen is the plain Other of Allie, the unattractive woman whose career would proceed unimpeded by sexual entanglements. The shots of the two women in mirrors, posed in positions reminiscent of the famous mirror shot in Bergman's *Persona* (1966), makes their psychological interdependence clear. In *Pacific Heights*, Drake Goodman grows increasingly violent in response to the 'bad influence' of Carter Hayes. At first glibly willing to commit white collar crime by, as he says, 'fudging the numbers a bit', Drake later viciously beats Carter and is about to strike him a murderous blow with a tyre iron when he is finally restrained by Patty's screaming plea. But like Nathaniel Hawthorne's Goodman before him, Drake has glimpsed the underlying moral ambiguity of human nature.

In *Bad Influence*, an updating of Hitchcock's *Strangers on a Train* (1951), Alex is the incarnation of what Michael calls the 'voice that tells you what to do some time', a therapeutic materialization of Michael's much-needed assertiveness train-ing. Like Bruno Antony to Guy Haines in Hitchcock's film, Alex is Michael's unrestrained id, the embodiment of Michelob's yuppie admonition that 'You can have it all'. As Alex shows Michael how to be more competitive and assertive, Michael's hair, like his personality, becomes increasingly Gekko-like. In the end, before going over the edge himself, Michael shoots Alex, who falls heavily from a pier, the water closing over him as he sinks back into the murky depths from which he had emerged, the creature from the black lagoon of Michael's mind now vanquished.

Even *Fatal Attraction*, which has almost uniformly been condemned for its scapegoating of the professional female, may be read in this way. It is possible to view the narrative as Dan Gallagher's horrifying mindscreen or psychodrama, wherein the results of his affair with Alex Forrest is, on one level, the return of his repressed dissatisfaction with his marriage.[19] Dan feels trapped by domesticity, his discontent imaged forth in the family's cramped apartment. He is clearly disap-pointed about the evening's prospects when he returns from walking the dog to find their daughter sleeping in his bed with his wife Beth. So he fantasizes a relationship with no distracting responsibilities in the form of Alex. But then, like a networking party turned nightmare, to assuage his guilt Dan projects the blame on to her – at one point he calls her 'sick' – making her a monstrous Other because she does not recognize what he calls 'the rules' for such affairs. Alex will not be 'reasonable', will not be treated like the sides of beef that hang outside her apartment building. She refuses to allow the removal of her voice, an ideological operation of the text which feminist critics such as Kaja Silverman and Mary Ann Doane have argued happens so often in Hollywood film. Alex telephones Dan insistently and leaves an audio cassette in his car which questions his masculinity – both instances of an assertive female voice that seems beyond his masculine control. Indeed, it is not Alex but Dan who is silenced, as her adamant refusal to have an abortion leaves him, as he admits, 'no say'.

Many commentators on yuppiedom have noted that yuppies are always threatened by the looming spectre of 'burnout' because they are 'workaholic[s] whose main identity and sense of self-worth is often supplied by [professional] success'.[20] Burnout is thus a fearful possibility that, like the portrait of Dorian Gray, haunts the yuppie's prized public image. It is no coincidence that Michael in *Bad Influence*, Drake Goodman in *Pacific Heights*, and Allie in *Single White Female* all show clear evidence of work-related stress. As one commentator puts it, 'You can, after all, stay on the fast track only so long, even in a $125 pair of running shoes.'[21] The important distinction is that the visage of Dorian Gray in yuppie horror films is handsome rather than grotesque. Here the craggy ugliness of a Rondo Hatton is replaced by the smooth charm of a Rob Lowe, for the ethical horrors of cupidity supersede the physical revulsion of the classic horror film. The fact that so many of these characters are at once ethically monstrous and physically attractive befits an age in which, as someone observes in *The Temp*, 'They still stab you in the back as much as in the 80s, only now they smile when they do it.' Indeed, it is exactly this view that animates the worldly narrative of *Ghost* (1990), a film that, while marginal as horror, is nevertheless strongly informed by yuppie angst, and Brett Easton Ellis's remarkable 1991 novel *American Psycho*, a book that perhaps stands in relation to yuppie horror as *Psycho* (1960) – to which its title obviously refers – does to the modern horror film. The book is a first-person chronicle by a handsome Wall Street mass murderer, Patrick Bateman. If yuppie consciousness and values fetishize appearances – 'Surface surface surface was all anyone found meaning in', Bateman observes[22] – then yuppie horror films show how frightening such surfaces can really be. 'I have a knife with a serrated blade in the pocket of my Valentino jacket,' Bateman matter-of-factly observes at one point,[23] demonstrating the truth of that sage comment in *The Temp*. It is perhaps no accident that Ellis's narrator often describes his perceptions in terms of film techniques such as pans, dissolves and slow motion.[24] Narrated with the same kind of dark humour as pervades *Psycho*, it is as if Norman has grown up and moved from a remote place off the main highway to life in the fast lane in the big city. Master Bates has become BateMAN – but ironically the onanism (a handy image of yuppiedom's self-possession) only suggested in the Hitchcock film is chillingly literal in the novel.

Because of the valorization of conspicuous wealth in the yuppie worldview (and one of the great jokes of Ellis' style in *American Psycho*), the monsters in yuppie horror films tend to threaten materiality more than mortality. For yuppies, in the words of the portrait in *Newsweek*, 'the perfection of their possessions enables them to rise above the messy turmoil of their emotional lives'.[25] Thus, yuppie horror films exploit the subculture's aspiration for material comfort, and the material success the characters so covet becomes frighteningly vulnerable and fragile, like the scale model of Patty and Drake's home in *Pacific Heights* that is shown smashing in close-up.

The vindictive Cady sums it up well in *Cape Fear* when he says, 'That house, that car, that wife and kid, they mean nothing to you now.' In these films, the Puritan-like material emblems of election come to seem suddenly damned. The appurtenances of an expensive lifestyle often turn deadly, like Claire's greenhouse in *The Hand That Rocks the Cradle* which becomes an elaborate weapon hailing lethal shards on her best friend, Marlene. The husband in *Unlawful Entry*, fetching a golf club to ward off a possible intruder in their home, jokes to his wife that if it turns out to be dangerous he'll come back for his driver. This yuppie joke is realized in *Something Wild* when Audrey uses one of Charlie's clubs to whack the attacking Ray, and in *Bad Influence*, where one of Michael's clubs (he owns a set although of course he doesn't play) serves as the murder weapon for Alex. *The Hand that Rocks the Cradle* devotes much of its time to chronicling objects that become 'unruly'. In an upscale yuppie home fitted with, as Elayne Rapping notes, tasteful 'houseware "touches" out of L.L. Bean and Bloomingdale's',[26] Peyton is like a yuppie gremlin, relocating material icons of yuppie status, such as a gold cigarette lighter, and thus encouraging a 'misreading' of their sub-cultural signification.

Perhaps, then, the quintessential moment of fright in the yuppie horror film is the image in *After Hours* – emphasized by Scorsese in slow motion – of aspiring yuppie Paul's lone \$20 bill flying out of the taxi window. In yuppie horror films, it would seem that to be underfunded is more frightening than being undead. So Charlie desperately clutches at his wallet in *Something Wild*, whereas he allows himself to be handcuffed to the bed by Lulu, whom he has just met, with barely a protest. Because yuppies are already 'possessed', these films suggest, they are more frightened by the sight of acid eating into the smooth finish of Dan's Volvo in *Fatal Attraction* than by, say, Uncle Ira no longer quite being Uncle Ira in *Invasion of the Body Snatchers* (1956).

The ideology of yuppie horror

While this yuppie cycle tends to rely primarily on the visual and narrative conventions of the classic horror film, on occasion their very discursive structure is also similar, employing what Tzvetan Todorov has called the *fantastic*, which critics have found to inform traditional horror films.[27] According to Todorov, the fantastic is characterized by a 'hesitation' that eludes either a realist explanation (the 'uncanny') or a supernatural one (the 'marvellous').

Such hesitation is found in those yuppie horror films which can be read as mindscreens, as already discussed, but perhaps the most interesting of the films in this regard is *The Temp*. Narrated from the viewpoint of the male protagonist, the film begins with him finishing a therapy session, and we soon learn that he has suffered from paranoid delusions in the past. He appears to have recovered, for he

Figure 18.1 Griffin Dunne and Linda Fiorentino in *After Hours* (1985). Courtesy of Warner and the Kobal Collection

is successful and competent in his high-powered executive position; but when an ambitious new secretary begins working for him, perceived rivals start dying in curious circumstances. Since we never see the secretary actually do anything ominous until the end, we can't be sure whether the protagonist's dark interpretation of events is correct or if the woman is really a terrific secretary and the deaths and other mishaps are merely a series of unhappy coincidences. This intriguing ambiguity is clearly resolved in the climax, though, where the patriarchal power of the narrator/male boss is forcefully reinstated with the defeat of the infernal secretary who has refused to stay in her allotted place in the corporate hierarchy. But until the film reaches for such predictable generic and ideological closure, it insistently questions patriarchal assumptions.

Fredric Jameson's observation that *Something Wild* is about patriarchy applies to many of these movies, which on another level, as my reading of *Fatal Attraction* suggests, are about masculinity in crisis.[28] This is hardly surprising, given that yuppie horror films necessarily question (by expressing an unease about) capitalist ideology. Indeed, to the very substantial extent to which yuppie horror films are about masculine panic, they are simply the most overt articulation of a theme that dominates contemporary Hollywood cinema, most obviously in the recent trend towards hyperbolic action movies, with their excessive display of masculine 'hardbodies'.

This is not to suggest, however, that all Yuppie horror movies in the end endorse the ideological status quo. For if we were to examine them according to Wood's 'basic formula for the horror film' – the way the texts define normality, the monster, and the relation between these two terms[29] – we would find they range from the reactionary to the progressive, as with any genre. In *Pacific Heights*, for example, all's well that ends well: Patty reconciles with Drake, sells the house for a tidy profit, and defeats Carter Hayes while adding further to her income, tax-free. The film thus endorses yuppie capitalist values and neutralizes any potential threat in the fact that Patty, as Carter says, has 'crossed the line' of acceptable behaviour. *Pacific Heights* is no Hitchcockian text.

By contrast, the ending of *Fatal Attraction* may be seen as more subversive. It is Beth who kills Alex, after which she and Dan embrace, reunited because she has submitted to the patriarchal imaginary; only then can marriage be 'happy'. The final shot is thus heavy with Sirkian irony: the camera pans to the fireplace mantle, the hearth of the family home, showing a photograph of the married couple – a still image – and a pair of bronzed baby shoes. Both objects undercut the notion that anything has changed in Dan and Beth's marriage; rather, the objects connote immobility and stasis, and offer a comment on the couple's embrace of traditional values. Similar is the ending of *After Hours*, when Paul returns from the nether world and arrives at the entrance to his midtown office. No longer what Andrew Marvell would call the iron gates of strife, they open of their own accord and, transformed by the golden light of dawn, seem to beckon Paul into the comfy heaven of his low-level executive job.

In their articulation of lurking dread, even the most conservative of these films are more interesting than bland yuppie movies like *Rain Man* (1988), wherein the yuppie is humanized and learns that there are more important things in life than imported sports cars, or *Grand Canyon*, in which the economic gap is dwarfed by the geographical one.[30] Jameson is right to call *Something Wild* and other such movies modern Gothic tales, although he incorrectly, I think, chooses to stress their reliance on nostalgia. For these movies, as I've argued here, are emphatically about now.

The fact that mainstream cinema has turned more to horror and the thriller than to, say, comedy and the musical, as it did in the past, to address fears about America's affluent but now struggling economy as well as the very nature of contemporary relationships, tells us how very deeply these anxieties are rooted. Indeed, these films tend to locate these larger cultural concerns at a more basic, personal level within the dynamic of intimate personal relationships – the perfect adaptation of the horror genre to the troubled narcissism of the post me-generation. In yuppie horror films, monsters do not roam the countryside, killing indiscriminately; instead, we find ourselves sleeping with the enemy, often literally.

One can discern a decided evolution within the cycle. In the earlier yuppie horror films the nightmarish situations were as often as not the result of recklessness rather than fiendishness. But as the recession has deepened, the monsters have tended to become increasingly malevolent: the big chill has become a wind from hell. (One might view the recent cycle of films based on old TV series – *The Addams Family* (1992), *The Beverly Hillbillies* (1993), *The Flintstones* (1994) and *Car 54, Where Are You?* (1994) – as the other side of yuppie anxiety. Truly based on nostalgic appeal, they recall both the historical 'better time' of the affluent 1960s, when the shows were first broadcast, and the ahistorical once-upon-a-time fantasy world of TV-land.)

Certainly, as I've already suggested, there are earlier horror films, such as *Rosemary's Baby* and *Race With the Devil*, that anticipate the yuppie cycle. *The Exorcist* is similar to Polanski's film in that it suggests that the demonic possession of the daughter is the result of the mother's putting her career before family. But of the several movies that one might cite as precursors of this modern horror cycle, only *Strangers on a Train*, in typical Hitchcock fashion, steadfastly refuses to locate or 'explain' the monstrous as supernatural. And while there are earlier movies that we might identify as examples of Stephen King's notion of economic horror, the yuppie horror cycle truly begins to appear around the time of the publication in 1985 of an article entitled 'Second thoughts on having it all' in *New York* magazine, described by one observer as an 'epochal event'.[31] Whether the yuppie protagonists are contained within their space in the movies of besiegement (*Fatal Attraction*, *Pacific Heights*, *The Hand That Rocks the Cradle*) or removed from it in the 'road movies' (*Something Wild*, *After Hours*), they share a frightening sense of alienation from a comfortable, privileged routine. Films that combine elements of both subclassifications (*Trespass*, *Judgment Night*) emphatically demonstrate that you can't take it with you, even if you have yuppie buying power.

Significantly, yuppie horror films exhibit minimal interest in gore and splatter effects. They avoid the kind of body horror characteristic of, say, George Romero or David Cronenberg, even though, as one writer puts it, 'the body is the yuppie's most prized possession'.[32] In these movies, as I've suggested, it is less life than 'lifestyle' that is threatened. *Disclosure* (1994) is filled with trendy dialogue about the dilemmas of contemporary sexual politics, and it suggests throughout a fear of the body that culminates, in the climactic scene where Michael Douglas is pursued by a virtual reality Demi Moore, in a complete rejection of the body. The greater concern with lifestyle in yuppie horror movies is perhaps nowhere more clear than in such movies as *The Firm* and *The Fugitive* (both 1993): the former is an upscale variation on such demonic cult horror films as Lewton's *The Seventh Victim* (1943); the latter little more than the hoary mechanics of the chase, situated within a yuppie context. Graphic body horror, by contrast, has become increasingly characteristic of the more mainstream horror film and of cyberpunk science fiction – the novels of William Gibson, or movies in which the body literally becomes a thing, as in *Robocop* (1987), *The Terminator* (1984), and such less distinguished clones as *Universal Soldier* (1992).

For similar reasons, fear of racial difference is not particularly important in yuppie horror movies. As in yuppie ideology, race is subsumed by economic difference. Hence, *Judgement Night* is careful to include a black among the group of four suburban men who carelessly venture, in a state-of-the-art mobile home, into the monstrous violence of inner city Detroit. By contrast, race had been an issue (albeit an infrequent one) in such earlier horror films as *White Zombie* (1932) and *I Walked With a Zombie* (1943), and has returned more recently in such mainstream horror movies as *The People Under the Stairs* (1991), *Candyman* (1992) and *Candyman II* (1995). But whether the monstrous Other in yuppie horror films is seemingly aristocratic (as in *Bad Influence*) or strictly blue collar (as in *Poison Ivy*), the fear exploited may be understood as the nightmarish result of the yuppie's typical narcissistic self-absorption.

Conclusion

If, as some would argue, yuppies are nothing more than a 'media mirage',[33] an imaginative creation of the culture industry, they nevertheless have had a powerful effect on advertising and marketing. Moreover, since yuppies come from the 'baby boomer' generation that constituted the teenagers to whom horror films became increasingly addressed in the 1950s and 1960s, they share an already established bond with the genre. Thus it is not surprising that Hollywood would seek to address these viewers who, in the words of one advertising executive, are themselves 'like a Hollywood movie, not real life'.[34]

Curiously, Rick Altman does not include horror in his examples of durable genres that have established a particularly coherent syntax, although the genre has been around since almost the beginning of cinema and, of course, before that in literature and folklore.[35] Surely, the yuppie horror film is a particularly vivid contemporary instance of a genre's semantic modification within its existing syntax to accommodate a newly defined potential audience. Indeed, horror is a rather flexible genre – 'extremely limber, extremely adaptable, extremely useful', in the words of Stephen King.[36] In fact, the yuppie horror film would seem a vivid demonstration of Altman's thesis that the 'relationship between the semantic and syntactic constitutes the very site of negotiation between Hollywood and its audience'.[37] And if this cycle of the horror film demonstrates the protean adaptability of genre, it also reveals the inevitable anxiety generated by the biggest monster of all, late capitalism.

Notes

1 See, for example, Robin Wood, *Hollywood from Vietnam to Reagan* (New York: Columbia University Press, 1986), Chapters 5 and 6; Carol J. Clover, *Men, Women and Chainsaws: Gender in the Modern Horror Film* (Princeton: Princeton University Press, 1992); and several of the essays in Barry Keith Grant (ed.), *Planks of Reason: Essays on the Horror Film* (Metuchen, NJ: Scarecrow Press, 1984).

2 Jerry Adler *et al.*, 'The year of the Yuppie', *Newsweek* (31 December 1984), p. 14; and John L. Hammond, 'Yuppies', *Public Opinion Quarterly*, no. 50 (Winter 1986), p. 496.

3 Marissa Piesman and Marilee Hartley, *The Yuppie Handbook: The State of the Art Manual for Young Urban Professionals* (New York: Long Shadow Books, 1984), p. 12.

4 Adler *et al.*, 'The year of the Yuppie', p. 19.

5 Jerry Savells, 'Who are the "Yuppies"? A popular view', *International Journal of Comparative Sociology*, vol. 27, nos. 3–4 (1986), p. 235.

6 Susan Kastner, 'So . . . where have all the Yuppies gone?', Toronto *Star* (17 April 1991), p. A4.

7 Savells, 'Who are the "Yuppies"?', p. 234.

8 Bruce Kawin, 'Children of the light', in Barry Keith Grant (ed.), *Film Genre Reader* (Austin: University of Texas Press, 1986), p. 237.

9 John Powers, 'Bleak chic', *American Film*, vol. 12, no. 5 (March 1987), p. 51.

10 Wood, *Hollywood from Vietnam to Reagan*, p. 90; Clover, *Men, Women and Chainsaws: Gender in the Modern Horror Film*, p. 30.

11 The importance of Ira Levin's fiction, including *Rosemary's Baby*, *The Stepford Wives* and *Sliver* to yuppie horror is significant and certainly a subject for further research.

12 Carol M. Ward, 'The Hollywood Yuppie: 1980–88', in Paul Loukides and Linda K. Fuller (eds), *Beyond the Stars: Stock Characters in American Popular Film* (Bowling Green, Ohio: Bowling Green University Popular Press, 1990), p. 97.

13 Stephen King, *Danse Macabre* (New York: Everest House, 1981), p. 138.

14 Barry Keith Grant, 'Looking upwards: reason and the visible in science fiction film', in Glenwood Irons (ed.), *Gender, Language, and Myth* (Toronto: University of Toronto Press, 1992), pp. 185–7.

15 Wood, *Hollywood from Vietnam to Reagan*, p. 79.

16 Roland Barthes, 'Myth today', in *Mythologies*, ed. and trans. Annette Lavers (New York: Hill and Wang, 1977), p. 151.

17 Savells, 'Who are the "Yuppies"?', p. 235.

18 Pam Cook, 'Scorsese's masquerade', *Sight and Sound*, vol. 1, no. 12 (April 1992), p. 15. 'Mindscreen' is the term used by Bruce Kawin to describe sequences of subjective vision in his *Mindscreen: Bergman, Godard and First-Person Film* (Princeton, N.J.: Princeton University Press, 1978).

19 It is worth noting that the action in Adrian Lyne's next film, *Jacob's Ladder* (1990), is revealed explicitly at the end to have occurred entirely in the mind of the protagonist in the moment of his death. The only other similar reading of the film of which I am aware is N. A. Morris, 'In defense of *Fatal Attraction*', *Movie*, no. 33 (Winter 1989), pp. 53–5.

20 Ward, 'The Hollywood Yuppie', p. 106.

21 Adler *et al.*, 'The year of the Yuppie', p. 24.

22 Brett Easton Ellis, *American Psycho* (New York: Vintage, 1991), p. 375.

23 Ellis, *American Psycho*, p. 52.

24 Ellis, *American Psycho*, pp. 5, 8, 114.

25 Adler, 'The year of the Yuppie', p. 19.

26 Elayne Rapping, '*The Hand that Rocks the Cradle*', *Cineaste*, vol. 19, nos. 2–3 (December 1992), p. 65.

27 Tzvetan Todorov, *The Fantastic: A Structural Approach to a Literary Genre*, trans. Richard Howard (Ithaca: Cornell University Press, 1975). For an application of Todorov's ideas to the horror film, see, for example, Tom Gunning, '"Like unto a leopard": figurative discourse in *Cat People* and Todorov's *The Fantastic*', *Wide Angle*, vol. 10, no. 3 (1988), pp. 30–9.

28 Fredric Jameson, *Postmodernism, or, the Cultural Logic of Late Capitalism* (Durham: Duke University Press, 1992), p. 291.

29 Wood, *Hollywood from Vietnam to Reagan*, p. 78.

30 In the context of romantic comedy, Steve Neale argues that the end of *Something Wild* 'manoeuvres its couple . . . into an "old-fashioned", "traditional" and ideologically conventional position'. 'The big romance or something wild?: romantic comedy today', *Screen*, vol. 33, no. 3 (Autumn 1992), p. 297.

31 George F. Will, 'Reality says you can't have it all', *Newsweek* (3 February 1986), p. 78. 'Second thoughts on having it all' appeared with no byline in *New York*, no. 18 (15 July 1985), pp. 32–50ff.

32 Adler *et al.*, 'The year of the Yuppie', p. 14.

33 Hammond, 'Yuppies', p. 496.

34 Kastner, 'So . . . where have all the Yuppies gone?', p. A4.

35 Rick Altman, 'A semantic/syntactic approach to film genre', in Barry Keith Grant (ed.), *Film Genre Reader II* (Austin: University of Texas Press, 1995), pp. 37–8.

36 King, *Danse Macabre*, p. 138.

37 Altman, 'A semantic/syntactic approach', p. 35.

Chapter 19

Would you take your child to see this film?

The cultural and social work of the family-adventure movie

Peter Krämer

One sunny afternoon in August 1994, I was watching the big summer movie of that year, *True Lies*, with a friend in Munich, and in the midst of all the magnificent mayhem on the screen, he suddenly turned round to me and said: 'Wouldn't family therapy be much cheaper?' What he referred to is the peculiar *raison d'être* for the action in this biggest and most expensive of all action movies: the hero and his wife have to learn to understand, and interact with, each other in a new way so as to revive their marriage, and once this is achieved the action-hero has to go through the motions all over again to overcome the alienation of his daughter. It was both annoying and strangely touching to realize that the spectacular attractions brought to the screen with the help of a reputed production budget of $120 million was ultimately geared to the completion of the simple dramatic feat of turning mummy and daddy and child into a happy family again.[1] Therapy would indeed have been cheaper. Yet, buying a ticket to see the family drama played out on the big screen is, of course, cheaper still, and in response to my friend's comment I wondered whether a trip to the cinema wouldn't have made the *True Lies* family just as happy as all the adventure they got involved in. It also occurred to me that, by offering itself to the audience as a substitute for the adventures undertaken by the family on the screen, this was perhaps what the film was trying to tell us, if it was trying to tell us anything at all: Enliven your family life – go to the movies together once in a while. Maybe, then, my friend and I became so self-conscious about, and frustrated with, the film's machinations and our own position as spectators precisely because we had left our families behind and thus had already failed to heed the advice *True Lies* was giving us.

In this chapter, I shall argue that the obsessive concern of many of Hollywood's biggest blockbusters with family issues indicates that they attempt to broaden their appeal beyond the core audience of teenagers and young adults to reach the family audience; that is, small groups of parents and children going to the movies together. Hence, many of today's action-adventure movies are, in fact, family films. At the same time, the traditional children's or family film has been upgraded with a heavy injection of spectacular adventure to appeal to teenagers and young adults as well as children and their parents. These two developments have resulted in a group of films which I would like to call family-adventure movies. It is my contention that family-adventure movies are the most successful production trend in American cinema since the late 1970s.[2] I shall suggest that the cultural work that the films' narratives perform to reconcile family members with each other on the screen translates into a kind of social work performed by the films on the familial units in the auditorium, creating shared experiences and opening up channels of communication. My discussion will focus on a number of massive box-office hits, combining textual analysis with a discussion of the films' marketing and reception. The key films are the top five entries in *Variety*'s list of all-time box-office hits, as of February 1996: *E.T. – The Extra-Terrestrial* (1982), *Jurassic Park* (1993), *Forrest Gump* (1994), *Star Wars* (1977) and *The Lion King* (1994).[3] Before embarking on my discussion of family-adventure movies, however, I wish to indicate how it intersects with some of the key concerns of academic criticism of contemporary Hollywood.

Fathers and sons in contemporary Hollywood criticism

Families and familial relations, most notably those between fathers and sons, figure largely in academic criticism of contemporary Hollywood cinema, especially where the work of Hollywood's most successful filmmakers George Lucas and Steven Spielberg is concerned. For Robin Wood, for example, the 'Lucas-Spielberg Syndrome' affecting most American films since the mid-1970s is constituted by a twist on the traditional category of the children's film, resulting in 'children's films conceived and marketed largely for adults – films that construct the adult spectator as a child, or, more precisely, as a childish adult, an adult who would like to be a child.'[4] The address of spectators in the auditorium as children is complemented by the 'Restoration of the Father' within the narratives on the screen, which Wood sees as 'the dominant project . . . of the contemporary Hollywood cinema, a veritable thematic metasystem embracing all the available genres and all the current cycles.'[5] The films' stories frequently focus on problematic father figures whose authority is initially being questioned, yet who will eventually 'be accepted and venerated', and on the 'Oedipal trajectory' of the young male hero who has to work through his problematic relationship with the father, learning to accept his power and to identify with him, so that 'he will one day in his turn *become* the father'.[6] The male spectator is invited to adopt the position of the young male hero, regressing to childhood and submitting to the power of the father in the story at the same time as he submits to the power of the spectacle and narrative drive of the film itself, 'totally passive, ready to be taken by the hand and led step by step through the narrative to participate emotionally in its reassuringly reactionary conclusion'.[7]

Wood's forceful analysis is representative of an important strand in contemporary Hollywood criticism.[8] Yet, unlike many other writers, Wood makes explicit the set of assumptions about audience composition, audience response and the quality of cinema-going experiences which underpin his work as well as that of other critics. Most importantly, Wood states that today's movie audience is largely made up of adults in search of regressive pleasures, implying that actual children constitute a negligible segment of this audience. Second, he claims that the audience is dominated by men who are 'all too ready to accept the films' invitation to infantile regression', whereas women are easily alienated from the experience on offer due to the films' patriarchal agenda. Thus, while men 'generally love E.T., women generally don't'.[9] Third, Wood distinguishes between 'the energetic, inquiring and often profoundly skeptical mind' possessed by 'real' and 'uncorrupted' children, and the infantile mind set contemporary Hollywood encourages in its adult spectators.[10] While he admits that he enjoys 'being reconstructed as a child, surrendering to the reactivation of a set of values and structures my adult self has long since repudiated', he can distance himself from this pleasurable experience and critically evaluate it as 'extremely reactionary, as all mindless and automatic pleasure tends to be'.[11] Using Wood's assumptions and claims as a point of departure, I am now going to take a look at family-adventure movies and their audiences, paying particular attention to the presence of children in the cinema auditorium, to the determining effect that gender may have on audience responses and to my own cinematic pleasures as well as those of others.

Parents, children and critics at the movies

At first sight, *The Lion King* confirms the critique of contemporary Hollywood put forward by Wood and other critics. The film tells the story of a young boy (the lion cub Simba) who wants to be king, a position currently held by his father. When his father is killed by Simba's jealous uncle, the boy is made to believe that he is responsible for the killing. He runs away from home and lives a life of forgetful hedonism, until he is encouraged to confront the past, learns the truth, overcomes the villainous uncle and finally assumes the position of his dead father, thus completing his 'Oedipal trajectory'. The press book for the film explains that 'Simba realizes that his father's spirit lives on in him and that he must accept the responsibility of his destined role.'[12] And Disney studio head Jerry Katzenberg described the film as 'a love story between a father and son' concerning 'the responsibility we have as torchbearers from one generation to the next'.[13] This would seem to suggest, in the terms of Wood's analysis, that the film offers adult males the opportunity to regress into a replay of their own Oedipal trajectories.

However, a look at actual audience composition and response complicates this conclusion.

When I went to see *The Lion King*, I found myself surrounded by hordes of children with adults in tow. As the only adult not accompanied by a child, I felt like an outsider and intruder. It seemed to me that I looked decidedly suspicious, as if I had the worst possible reasons for mingling with all these kids in the darkened movie theatre. I almost feared that I would be refused entry, yet once inside I soon forgot about my dubious status and lost myself in the film. Instead of feeling distanced from the children around me, in a very real sense I became one of them, perhaps recovering the sense of magic which had infused the fairytales my mother read to me when I was a child, and the first films I ever saw at the cinema with her. Memorably, these early cinema experiences included Disney's *The Jungle Book* (1967), the story of an orphan boy who has to leave the people who have loved and nurtured him like parents. *The Jungle Book* is very much a story of separation and loss, told from a child's point of view, as is *The Lion King* for a substantial part of its duration. Coming out of the cinema, *The Lion King* partly felt like a revisitation of that crucial earlier movie experience, and my status as a lone adult contrasted sharply not only with the groups of parents and children leaving the cinema with me, but also with the memory of going to the cinema with my mother. This added another layer to the experience of separation and loss that *The Lion King* had played upon.

Like Robin Wood, then, I admit to the pleasures of 'being reconstructed as a child'. However, I don't think that these pleasures are in any way 'automatic' and 'mindless'. Instead they are likely to be bracketed by reflections on one's present status as an adult and one's relationship to children, as well as on memories of past moviegoing experiences as a child and the relationship with one's parents. Furthermore, even when the films' stories concentrate on the relationship between fathers and sons, mothers are likely to have a prominent role, taking children by the hand both in the movie theatre in the present and in memories of the past. On and off the screen, rivalry and identification with the father is only part of the (Oedipal) story.[14] Finally, the onscreen representation of childhood, like the off-screen memories of childhood which are being evoked, is by no means idealized. Far from being depicted as a paradisical state, characterized by endless pleasure, straightforward wish-fulfilment and irresponsibility, childhood emerges as a difficult phase indeed.

According to Wood the appeal of contemporary Hollywood's regressive fantasies is 'the urge to evade responsibility – responsibility for actions, decisions, thought, responsibility for changing things: children do not have to be responsible, there are older people to look after them.'[15] *The Lion King*, however, shows exactly the reverse. Here, the child feels responsible for something he hasn't done, and the guilt arising from this keeps him in a state of suspended maturation. There is a hint that in Simba's mind, the killing of his father is connected to his impatient declaration 'I just can't wait to be king' towards the beginning of the film, implying as it does the death of the present king. Thus, the death of the father is an implied wish come true.[16] Simba's transformation later in the film is based on his ability to gain a realistic view of the relationship between his wishes, thoughts and actions, on the one hand, and developments in the world around him, on the other hand. This allows him to understand what he is, and is not, responsible for. The 'escapist' experience that contemporary Hollywood is said to offer its audiences (equivalent to Simba's years of suspended maturation), then, is precisely what *The Lion King* reflects upon, examining the psychological causes of the need to escape from responsibility (here identified as an overwhelming and misguided sense of responsibility) and highlighting the need to overcome the escapist condition.

So far, my analysis has approached *The Lion King* from an adult point of view, but most of what I have said about the ways in which the film tries to affect audiences also applies to the children in the audience. However, what is perceived by an adult as a fantastic evocation of past experiences is more likely to be seen by a child as a realistic extension of everyday feelings and experiences. Indeed, in a critical attack on Disney's animated features, focusing on *The Lion King*, Matt Roth accuses Disney of a kind of emotional hyperrealism – 'that obsessive plumbing of horrors more real to children than death: parental loss, withdrawal of love, exile from family and friends, and blame for unintended acts of destruction.'[17] Roth sees this as an attempt 'to induce (emotional trauma) in young children' so as to open them up for the reassuring 'fascist' principles Disney 'feels it must implant in each new generation'.[18] While I disagree with his conclusion, Roth's description of the severity and realism of Disney's treatment of childhood experiences would seem to be apt.[19]

If screen representations can be seen in terms of emotional realism rather than fantasy, it is also possible to approach the social and psychological experiences of audiences through observation rather than psychoanalytic theoretization. This allows, among other things, for a far less deterministic view of the role of gender in the shaping of audience responses. Discussions of male-centred films such as *The Lion King* and *E.T.* with students, for example, do not confirm Wood's contention that male responses to these films and their male protagonists are stronger and more positive, whereas females are easily alienated from the films' oedipal concerns. As with *The Lion King*, at first sight *E.T.* would seem to be a perfect example for Wood's critique. The film tells the story of a 10-year-old boy whose parents have recently separated. Elliott misses his father, perhaps also resenting him for going away. When he befriends an alien creature who hides in his shed, the alien comes to serve as both a kid brother and a wise old man, an ideal yet temporary father figure, who eventually has to leave the boy who loves him. In the heart-breaking yet reassuring farewell scene at the end of the film, E.T. tells the boy that he will always be with him, right there in his head. Now, far from rejecting the film for its oedipality, female students tend to be more willing than males to shed the tears the film works so hard to provoke, and to talk about this emotional experience in class. Furthermore, while all students freely admit to having wept when they first saw the film as children (often during one of their first ever visits to the cinema), they are somewhat surprised and puzzled by the fact that the film still has the power to move them. Thus, students' responses and reflections are influenced by their assumptions about what is, or is not, an appropriate emotional response in terms of both sex and age, rather than by the force of same-sex identification with screen characters.[20]

When asked about the significance of the protagonists' sex, students suggested that the fact that Elliott is male, and E.T. appears to be male as well, adds to the drama. They argued that females are much more open to intimate friendships and shared emotional experiences, whereas boys have to work much harder at them. The intimate bond which is being established between Elliott and E.T., and Elliott's extreme expressions of grief and jubilation, especially in the scene in which the alien first dies and then comes back to life, are all the more dramatic and effective for the difficulties usually encountered by boys in handling their emotions. To take this line of argument further, it is possible to say that, rather than constructing their spectators as male, films like *E.T.* are in effect working to 'feminize' both their young male protagonists and their male audiences; that is, to allow them to experience and freely express emotions (in the darkness and an-onymity of the movie theatre) in a way which is usually considered to be typically female.[21] At the same time, it is true that female spectators are encouraged to identify with the young male hero rather than with the film's female characters. Elliott's mother, recently abandoned by her husband and struggling to earn a living and raise three kids all on her own, is a sympathetic character, especially for adult female spectators, and Elliott's little sister Gertie gets a chance to teach E.T. to speak and to dress him up in women's clothes. Yet, the narrative is determined to a large extent by Elliott's inquisitive mind, ingenuity and decisive action, which establishes him as the main point of identification.

In an essay on the problems of writing women's history, Sue Zschoche regrets 'the poverty of imagination that characterizes the stories told about women's lives', which may make it necessary for women to identify with great men in order to experience vicarious heroic action. The example she gives concerns her daughter, who developed an obsession with *E.T.* at the age of 3, watching the film over and over again. The little girl soon became quite convinced that she really would find E.T. herself, and at that point she 'announced that henceforth and forevermore, she was to be called Elliot'.[22] While Zschoche sees this as a symptom of a male-oriented culture unwilling to grant heroic status to women, the anecdote also illustrates the openness of films such as *E.T.* for cross-sex identification.[23] What both girls and boys are encouraged to identify with is not so much a clearly gendered character than a child figure who combines masculine and feminine traits (heroism and empathy, stoicism and expressiveness) in the same way that it combines traits usually associated with children (an active imagination and a willingness to believe in the impossible), with a strong sense of responsibility for, and active commitment to, the welfare of another being which is surprisingly mature.

By transcending culturally encoded dualities of sex and age, the child figure in E.T. and The Lion King is turned into an idealized point of identification for both males and females, children and adults.[24] This identification is further enhanced through the parallels between the qualities displayed by the child on the screen and the conditions of spectatorship in the auditorium. For example, Elliott's ability to empathize with E.T. mirrors the audience's need to empathize with Elliott, which is a precondition for their enjoyment of the film. Also, Elliott's willingness to believe in the existence of E.T. corresponds to the audience's necessary suspension of disbelief with respect to the film they are watching, his expressions of grief and joy are echoed by those provoked in the auditorium, and his final farewell to E.T. (the film's very last shot is a close-up of Elliott's composed face staring into space) prefigures the audience's farewell to E.T., the movie. This farewell results in a return to reality after the excitement of fantastic adventure, which allowed both Elliott and the audience to deal with issues and emotions that are part and parcel of everyday life yet are difficult to deal with there. The film's focus on the problematic relationship between children and adults is closely connected to the immediate concerns of the familial units of parents and children making up a large proportion of the audience. The narrative importance of divorce in E.T. would seem to connect directly with the social reality of divorce or dysfunctional family life affecting many people in the auditorium, in the same way that the death of the father in The Lion King taps directly into children's fears.

Furthermore, in both films the central male child is integrated into a group of people of different sex and age who share many of his experiences and, to a greater or lesser extent, participate in his heroic action, also joining him in the film's concluding scene. Elliott is joined in his adventures by, and through them is finally united with, his siblings, his brother's friends and eventually even his mother and 'Keys', the scientist. Simba is helped along throughout the film, and joined in the final tableau, by his father's adviser Zazu, the wise old man Rafiki, his irresponsible, hedonistic jungle friends Timon and Pumbaa, and his girlfriend Nala. Identification with the heroic male child, then, also means vicarious participation in group experiences and efforts, which again mirrors the very conditions of cinema spectatorship. Crucially, the group that is being assembled at the end of these films is, just like the target audience, a mixture of men and women, children and adults. At the centre of this group is the family unit, yet the group extends well beyond this unit to include people who have bonded with members of the central family in the course of the adventures depicted in the film. Not only do the films work to strengthen the bonds between family members, then, but they also incorporate these families into a wider community, both on the screen and in the auditorium.[25]

All of this is perhaps not too surprising in the light of the fact that both *The Lion King* and *E.T.* are effectively children's films, a rather loose, yet easily identifiable category defined by the films' primary appeal to children, which is usually achieved through child and/or animal protagonists. It could be argued, then, that commercially successful children's films will tend to surround their young protagonists with adults so as to represent on the screen the very adults who are expected to accompany children to the cinema, and who are thus offered two points of entry into the film's narrative scenarios – a regressive identification with the child protagonist and a mature identification with one of the adults. Having said this, most of the above analysis of *The Lion King* and *E.T.* would also seem to apply to action-adventure films which do not centre on child protagonists and are not primarily aimed at children.

Star Wars is a striking example. Marketing research before the film's release in May 1977 showed that on the basis of the film's title and a brief description of its story and main attractions, interest in *Star Wars* was highest among young men, whereas women and older people (including parents) were put off by the film's generic classification, science-fiction, which was associated with technology and the lack of a human dimension.[26] The original advertising campaign, which emphasized the film's mythic and epic qualities, its fantasy and romanticism to overcome the resistance of female and mature cinemagoers, was directed primarily at 12- to 24-year-olds and secondarily at 25- to 35-year-olds. Following the enormously successful release of the film, subsequent advertising campaigns for re-releases in the summer of 1978 and 1979 were aimed primarily at people over 35. According to media analyst Olen J. Earnest, the theme of these later campaigns 'was a reminder to older moviegoers of the fun of the Saturday matinee, Errol Flynn swashbuckling entertainment experiences of their younger moviegoing days – or how to be a kid again for two hours'.[27]

While childhood was a central concern in the marketing and reception of *Star Wars*, there was little consideration of actual children. Nevertheless, the film operates very much like the children's films discussed earlier. After its action-packed opening, *Star Wars* focuses for quite some time on the interaction and misadventures of the two robot characters 3-CPO and R2-D2, a rather childish comic duo, not that far removed from young Simba and Nala, or Timon and Pumbaa, or the children in *E.T.* The film then shifts focus to its teenage hero, Luke Skywalker, an orphan who lives and works on the farm of his aunt and uncle, wishing to leave this humble existence behind to join a military academy and become a warrior like his father. His wish is fulfilled under tragic circumstances, when his foster parents are killed, which allows, and indeed forces him to go off to save the princess and the known universe from domination by the evil empire. In his adventures, he is accompanied and supported by a substitute father (Obi-Wan Kenobi), a kind of older brother (Han Solo) and a young woman (Princess Leia) who he never quite gets romantically involved with, as well as assorted creatures and robots, most of whom are assembled in the concluding tableau of the film. This tableau emphasizes heroic group effort and community spirit rather than individual heroism and romantic coupling, and includes a final turn by the main protagonists towards the camera and the applause of the assembled rebel forces, mirroring quite precisely the cinema audience's (hoped for) response to the film itself.

In the sequels *The Empire Strikes Back* (1980) and *Return of the Jedi* (1983), the familial configurations become even more central and literal. The villain (Darth Vader) turns out to be Luke's father, and the princess his sister. With the continuing support of two substitute fathers (Obi Wan-Kenobi and Yoda), Luke finally confronts his real father, and mobilizes the remnants of Vader's paternal feelings to turn him against his master, the evil emperor. By killing the emperor, Luke's father redeems himself. The trilogy's final tableau again features a celebration, assembling Luke and his companions as well as a cross-section of friendly alien creatures for a party. At the very end, a thoughtful Luke encounters the spirits of his three fathers (presented through superimposition), who are dead, yet who will remain with him forever precisely as projections (much like the film itself). Again, as in *The Lion King* and *E.T.*, the young male protagonist is incorporated into a community, which has been brought together more closely by the film's adventures, and is overseen by the spirits of dead or absent fathers. Again, the audience is invited to see itself on the screen – men and women, children and adults, celebrating the end of the adventure (which has been a wish come true) and also saying an emotional farewell (to fathers and to the film itself). Given all the similarities with children's films such as *The Lion King* and *E.T.*, it is not surprising to find out that, despite the initial marketing focus on teenagers and young adults, in the long run *Star Wars* has been recognized as a film for the whole family. In an interview on the occasion of the enormously successful release of the *Star Wars* special edition in February 1997, Twentieth Century Fox chairman Tom Sherak cited surveys which showed that one-third of the audience for this latest re-release were families.[28]

This emphasis on the family is also at the very heart of both the marketing and the narrative of *Jurassic Park* (1993). However, while the film's multimedia marketing and merchandising campaign was largely based on the apparently irresistible appeal of dinosaurs to children, and its world première took place in the White House in aid of the Children's Defence Fund, reviewers warned parents that the film may be too scary for pre-teenage children, and Spielberg declared that he wouldn't let his own children, all under the age of 10, see the film.[29] Such public concern only served to foreground and intensify *Jurassic Park*'s special relationship with children and their families, which is explicitly addressed in the film itself. After its brief action-packed opening sequence, familial concerns are raised with a reference to the fact that Hammond, the amusement park's owner, has a daughter who is going through a divorce, which later justifies the presence of his grandchildren Tim and Alexis in the park (the mother needs some time on her own to work things out). The scientist couple (Alan Grant and Ellie Saddler) is then introduced in a scene which focuses on a child who is mysteriously present at the site of their latest archaeological dig. The boy is not impressed by all the talk about dinosaurs, until Grant turns to him, describing, and partly enacting, in great and gruesome detail, what velociraptors would do to him, if he ever encountered them (namely slice him open and start eating him while he's still alive). The film here quite self-consciously sends a warning signal to the children in the auditorium, preparing them for the violence to come, much of which is directed against Hammond's grandchildren. The scene continues with a conversation between Grant and Saddler about his dislike of children and her wish to have children of her own. While this wish is not granted in the film, the subsequent adventure in Jurassic Park forces Grant to protect Tim and Alexis and encourages him to form a strong emotional bond with them, so that in the final tableau in the helicopter which takes them away from the island, the children happily rest in his arms, with a smiling Saddler looking on. Not coincidentally, this development is paralleled in one of the dinosaur subplots. Despite the fact that all the genetically engineered dinosaurs in Jurassic Park are female, they do eventually reproduce (after some of them spontaneously change sex), because, as the chaos theoretician Malcolm says: 'Life cannot be contained. . . . Life finds a way.' Both in Grant and in the dinosaurs, reproductive and familial instincts cannot be suppressed.

Jurassic Park also contains the most extensive reflections on its own status as family entertainment of all the films discussed so far. When he first appears at Grant and Saddler's dig, Hammond (played by film director Richard Attenborough) says about his amusement park, which carries the same title as the film: 'Our attractions will drive kids out of their minds. And not just kids – everyone!' In the park's main building, which is filled with merchandise prominently featuring the film's logo, Hammond describes the difference between Jurassic Park and other amusement parks in terms not dissimilar to the publicity surrounding the film's computer generated images which literally brought dinosaurs to life on the screen: 'I'm not talking just about rides, you know. Everybody has rides. No, we have made living biological attractions, so astounding that they'll capture the imagination of the entire planet.' When the corporate lawyer talks about the enormous fees people will be willing to pay for entry into the park, Hammond says that the park is 'not only for the super-rich. Everyone in the world has the right to enjoy these animals'. And when his grandchildren arrive, Hammond tells his companions that now they are going to 'spend a little time with our target audience'.

Thus, the film clearly spells out what kind of entertainment it is meant to be: *Jurassic Park* offers an exciting, almost life-like adventure, which is affordable for everyone and appeals first and foremost to children but is also attractive for teenagers and adults. In response to possible accusations that its attractions are either too mechanical, lacking a human dimension, or too frightening for kids, the film tells a little morality tale. Hammond is made to realize that he's gone too far with his park: 'With this place, I wanted to show them [his audience] something that wasn't an illusion, something that was real.' Ellie Saddler replies that Hammond's idea of total control over his creation was an illusion, and that what matters much more than such control 'is the people we love'. At the heart of popular entertainment, then, is not technological power and control but love, both for the characters in the fictions and for the people in the auditorium. As in the other films discussed so far, *Jurassic Park*'s final tableau depicts the strong emotional bond which has been forged between the visitors to Jurassic Park, mirroring the bond which the adventure of the film is meant to have forged among members of the cinema audience.

The discussion of these four films has demonstrated that in contemporary Hollywood cinema, there is indeed a convergence of the children's/family film and the action-adventure movie resulting in what I have called family-adventure movies. These films are imbued with sentimentality, spectacle and a sense of wonder, telling stories about the pain and longing caused by dysfunctional or incomplete families (usually with absent or dead fathers), about childish wishes and nightmares magically coming true and the responsibilities that go along with this, about the power of shared adventures to unite the young male protagonist with other members of his family and a community beyond the boundaries of the family, and about the irrevocability of loss and separation (the family remains incomplete, the father does not return). Indeed by foregrounding the cinematic spectacle of special effects and precisely choreographed action, and by constantly referring to their own status as cinematic entertainment for a captive audience, these films offer themselves as a temporary relief from the real-life problems which their stories focus on but can never solve. Here, the young male protagonists, and the groups they are part of, serve as ideal representatives of a receptive audience, and the films' sensuous rides and magical transformations provide fleeting moments of unselfconscious happiness for this audience, which, like the group in the films' final tableau, eventually will have to leave the film adventure behind and re-enter the more mundane world of problematic social relationships and painful feelings. In terms of their marketing and their critical reception, the films are widely understood as familial experiences, and they are best enjoyed as part of a family outing, or as an occasion to contemplate one's own place in familial networks, past and present. Yet, although they tend to ignore or marginalize romantic love and courtship, two of the most important concerns of the cinema's primary audience of teenagers and young adults, the films are able to please this constituency with their spectacle and emotional impact.

The family-adventure movie and the family audience at the box office

In the light of the ability of family-adventure movies to appeal to all audience segments, it is not surprising to find that they dominate box-office charts. Sixteen of the top twenty films in *Variety*'s list of all-time top grossers can be identified as family-adventure movies (see Appendix). While these films do not necessarily reproduce every aspect of the complex model developed in the previous section, they all share certain basic characteristics. They are intended, and manage, to appeal to all age groups, especially children and their parents, by combining spectacular, often fantastic or magical action with a highly emotional concern with familial relationships, and also by offering two distinct points of entry into the cinematic experiences they provide (childish delight and absorption on the one hand, adult self-awareness and nostalgia on the other hand).

These films are fairly evenly distributed across the period 1977–95, with most years (thirteen out of nineteen) seeing the release of one or two extremely successful family-adventure movies in late spring/early summer or in the second half of November. The US market share of each of these films in its year of release was about 5–10 per cent, and in most cases these family-adventure movies grossed considerably more money than their nearest competitors. The most extreme example is *E.T.*, which grossed more than twice as much as any other film released in 1982 and had a market share of over 10 per cent, which means that more than one out of every ten cinema tickets bought in the United States during that year was for this one film.[30]

What does the market dominance of family-adventure films tell us about the cinemagoing habits and experiences of the American population? It is a well-known fact that the majority of frequent cinemagoers (that is those who go at least once a month) are young people, and that most cinema tickets are sold to people under 30.[31] The vast majority (up to 80 per cent) of people over 30 go to the cinema only rarely (that is between one and six times a year) or not at all; this is especially true of adults without children, 50 per cent of whom attend once a year or never, whereas for adults with children the figure is only about 35 per cent.[32] This suggests that the American cinema audience is chiefly made up of young cinemagoers who attend regularly and of family units who attend only on special occasions. These occasions would seem to be provided primarily by family-adventure movies, which are conveniently released in the run-up to, or during, school holidays. A release between the end of May and mid-July is the springboard for a long run during the summer holidays, and a November release is the ideal launching pad for a successful run during the Christmas season.[33] There is considerable evidence, then, to suggest that it is the rare holiday outings of groups of parents and children which, complemented by the core youth audience, turn a small number of family-adventure movies into superhits. These superhits provide the majority of the American population who go to the movies very rarely with their only cinematic experiences, while also providing the film industry with a considerable portion of its revenues from theatrical exhibition and related markets such as video, pay-TV and merchandising. Thus, family-adventure movies are central both to the economics of the American film industry and to the moviegoing experiences of the American public.

Conclusion: the cultural and social work of *Forrest Gump*

What, then, is the point of going to the cinema for the vast audiences which family-adventure movies attract? By way of conclusion, I would like to indicate briefly how this question may be approached with reference to *Forrest Gump*.[34] A starting point is provided by speculations about, and observations of, audience responses in the press. In his *Variety* review, for example, Todd McCarthy writes that *Forrest Gump* 'offers up a non-stop barrage of emotional and iconographic identification points that will make the postwar generation feel they're seeing their lives passing on screen.'[35] Martin Walker notes the special appeal of the film's version of history for thirtysomething and fortysomething adults: 'As the baby-boomers . . . pass through the decades and become parents, professors, senior managers and even president, they feel the need for some discrete (*sic*) but deliberate revisionism of their pasts.'[36] He goes on to argue that the film achieves this by being multifaceted and quite open to a variety of political readings, with both liberal and conservative critics attacking the film, and with both political camps also celebrating it. In *Time* magazine, Richard Corliss examines the movie crowds themselves: 'You see them – folks of all ages and both sexes – floating out of the movie theater on waves of honorable sentiment.' Having 'completed an upbeat encounter session with America's recent past' and an 'emotional journey', each audience segment takes something different away from the experience: 'For younger viewers . . . *Forrest Gump* serves as a gentle introduction to the '60s. . . . And to those who raged, suffered or sinned through that insane decade, the movie offers absolution with a love pat.'[37] These commentators all imply that the release of *Forrest Gump* became an occasion for baby-boomers to reflect on their generational identity and on the wider historical context for their individual biographies, as well as an opportunity to communicate these reflections and personal experiences to the younger generations.

Indeed, a Gallup study showed that the audience of *Forrest Gump* was dominated by older people: 40 per cent of the audience were 40–65 years old and 35 per cent were in the 12–24 age range.[38] This suggests that the audience did indeed to a large extent consist of baby-boomers taking their children, both little kids and young adults, to share the experience of this film with them. The survey also registered unusually high approval ratings for *Forrest Gump* among all audience segments. Both teenagers and old people, both men and women, both African-Americans and other ethnic groups highly recommended this film. In fact, despite severe criticism of the film's sexism and racism, *Forrest Gump* received a considerably higher approval rating from women than it did from men, and even a slightly higher rating from African-Americans than it did from non-blacks.[39] Again, this confirms the impression that *Forrest Gump* became an occasion for self-reflection and communication across the boundaries of age, sex and ethnicity.[40]

As with other family-adventure films, the social work that *Forrest Gump* performs on the familial units in the auditorium derives from the cultural work it performs on the families on the screen (moving Forrest Gump from the position of the child in one single-parent family – mother and son – to the position of parent in another: father and son). As I have argued throughout this chapter, this mirroring relationship is the basis for the significance and success of family-adventure films. Thus, in order to get the point of these films, fully to experience and appreciate what they are trying to do, it may indeed be necessary for audience members, including critics, to take a child along to the cinema, or to be taken along as a child, or at least to be willing to contemplate one's place in families past and present.

Appendix: Twenty top grossers at the North-American box office

According to Leonard Klady, ' "Apollo" launched on all-time b.o. list' (*Variety*, 26 February 1996, p. 46). This list is based on ticket sales in North America (including Canada) for the original release and subsequent reissues. It is not adjusted for inflation. Box-office figures are rounded. Where the exact release date could not be obtained, I have given the date of the film's review in *Variety*, which usually appears within days of the film's release. Family-adventure movies appear in bold.

1	***E.T. – The Extra Terrestrial*** (released 11 June 1982)	$400 million
2	***Jurassic Park*** (released 10 June 1993)	$357 million
3	***Forrest Gump*** (released 6 July 1994)	$330 million
4	***Star Wars*** (released 25 May 1977)	$322 million
5	***The Lion King*** (released 15 June 1994)	$313 million

6	*Home Alone* (released 16 November 1990)	$286 million
7	*Return Of The Jedi* (released 25 May 1983)	$264 million
8	*Jaws* (released 20 June 1975)	$260 million
9	*Batman* (released 2 June 1989)	$251 million
10	*Raiders Of The Lost Ark* (released 2 June 1981)	$242 million
11	*Ghostbusters* (1984; reviewed on 6 June)	$239 million
12	*Beverly Hills Cop* (1984; reviewed on 28 November)	$235 million
13	*The Empire Strikes Back* (released 21 May 1980)	$223 million
14	*Mrs Doubtfire* (released 24 November 1993)	$219 million
15	*Ghost* (released 13 July 1990)	$218 million
16	*Aladdin* (released 11 November 1992)	$217 million
17	*Back To The Future* (1985; reviewed on 26 June)	$208 million
18	*Terminator 2: Judgment Day* (released 3 July 1991)	$205 million
19	*Indiana Jones And The Last Crusade* (released 24 May 1989)	$197 million
20	*Gone With The Wind* (1939)	$192 million

Notes

1 Cf. Jose Arroyo, 'Cameron and the comic', *Sight and Sound*, vol. 4, no. 9 (September 1994), pp. 26–8.

2 By using the term 'production trend' rather than 'genre' for the classification of films, I follow Tino Balio's example. Production trends can be identified by both textual features (such as story, iconography and forms of spectacle) and extratextual features (such as target audience, release pattern, budget, cultural status and key personnel). See Tino Balio, *Grand Design: Hollywood as a Modern Business Enterprise, 1930–1939* (Berkeley: University of California Press, 1995), Chapter 7.

3 Leonard Klady, '"Apollo" launched on all-time b.o. list', *Variety*, 26 February 1996, p. 46. See Appendix 1.

4 Robin Wood, *Hollywood from Vietnam to Reagan* (New York: Columbia University Press, 1986), pp. 162–3.

5 Ibid., p. 172.

6 Robin Wood, ''80s Hollywood: dominant tendencies', *CineAction!*, no. 1 (Spring 1985), p. 3.

7 Ibid., p. 5.

8 This critical tradition extends from Steve Neale, 'Hollywood strikes back: special effects in recent American cinema', *Screen*, vol. 21, no. 3 (1980), pp. 101–5, to Sarah Harwood, *Family Fictions: Representations of the Family in 1980s Hollywood Cinema* (London: Macmillan, 1997). Cf. Andrew Gordon, 'Science-fiction and fantasy film criticism: the case of Lucas and Spielberg', *Journal of the Fantastic in the Arts*, vol. 2, no. 2 (1989), pp. 80–94.

9 Wood, ''80s Hollywood', p. 5.

10 Ibid. p. 5.

11 Wood, *Hollywood from Vietnam to Reagan*, p. 164.

12 Walt Disney Pictures Fact Sheet, *The Lion King* microfiche, British Film Institute (BFI). Press material circulated by distributors is worth studying because its statements find

their way into a wide range of publications, thus shaping the expectations of prospective film audiences.

13 Katzenberg quoted in J. Hoberman, 'The mouse roars', *Village Voice*, 21 June 1994, p. 45.

14 Wood sees the 'Expulsion of the mother' as one of the key aspects of contemporary Hollywood cinema: 'once the Oedipal trajectory has been completed and the identification with the father achieved, she is entirely dispensable and something of an encumbrance' (''80s Hollywood', p. 3).

15 Wood, *Hollywood From Vietnam to Reagan*, p. 165.

16 Similarly, *Home Alone* (1990, no. 6 in the *Variety* list of all-time box-office hits) focuses on the problematic status of childish wishes and wish-fulfilment fantasies, that is on the pleasures and terrors of wishes (apparently) coming true. This is highlighted in the press book: 'Once little Kevin comes to terms with this scary reality, that his family is really gone (something he wished for in a fit of anger the previous night), he must fend for himself in the everyday chores of housekeeping' (*Home Alone* microfiche, BFI).

17 Matt Roth, '*The Lion King*: a short history of Disney-fascism', *Jump Cut*, no. 40, p. 15.

18 Ibid., pp. 15, 18.

19 Again, there are parallels with *Home Alone*. The press book quotes director Chris Columbus who described the film as 'a combination of kids' fears and fantasies of being left home alone'. Despite its excessive comic spectacle, several British critics welcomed the film as a realistic alternative to 'machine-tooled fantasies in plastic and rubber' such as *Teenage Mutant Ninja Turtles* (1990); see, for example, Geoff Brown, 'Exploitation with a human face', *The Times*, 20 December 1990, p. 17. Interestingly, the press book also quotes Catherine O'Hara, who plays the mother, saying that she 'liked the idea that a good, normal kind of family, good parents, could make such a stupid mistake' (*Home Alone* microfiche, BFI). The film deals extensively with the mother's feelings of guilt and her desperate attempt to get back to her son.

20 Cf. Sue Harper and Vincent Porter, 'Moved to tears: weeping in the cinema in postwar Britain', *Screen*, vol. 37, no. 2 (Summer 1996), pp. 152–73, and Steve Neale, 'Melodrama and tears', *Screen* vol. 27, no. 6 (November–December 1986), pp. 6–22.

21 The relationship between traditional gender roles and emotional and physical excess on screen and in the auditorium has been explored by Linda Williams in 'Learning to scream', *Sight and Sound*, vol. 1, no. 12 (December 1994), pp. 14–17, and 'Film bodies: gender, genre and excess', *Film Quarterly*, vol. 44, no. 4 (1991), pp. 2–13. See also Carol J. Clover, *Men, Women and Chainsaws: Gender in the Modern Horror Film* (London: BFI, 1992).

22 Sue Zschoche, '*E.T.*, women's history, and the problem of Elliot', *American Studies*, vol. 36, no. 2 (Fall 1995), p. 100.

23 Interestingly, Zschoche notes that her daughter's next obsession were the Oz books, whose heroic central figure is 'a girl on a great quest' (ibid., p. 109). The popularity of these books and of other children's classics such as Lewis Carroll's Alice books indicate that there are powerful models for stories about girl adventurers, but these are largely ignored in contemporary popular culture.

24 The films could also be said actively to encourage identification across racial and ethnic boundaries. After all, the story of *E.T.* revolves around the possibility of transcending such boundaries (here between human being and alien). While *The Lion King* has been attacked for being racist, critics have also pointed out 'just how black it is'

(Hoberman, 'The mouse roars'), referring in particular to the range of black voices featured in the film.

25 While *Home Alone* is largely centred on the actions of a single young male protagonist, it also is concerned both with the reunion of the family at the end of the film and with the strengthening of the protagonist's bond with other members of the suburban community, exemplified by the old neighbour, who, due to the boy's intervention, is reunited with his own son in the final tableau.

26 Olen J. Earnest, '*Star Wars*: A case study of motion picture marketing', *Current Research in Film*, vol. 1 (1985), pp. 1–18.

27 Ibid., p. 17.

28 Quoted in Claudia Puig, '*Star Wars* makes a new killing at the box office', *Guardian*, 4 February 1997, p. 13.

29 As reported in the British press; see, for example, Martin Walker, 'Fabulous beasts stumble to extinction in White House', *Guardian*, 6 June 1993, p. 24; Phil Reeves, 'Dino-fever grips nation as cultural tyrant is born', *Independent on Sunday*, 18 June 1993, p. 13; Jonathan Romney, 'Toys for a movie brat', *Guardian*, 21 June 1993, Section 2, pp. 2–3. Cf. Henry Sheehan, 'The fears of children', *Sight and Sound*, vol. 3, no. 7 (July 1993), p. 10. There was similar concern about *The Lion King*, especially about the terrifying and potentially traumatizing impact of the scene in which the father dies. As reported in 'Hamlet with fur makes a box office killing', *Daily Telegraph*, 21 June 1994, p. 13, and James Bone, 'Critics fear Disney hit may disturb children', *The Times*, 22 June 1994, p. 6.

30 These calculations are based on the box-office grosses in the films' year of release which are derived from Cobbett Steinberg, *Reel Facts* (New York: Vintage, 1981), pp. 444–5, and 'The 1980s: a reference guide to motion pictures, television, VCR, and cable', *The Velvet Light Trap*, no. 27 (Spring 1991), p. 78. Overall annual box-office revenues are listed in 'The 1980s'; Joel W. Finler, *The Hollywood Story* (London: Octopus, 1988), p. 288; Leonard Klady, 'Numbers game at showest', *Variety*, 10 March 1997, p. 15; and Ralf Ludemann, 'Pay-TV paves the way ahead', *Screen International*, 24 January 1997, p. 74. The dominance of this production trend at the North American box office translates into success in other markets, with a small number of family-adventure films dominating the international theatrical and video market since the mid-1970s, each generating revenues in the region of $1–2 billion. See, for example, the list of all-time international top grossers in *Variety*, 3 June 1996, p. 70, and the list of all-time top sell-through videos in Adam Sandler, 'Biz ponders Oscar's effect on *Gump* vid', *Variety*, 24 April 1995, p. 7; also an *Entertainment Weekly* survey calculating total income generated from box-office admissions and video sales and rentals, which is reproduced in a supplement to the August 1994 issue of *Empire* magazine, entitled '101 things you never knew about the movies', p. 32.

31 This was first discovered when Hollywood started to do market research in the 1940s. The age distribution of the cinema audience was remarkably stable between the 1950s and the 1970s with about 75 per cent of all tickets bought by people under 30. Yet since the 1980s this dominance of young people has been decreasing (moving closer to the 50 per cent mark). See Thomas Doherty, *Teenagers and Teenpics: The Juvenilization of American Movies in the 1950s* (Boston: Unwin Hyman, 1988), pp. 62–3, 157, 231; Garth Jowett, *Film: The Democratic Art* (Boston: Little, Brown, 1976), pp. 476, 485; Justin Wyatt, *High Concept: Movies and Marketing in Hollywood* (Austin: University of Texas Press, 1994), p. 178; 'Industry economic review and audience profile', *The Movie*

Business Book, ed. Jason E. Squire (New York: Fireside, 1992, 2nd edition), pp. 388–9.

32 'Industry economic review', pp. 389–90.

33 Cf. John Izod, *Hollywood and the Box Office, 1895–1986* (London: Macmillan, 1988), pp. 181–2.

34 Academic critics have taken issue with the history lessons the film provides, in particular with its marginalization and negative representation of women, African-Americans and the counterculture. See Thomas B. Byers, 'History re-membered: *Forrest Gump*, postfeminist masculinity, and the burial of the counterculture', *Modern Fiction Studies*, vol. 42, no. 2 (Summer 1996), pp. 419–44; Fred Pfeil, *White Guys: Studies in Postmodern Domination and Difference* (London: Verso, 1995), pp. 251–7. A more sympathetic view is offered by Peter N. Chumo II, ' "You've got to put the past behind you before you can move on": *Forrest Gump* and national reconciliation', *Journal of Popular Film and Television* vol. 23 (1995), pp. 2–7.

35 *Variety*, 11 July 1994.

36 Martin Walker, 'Making saccharine taste sour', *Sight and Sound*, vol. 14, no. 10 (October 1994), p. 16.

37 Richard Corliss, 'The world according to Gump', *Time*, 1 August 1994, pp. 41–2.

38 Leonard Klady, 'B.O. bets on youth despite a solid spread', *Variety*, 10 April 1996, p. 14.

39 Ibid.

40 A more detailed study of how this might work in concrete terms could be modelled on sociological field work conducted at the site where the baby-boom hit *Field of Dreams* (1989) was shot. See Roger C. Aden, Rita L. Rahoi and Christina S. Beck, ' "Dreams are born on places like this": the process of interpretive community formation at the *Field of Dreams* site', *Communication Quarterly*, vol. 43, no. 4 (Fall 1995), pp. 368–80.

Select bibliography

Aksoy, Asu and Robins, Kevin, 'Hollywood for the 21st century: global competition for critical mass in image markets', *Cambridge Journal of Economics*, vol. 16, no. 1 (1992), pp. 1–22.

Alloway, Lawrence, *Violent America: The Movies, 1946–64* (New York: MOMA, 1971).

Altman, Rick, *Sound Theory, Sound Practice* (New York and London: Routledge, 1992).

Alvey, Mark, 'The independents: rethinking the television studio system,' in Lynn Spigel and Michael Curtin (eds), *The Revolution Wasn't Televised: Sixties Television and Social Conflict* (London: Routledge, 1997).

Anderson, Christopher, *Hollywood TV: The Studio System in the Fifties* (Austin: University of Texas Press, 1994).

Balio, Tino, *United Artists: The Company That Changed the Film Industry* (Madison: University of Wisconsin Press, 1989).

Balio, Tino, 'When is an independent producer independent? The case of United Artists after 1948', *The Velvet Light Trap*, no. 22 (1986), pp. 53–64.

Balio, Tino (ed.), *The American Film Industry* 2nd edn (Madison: University of Wisconsin, 1985).

Balio, Tino (ed.), *Hollywood in the Age of Television* (Boston: Unwin Hyman, 1990).

Barr, Charles, 'CinemaScope: before and after', *Film Quarterly*, vol. 16, no. 4 (1963), pp. 4–24.

Bart, Peter, *Fade Out: The Calamitous Final Days of MGM* (New York: Morrow, 1990).

Bazin, André, 'The evolution of the language of cinema', in *What is Cinema?* vol. 1, trans. Hugh Gray (Berkeley: University of California Press, 1967).

Bazin, André, 'The evolution of the western', in *What is Cinema ?* vol. II, trans. Hugh Gray (Berkeley: University of California Press, 1971).

Belton, John, 'The bionic eye: zoom esthetics', *Cineaste*, vol. 9, no. 1 (1980–1), pp. 20–7.

Belton, John, *Widescreen Cinema* (Cambridge: Harvard University Press, 1992).

Belton, John, *American Cinema/American Culture* (New York: McGraw Hill, 1994).

Bernadoni, James, *The New Hollywood: What the Movies Did with the New Freedoms of the Seventies* (Jefferson: McFarland Press, 1991).

Bernstein, Matthew, 'Hollywood's semi-independent production', *Cinema Journal*, vol. 32, no. 3 (Spring 1993), pp. 41–54.

Blacker, Irwin R., *The Elements of Screen-writing: A Guide for Film and Television Writers* (New York: Collier Books, 1986).

Block, Alex Ben, *Outfoxed: The Inside Story of America's Fourth Television Network* (New York: St Martin's Press, 1990).

Boddy, William, *Fifties Television: The Industry and its Critics* (Champaign: University of Illinois Press, 1990).

Bordwell, David, *Narration in the Fiction Film* (London: Methuen, 1985).

Bordwell, David, Staiger, Janet and Thompson, Kristin, *The Classical Hollywood Cinema: Film Style and Mode of Production to 1960* (London: Routledge, 1985).

Britton, Andrew, 'The philosophy of the pigeon hole: Wisconsin formalism and the "classical style"', *CineAction!*, no. 15 (Winter 1988/9), pp. 47–63.

Brownstein, Ronald, *The Power and the Glitter* (New York: Pantheon, 1990).

Bruck, Connie, *Master of the Game: How Steve Ross Rode the Light Fantastic from Undertaker to Creator of the Largest Media Conglomerate in the World* (New York: Simon & Schuster, 1994).

Cham, Mbye B., and Andrade-Watkins, Claire (eds), *Critical Perspectives on Black Independent Cinema* (Cambridge, Mass.: MIT Press, 1988).

Chion, Michel, *Audio-Vision: Sound on Screen* (New York: Columbia University Press, 1994).

Clover, Carol J. *Men, Women and Chainsaws: Gender in the Modern Horror Film* (London: BFI Publishing, 1992).

Collins, Jim, Radner, Hilary and Preacher Collins, Ava (eds) *Film Theory Goes to the Movies* (New York: Routledge, 1993).

Cook, Pam, 'Outrage (1950)', in Annette Kuhn (ed.), *Queen of the 'B's: Ida Lupino Behind the Camera* (London: Flicks Books, 1995).

Corrigan, Tim, *A Cinema Without Walls: Movies and Culture After Vietnam* (London: Routledge, 1991).

Curtin, Michael, 'On edge: culture industries in the neo-network era', in Ohmann (ed.), *Making and Selling Culture*.

Dale, Martin, *The Movie Game: The Film Business in Britain, Europe, and America* (London: Cassell, 1997).

Darby, William and Dubois, Jack, *American Film Music: Major Composers, Techniques, Trends, 1915–90* (Washington, DC: MacFarland, 1982).

Davidson, Bill, 'MCA', *Show*, February 1962, pp. 50–53 and March 1962, pp. 68–71.

Denisoff, R. Serge and Plasketes, George, 'Synergy in 1980s film and music: formula for success or industry mythology?', *Film History*, vol. 4 (1990), pp. 257–76.

Denisoff, R. Serge and Romanowski, William D., *Risky Business: Rock in Film* (London/New Brunswick, NJ: Transaction, 1991).

Dewey, Donald, *James Stewart: A Biography* (Atlanta: Turner Publishing, 1996).

Diawara, Manthia (ed.), *Black American Cinema* (New York: Routledge, 1993).

Dick, Bernard F., *City of Dreams: The Making and Unmaking of Universal Pictures* (Lexington: University Press of Kentucky, 1997).

Doane, Mary Ann, *The Desire to Desire: The Woman's Film of the 1940s* (Basingstoke: Macmillan, 1987).

Docherty, Thomas (ed.), *Postmodernism: A Reader* (London: Harvester Wheatsheaf, 1993).

Doherty, Thomas, *Teenagers and Teenpics: The Juvenilization of American Movies in the 1950s* (Boston: Unwin Hyman, 1988).

Donnelly, K.J., 'Altered status: a review of music in postmodern cinema and culture', in Steven Earnshaw (ed.), *Postmodern Surroundings* (Amsterdam: Rodopi, 1994).

Earnest, Olen J., '*Star Wars:* a case study of motion picture marketing', *Current Research in Film* 1 (1985), pp. 1–18.

Eidsvik, Charles, 'Machines of the invisible: changes in technology in the age of video', *Film Quarterly*, vol. 42, no. 2 (Winter 1988–9), pp. 18–23.

Eitzen, Dirk, 'Evolution, functionalism, and the study of the American cinema', *The Velvet Light Trap*, no. 28 (Fall 1991), pp. 73–85.

Eller, Claudia, 'Media's mega-deal makers', *The Los Angeles Times*, 18 July 1996, p. D6.

Eller, Claudia and Frook, John Evan, 'Mickey munches on Miramax', *Variety*, 3 May 1993, pp. 1, 60–2.

Ellwood, D. and Kroes, R. (eds), *Hollywood and Europe* (Amsterdam: Vrije Universiteit, 1994).

Elsaesser, Thomas, 'The pathos of failure: American films in the 70s – notes on the unmotivated hero', *Monogram*, no. 6 (1975), pp. 13–19.

Farber, Manny, 'The gimp', in *Negative Space* (New York: Praeger, 1971).

Farber, Stephen, *The Movie Rating Game* (Washington, DC: Public Affairs Press, 1972).

Finney, Angus, *The State of European Cinema: A New Dose of Reality* (London: Cassell, 1996).

Fisher, Bob, 'Dawning of the digital age', *American Cinematographer*, vol. 73, no. 4 (April 1992), pp. 70–86.

Frook, John E., 'Call Harvey Mickey Mouth', *Variety*, 29 November 1993, pp. 1, 75.

Gallagher, Tag, *John Ford: The Man and his Films* (Berkeley: University of California, 1986).

Gelmis, Joseph, *The Film Director as Superstar* (Harmondsworth: Penguin, 1970).

Goldman, William, *Adventures in the Screen Trade* (New York: Warner Books, 1983).

Gomery, Douglas, 'The American film industry of the 1970s: stasis in the "New Hollywood"', *Wide Angle*, vol. 5, no. 4 (1983), pp. 52–9.

Gomery, Douglas, 'Failed opportunities: the integration of the US motion picture and television industries', *Quarterly Review of Film Studies*, vol. 9, no. 3 (Summer 1984), pp. 219–23.

Gomery, Douglas, *The Hollywood Studio System* (New York: St Martin's Press, 1986).

Gomery, Douglas, *Shared Pleasures: A History of Movie Presentation in the United States* (London: BFI, 1992).

Gomery, Douglas, 'Toward a new media economics', in David Bordwell and Noël Carroll (eds), *Post-Theory: Reconstructing Film Studies* (Madison: University of Wisconsin Press, 1996).

Gorbman, Claudia, *Unheard Melodies: Narrative Film Music* (London: BFI, 1987).

Gordon, Andrew, 'Science-fiction and fantasy film criticism: the case of Lucas and Spielberg', *Journal of the Fantastic in the Arts*, vol. 2, no. 2 (1989), pp. 80–94.

Grant, Barry Keith, 'Looking upwards: reason and the visible in science fiction film', in Glenwood Irons (ed.), *Gender, Language, and Myth* (Toronto: University of Toronto Press, 1992).

Grover, Ronald, 'Nightmares, turtles – and profits', *Business Week*, 30 September 1991, pp. 52–6.

Guerrero, Ed, *Framing Blackness* (Philadelphia: Temple University Press, 1993).

Gustafson, Robert, '"What's happening to our pix biz?" From Warner Bros to Warner Communications, Inc.', in Balio (ed.), *The American Film Industry*.

Handzo, Stephen, 'The sound of sound – a brief history of the reproduction of sound in movie theatres', *Cineaste*, vol. 21, nos. 1–2 (1995) pp. 68–71.

Hansen, Miriam, 'Early cinema, late cinema: permutations of the public sphere', *Screen*, vol. 34, no. 3 (Autumn 1993), pp. 197–210.

Harwood, Sara, *Family Fictions: Representations of the Family in 1980s Hollywood Cinema* (London: Macmillan, 1997).

Hayward, Philip and Wollen, Tana (eds), *Future Visions: New Technologies of the Screen* (London: British Film Institute, 1993).

Hillier, Jim, *The New Hollywood* (London: Studio Vista, 1992).

Hilmes, Michelle, *Hollywood and Broadcasting: From Radio to Cable* (Urbana: University of Illinois Press, 1990).

Hoberman, J., *Vulgar Modernism: Writing on Movies and Other Media* (Philadelphia: Temple University Press, 1991).

Holmlund, Chris, '"Cruisin' for a bruisin'": Hollywood's deadly (lesbian) dolls', *Cinema Journal*, vol. 34, no. 1 (Fall 1994), pp. 31–51.

Huyssen, Andreas, *After the Great Divide: Modernism, Mass Culture and Postmodernism* (London: Macmillan, 1988).

Izod, John, *Hollywood and the Box Office, 1895–1986* (London: Macmillan, 1988).

Jameson, Fredric, *Postmodernism, or The Cultural Logic of Late Capitalism* (London: Verso, 1991).

Jeffords, Susan, *Hard Bodies: Hollywood Masculinity in the Reagan Era* (New Brunswick: Rutgers University Press, 1994).

Jenkins, Henry, 'Historical poetics', in Joanne Hollows and Mark Jancovich, *Approaches to Popular Film* (Manchester: Manchester University Press, 1995).

Joannides, Paul, 'The aesthetics of the zoom lens', *Sight and Sound*, vol. 40, no. 1 (1970–1), pp. 40–2.

Jones, Jacquie, 'The new ghetto aesthetic', *Wide Angle*, vol. 13, nos. 3–4 (July–October 1991), pp. 32–43.

Jowett, Garth, *Film: The Democratic Art* (Boston, Mass.: Little, Brown, 1976).

Kalinak, Kathryn, *Settling the Score: Music and the Classical Hollywood Film* (Madison: University of Wisconsin Press, 1992).

Kent, Nicholas, *Naked Hollywood: Money, Power and the Movies* (London: BBC, 1991).

Klinger, Barbara, *Melodrama and Meaning: History, Culture and the Films of Douglas Sirk* (Bloomington and Indianapolis: Indiana University Press, 1994).

Kerbel, Michael, 'Edited for television, 1: scanning', *Film Comment*, vol. 13, no. 3 (1977), pp. 28–30.

Krämer, Peter, 'The lure of the big picture: film, television and Hollywood', in John Hill and Martin McLoone, *Big Picture, Small Screen: The Relations between Film and Television* (Luton: University of Luton/John Libbey, 1996).

Krämer, Peter, 'Post-classical Hollywood film: concepts and debates', in John Hill and Pamela Church Gibson (eds), *The Oxford Guide to Film Studies* (Oxford: Oxford University Press, 1998).

Lafferty, William, 'Feature films on prime-time television', in T. Balio (ed.), *Hollywood in the Age of Television* (Boston, Mass.: Unwin Hyman, 1990).

Lee, Spike, *Spike Lee's Gotta Have It: Inside Guerrilla Filmmaking* (New York: Fireside Press, 1987).

Lewis, Jon, *Whom God Wishes to Destroy: Francis Coppola and the New Hollywood* (Durham and London: Duke University Press, 1995).

Litwak, Mark, *Reel Power: The Struggle for Influence and Success in the New Hollywood* (Los Angeles: Silman-James Press, 1994).

Lyons, Charles, *The New Censors: Movies and the Culture Wars* (Philadelphia: Temple University Press, 1997).

MacCann, Richard Dyer, *Hollywood in Transition* (Boston, Mass.: Houghton Mifflin, 1962).

Madsen, Axel, *The New Hollywood* (New York: Crowell, 1975).

Maltby, Richard, *Harmless Entertainment: Hollywood and the Ideology of Consensus* (Metuchen: Scarecrow Press, 1983).

Maltby, Richard, *Hollywood Cinema: An Introduction* (Oxford: Blackwell, 1995).

Maltby, Richard, '"A brief romantic interlude": Dick and Jane go to 3½ seconds of the classical Hollywood cinema', in David Bordwell and Noël Carroll (eds), *Post-Theory: Reconstructing Film Studies* (Madison: University of Wisconsin Press, 1996).

Marion, Frances, *How to Write and Sell Film Stories* (New York: Colvici Friede, 1937).

Marshall, Stuart, 'Video: from art to independence: a short history of a new technology', *Screen*, vol. 26, no. 2 (March/April 1985), pp. 66–71.

Matthews, Tom, 'Entretien avec Skip Lievsay', *24 Images* 60 (1992), pp. 24–8.

Meisel, Myron, 'New Line's nightmare spurs ambitious expansion program', *The Film Journal*, April 1986, p. 37.

Miller, Mark Crispin (ed.), *Seeing Through Movies* (New York: Pantheon Books, 1990).

Monaco, James, *American Film Now* (New York: Oxford University Press, 1979).

Moran, Albert (ed.), *Film Policy: International, National, and Regional Perspectives* (London: Routledge, 1996).

Natoli, Joseph, *Hauntings: Popular Film and American Culture, 1990–1992* (Albany: State University of New York Press, 1994).

Neale, Steve, '"New Hollywood cinema"', *Screen*, vol. 17, no. 2 (1976), pp. 117–22.

Negroponte, Nicholas, *Being Digital* (London: Hodder and Stoughton, 1995).

Newman, Kim, 'Exploitation and the mainstream', in Nowell-Smith (ed.), *The Oxford History of World Cinema*.

Nowell-Smith, Geoffrey (ed.), *The Oxford History of World Cinema* (Oxford: Oxford University Press, 1996).

Nowell-Smith, Geoffrey, 'Introduction: the modern cinema', in Nowell-Smith (ed), *The Oxford History of World Cinema*.

Ohmann, Richard (ed.), *Making and Selling Culture* (Hanover: Wesleyan University Press, 1996).

Pearson, Roberta E. and Uricchio, William (eds), *The Many Lives of the Batman* (London: BFI, 1991).

Pierson, John, *Spike, Mike, Slackers, and Dykes: A Guided Tour across a Decade of Independent American Cinema* (London: Faber, 1996).

Polan, Dana, 'Globalism's localisms', in Rob Wilson and Wimal Dissanayake (eds), *Global/Local: Cultural Production and the Transnational Imaginary* (Durham: Duke University Press, 1996).

Prendergast, Roy M., *A Neglected Art: Film Music* (New York: New York University Press, 1977).

Pye, Michael and Myles, Lynda, *The Movie Brats* (London: Studio Vista, 1985).

Ray, Robert, *A Certain Tendency of the Hollywood Cinema* (Princeton: Princeton University Press, 1985).

Rebello, Stephen, *Alfred Hitchcock and the Making of Psycho* (New York: Dembner Books, 1990).

Reid, Mark A., *Redefining Black Film* (Berkeley: University of California, 1993).

Rhines, Jesse Algeron, *Black Film/White Money* (New Brunswick: Rutgers University Press, 1996).

Salt, Barry, *Film Style and Technology: History and Analysis*, 2nd edn (London: Starword, 1992).

Schatz, Thomas, *Old Hollywood, New Hollywood: Ritual, Art, and Industry* (Ann Arbor: UMI Press, 1983).

Schatz, Thomas, 'The New Hollywood', in Collins *et al.* (eds), *Film Theory Goes to the Movies*.

Schuyten, Peter J., 'How MCA rediscovered movieland's golden lobe', *Fortune*, November 1976, pp. 122–4, 212–24.

Serafine, Frank, 'Creating the undersea sounds of *Red October*', *American Cinematographer*, vol. 71, no. 9 (September 1990), pp. 67–72.

Squire, Jason E., *The Movie Business Book*, 2nd edn (New York: Fireside, 1992).

Storper, Michael, 'The transition to flexible specialization in the US film industry: external economies, the division of labour and the crossing of industrial divides', in Ash Amin (ed.), *Post-Fordism: A Reader* (Oxford: Blackwell, 1994).

Storper, Michael and Christopherson, Susan, 'Flexible specialisation and regional industrial agglomerations: the case of the US motion picture industry', *Annals of the Association of American Geographers*, vol. 77, no. 1 (1987), pp. 104–17.

Taylor, John, *Storming the Magic Kingdom: Wall Street, the Raiders, and the Battle for Disney* (New York: Knopf, 1987).

Thompson, Anne, 'Will success spoil the Weinstein brothers?', *Film Comment*, 25: 4 (July–August 1989), pp. 72–6.

Thompson, Kristin, 'Narrative structure in early classical cinema', in John Fullerton (ed.), *Celebrating 1895* (University of Luton/John Libbey, forthcoming).

Traube, Elizabeth, *Dreaming Identities: Class, Gender, and Generation in 1980s Hollywood Movies* (Boulder: Westview Press, 1992).

The Velvet Light Trap, no. 21 (1985) – special issue on widescreen.

The Velvet Light Trap, no. 22 (1986) – special issue on Hollywood Independents.

Vianello, Robert, 'The rise of the telefilm and the networks' hegemony over the motion picture industry', *Quarterly Review of Film Studies*, vol. 9, no. 3 (Summer 1984), pp. 204–18.

Virillo, Paul, *War and Cinema* (London: Verso, 1989).

Vogel, Harold J., *Entertainment Industry Economics* (Cambridge: Cambridge University Press, 1990).

Warner, Frank, 'The sound of silence and things that go "flash" in the night', *American Cinematographer* (LTV, 1984), pp. 62–72.

Wasko, Janet, *Hollywood in the Information Age: Beyond the Silver Screen* (Cambridge: Polity Press, 1994).

Weegee and Harris, Mel, *Naked City* (New York: Farrar, Straus and Giroux, 1953).

Weis, Elizabeth, 'Sync tanks – the art and technique of postproduction sound', *Cineaste*, vol. 21 (1995), pp. 56–61.

Weis, Elizabeth and Belton, John, *Film Sound: Theory and Practice* (New York: Columbia University Press, 1992).

Williams, Christopher, 'After the classic, the classical and ideology: the differences of realism', *Screen*, vol. 35, no. 3 (1994), pp. 275–92.

Williams, Linda, *Hard Core: Power, Pleasure and the 'Frenzy of the Visible'* (London: Pandora, 1991).

Williams, Linda, 'Learning to scream', *Sight and Sound*, vol. 4, no. 12 (December 1994), pp. 14–17.

Williams, Linda, 'Sex and sensation', in Nowell-Smith (ed.), *The Oxford History of World Cinema*.

Wood, Robin, ' '80s Hollywood: dominant tendencies', *CineAction!*, vol. 1 (Spring 1985), pp. 2–5.

Wood, Robin, *Hollywood from Vietnam to Reagan* (New York: Columbia University Press, 1986).

Wyatt, Justin, *High Concept: Movies and Marketing in Hollywood* (Austin: University of Texas Press, 1994).

Wyatt, Justin, 'Economic constraints/economic opportunities: Robert Altman as auteur', *The Velvet Light Trap*, no. 38 (Fall 1996), pp. 51–67.

Yearwood, Gladstone (ed.), *Black Cinema Aesthetics* (Athens: Ohio University Press, 1982).

Young, Josh, 'New Line Cinema: it was a very good year', *The New York Times*, 18 September 1994, pp. H13, 20–1.

Index

Page numbers in **bold type** indicate where there is an illustration.